The security dimensions of EU enlargement

Manchester University Press

The security dimensions of EU enlargement
Wider Europe, weaker Europe?

edited by David Brown and Alistair J.K. Shepherd

MANCHESTER UNIVERSITY PRESS

MANCHESTER AND NEW YORK • distributed exclusively in the USA by Palgrave

Copyright © Manchester University Press 2007

While copyright in the volume as a whole is vested in Manchester University Press, copyright in individual chapters belongs to their respective authors, and no chapter may be reproduced wholly or in part without the express permission in writing of both author and publisher.

Published by Manchester University Press
Oxford Road, Manchester M13 9NR, UK
and Room 400, 175 Fifth Avenue, New York, NY 10010, USA
www.manchesteruniversitypress.co.uk

Distributed exclusively in the USA by
Palgrave, 175 Fifth Avenue, New York, NY 10010, USA

Distributed exclusively in Canada by
UBC Press, University of British Columbia, 2029 West Mall, Vancouver, BC, Canada
V6T 1Z2

British Library Cataloguing-in-Publication Data
A catalogue record for this book is available from the British Library

Library of Congress Cataloging-in-Publication Data applied for

ISBN 978 0 7190 7280 2 *hardback*

First published 2007

16 15 14 13 12 11 10 09 08 07   10 9 8 7 6 5 4 3 2 1

Typeset in ITC Charter with Eras display
by Servis Filmsetting Ltd, Manchester
Printed in Great Britain
by CPI, Bath

Contents

LIST OF TABLES	page vi
LIST OF ABBREVIATIONS	vii
NOTES ON CONTRIBUTORS	x
ACKNOWLEDGMENTS	xiii

	Introduction: security and enlargement into the twenty-first century *Alistair J.K. Shepherd*	1
1	EU enlargement and NATO: the Balkan experience *Martin A. Smith*	7
2	The implications of EU enlargement for the European security and defence policy *Alistair J.K. Shepherd*	20
3	The impact of enlargement on the EU's counter-terrorist framework *David Brown*	38
4	The external shield of internal security: the EU's emerging common external border management *Jörg Monar*	54
5	EU enlargement and organised crime: Transdniestria as a case study *Graeme P. Herd* and *Anne C. Aldis*	69
6	Enlargement and human rights law: norms and realities *Karim A.A. Khan* and *Anna Kotzeva*	86
7	An assessment of the Baltic States contribution to EU efforts to prevent proliferation and combat illicit arms trafficking *Paul Holtom*	99
8	Russia–EU relations: opportunities for a security dialogue *Dmitry Polikanov*	115
9	Russia–EU relations and the Chechen issue *Tracey C. German*	129
10	A leap forward to Europe: the impact of the 'Orange Revolution' on EU–Ukraine relations *Rosaria Puglisi*	144
11	The EU and Turkey: bridge or barrier? *Bill Park*	157
12	EU Enlargement and security in the Mediterranean region *Roderick Pace*	174
13	A successful Stability Pact: European Union policy in South-east Europe *Anthony Welch*	191
	Conclusion: the security implications of EU enlargement *David Brown*	207

SELECT BIBLIOGRAPHY	222
INDEX	229

Tables

2.1	Estimated commitments to the EU Headline Goal	*page* 29
2.2	New member states contributions to Operation Althea and the EUPM (August 2005)	30
2.3	Defence expenditure and expenditure as percentage of GDP: ten new member states	31
7.1	Seizures of illegally held firearms in Lithuania	105
7.2	Quantities of illegally held weapons, ammunition and explosive materials and devices discovered in the Kaliningrad region	107
8.1	Figures matrix of EU–Russia relations	115

Abbreviations

ABC	Air Borders Centre
ACPO	Association of Chief Police Officers
ACT	Ad Hoc Centre for Border Guard Training
AFSJ	Area of Freedom Security and Justice
AFTA	Agadir Free Trade Area
AKP	Justice and Development Party
BAM	Border Assistance Mission
BiH	Bosnia and Herzegovina
BSEC	Black Sea Economic Cooperation Organisation
CARDS	Community Assistance for Reconstruction, Development and Stabilisation
CEE	Central and Eastern Europe
CFE	Conventional Forces Europe
CFSP	Common Foreign and Security Policy
CIRAM	Common Integrated Risk Analysis Model
CIS	Commonwealth of Independent States
CLB	Centre for Land Borders
COARM	Conventional Arms Exports Working Group
CSCM	Conference on Security and Cooperation in the Mediterranean
CSP	Country Strategy Paper
CSR	Common Strategy on Russia
CWC	Chemical Weapons Convention
DFID	Department for International Development
DRC	Democratic Republic of the Congo
DSACEUR	Deputy Supreme Allied Commander Europe
EAW	European Arrest Warrant
EC	European Community
ECHO	European Community Humanitarian Aid Department
ECHR	European Convention on Human Rights
ECJ	European Court of Justice
ECO	Economic Cooperation Organisation
ECtHR	European Court of Human Rights
EEZ	Exclusive Economic Zone
EIDHR	European Initiative for Democracy and Human Rights
EIT	Essentially Identical Transfers
EMFTA	European Mediterranean Free Trade Area
EMP	European Mediterranean Partnership
ENP	European Neighbourhood Policy
ERRF	European Rapid Reaction Force
ESDP	European Security and Defence Policy
ESBC	Eastern Sea Borders Centre
ESS	European Security Strategy
EUCPN	European Union Crime Prevention Network

EUFOR	European Union Force
EUMC	European Military Committee
EUMS	European Military Staff
EUPM	European Union Police Mission
EUROPOL	European Police Office
FSB	Federal Security Bureau
FSU	Former Soviet Union
FYROM	Former Yugoslav Republic of Macedonia
GDP	Gross Domestic Product
GMP	Global Mediterranean Policy
GRECO	Group of States Against Corruption
GUAM	Georgia, Ukraine, Azerbaijan, Moldova
HHG	Helsinki Headline Goal
JHA	Justice and Home Affairs
IAEA	International Atomic Energy Agency
ICC	International Criminal Court
IEA	International Energy Agency
IFOR	Implementation Force
IRA	Irish Republican Army
ISAF	International Security Assistance Force
KFOR	Kosovo Force
MTS	Medium Term Strategy
NAC	North Atlantic Council
NATO	North Atlantic Treaty Organisation
NBC	Nuclear, Biological and Chemical
NCIS	National Criminal Intelligence Service
NGO	Non-Governmental Organisation
NIP	National Indicative Programme
NMS	New Member State(s)
NPT	Non-Proliferation Treaty
NRF	NATO Response Force
NSC	National Security Council
OIC	Organisation of the Islamic Conference
OIDHR	Office for Democratic Institutions and Human Rights
OSCE	Organisation for Security and Cooperation in Europe
PCA	Partnership and Cooperation Agreement
PfP	Partnership for Peace
PKK	Kurdish Workers Party
PMR	Pridnestrovskaya Moldavskaya Respublika (Transdniestria)
PSC	Political and Security Committee
RAC	Risk Analysis Centre
PHARE	Pologne, Hongrie Assistance à la Reconstruction Economique
SAA	Stability and Association Agreement
SALW	Small Arms and Light Weapons
SAP	Stabilisation and Association Process
SEEBRIG	South-Eastern Europe Brigade
SES	Single Economic Space
SFOR	Stabilisation Force

LIST OF ABBREVIATIONS

SIAC	Special Immigration Appeals Commission
SIS	Schengen Information System
SME	Small and Medium Enterprise
TACIS	Technical Aid to the Commonwealth of Independent States
TEU	Treaty on European Union
TGS	Turkish General Staff
UKHL	United Kingdom, House of Lords
UNMIK	United Nations Interim Mission
UNPROFOR	United Nations Protection Force
USAID	United States Aid
UNSC	United Nations Security Council
USSR	Union of Soviet Socialist Republics
WEU	Western European Union
WMD	Weapons of Mass Destruction
WTO	World Trade Organisation

Notes on contributors

Anne C. Aldis is Director of the Conflict Studies Research Centre, UK Defence Academy. Her work focuses on international security, conflict resolution and defence diplomacy, primarily in southern and eastern Europe, the Caucasus and Central Asia. She has recently published (with Graeme Herd) *Soft Security Threats and European Security* (Routledge, 2005) and *The Ideological War on Terror* (Routledge, 2006); and, with Roger McDermott, *Russian Military Reform 1992–2002* (Frank Cass, 2003).

David Brown is a Senior Lecturer in Defence and International Affairs at the Royal Military Academy Sandhurst. His main research interests are in terrorism and European internal security and police co-operation. His recent articles include: 'Defending the fortress: assessing the European Union's response to trafficking', *European Security* (2004) and 'NATO and terrorism', *Contemporary Security Policy* (2005). He is currently finalising his monograph on the EU's contribution to counter-terrorism, *Unsteady Foundations? The European Union's Counter-Terrorist Strategy 1991–2006* (Manchester University Press, 2007).

Tracey C. German is a Lecturer in Defence Studies at the Joint Services Command and Staff College, King's College London. Her current research interests are the impact of the on-going Chechen conflict, security in the Caucasus region and energy issues in the former Soviet states. Her recent publications include: *Russia's Chechen War* (Routledge, 2003); 'Post-Soviet security politics', in *Security Dynamics in the Former Soviet Bloc: Integration or Isolation?* (Routledge, 2003); and 'The Pankiski Gorge: Georgia's Achilles' heel in its relations with Russia?', *Central Asian Survey* (March 2004).

Graeme P. Herd is a resident Faculty Member at the Geneva Centre for Security Policy and an Associate Fellow of Chatham House, London. He has published an extensive range of articles on contemporary European security politics. His latest books include *Soft Security Threats and European Security* (Routledge, 2005), co-edited with Anne Aldis and *Divided West: European Security and Transatlantic Relations* (Chatham House, 2006), co-authored with Tuomas Forsberg.

Paul Holtom is a researcher in SIPRI's Arms Transfer Project. Prior to this he was a research fellow at the Centre for Border Studies, the University of Glamorgan. His research on control regimes on SALW and measures to combat arms trafficking in the Baltic States, Poland and Russia – *Arms Transit Trade in the Baltic Region* – was published in 2003 in collaboration with the INGO Saferworld. He has recently completed a small arms survey of Albania, *Turning the Page: Small Arms and Light Weapons in Albania* (Saferworld, 2005).

Karim A.A. Khan is a member of 2 Hare Court, Temple and specialises in international criminal and human rights law. He has worked on the UN International Criminal Tribunals for the Former Yugoslavia and Rwanda, the Special Courts in East Timor and Sierra Leone and provided legal advice to the ICJ. He is also a Senior Research Fellow, King's College, London. Recently, he has co-authored (with Rodney Dixon) *Archbold International Criminal Courts* (Sweet and Maxwell, 2005) and co-edited *International Criminal Law Reports* (ICLR) and *International Criminal Evidence* (Cameron May, 2006).

NOTES ON CONTRIBUTORS

Anna Kotzeva is a barrister at 1 Temple Gardens, London and is currently working as a legal officer in the Office of the Prosecutor of the ICTY. She has substantial experience in the ECHR and has advised the Home Office 'in house' in relation to treaty obligations and implementation issues. In addition to a number of articles in the *Solicitors Journal*, she is the co-author (with Robin Tam) of the *Asylum and Human Rights Appeals Handbook* (Oxford University Press, 2006).

Jörg Monar holds the Marie Curie Chair of Excellence and is Director of the SECURINT project at Université Robert Schuman of Strasbourg. He is also specialist adviser to the House of Lords EU Committee and has acted as consultant to the European Parliament and to a number of European governments. He has published over 170 books, articles and chapters on the political, institutional and legal development of the EU. His research focus is on EU governance and treaty reform, external relations and justice and home affairs.

Roderick Pace is a Lecturer in International Relations and European Studies, Director of the European Documentation and Research Centre (EDRC) and a member of the Islands and Small States Institute (ISSI) of the University of Malta. He was involved in Malta's EU accession process. His research interests include theories of European integration, Euro-Mediterranean studies and small states in international affairs. He has published numerous articles on these themes. He is also the author of *Microstate Security in the Global System: EU–Malta Relations* (Midsea Books, 2001).

Bill Park is a Senior Lecturer in Defence Studies at the Joint Services Command and Staff College, King's College, London. His current research interest is primarily Turkish foreign and security policy. He has given evidence to both House of Lords and House of Commons Select Committees on Turkey. He has published widely on NATO and Turkish foreign and security policy, including *Defending the West: A History of NATO* (Wheatsheaf, 1986); *Rethinking Security in Post-Cold War Europe* (Longmans, 1998) with Wyn Rees; and a number of articles on Turkey's foreign and security policy.

Dmitry Polikanov is Director of International Relations at the All-Russia Public Opinion Research Center (VCIOM). He has worked as Research Fellow and Deputy Director in the PIR Center for Policy Studies and as Communications Adviser for the Moscow delegation of the ICRC. Author of over 70 publications on international affairs, Russian foreign and domestic policy, he also lectures at the NATO School, the Moscow Party School and the School of Public Politics in Russia.

Rosaria Puglisi is Political Advisor to the EU Special Representative for Moldova. In the period 2003–05, she was Political Officer at the Delegation of the European Commission to Ukraine, having previously worked as a research Fellow in post-Soviet politics at the University of Leeds. She is author of *Economic Elites and Russian–Ukraine Relations* (Routledge, 2005); 'The rise of the Ukrainian oligarchs', *Democratization* (2003) and 'Clashing agendas? Economic Interests, elite coalitions and prospects for cooperation between Russia and Ukraine', *Europe–Asia Studies* (2003).

Alistair J.K. Shepherd is a Lecturer in Contemporary European Security in the Department of International Politics, University of Wales, Aberystwyth. His central research areas are European security and transatlantic relations. He has written a number of articles on the emergence of a military capability for the EU, including 'Irrelevant or indispensable? ESDP, the "War on Terror" and the fallout from Iraq', *International Politics* (2006). He is also co-author (with Trevor Salmon) of *Towards a European Army: A Military Power in the Making?* (Lynne Rienner, 2003).

Martin A. Smith is a Senior Lecturer in Defence and International Affairs at the Royal Military Academy Sandhurst. His main research interests are in the areas of international and European security, with a particular focus on the post-Cold War evolution of NATO. His most recent book, *Russia and NATO since 1991*, was published by Routledge in December 2005. He is currently working on a book addressing the nature and distribution of power in the post-Cold War world. This will be published by Polity Press in 2007.

Anthony Welch was a Brigadier in the British Army. Subsequently, he worked for the UN as Chef de Cabinet to the Special Representative of the Secretary General for the former Yugoslavia and then as Conflict and Security Advisor for the UK's Department for International Development (DFID). In 1999, he was appointed Head of the DFID Office in Kosovo and later became the UN Regional Administrator, Mitrovica. Currently, he is in Kosovo as the Coordinator of the Internal Security Sector Review, prior to decisions on the final status of the province.

Acknowledgments

We would like to thank those who took the time to give us their comments and advice, in particular Richard Shepherd, Roger Scully and Martin Smith. We are very grateful for the support of our family and friends; Judith especially has been an endless source of support and encouragement.

Introduction: security and enlargement into the twenty-first century

Alistair J.K. Shepherd

The European Union's (EU) leap from fifteen to twenty-five members consigns to history the Cold War legacy of separate and sometimes hostile camps in Eastern and Western Europe. The 2004 EU enlargement has widened the European security community, incorporating ten member states to its south and east. However, security concerns remain, and, in some cases, have been heightened.

The first EU enlargement of the twenty-first century coincides with a period of international tension and transition. Tensions have been apparent over: the war in Iraq, the 'War on Terror', immigration, organised crime, ethnic confrontation, human rights, energy resources and the proliferation of weapons of mass destruction (WMD). In parallel, within the EU, there is a sense of transition and political tension over: the failed EU Constitution, the direction and extent of future enlargement, economic and budgetary difficulties, nature of border security, direction of police and judicial co-operation and differing visions of the European Security and Defence Policy (ESDP). The addition of ten new states impacts on how the EU perceives and tackles these tensions and transitions, thereby shaping the EU's overall security role.

This raises the first central theme of this volume – internal cohesion. Can a union numbering twenty-five states (and rising) achieve consensus on any issue, let alone something as sensitive as security policy? While it may be a little early to pass definitive judgement, the fifteen states in the EU prior to the 2004 enlargement have already encountered difficulties reaching consensus on security issues. Consensus may become more elusive with the addition of a further ten states. This volume explores how the widening of interests, agendas and capabilities will affect the deepening of integration. It also examines the impact that enlargement will have on leadership within the EU, a pre-requisite for policy coherence. Across the chapters, a key theme emerges: enlargement has not always introduced new problems, but has crystallised crucial problems that the EU seems to have been avoiding. What is less clear is whether the EU will now make a concerted effort to address them. The evidence available since May 2004 suggests that the EU may have missed the opportunity presented by enlargement to pause and fully implement existing security policies. Instead, the EU has continued to develop further initiatives and headline goals.

This perpetual forward motion may create problems because, despite the EU being the best example of a security community in today's international system, it still has a number of pressing security concerns, both internally and externally, for which they have not yet fully implemented their existing policies. While the EU no longer fears war, the threats of terrorism, organised crime and illegal immigration have risen to the top of its internal security agenda. Externally, it has a 'neighbourhood' that is far less stable and is often the source of these internal security threats. This raises another theme central to any discussion on security in an enlarged EU: the merging of the concepts of internal and external security. Terrorism, organised crime, illegal immigration, trafficking and ethnic tensions cannot be simply labelled as external or internal security threats. They are, by their very nature, trans-boundary issues and, in many respects, they explicitly seek to dissolve boundaries and borders. These security concerns also highlight the shifting emphasis between hard and soft security. While the EU is actually equipping itself for harder security missions, as examined by Alistair Shepherd in Chapter 2, the types of security issues analysed in many of the chapters deal with soft security, although the alleged softness of these security issues does not preclude the need for a harder edge to the EU's security capabilities.

The EU has made genuine progress in developing its security policies since the launch of the Common Foreign and Security Policy (CFSP) and Justice and Home Affairs (JHA) in the Treaty on European Union (TEU). However, ambitious rhetoric, scoreboards and headline goals have tended to overshadow actual progress, entrenching the notion of a capabilities–expectations gap.[1] Rhetoric running ahead of progress can be seen in both the development of ESDP and in the EU's counter terrorism efforts, as examined by Alistair Shepherd in Chapter 2 and David Brown in Chapter 3. In the context of ESDP, enlargement presented an opportunity to reinvigorate the waning political will to develop the necessary military capabilities to complement the EU's new and existing civilian capabilities. The new member states showed genuine will to reform and improve their military capabilities to adjust to the changed security environment, even if they barely had the financial resources to do so. If such political will could be uniformly applied across the EU, it would greatly benefit both current and future EU crisis management operations, particularly in the Balkans.

Coupled with a greater degree of political will, the new member states have also shifted the political balance within the EU towards a more Atlanticist approach to security. The new member states are determined to ensure the primacy of the North Atlantic Treaty Organisation (NATO) and the continuing engagement of the United States in European security. The centrality of the EU–NATO relationship to European security cannot be overstated, and Martin Smith (in Chapter 1) examines the evolution of this relationship with regard to their respective enlargement strategies and their burden-sharing approach in the Balkans. Smith argues that the EU and NATO have moved from perceiving the relationship as competitive to acknowledging that it is, in fact, complementary. As membership of NATO and the EU continues to converge in the coming years, this complimentarity is likely to strengthen further.

Returning to the development of an EU counter-terrorist policy, David Brown argues that the 2004 enlargement was an opportunity to pause, take stock and refocus efforts, rather than simply continuing the momentum of rhetoric. The perpetual stream of declarations, initiatives and policies has left an implementation gap in their wake, consigning many initiatives to the status of distractions and diverting valuable resources. Both in the field of military capabilities and counter-terrorism, the EU's credibility is undermined by its failure to meet expectations. The focus in these areas, and across the realm of security, should be on how the EU can 'add value' to the existing policies and capabilities of the member states. With the addition of ten new states, the 'presence'[2] of the EU on the international stage has increased greatly, yet its 'actorness'[3] has not seen a comparable improvement.

While pushing ahead with existing policy initiatives, the EU has tended to be slow in practically addressing many problems in its neighbourhood. This is clearly demonstrated by Graeme Herd and Anne Aldis in their chapter on organised crime (Chapter 5). The EU's lack of political will to engage in the problems crippling Moldova before 2004, organised crime being central to these problems, has damaged the EU's credibility as a security provider. On a more positive note, it may well have been the 2004 enlargement (and the 2007 enlargement to include Romania) that forced the EU to recognise the urgency of Moldova's predicament. Enlargement has also highlighted the problem of arms trafficking in the Baltic States and the difficulties of progressing from legislation to implementation. Paul Holtom, in Chapter 7, clearly demonstrates that, while these states, like the EU in many areas, have been strong on rhetoric, they have not been able to make the transition from gateways to gatekeepers in the transit of illicit arms. The culture of customs, border and law enforcement agencies needs to be transformed, and these states, like the EU, need to ensure they have the capability to turn rhetoric into legislation and legislation into implementation.

These new, soft security issues are of increasing importance across the new member states and the EU's wider neighbourhood, particularly those of Central and Eastern Europe (CEE). A key concern for these new member states, and for the EU as a whole, is the issue of border security. Jorg Monar, in Chapter 4, provides a detailed exposition of the EU's efforts to improve border controls and the additional challenges generated by the 2004, and future, enlargements. His analysis highlights the strong security rationale behind the EU's approach to border management. Border policy has been a significant concern for the EU since the 1980s, as evidenced by the development of the Schengen Agreement. After over twenty years of carefully orchestrated incremental progress, there were fears that enlargement to include poorer states with few effective capabilities would weaken the EU's external border regime. Hence, the new member states accession to the full Schengen part of the *acquis communautaire* has been delayed. However, Monar argues that, contrary to fears, enlargement has not significantly weakened the external border system and, more broadly, progress has continued with the development of the Area of Freedom, Security and Justice (AFSJ).

Elements of the new security agenda are also at the forefront of security concerns in the Mediterranean region, as demonstrated by Roderick Pace in Chapter 12. Key issues in the Mediterranean Basin include immigration, energy security and natural resources. By acceding to the EU, Malta has moved the EU much close to the major source and transit states for illegal immigration. Malta and Cyprus' accession has also put the EU at the geographical heart of a number of potential resource disputes, ranging from fishing rights to oil and gas supplies. However, Pace also emphasises that the Mediterranean region has a number of hard security concerns, such as terrorism and WMD proliferation, both linked to the Middle East conflict. While the Euro-Mediterranean Partnership (EMP) tried to avoid engaging in the politics of the Middle East Peace Process, these types of security concerns mean it has been very difficult to do so. The EU has tentatively taken its first operational steps in helping to facilitate a de-escalation of tension in the Israel–Palestine conflict, launching a police training and a border-monitoring mission. However, to stabilise the entire Mediterranean region further will require practical and political engagement to follow.

The Mediterranean dimension of EU security policy takes on an even greater significance when looking towards future enlargements. While by no means a foregone conclusion, the start of negotiations in October 2005 has moved Turkish membership of the EU a step closer. Hence, the EU's long-standing question of how to handle Turkey cannot be left unanswered for much longer. Bill Park, in Chapter 11, addresses the decision in terms of conceptualising Turkey as either a bridge or barrier for the EU. Geo-strategically, Turkey is vital to European security, neighbouring as it does the Middle East and the Caucuses and the Caspian, Black and Mediterranean Seas. Both conceptualisations of Turkey as a bridge and as a barrier have supporters within the EU. Some wish to envisage Turkey as a barrier to the instability of these regions, while others hope that Turkey can act as bridge to export stability to these regions. Regardless of the outcome of this debate, EU–Turkey relations will be increasingly significant for Europe's security.

Of at least equal significance is Russia. With a clear ability to influence the security of the EU, despite not seeking membership, the nature of Russia's role in European, and international, security is crucial. Dmitry Polikanov, in Chapter 8, argues that the EU–Russia relationship appears to have stagnated in recent years. He suggests two central reasons for this stagnation: the EU's internal incoherence and the growing ambiguity in Russian foreign policy. As with EU policy initiatives across a variety of security areas, an emerging theme is the difference between rhetoric and reality in this relationship. Polikanov's analysis of the relationship concludes that neither the EU nor Russia can decide if these two powers, both with global aspirations, are partners or competitors.

Since 1994, this relationship has been clouded by the conflict in Chechnya, an issue explored by Tracey German in Chapter 9. In her analysis of the Chechen conflict, German highlights the crucial differences in EU and Russian perceptions of security, reinforcing the central message of Polikanov. Her exploration of this highly sensitive political issue highlights EU–Russia differences between values and interests and between hard and soft approaches to security. These differences are most clearly expressed in the EU's expectations for Russia's handling of the Chechen conflict and Russia's actual approach. Once again, differences in rhetoric and reality, theory and practice, are apparent in the EU's handling of Russia's Chechnya policy, denouncing it in one forum and ignoring, or even indirectly legitimising, it in another.

Of fundamental concern to the EU's approach to Chechnya, and to security more broadly, is the emphasis on human rights. With the incorporation of eight relatively new democracies into the EU, ensuring human rights standards are upheld and spread beyond the new EU borders has been central to the enlargement process. During the accession process, the EU has a great deal of leverage over candidate states, obliging them to fulfil all criteria prior to membership, including those on human rights and fundamental freedoms. However, once these states have entered the EU, leverage is significantly reduced. However, Karim Khan and Anna Kotzeva, in Chapter 6, argue that, due to the 'War on Terror', the human rights security nexus has remained at the forefront of EU security policy. Therefore, leverage can still be exerted on a state that seems to be allowing human rights to diminish in importance. Yet, Kahn and Kotzeva admit that, when push comes to shove, state security does seem to take precedence over an individual's human rights, even in an established liberal democracy like the United Kingdom. This is significant, as human rights have a central role in the EU's perception and projection of security. Human rights are at the heart of the EU's values and an inability to uphold them risks undermining its credibility.

The loss of credibility was perhaps most apparent in the Western Balkans. This is a region that has seen some of the worst human rights abuses in Europe's post-Cold War history. In Chapter 13, Anthony Welch challenges the EU to do better in the Western Balkans, where human rights violations have been at the centre of the violent break up of Yugoslavia. Welch argues that the problems and failures of the EU's Stability Pact for South-eastern Europe will widen the chasm between the EU and those parts of the Balkans that remain, at least in the short to medium term, outside the Union. Politically and economically, the EU must learn the lessons of past failures and encourage the development of a political and economic climate not based on marginalisation and fear. Relations within and across the states of the Western Balkans must be normalised and stabilised. The EU and other international organisations must put the needs of the people of these war-torn states at the forefront of their policies. Longer term, how the EU deals with this region will be central to the EU's strategy for spreading stability beyond its borders in future years.

The ability to normalise and stabilise relations, entrench democracy and encourage economic development will also be vital in the EU's relationship with Ukraine. Rosaria Puglisi, in Chapter 10, explores the prospects for EU relations with Ukraine, one of the EU's largest potential member states. With the accession of Poland and the 'Orange Revolution' of 2004–05, Ukraine's strategic outlook shifted significantly westward. Yet, developments through 2005–06 have brought into question the durability of the 'Orange Revolution' and hence the long-term strategic orientation of Ukraine. Domestic political instability and rising tensions with Russia will prove a stern test of the revolutionary enthusiasm that so captivated Europe in 2004–05. A secure Ukraine should enhance stability along an important section of the EU's eastern border. However, it also raises a number of questions and brings a number of security concerns closer to the EU. For example, Moldova's fragile condition is of major concern to both Ukraine and the EU. Yet, as mentioned earlier, the EU has taken a long time to become fully engaged in this crisis, only recently agreeing to assist Ukraine in a border-monitoring mission along the Moldova–Ukraine border and becoming more proactive in negotiations.

As this introduction illustrates, this book takes a holistic approach to security. Rather than focus on one specific aspect of the security agenda in relation to enlargement, this volume tackles a range of different security issues. The book also adopts a broad geographical scope, by examining key security relationships with states and regions in the EU's self-declared neighbourhood, namely Russia, Ukraine, Turkey, the Greater Middle East and the Balkans.

This volume aims to analyse these fundamental functional and geographical security priorities. Underlying this critical survey of Europe's security is a core theme: the impact of enlargement on the security of the EU. The central question is whether the EU is more or less secure post-enlargement. By addressing the range of contemporary security issues facing the EU, from traditional state-centred, military issues to new, transnational issues, focused on the security of the region, community or individual, this book highlights the substantive issues at the core of any future EU security policy.

These issues and threats facing the EU can no longer be simply labelled internal or external and therefore the EU, as well as the new member states, will have to adjust to this evolving security environment. Most importantly, to tackle the range of security issues facing the EU, the community needs to improve its political will, sense of leadership and material capability. The EU will have to ensure that enlargement does not further disrupt its internal cohesion and adds to, rather than detracts from, its ability to externally project security and stability into its neighbourhood. Donald Rumsfeld's conceptualisation of 'old' and 'new' Europe must not be set in stone, nor must the EU allow its perception of security to remain static. Nevertheless, the EU must be realistic in its objectives and maintain a balance between constantly trying to stay relevant in the field of security and ensuring it fulfils its existing expectations. While the EU has widened its security community, contributing to the stability of a large swath of Central and Eastern Europe, security concerns remain and are an ever-increasing priority on its policy agenda. This security agenda focuses on the EU's efforts to secure the community's values and interests, as well as its ability to project stability and security outside of the security community. Having raised expectations on both fronts, the EU needs to work hard to establish its credentials as a provider of security.

Notes

1 Christopher Hill, 'The capability–expectations gap, or conceptualising Europe's international role', *Journal of Common Market Studies*, 31:3 (1993), pp. 305–28.
2 See David Allen and Michael Smith, 'Western Europe's presence in the contemporary international arena', *Review of International Studies*, 16:1 (1990), pp. 19–37.
3 See C. Cosgrove and K. Twitchett (eds), *The New International Actors: The UN and the EEC* (London: Macmillan, 1970); Charlotte Bretherton and John Vogler, *The European Union as a Global Actor* (London: Routledge, 1999); Karen Smith, *EU Foreign Policy in a Changing World* (London: Polity, 2003).

1

EU enlargement and NATO: the Balkan experience

Martin A. Smith[1]

During the 1990s, both the EU and NATO enlarged their memberships: the EU by taking in Austria, Finland and Sweden in 1995 and NATO by admitting the Czech Republic, Hungary and Poland four years later. These two enlargement processes were not officially linked. In the wake of the developing EU enlargement process in the early 1990s, NATO members had apparently contented themselves with the inclusion of a paragraph in their own 1995 'Study on NATO Enlargement' (the document that can be said to have officially begun NATO's enlargement process). The study stated that:

> The enlargement of the two organisations will proceed autonomously, according to their respective internal dynamics and processes. This means they are unlikely to proceed at precisely the same pace. But the Alliance views its own enlargement and that of the EU as mutually supportive and parallel processes, which together will make a significant contribution to strengthening Europe's security structure. Thus, each organisation should ensure that their respective processes are in fact mutually supportive of the goal of enhancing European stability and security. While no rigid parallelism is foreseen, each organisation will need to consider developments in the other.[2]

In fact, the EU and NATO enlargement processes during the 1990s were characterised by what Smith and Timmins have called 'incremental linkage'.[3] Although not formally or structurally linked, it was apparent that a move forward in one institution's enlargement process would, within a relatively short period of time, produce an 'answering call' from the other, in terms of a corresponding move. As a result, in practice, neither institution's enlargement dynamic was allowed, by its member states, to move decisively ahead of the other.

On the NATO side, the main impetus for the creation and maintenance of this informal incremental linkage came from the US and its Atlanticist allies in Europe. They were motivated, firstly, by concerns that, if EU enlargement was allowed to proceed into Central and Eastern Europe and the Balkan region significantly ahead of NATO's own enlargement process, then what US officials had called 'underlapping security guarantees' might develop.[4] In other words, EU members might find themselves being drawn into conflicts in these relatively unstable regions and, not having an established system of security guarantees through the EU itself, might then call on

NATO to intervene, even though the states directly concerned might not themselves be NATO members. In addition, there was also, undoubtedly, a sense at the time of what might be called 'institutional Darwinism', namely a feeling that the two institutions were in a kind of competition with regard to embracing non-member countries in Europe. It was felt that there would be potentially debilitating consequences for the 'loser' if one was allowed to get too far ahead of the other in this 'great game'. Hence, there was an innate reluctance to allow either to do so. In sum, the motivation behind the development of incremental linkage was essentially competitive, rather than co-operative.

Enlargement in the new millennium: incremental linkage continued?

The very fact that the most important enlargement rounds in the histories of both organisations were completed within one month of each other, in the spring of 2004, lends weight to the proposition that the member states of both institutions remained concerned to ensure that neither got significantly ahead of the other in the enlargement stakes. An examination of key agreed statements by EU and NATO ministers provides additional support for the contention that incremental linkage between their respective enlargement processes has been maintained into the twenty-first century.

Within less than a week of each other, in December 1999, the two institutions' senior decision-taking forums – the European Council and the North Atlantic Council (NAC) respectively – committed their members in principle to moving ahead with enlargement. The European Council declared that 'the Union should be in a position to welcome new member states from the end of 2002, as soon as they have demonstrated their ability to assume the obligations of membership and once the negotiating process has been successfully completed'.[5] Four days later, the NAC, meeting at foreign minister level,[6] reaffirmed NATO's 'commitment to remain open to new members'. It added that 'the Alliance expects to extend further invitations in coming years to nations willing and able to assume the responsibilities and obligations of membership'.[7] The EU's declared choice of 2002 as the target year for signing accession agreements with prospective new members was also significant. In April 1999, at a summit meeting called to mark NATO's fiftieth anniversary, its members' leaders, having agreed that the door remained open to further enlargement, also stated that they themselves would 'review' progress towards that goal 'no later than' 2002.[8]

Thus, by the beginning of the new millennium, the members of both institutions had established an in-principle commitment to moving ahead with further rounds of enlargement within a directly comparable timeframe. The rhetorical (and practical) pace quickened from 2001. In June of that year, the European Council declared that 'the enlargement process is irreversible' and reaffirmed the 2002 date for the completion of accession negotiations. These types of EU statements had also begun to add another date – 2004 – as the deadline for the new members to actually join the institution and assume the obligations of membership (this date was chosen so as to enable them to take part in the European Parliament elections due that year).[9] Thus was born the *de facto* 2004 deadline for the enlargement of *both* institutions' memberships. At the end of 2001, NATO members duly issued their answering call. They declared at their December foreign ministers' meeting that the next NATO summit, in Prague in November 2002, would 'launch the next round of NATO enlargement'.[10] It duly did do, with a stated commitment that the NATO process would be completed by May 2004.[11]

During 2002, as anticipated, both the EU and NATO officially identified those states that their members wished to invite to join the ranks and invited them to conclude negotiations on accession.[12] There were multiple points of comparison between the would-be new members on the respective guest lists. Both the EU and NATO had identified the three Baltic States, Slovenia, Slovakia, Romania and Bulgaria as candidates for accession. In addition, the EU was also negotiating with NATO's three newest members: the Czech Republic, Hungary and Poland. Their accession would enable the EU to catch up with NATO, in terms of enlarging into former Soviet bloc territory in Central Europe. The only differences between the EU and NATO were that Cyprus and Malta were negotiating for membership of the former, but not the latter.

It is clear from this brief discussion that distinct, informal but, at the same time, noticeable and important linkages between the two enlargement processes were in evidence through the 1990s and leading up to the 2004 enlargements. In spite of this, the absence, to date, of *formal* linkage between them has concerned some observers. For them, this deficiency opens up the possibility of what Adrian Hyde-Price has called 'antinomies' developing in relations between the EU and NATO and in their overall approaches to Europe's security challenges.[13] The discussions in the sections that follow aim to assess whether such antinomies are, in fact, observable. They will focus on what has been Europe's most significant region in terms of security challenges and international responses since the end of the Cold War: the Balkans.

The Balkans: competition or complementarity?

The region under consideration here is, in NATO parlance, generally referred to as 'South-eastern Europe' and, in EU speak, as the 'Western Balkans'. Essentially, these descriptors cover the successor states of the former Yugoslavia,[14] together with Albania. Other neighbours, being either EU and/or NATO members or slated to join, are usually diplomatically excluded from descriptive association with these strife-prone states.

NATO's interest in this region can be traced back to 1992 and the first deployment of its collective military assets in support of the United Nations Protection Force (UNPROFOR) during the civil war in Bosnia–Herzegovina (BiH). During the course of the 1990s, its military contribution became extensive. In 1995–96, a multinational Implementation Force (IFOR) of 60,000 troops was deployed to Bosnia, within a NATO command and control framework, to help police the implementation of the recently signed Dayton peace accords. A further 40,000 soldiers were sent to Kosovo as part of the NATO-led Kosovo Force (KFOR) in June 1999, following Operation Allied Force, the coercive air campaign which forced the Serbs to relinquish *de facto* control over that province.

Following early, abortive, diplomatic efforts to prevent the break-up of Yugoslavia degenerating into civil war in 1991–92, the EU was relatively quiescent in the region until the end of the NATO-Serb conflict over Kosovo in mid 1999. Thereafter, it became significantly more proactive. Firstly, in June 1999, the 'Stability Pact' was launched for the states of the region, embracing negotiations on security, democratisation and economic reconstruction.[15] Later that same year, Javier Solana, who had been NATO Secretary-General during the Kosovo conflict, was appointed to be the EU's first 'High Representative for the Common Foreign and Security Policy'. He displayed a strong personal interest in the Balkan region and, by the summer of 2002, was reported to be spending about 60 per cent of his time dealing with it.[16]

In every sense, the 1999–2004 round of enlargement played an important role in bringing the EU closer to the Balkans than it ever had been before. In 2004, Slovenia became the first former Yugoslav republic to join both the EU and NATO. NATO also admitted Bulgaria and Romania, neighbouring states of the former Yugoslavia, both of which are also slated to join the EU in 2007. As part of the process of preparing the ground for enlargement, the EU sought to further enhance its relations with the former Yugoslav states. The main fruit of this renewed interest has been the so-called 'Stabilisation and Association' process. This holds out the ultimate prospect of states in the 'Western Balkans' being allowed to join the EU, on condition that they prove willing to make extensive reforms to their economic and political structures and are co-operative in helping to apprehend remaining indicted war criminals from the Balkan conflicts of the 1990s.[17] NATO, for its part, has declared that 'the door remains open' to future enlargements and has specifically identified Croatia, Albania and the Former Yugoslav Republic of Macedonia (FYROM) as states that are working towards eventual membership.[18]

The cumulative effect of this state of affairs is that the Balkan region has increasingly been emerging as the place 'where theory becomes reality in the NATO–EU relationship'. The same analyst also rightly added that 'whatever the discussion in Brussels is regarding NATO and the EU, the place where the relationship is most put to the test is the Balkans. A smoothly functioning relationship there will have positive ramifications at a more political level.'[19] That is why it is appropriate here to assess the nature and character of contemporary EU–NATO activities and relations in the Balkan region.

Until the end of the 1990s, the two institutions essentially had little formalised contact with each other in any respect. The peace agreements for both Bosnia and Kosovo had set in place a basic division of labour approach to the international pacification and stabilisation efforts in both these places, with a similar structure for each. The UN sat on top, nominally at least, and tried to provide a sense of overall strategic direction. Underneath it, the NATO forces undertook peace-keeping duties and also dealt with specific military tasks, such as searching for illicit arms caches and indicted war criminals. The EU, meanwhile, took the lead in seeking to promote economic reconstruction and development, whilst the Organisation for Security and Co-operation in Europe (OSCE) headed up election supervision responsibilities.

This situation has begun to change in the new millennium. The first change came with the EU takeover of the UN Police Mission in Bosnia in January 2003. The most obvious and important consequences of the change for EU-NATO relations have been the transition from NATO to EU-led peace-keeping and stabilisation forces in, firstly, FYROM, in the spring of 2003 and, subsequently, Bosnia at the end of 2004. This has necessitated a significant increase in operational co-operation between and across the two institutions, based on the hitherto unused Berlin Plus arrangements.[20] It has also led to suggestions that the EU is in the process of 'taking over in the Balkans', as NATO and the US increasingly focus their interests outside Europe, as part of the Bush administration's global 'War on Terror'.

In December 2004, for example, just as the EU was preparing to assume peace-keeping duties in Bosnia, a report published by the Assembly of the Western European Union (WEU) (which now bills itself as the 'Interparliamentary European Security and Defence Assembly') asserted that:

> Althea [the EU military operation in Bosnia] is more than simply a military crisis-management mission, or the substitution of a NATO force by an EU one. It marks a stage towards the EU's political objective gradually to take over the crisis management of all aspects of Balkan affairs: political, security, economic and social. This aim is clearly stated in the European Security Strategy adopted by the European Council in Brussels, on 12 December 2003.[21]

Elsewhere, this same report argued that the EU operation in Bosnia, 'while it takes account of the US view of Balkans security, is independent of the United States'.[22] A quasi-conspiratorial interpretation of developments – suggesting that EU members in some way 'aim' to progressively diminish NATO's role in European security affairs – has also been put forward by some, on the basis of their reading of the proposed EU Constitution. Jeffrey Cimbalo, for example, has argued that, if the Constitution is ever finally adopted (now a very sizeable 'if' in view of its rejection in the French and Dutch ratification referendums in the summer of 2005), 'the new Europe would focus on aggrandising EU power at the expense of NATO'.[23]

These concerns are exaggerated. The 2003 European Security Strategy (ESS) referred to in the WEU report is clear that 'one of the core elements of the international system is the transatlantic relationship. This is not only in our bilateral interest but strengthens the international community as a whole. NATO is an important expression of this relationship.' Lest there still be room for doubt, the basic point is reiterated later in the same document. Here, it is asserted that 'the transatlantic relationship is irreplaceable'.[24]

Old-style Atlanticists might be perturbed to see NATO referred to as 'an' rather than 'the' institutional embodiment of the transatlantic relationship, yet this formulation does no more than reflect objective realities. The EU has a distinct transatlantic relationship of its own, via a programme of institutionalised summit meetings between the US President and senior administration officials, on the one hand, and the Commission

President and current EU Presidency state on the other. Some might also argue that the OSCE serves as an additional transatlantic consultative and discussion forum.

One has to work very hard, even reading between the lines, to detect any 'clear statement' in the ESS about an EU aim to take over in the Balkans. On the contrary, the text of the document seems clear in recognising that the EU cannot realistically aspire to bring long-term peace and stability to the region on its own. Thus, it is stated that:

> Our task is to promote a ring of well-governed countries to the East of the European Union and on the borders of the Mediterranean with whom we can enjoy close and cooperative relations. The importance of this is best illustrated in the Balkans. *Through our concerted efforts with the US, Russia, NATO and other international partners*, the stability of the region is no longer threatened by the outbreak of major conflict [emphasis added].[25]

And again, later:

> The European Union has made progress towards a coherent foreign policy and effective crisis management. We have instruments in place that can be used effectively, as we have demonstrated in the Balkans and beyond. But if we are to make a contribution that matches our potential, we need to be more active, more coherent and more capable. *And we need to work with others* [emphasis added].[26]

In July 2003, five months before EU members endorsed the ESS, NATO and the EU had agreed to pursue a 'concerted approach for the Western Balkans'. What this meant in practice was agreement on the core areas of concern that needed to be addressed, together with outline agreement on the main roles that each institution would undertake. There was also a pledge to step up inter-institutional consultation and co-ordination.[27] It has been described as 'the only formal agreement between the two organisations'.[28] Although it is not, in fact, the only co-operative agreement *per se* (a number of accords have been put in place to give practical effect to the Berlin Plus arrangements), it is certainly true that the 'concerted approach' represents a precedent for theatre-specific operationally focused understandings between the organisations and their respective member states.

The catalyst for the agreement seems to have come about as a result of some problems in the handover from NATO to the EU of the stabilisation mission in FYROM. These reportedly related to the sharing of information and co-ordination issues.[29] It seems likely that they were the product, not of deliberate obstruction or ill-will on either side, but rather of the simple fact that this was the first occasion in practice when NATO members had agreed to formally hand a military operation over to another international institution. It was also, of course, the first time that the EU had undertaken to be responsible for a military operation. No template for a smooth transition existed, therefore, on either side. The July 2003 agreement can thus be seen as an attempt to establish ground rules, both for FYROM and also for other theatres in the region. As such, it pointed clearly towards acceptance of the view, on both sides, that NATO and the EU were likely to be working *together* in the Balkans for the foreseeable future.

It is, however, in relation to the practicalities of the EU-led operations in FYROM and Bosnia that the lack of substance in suggestions that the EU might wish to displace NATO from the Balkans can most clearly be seen. In both operations, the EU-led forces have been crucially dependent upon NATO military assets and resources. As noted earlier, they operate under arrangements that are known in NATO-speak as Berlin Plus. In practice, this means that the EU forces have relied largely on NATO command and planning structures, with a chain of command leading from NATO's senior military headquarters in Belgium and the Deputy Supreme Allied Commander Europe (DSACEUR). Although the DSACEUR is, by tradition, always a European national, the command chain also reportedly runs through the NATO southern command, which is a US-led headquarters. The command structure has evidently been carefully designed to avoid the appearance of EU forces being placed *directly* under US command.[30] Yet, it is not the case that the operations have been conducted, as the 2004 WEU report referred to earlier appears to suggest, *completely* independently of the US. Whilst they may be formally politically independent, in the sense that they have been placed under the overall direction of the EU Council, by agreeing to utilise the Berlin Plus arrangements, EU members have accepted 'logically, the United States having some influence over the operation[s]'.[31]

In addition, suggestions that either NATO or the US are in the process of *withdrawing* (as opposed to *drawing down*) their presence and force levels in the Balkans are wide of the mark. By far the largest military deployment in the region – over 20,000 troops, which are still committed to KFOR – remains under NATO command. When it was first deployed in 1999, 15 per cent of KFOR was made up of US troops. The ratio had fallen to 9 per cent by 2004 (the last full year for which figures were available at the time of writing). However, this still represented a US commitment of over 2,000 troops.[32]

NATO has also retained military headquarters in both FYROM and Bosnia, following the formal handover to EU-led forces there. Both NATO headquarters Sarajevo and NATO headquarters Skopje are small (with around 200 personnel in each) and their presence may thus be said to be mainly symbolic. However, the symbolism is potent, in several respects. To begin with, the continued NATO presence is a tangible demonstration on the ground of the implementation of the July 2003 EU–NATO agreement on tackling key Balkan challenges together. The NATO headquarters thus have specific assigned tasks. Chief amongst them, in both Bosnia and FYROM, is working with governments to secure defence sector reforms. In Bosnia, in addition, the NATO force is tasked with continuing the quest to apprehend remaining indicted war criminals and with tracking any attempt by militant Islamists to establish a foothold in that state.[33]

A continuing NATO and US presence has also been required in order to provide an underlying degree of reassurance to the locals that EU forces by themselves cannot provide. This has been the case in Bosnia especially, where the record of the 1990s conflict implies for many Bosnians, of all ethnic backgrounds, that the EU on its own is unable to deal effectively with a serious security breakdown and the carnage that can result.[34] Therefore, in Bosnia, in addition to the NATO headquarters in Sarajevo, the US also retains a national military base at Tuzla, primarily to enable it to airlift in additional military forces, should it decide that the security situation in future makes reinforcement necessary.[35]

All told, around 250 US military personnel continue to serve in Bosnia, at either the national or the NATO headquarters. Their numbers are down from the 1,000 or so who served with the NATO-led Stabilisation Force (SFOR) at the time that it was replaced by the EU force in December 2004.[36] This obviously represents a notable drawing down of the US presence. It is likely that one reason the Bush administration embraced the idea of the EU replacing SFOR was that this US draw-down would enable the US to assuage those amongst its own supporters who believed the 2000 Bush presidential election campaign had pledged to withdraw from the Balkans altogether.

What is also striking, on the other hand, is the extent to which there has been a dearth of pressure from within the EU – or amongst European members of NATO – for the US and NATO to turn the Balkans over entirely to the EU. Voices supporting this could sometimes be heard back in the late 1990s, before EU members had found agreement on operationalising their rhetorical commitments to create a viable ESDP. Since the EU actually began to make tangible military commitments to the Balkans, however, these voices have largely fallen silent. Instead, there has been a reiteration of what became a *de facto* mantra during the second half of the 1990s: the US and Europe went into the Balkans together and they will leave together.

A new division of labour?

An interim conclusion can be drawn here from this analysis of the recent record of the EU and NATO in the Balkans. Michael Clarke and Paul Cornish have argued that 'the "competition" between them for a defence role is greatly overdrawn in a highly charged political debate in the UK'.[37] This sound judgement can also be applied to the debates in other EU and NATO member states. As the discussions above have demonstrated, the record since the start of the new millennium has, in fact, been one increasingly marked by co-operation rather than competition between the two institutions.

Some have seen the increasing lack of rancour in debates about the roles of the EU and NATO as being due to a growing *de facto* division of labour between them. This term has been used in two distinct senses. Firstly, it is sometimes employed to describe the perceived situation within the Balkan region. In this scenario, the EU has taken on quasi-military tasks in relatively stable and secure environments in Bosnia and FYROM, with NATO retaining control in more volatile Kosovo. NATO has retained a baseline presence in Bosnia and FYROM too, as noted above, so that it can bring a harder military edge to bear effectively and efficiently should necessity dictate in the future.

This view has much to commend it. The July 2003 agreement between the two institutions did indeed lay out a framework for a division of labour between them and the complementarity of approach that the agreement sought to entrench appears, thus far, to have been solidified in practice. This has been most apparent in Bosnia, where the small NATO force has existed alongside the larger EU one for the purpose of undertaking a number of agreed and specified military tasks.

What is less clear, however, is whether the increasing EU commitment to operations in the Balkans is helping to promote the second kind of division of labour that is sometimes mentioned. This sees security roles and tasks within Europe as a whole coming increasingly within the purview of the EU, whilst NATO focuses mainly on threats and challenges in other regions. The view is also sometimes expressed that one side of this equation feeds directly into the other, because the EU's Balkan commitments help to free up NATO resources and attention for the wider global tasks.[38]

Over the course of 2002, NATO members effectively decided to eliminate the remaining vestiges of the Cold War understanding, which held that NATO had no institutional roles to play outside of Europe. They formally recognised international terrorism and the proliferation of WMD as being core security threats. In addition, they adopted elements of US thinking on 'effects-based operations', a significant part of which rests on the premise that military power should be projected quickly and effectively to trouble spots beyond the territory of NATO member states. In this respect, the most important practical decision, taken at the NATO Prague summit in November 2002, was to begin to create a multinational NATO Response Force (NRF), which could be deployed 'wherever needed' around the world. This force is due to be fully operational by the autumn of 2006.[39]

Developments on the ground since 2002 may also indicate that NATO is increasingly focusing its interests and efforts outside of Europe. In August 2003, it began to provide a multinational headquarters facility in Kabul, Afghanistan for the International Security Assistance Force (ISAF) that was based there. This was the first time in its history that a formal NATO operation (that is, one involving deployment of its multinational military assets) had been mounted outside Europe. Over the course of 2004 and 2005, agreement was also reached amongst member states to use NATO multinational teams to assist in the training of indigenous security forces inside Iraq.

There is little doubt as to where the major impetus behind these developments has come from: the US. Many prominent US officials and analysts have articulated and developed the view that international security threats and challenges in the post-September 11 era necessitate NATO refocusing on extra-European commitments. In congressional testimony in April 2003, for example, Nicholas Burns, the then US Ambassador to NATO stated that:

> If NATO's past was centred in countering the Soviet threat to Western Europe, its future must be devoted to meeting the greatest security challenge this generation faces – the toxic mix of terrorism, states that sponsor terrorism, and weapons of mass destruction far from Europe's shores. NATO needs to pivot from its inward focus on Europe – which was necessary and appropriate during the Cold War – to an outward focus on the arc of countries where most of the threats are today – in Central and South Asia, and in the Middle East.[40]

Well-known analyst Ronald Asmus told the same hearings:

> The core question facing NATO today is simple: what should be this Alliance's main mission in a world where Europe is increasingly secure and many if not all of the major threats we are likely to face in the future will come from new sources beyond the

continent? Should NATO's job be limited to maintaining the peace on an increasingly secure continent – a worthwhile objective but hardly America's only or most important concern? Or should the Alliance retool itself to address new threats to its members' security irrespective of where they emanate from? To be blunt, do we and our allies want NATO to have a significant role in the future Afghanistan and Iraqs that we will inevitably face?[41]

It would be wrong, however, to suggest that it is simply a question of the US pushing for NATO to move outside Europe and leaving the EU to deal with remaining security challenges in the Balkans. The discussions above have demonstrated that the US has deemed it important – for political, security and operational reasons – to continue to retain both a NATO and a national military presence in the Balkan region. While this is at a historically low level in terms of numbers of troops on the ground, NATO has developed the capacity to move in reinforcements quickly if required, as happened at the time of serious ethnic disturbances in Kosovo in March 2004.

In short, there has been an enduring sense, in both the US and amongst NATO members in Europe, that security tasks in the Balkans remain sufficiently important as to justify continued US and NATO interest and engagement. The priorities of both NATO and the EU's new member states have reinforced this sense of importance. Hence, as noted above, the Bush administration has persevered with the 'in together, out together' doctrine first propounded by its predecessor in the 1990s.[42]

The US has also been consistently interested in trying to persuade a broad cross-section of its allies in Europe to contribute militarily to its major campaigns in Afghanistan and, especially, Iraq. To this end, there has been official US reluctance to see any division of labour arrangements being formalised *within* NATO. As Ambassador Burns noted during his congressional testimony in April 2003, 'we do not want to see it develop. We do not want to see a two-tiered alliance where the United States is uniquely capable of projecting force, of doing the fighting, and our European allies cannot be with us'.[43] This thinking lay behind the US initiative to create the NRF. In purely military terms, the US, with its unrivalled national force projection capabilities, surely has no need of another, multinational, expeditionary formation. The point of the NRF, therefore, is mainly political – to provide a framework and a means for attempting to ensure that a cross-section of NATO allies participate alongside the US in military operations outside Europe. It could even be argued that there has been a *de facto* trade-off between continued US involvement in the Balkans and (albeit in some cases tentative) European support for NATO's growing portfolio of extra-European operations.

Conclusion

To return to an underlying theme of this book, how important has EU enlargement been in helping to explain its greater involvement in the Balkan region since the turn of the millennium? It would be foolish to suggest that it has played no role. The 2004 round of enlargement extended the EU's membership into the Balkan region, after all. On the other hand, it is possible to argue that the EU and its member states were moving towards taking on more significant roles in the Balkans in any event, due to two other factors. The first has been the personal interest in the region of High Representative Solana who, it may be recalled, had also been preoccupied with Balkan issues during his tenure as NATO Secretary-General in the second half of the 1990s. His time in office saw the first deployments of NATO peace-keeping forces to Bosnia, as well as the Kosovo war. The second causal explanation for greater EU interest in the region in the present decade can be found in the formal creation of the ESDP in 1999 (a development inspired partly by reactions to perceived European over-dependence on the US during the Kosovo conflict). Once the member states had declared that the EU was prepared to take on certain military tasks (largely relating to peace-keeping and humanitarian operations) and identified force goals, a process was set in motion whereby it became reasonable to expect them to begin to seek out opportunities to test their new capabilities. Thus, in spring 2003, the EU took the relatively 'easy first step'[44] in FYROM and followed that up in Bosnia at the end of 2004. This latter commitment is undoubtedly more demanding. Yet, EU members have had the assurance that NATO and the US remain 'on the horizon' in the region and can be expected to become involved promptly if anything goes seriously wrong.

NATO's own 2004 round of enlargement mirrored that of the EU by moving its membership deep into the Balkans. It is, thus, hardly surprising that it has not withdrawn from the region. Given the EU's enhanced degree of involvement, and in terms of overall security in the Balkans, it is essential that the EU and NATO develop means and methods of co-operation, in order to ensure that each makes a worthwhile contribution and relations between them do not become either duplicative or competitive. Thus far, concerns about a competitive situation developing have proved to be without foundation. Given the politicking and sometimes public bickering and expressions of rivalry that were apparent on occasion during the 1990s, this might appear to be surprising. The 1990s were a time of rhetorical posturing, however, especially for the EU, which did not then have any actual operational defence and security capability. The current decade has witnessed a transition to such an operational capacity and, as this has developed, the rhetoric has been increasingly replaced by a realisation that successful operations on the ground require both effective demarcation and efficient co-operation with NATO. The 'Atlanticist' perspective of the 2004 and likely future enlargements will reinforce this approach.

Notes

1 The views expressed here are personal and do not represent the opinions or views of the British Government, Ministry of Defence or the Royal Military Academy Sandhurst.
2 *Study on NATO Enlargement* (Brussels: NATO, 1995), p. 8.
3 Martin A. Smith and Graham Timmins, 'The European Union and NATO enlargement debates in comparative perspective: a case of incremental linkage?', *West European Politics*, 22:3 (July 1999), pp. 22–40 and Martin A. Smith and Graham Timmins, *Building a Bigger Europe: EU and NATO Enlargement in Comparative Perspective* (Aldershot: Ashgate, 2000).
4 Author's interview with a member of the US Mission to NATO, October 1993.

5 Council of the European Union, *Conclusions of the Helsinki European Council* (Brussels, December 1999).
6 The North Atlantic Council can meet in any one of four different formats: permanent representatives, defence ministers, foreign ministers and heads of state and government.
7 NATO Press Release M-NAC-2(99)166, www.nato.int/docu/pr/1999/p99-166e.htm.
8 NATO Press Release NAC-S(99)64, www.nato.int/docu/pr/1999/p99-064e.htm.
9 Council of the European Union, *Conclusions of the Göteborg European Council* (Brussels, June 2001).
10 NATO Press Release M-NAC-2(2001)158, www.nato.int/docu/pr/2001/p01-158e.htm.
11 Prague Summit Declaration, Press Release 2002 127, www.nato.int/docu/pr/2002/p02-127e.htm.
12 Council of the European Union, *Conclusions of the Seville European Council* (Brussels, June 2002) and NATO Press Release (2002)127, www.nato.int/docu/pr/2002/p02-127e.htm.
13 Adrian Hyde-Price, 'The antinomies of European security: dual enlargement and the reshaping of European order', *Contemporary Security Policy*, 21:3 (December 2000), pp. 139–67.
14 BiH, Croatia, FYROM, Serbia and Montenegro and Slovenia.
15 For analysis of the early record of the Stability Pact see Paul Latawski, 'South-east Europe: collision of norms and identity?', in Martin A. Smith and Graham Timmins (eds), *Uncertain Europe: Building a New European Security Order?* (London: Routledge, 2001).
16 Author's interview with EU official, July 2002.
17 See Marco Minniti, *South East European Security and the Role of the NATO–EU Partnership* (Brussels: NATO Parliamentary Assembly, 2004), pp. 12–13.
18 NATO Press Release (2004)096, www.nato.int/docu/pr/2004/p04-096e.htm.
19 John Smith, *NATO's Ongoing Role in Balkan Security* (Brussels: NATO Parliamentary Assembly, 2005), p. 1.
20 Based on 1996 Berlin NATO ministerial, see Press Communiqué M-NAC-1(96)63, www.nato.int/docu/pr/1996/p96-063e.htm and 1999 NATO summit in Washington: see Press Release NAC-S-(99)64, www.nato.int/docu/pr/1999/p99-064e.htm.
21 Assembly of Western European Union, *The Deployment of European Forces in the Balkans* (Paris: Assembly of Western European Union, 2004), p. 12.
22 John Wilkinson, *The Deployment of European Forces* (2004), p. 13.
23 Jeffrey Cimbalo, 'Saving NATO From Europe', *Foreign Affairs*, 83:6 (November/December 2004), p. 111; Bart van Winsen, *The European Security and Defence Policy following EU and NATO Enlargement – Reply to the Annual Report of the Council* (Paris: Assembly of Western European Union, 2004), pp. 11–12.
24 *A Secure Europe in a Better World: European Security Strategy* (Brussels: European Union, 2003), p. 9 and p. 13.
25 Ibid., p. 8.
26 Ibid., p. 11.
27 NATO Press Release (2003)089, www.nato.int/docu/pr/2003/p03-089e.htm.
28 Marco Minniti, *NATO–EU Security Co-operation* (Brussels: NATO Parliamentary Assembly, 2005), p. 2.
29 Ibid., p. 4; John Smith, *The Development of Response Forces in NATO and the EU and the Evolving NATO–EU Relationship* (Brussels: NATO Parliamentary Assembly, 2004), para. 39.
30 See Julian Lindley-French, 'The ties that bind', *NATO Review* (Autumn 2003), www.nato.int/docu/review/2003/issue3/english/art2.html; Lionel Ponsard, 'The dawning of a new security era?', *NATO Review* (Autumn 2004), www.nato.int/docu/review/2004/issue3/english/art3.html; Smith, *The Development of Response Forces in NATO and the EU*, para. 37.
31 John Wilkinson, *The European Union's Stabilisation Missions in South-east Europe* (Paris: Assembly of Western European Union, 2004), p. 16.
32 Gustav Lindstrom, 'EU–US burdensharing: who does what?', *Chaillot Paper*, 82 (2005), pp. 42–3.

33 Robert Serry, 'NATO's Balkan odyssey', *NATO Review* (Winter 2003), www.nato.int/docu/review/2003/issue4/english/art3.html; John Wilkinson, *The European Union's Stabilisation Missions in South-east Europe*, p. 15; Marco Minniti, *NATO-EU Security Co-operation*, p. 3.
34 See House Committee on International Relations, *Bosnia and Herzegovina: Unfinished Business*, 109th Congress First Session (Washington, DC: US Government Printing Office, 2005), pp. 24–6; Smith, *The Development of Response Forces in NATO and the EU*, para. 48; Ponsard, 'The dawning of a new security era?'.
35 See Robert Serry and Christopher Bennett, 'Staying the course', *NATO Review* (Winter 2004), www.nato.int/docu/review/2004/issue4/english/art3.html.
36 Terri Lukach, 'Bosnia mission continues for 250 US troops', *American Forces Information Service News Articles* (September 2005), www.defenselink.mil/.
37 Michael Clarke and Paul Cornish, 'The European defence project and the Prague summit', *International Affairs*, 78:4 (October 2002), p. 786.
38 See Dieter Dettke, House Committee on International Relations, *The Future of Transatlantic Relations: A View From Europe*, 108th Congress First Session (Washington, DC: US Government Printing Office, 2003), p. 19.
39 See Reykjavik Summit, Press Release M-NAC-1(2002)59, www.nato.int/docu/pr/2002/p02-059e.htm; Prague summit communiqué; Press Release (2002)127, www.nato.int/docu/pr/2002/p02-127e.htm.
40 Senate Committee on Foreign Relations, *NATO Enlargement: Qualifications and Contributions – Parts I–IV*, 108th Congress First Session (Washington, DC: US Government Printing Office, 2003), www.access.gpo.gov/congress/senate.
41 *NATO Enlargement*.
42 See Nancy Soderberg, *The Superpower Myth* (New Jersey: Wiley & Sons, 2005), pp. 116–17.
43 *NATO Enlargement*.
44 John Smith, *The Development of Response Forces in NATO and the EU*, para. 38.

2

The implications of EU enlargement for the European security and defence policy

Alistair J.K. Shepherd

Introduction

The EU's enlargement from fifteen to twenty-five members brings both risks and opportunities for the EU's most challenging policy initiative, the ESDP. It crystallises the fundamental questions at its heart. What policy priorities and common interests shape ESDP? What capabilities does ESDP possess and what does it still need? What sort of leadership will be required to develop greater cohesion? The perspectives brought by the new member states (NMS) may complicate the questions, but may also provide new solutions.

The risks of enlargement were evident even before the NMS had formally joined the EU. During the 2003 Iraq crisis, all the CEE states joining, or hoping to join, the EU supported US policy, while a slim majority of the pre-2004 EU member states (EU fifteen) were opposed. While Iraq was the most high profile split of recent times, it does suggest that enlargement exacerbates the core problem of generating coherence, broadens the range of policies and interests to be accommodated and deepens differences in this area. Difficulties may also arise in managing a wider array of civilian and military capabilities. Indeed, the often-recited problem of a 'capabilities gap' in the transatlantic relationship may be replicated *within* the EU.

However, the enlarged EU brings important opportunities too. Enlargement has the potential to give the EU an even stronger voice on the international stage, greater presence and even more ability to 'act'.[1] Given the increased number of states, the EU voice (when speaking as one) may also carry more legitimacy.[2] Furthermore, the accession of these ten states may endow the EU with some of the extra capabilities it needs to develop an autonomous military capability, the objective of the 1999 Helsinki Headline Goal (HHG) and the Headline Goal 2010.[3] Many of the new CEE member states, such as Poland and Slovakia, were contributing to operations in the Balkans, Afghanistan and Iraq under both NATO and EU auspices before formally acceding to these organisations. Finally, despite the potential for further incoherence, the NMS may have the effect of producing a clearer majority, in favour of the Atlanticist perspective, in EU discussions on international security. However, this may not be welcome among those with a 'Europeanist' preference for ESDP.

The 2004 EU enlargement coincides with a period of international tension and transition, characterised by Iraq, the 'War on Terror' and Iran's nuclear ambitions. Within the EU, there is tension too: the failed EU Constitution, future enlargement, economic and budgetary difficulties and differing visions of ESDP's scope and its relationship to NATO are indicators of this. This chapter analyses the impact of the 2004 EU enlargement on the ESDP by tackling the three areas crystallised by enlargement. Firstly, the chapter provides an overview of the foreign policy priorities and interests of the NMS, highlighting areas of match and mismatch with those of the EU fifteen. Secondly, the chapter examines the capabilities the NMS bring to ESDP to tackle these policies, to determine whether a new capabilities gap will emerge or whether enlargement will help overcome the capability shortfalls. Thirdly, the chapter assesses the impact of enlargement on ESDP decision making and leadership. Without clear leadership and effective decision making, the policies and capabilities may be ineffective and ESDP disjointed. Finally, the chapter concludes with an overall assessment of the opportunities and risks enlargement brings to ESDP and thus its ability to enhance the EU's role in international security. First, the chapter turns to the key foreign and security policies of the NMS.

Policies and priorities of the new member states

The accession of ten new states to the EU clearly widens the range of foreign, security and defence policies that the EU must try to co-ordinate. A common basis from which CFSP and ESDP could move forward was provided by the requirement that all NMS adopt and fulfil the obligations of the *acquis communautaire*, including the specific chapter on the CFSP. The chapter on CFSP was not problematic, because all the NMS had, to prove their EU credentials, voluntarily been aligning themselves with virtually all EU common positions and *demarches* well before joining the EU.[4] This alignment suggested that both the NMS' international outlook and their core values were broadly in line with those of the EU fifteen. This was reinforced by the NMS' security strategies, foreign and defence policies and their military reforms, which broadly followed the pattern of the EU fifteen and, importantly from their perspective, the US.

In the 1990s, the overwhelming priority in the foreign and security policies of the NMS was to join the EU and NATO. Now they have joined these organisations, it is apparent that the NMS' foreign, security and defence policies have a double impact on ESDP. Firstly, it is clear that the NMS bring their own preferences, policies and interests to bear, thereby complicating an already contentious policy. The 2003 European rift suggests that, when their own interests are strong, the NMS will not be as compliant as some, like President Chirac, perhaps wanted. Secondly, the security strategies of the NMS also demonstrate significant overlap with the ESS, thereby potentially consolidating EU priorities and adding weight to its initiatives. This section will explore five key areas where the perspectives of the NMS may complicate existing differences in the EU: Iraq, the role of the US and NATO, Russia, the nature of security and the geographical focus of EU foreign and security policy. The section will then conclude by analysing the areas of policy consensus.

Iraq 2003

The fault lines that opened up across Europe in 2003 over Iraq appeared ominous for the development of a cohesive CFSP and an effective ESDP. Yet, as Menon argues, Iraq may also be seen as an opportunity, crystallising the problems and alternative ambitions within ESDP.[5] This chapter argues that enlargement has had a similar effect. The NMS strongly supported the US position, as noted in Donald Rumsfeld's evocation of 'new' and 'old' Europe. All the CEE NMS, and three candidate states, signed letters supporting US policy on the enforcement of UN Security Council (UNSC) Resolution 1441. The Czech Republic, Hungary, Poland and Slovakia appended their names to a letter signed by the leaders of five EU states (Denmark, Italy, Portugal, Spain and the UK) supporting the US campaign to disarm Iraq.[6] This letter formulated its support in terms of the need for the UNSC to fulfil its obligations, arguing that 'the Security Council must maintain its credibility by ensuring full compliance with its resolutions'.[7]

A more strongly worded statement followed from the 'Vilnius Ten': Albania, Bulgaria, Croatia, Estonia, FYROM, Latvia, Lithuania, Romania, Slovakia and Slovenia. In their joint statement, they declared that 'we are prepared to contribute to an international coalition to enforce its provisions and the disarmament of Iraq'.[8] The robustness of their statement may be attributed to two factors. Firstly, it aimed to prove their Atlanticist (hence NATO) credentials. Secondly, it may also be linked to the still unclear role played by a US lobbyist, Bruce Jackson, an advisor to CEE states for several years and promoter of their inclusion in NATO. The Deputy Chief of Mission in the Lithuanian Embassy in Washington has described his role as 'considerable'.[9] The importance of these letters was that they provided a clear political statement in favour of US leadership and, therefore, in favour of an Atlanticist ESDP.

While the desire to enforce UNSC Resolution 1441 was well supported, the timing and means were not supported in Rumsfeld's 'Old Europe' of France and Germany. In March 2003, then German Foreign Minister, Joschka Fischer, reiterated the position that the German government had held since 2002, stating that, 'Germany emphatically rejects the impending war.'[10] However, the French position on the use of force in Iraq was not, at least until a few weeks prior to the war, as clear-cut. In February 2003, then French Foreign Minister, Dominique de Villepin, stated, 'we do not exclude the possibility that force may have to be used one day if the inspectors' reports concluded that it was impossible to continue with inspections'.[11] The French argued for increased, even armed, inspections for a period of three to six months. Then, if compliance was still withheld, force could be used, legitimised by a new UNSC Resolution. Their position was hardened by the perceived 'with us or against us' attitude of US policy. By March 2003, there were clear 'for' and 'against' camps within Europe, with the CEE states of 'new' Europe strongly supporting the US.

Divisions were further exacerbated by President Chirac, who demanded that the CEE states adopt the Franco-German position. He noted that the CEE states had 'lost a good opportunity to keep quiet', calling their support for the US 'infantile' and 'reckless'.[12] There was even an implicit threat that they might have their membership blocked by a French referendum. Although the other EU states and the Commission rejected Chirac's criticism, the incident further reinforced the notion of 'old' and 'new' Europe. To paper over these tensions, the EU worked hard to produce a common, although rather ambiguous, position. The conclusions of the February 2003 Extraordinary European Council stated that, 'War is not inevitable. Force should only be used as a last resort.'[13] The statement assigned the UN a central role, but did not completely rule out the use of force. The disagreement was not so much about using force, but about agreeing on the point of last resort.

It is unsurprising that such divisions developed over Iraq, raising, as it did, fundamental issues of war and peace, the legitimacy of the use of force, the role of the UN, the future of the Middle East and the nature of the transatlantic relationship.[14] However, indecision, divergence and ambiguity over EU security policy are not new. Indeed, they have been one reason why ESDP has only developed as far as it has. What the divisions did was dramatically intensify the long-running debate on US leadership in Europe.

Relations with the US and NATO

On this issue, the CEE states are clear and adamant: the US should continue to lead and do so through NATO. This position is echoed by the UK and other Atlanticist states. However, the CEE states do not want to choose between the US and Europe. They want to maintain close links with the US, while being part of an increasingly influential EU. The Hungarian security strategy is unequivocal: 'It is Hungary's goal to remain a strategic partner of the United States, as well as a member of the European Union, and to be a NATO-ally, contributing to a stronger European engagement.'[15] Grandiose political posturing significantly influenced the position of the CEE states. These states were either new or soon-to-be NATO members. It would have been unwise to create a rift with the US so close to NATO membership. Economic ties with the EU are crucial, but, on matters of hard security, the CEE states view NATO as the primary guarantor. Hence, the US, as the hegemon in NATO, was seen as the key state to ally with. As the Slovenian Foreign Minister noted in late 2002, 'Slovenes regard NATO as the prime guarantor of peace, security and stability in the Euro-Atlantic area.'[16]

A central element of a stable Euro-Atlantic area is a stable Russia. Lingering concerns about the direction of Russian foreign and domestic policy were central to the NMS pursuit of NATO membership. However, that rationale was largely based on what NATO *was* previously, as opposed to what NATO has now *become*. While still at the ideological heart of NATO, Article 5 has been overshadowed by NATO's attempt to become a major global crisis management organisation. After the 2002 Prague summit, NATO's *raison d'etre* moved further from Article 5, positioning itself at the heart of the 'War on Terror' and even as a key contributor in efforts to counter WMD proliferation.[17] While several CEE states have been contributing to some of these new operations, it is not the kind of NATO they hoped to join when they applied.

Perhaps that is partly why, as ESDP developed, there has been a gradual increase in CEE support for it. Initially, there were serious concerns that it would either undermine NATO or fail entirely, coupled with lingering unease about pooling sovereignty. As the institutional structures and military commitments became operational in the Balkans and Central Africa, so the NMS became more supportive of the project. Yet, the centrality of NATO remains. The acceptance of ESDP has been on the basis of a clearly defined EU–NATO relationship. The 2002 EU–NATO Copenhagen Agreement, finalising the Berlin Plus arrangements, and the December 2003 Agreement on NATO/EU Consultation, Planning and Operations, has largely assured this.[18] CEE support for ESDP is based primarily on its ability to complement NATO; its ability to improve the EU's security capabilities is secondary. This adds weight to the British preference for an Atlanticist ESDP, rather than the Franco-German vision of an entirely separate capability. Across CEE, there has been a pragmatic acceptance of ESDP, first as a benefit to NATO (and hence the US) and, second, as a requirement for the EU to fulfil CFSP's potential, especially given the Balkan experiences of the 1990s.

Both the positioning of the CEE states over Iraq and their preference for NATO as Europe's security and defence organisation demonstrates their clear preference for US leadership in European security. One key reason for this is the NMS' lingering concerns about Russia's potential as a source of instability or threat.

Russia

The CEE states view of Russia as a potential source of instability is the key difference with the EU fifteen. While acknowledging the necessity for diplomatic niceties, Poland was less than pleased with the way Russia was (or rather was not) dealt with in the ESS. Poland found it 'myopic' that Russia was exclusively seen as a partner, without also acknowledging it as a potential source of security problems.[19] While Poland requires good relations with Russia, especially over Kaliningrad, it does not feel that the EU is being robust enough in pushing Russia to reform. These concerns may actually be increasing. In 2001, in common with all the NMS, Estonia declared that, 'it does not see a direct military threat to its security neither now, nor in the foreseeable future'.[20] Yet, despite accession to both NATO and the EU, Estonia's 2004 security strategy subtly reintroduces the potential for a reoccurrence of a military threat in the long term,[21] hinting at increasing concern over Russia and suggesting that traditional threats still have a higher priority in the NMS than in the EU fifteen. As the Polish example demonstrates, these lingering concerns highlight the difference between the EU fifteen and the NMS. Even assuming a harsher assessment of Russia's potential as a source of insecurity by CEE states, it is perhaps the EU, rather than NATO, which is better placed to tackle potential problems, such as border issues, energy security and organised crime. These problems are seen as being at the heart of Europe's 'new' security agenda and shape the way security is perceived within the enlarged EU.

Nature of security

Aside from the usual priority of ensuring political independence and territorial integrity, the key security concerns of the NMS include the well-established repertoire of: WMD, terrorism, South-eastern Europe, the Middle East and North Africa, ethnic and religious disputes, the environment, organised crime and promoting freedom, democracy, international law and human rights.[22] These concerns, central to the 'new security agenda', mirror those of the ESS, agreed in December 2003.[23]

This new focus illustrates how security in Europe has changed since 1991. There has been a convergence in the perceptions of security across the enlarged EU. None of the NMS sees an *immediate* direct military threat to their security. Even Estonia couches its concerns as a long-term risk, a view also held within the EU fifteen. The UK declares 'there is currently no major conventional threat to Europe', while Germany states that 'at present, and in the foreseeable future, there is no conventional threat to the German territory'.[24] Yet, in the NMS, traditional military security threats are still a greater concern than in the EU fifteen.

Despite the lingering traditional security threats, the impact of EU enlargement has been to elevate the priority of some aspects of the 'new security agenda' and raise the profile of non-military security issues, such as minorities, human rights, identity and the consolidation of democracy, rule of law and free markets.[25] These issues, covered by the ESS, broaden the possible threats and operations that ESDP may have a role in tackling. This presents another important trend: ESDP will have to be co-ordinated closely with policies and instruments from Pillar Three in order to effectively tackle these types of issues. This objective is highlighted by the ESS, which stresses the need for better co-ordination between external action and internal security policies.[26] Enlargement has, therefore, crystallised the need for the EU to deal with security in a comprehensive manner and to develop much greater co-operation, even integration, between the EU's external and internal security policies. This has major implications for the EU's institutional structures and decision-making regimes. The overlap between internal and external security is most clearly seen in the NMS prioritisation of stabilising the EU's immediate neighbourhood.

Regional priorities

Much of the 'new' security agenda is of particular relevance to the regions immediately adjacent to the enlarged EU. As the EU has moved further east, tensions, crises and failures in the states of the Former Soviet Union (FSU) become of greater concern, due to their geographical proximity to EU borders. Potential trouble spots such as Belarus, Moldova, Georgia, Chechnya and the rest of the Caucasus and the Caspian

Basin acquire increasing importance for the EU.[27] The EU has acknowledged this through the ESS' objective of 'building security in our neighbourhood'[28] and the Commission's formulation of a European Neighbourhood Policy (ENP). With enlargement, the NMS will push for a still more significant *Ostpolitik*, to ensure the insider/outsider concept is not entrenched in relations with those left out of the 2004 or subsequent enlargements. This pressure can be seen in Polish concerns over tight border controls with Ukraine, and in relations with Russia over Kaliningrad.[29] After the enlargement in 2007 brings Romania into the EU, the instability of Moldova will be brought right to the EU's border.

To the south, Cyprus and Malta's entry into the EU requires acceleration of the Barcelona Process to improve policies towards the southern Mediterranean. Since accession to the EU, Malta is a favoured destination for immigrants wishing to enter the EU. Yet, its small size and limited resources hampers effective response and has led to calls for increased EU assistance in handling this problem. Meanwhile, the inclusion of Cyprus puts a sharper focus on the EU's relationship with Turkey. In particular, like it or not, Turkey will eventually have to deal with the Cyprus problem during its accession negotiations. However, at least Turkey's negotiations have started. The process will be long and, at times, difficult for both sides, but, compared with the ENP states, EU membership is more tangible. For the states remaining outside, the 'outsider' label becomes a serious political issue. Relations with those states to the east of the EU, in the Former Yugoslavia, the Black Sea basin and the Caucasus, have to be managed carefully to ensure no new permanent division is established. As EU membership is an unrealistic option for some states (e.g. the Caucasus), a range of policy options short of membership will be required to facilitate reform and enhance stability and security.

For the NMS, the regional focus is far more pressing, with several of the EU fifteen possessing a more global outlook. The ESS, while raising the importance of 'building security in our neighbourhood', is also a global document. It is not that the NMS do not have worldwide interests or do not contribute to diplomatic and security missions around the world. It is just that developments in the FSU are more important than crisis management in Central Africa for the CEE states, while trans-Mediterranean migration will be more important to Malta than organised crime syndicates in Kaliningrad. Nevertheless, the issues emanating from these regions are of concern to all in the enlarged EU and there is a clear consensus on identifying these problems and threats.

An enlarged consensus

Having examined five areas where differences may arise, it is also important to highlight areas of consensus. The divisions over Iraq and the diverging priorities have not created permanent splits. Instead, the EU is returning to its tradition of variable combinations of agreement and disagreement across policy areas. As suggested earlier, security strategies across the enlarged EU are very similar and there is agreement on a number of difficult policy areas.

In the Balkans, the EU member states, including the NMS, make up the vast majority of the peace-keeping troops (see below). On Iran, the French, German and UK foreign ministers managed to extract an agreement on behalf of the EU on International Atomic Energy Agency (IAEA) inspections of Iran's nuclear facilities (although that subsequently fell through). In relation to the UN, it is clear from the ESS and statements from the NMS that all EU states believe the 'United Nations Security Council has the primary responsibility for the maintenance of international peace and security'.[30] With regard to the Middle East Peace Process, there is wide-ranging support for the 'Road-Map' and EU monitors have deployed on the Gaza–Egypt border.[31] Finally, regarding the EU's immediate neighbourhood, the NMS may end up leading policy developments.[32] Despite Iraq, the NMS also appear to agree with the majority of the EU fifteen in favouring multilateral solutions to international crises, as seen in their support for the EU Strategy against the Proliferation of Weapons of Mass Destruction and the adoption, in June 2004, of the EU Plan of Action on Combating Terrorism.[33] On the other hand, Osica argues that the CEE states may be actually less trusting of the UN, given Russia's Security Council veto.[34] That said, enlargement has not damaged the consensus on the fundamental security concerns facing the EU.

The NMS have also been active in both civilian and military operations. They have approached these operations with the same political pragmatism that has shaped their attitude to EU–NATO relations: support the EU while keeping the US on side. This pragmatism continues in their approach to capabilities. The following section explores the capabilities available to the NMS, to assess both the potential benefits and problems they may bring to ESDP.

(Military) capabilities of new member states

Military reform

The NMS, aside from Cyprus and Malta, which are excluded from ESDP operations with recourse to NATO assets, can be split into two broad categories. First, there are those that are attempting fundamental reform of their armed forces, to move away from large standing forces, top heavy command structures and a focus on heavy armour, towards smaller more mobile, flexible and deployable forces. These states – the Czech Republic, Hungary, Poland and Slovakia (and Bulgaria and Romania for the 2007 enlargement) – also have to replace or overhaul much of their equipment to ensure interoperability. The second group of states – Estonia, Latvia, Lithuania and Slovenia – have the equally difficult job of creating entirely new armed forces, as these states did not have any until their independence in the early 1990s.

Their security strategies make it clear that the primary driving force behind such reforms has been NATO membership, rather than the development of ESDP. Hence, the US Revolution in Military Affairs influenced the transformation more than the requirements of the European Rapid Reaction Force (ERRF). Indeed, for the Czech Republic, Hungary and Poland, ESDP did not even exist when they signed up to join NATO. Thus, for these three states especially, but also for other new EU members, NATO and the US have had a significant influence on their military evolution. While there have been criticisms of the pace and nature of defence reform,[35] and simultaneous preparation for EU entry has clearly added to their burden, most commentators agree that defence reform has seen significant progress in the CEE states.[36]

Capability commitments

Despite initial reservations about ESDP, all the NMS made commitments to the HHG and are also contributing to the battlegroups being developed under the Headline Goal 2010. The ten states that joined the EU in 2004 have approximately 280,700 troops (Poland accounting for half of them), of which about 92,000 (67,500 Polish) are conscripts.[37] However, the number of conscripts is falling, as the Czech Republic, Hungary, Slovenia and Slovakia (2006) phase out conscription and Poland reduces the length of conscription.[38] As well as financial considerations, the experience of several CEE states in NATO's Balkan operations in the 1990s confirmed the problematic nature of conscription for operations now envisaged by the EU (and NATO).[39] Thus, on paper, there are approximately 188,000 non-conscript troops, minus those already deployed, which could be used for operations overseas, already an improvement since the beginning of the decade. It is primarily from these forces that contributions to the ERRF are drawn. Yet, as in the EU fifteen, the quality and availability of these troops still needs improvement. A particular problem common to all is that these commitments are 'dual-hatted' as forces also earmarked for NATO operations, may already be deployed. Despite these problems, by the end of 2004, Poland had over 10,000 troops deployed in various operations around the world.[40] Table 2.1 illustrates the estimated commitments made to the HHG by the NMS.

Their overall approach in earmarking capabilities has been to provide small, but realisable and hopefully effective, military units, often with a specialist capability. This role specialisation and pooling of capabilities has been largely determined by budgetary constraints (see below). However, it also corresponds with proposals from several other EU states for such an approach (e.g. the Dutch Patriot capability).[41] Examples of such specialist capabilities include: Hungary's engineering capabilities, Slovakia's bio-chemical warfare capability, Latvia's explosive ordinance unit and the Baltic's pan-Baltic radar network. Meanwhile, Romania and Bulgaria are also developing specialist capabilities, such as chemical and biological reconnaissance units and field hospitals.

Some contributions have already, on a relatively small scale, been made operational in Bosnia, through Operation Althea and the EU Police Mission (EUPM), and in FYROM, through Operation Concordia and Proxima.[42] They demonstrate the pragmatic approach taken to ESDP, with CEE states willing to contribute to EU

Table 2.1 **Estimated commitments to the EU Headline Goal**

Country	Land forces	Aerial forces	Naval forces
Cyprus	Non-combat troops – support and services only (30 policemen)		
Czech Republic	Mechanised infantry battalion, special forces, medical battalion, NBC company (1,000 troops total)	Helicopter unit	N/A
Estonia	Light infantry battalion, military police unit, mine clearance platoon		2 naval vessels
Hungary	Air defence unit and mechanised infantry battalion (350 troops)		
Latvia	Infantry battalion, explosive ordinance disposal unit, military police unit; field medical unit		2 mine sweepers, 1 fast patrol boat
Lithuania	3 motorised battalions, medical and engineer units	2 helicopters, 2 cargo aircraft	2 mine hunters
Malta	Light infantry platoon (30 troops)		
Poland	Framework brigade – 1,300 troops, military police unit	Aerial search and rescue group	Naval support group
Slovakia	Mechanised company, mine clearance unit, military police unit, field hospital	4 Mi-17 transport helicopters	
Slovenia	Infantry company, military police unit, medical unit	Transport helicopter/ air force unit	

Sources: Commission of the European Union, *Regular Reports on Progress towards Accession* (for all ten states) (2002); Cypriot Ministry of Foreign Affairs, *Cyprus and the Common Foreign and Security Policy* (October 2003), www.mfa.cy/mfa/mfa.nsf/EUCFSP_ESDP? open form; Czech Ministry of Foreign Affairs, *The Czech Republic and European Union* (August 2006), www.czechembassy.org/wwwo/mzv/default.asp?id=5088&ido=4591&idj=2; Estonian Ministry of Foreign Affairs, *Estonia and the Common Foreign and Security Policy of the European Union* (16 May 2001), www.vm.ee/eng/euro/kat_315/2761.html; Lithuanian Ministry of Foreign Affairs European Integration Department, *Co-operation between Lithuania and the European Union* (20 May 2002), www.urm.1t/data/3/EF219141058_eida4.htm; Maltese Ministry of Foreign Affairs, *Prime Minister Participates in Meeting with EU Defence Ministers from Candidate Countries with EU Defence Ministers* (May 2002), www.foreign.gov.mt/pr/docsgov/2002/pr020515b-ESDP-doi657.htm; and Antonio Missiroli, *Bigger EU, Wider CFSP, Stronger ESDP? The view from Central Europe* (Paris: EU Institute for Security Studies, April 2002).

operations, while continuing to argue for NATO's primacy. In Bosnia, as shown below, the NMS are contributing 600 military personnel to the total of 6,656 in Operation Althea and forty-eight police personnel out of the 425 in the EUPM (see table 2.2).[43]

Table 2.2 **New member states contributions to Operation Althea and the EUPM (August 2005)**

Country	Operation Althea	EUPM
Cyprus[a]	0	6
Czech Republic	89	7
Estonia	2	2
Hungary	122	5
Latvia	3	4
Lithuania	1	2
Malta[a]	0	2
Poland	226	11
Slovakia	4	6
Slovenia	153	3
Total	600	48

Note: [a] Cyprus and Malta cannot take part in EU military operations conducted using NATO assets.

Sources: EUFOR, 'EUFOR Troop Strength', (10 August 2005), www.euforbih/organisation050810_strength.htm and EUPM; 'Weekly establishment of EUPM personnel by countries – Member States' (26 August 2005), www.eupm.org/documents/weekly.pdf; European Council, *Presidency Conclusions, Annex II, Declaration of the Council Meeting in Copenhagen on 12 December 2002* (Copenhagen: 12–13 December 2002).

Meanwhile, for Operation Concordia, eight, then accession states, contributed twenty-seven troops to the 357 strong force, seventeen of which were from Poland. Today, nine of the NMS are contributing to Operation Proxima (170 international police and civilian personnel, supported by 150 local support staff).[44] While these numbers are perhaps not significant militarily, they are of political significance. The contributions demonstrate a willingness to participate and the ability to perform Petersberg tasks under foreign and multinational command arrangements. While the political will is apparent, so is the rather under-resourced nature of these states' military and civilian crisis management capabilities. On the military side of the equation, with 600 troops deployed, the NMS provide just over 10 per cent of EU troops (5,798). However, this amounts to under 10 per cent of the 6,656 total and less than the non-EU contributors (858 troops).[45] On the civilian side, they are only slightly better represented, providing forty-eight personnel, about 13 per cent of the EU contingent (11 per cent of the total), again less than non-EU states (fifty-four personnel), such as Turkey, Ukraine, Canada and others.[46]

These contributions, as well as other deployments under NATO, the UN and OSCE, demonstrate their willingness to participate in peace-keeping missions. Meanwhile, their participation in Kosovo (1,506 personnel) and Afghanistan (252 personnel)[47] also indicates a willingness to engage in peace enforcement operations. While the CEE states were quite prominent in Operation Iraqi Freedom (contributing 6,058 personnel, two-thirds of which were from Poland and Ukraine),[48] these states have now started withdrawing from Iraq or scaling down their involvement. While

Table 2.3 **Defence expenditure and expenditure as percentage of GDP: ten new member states**

Country	Defence expenditure (US$m) 2002	Defence expenditure (US$m) 2003	Defence expenditure as % GDP 2002	Defence expenditure as % GDP 2003
Cyprus	240	294	2.4	2.3
Czech Republic	1,482	1,900	2.0	2.2
Estonia	99	172	1.5	2.0
Hungary	1,145	1,589	1.8	1.9
Latvia	113	194	1.3	1.9
Lithuania	247	342	1.8	1.8
Malta	74	95	1.9	2.1
Poland	3,596	4,095	1.9	2.0
Slovakia	464	627	1.9	1.9
Slovenia	275	378	1.2	1.4

Source: IISS, *Military Balance 2004–05*.

partly driven by over-stretch and public opinion at home, this may indicate a change in policy and a possible weakening in support for some US policies. In addition, the NMS have made pledges regarding the establishment of battlegroups, a concept that fits neatly with the notion of role specialisation. Currently, the NMS will contribute to at least three of the proposed thirteen battlegroups. The Poles will form the bulk of a battlegroup developed with Germany, Latvia, Lithuania and Slovakia.[49] The Czechs are forming a unit with the Germans and Austrians, while Hungary and Slovenia are to co-operate with Italy.[50]

Defence budget constraints

However, despite the political will, defence reforms have not all been as smooth, quick or fundamental as sometimes suggested in official publications. Key problems continue in reducing the size of the armed forces, redistributing defence spending and increasing the overall percentage of GDP allocated to defence.[51] On the positive side, defence budgets across the NMS have been rising (see table 2.3). For the CEE states, this is primarily due to NATO membership, with several CEE states close to, or above, spending 2 per cent of GDP on defence, a broad NATO target that the EU has implicitly adopted. However, given their much smaller GDPs, there is still a funding shortfall. For example, Poland commits 2 per cent of its GDP to defence, compared to just 1.2 per cent in Spain (similar population), yet Spain spends a total of $9.9bn and Poland $4.1bn on defence.[52]

The percentage of GDP spent on defence again shows the political will to prioritise defence, although the actual resources available are far more limited. In contrast, several of the EU fifteen states do not meet the 2 per cent target. On average, the percentage of GDP spent on defence is higher in the NMS (1.97 per cent) than in the EU fifteen (1.73 per cent). The difference is even greater if the four candidate states are included (2.24 per cent).[53] This problem is exacerbated by the distribution of spending, with a large proportion still being absorbed by personnel costs, instead of spending on equipment, procurement and research and development. This is a general problem and must be addressed if ESDP is to be effective. The level of resources in the NMS is unlikely to be sufficient to significantly impact on the shortfalls listed in the Capability Improvement Chart II/2004, which identifies sixty-four shortfalls, of which just seven have been solved and four have seen some improvement.[54] The procurement dilemma, especially for NMS, is how to balance the desire for national defence capabilities with EU (and NATO) pressures for capabilities more suited to crisis management, peace enforcement and force projection.[55]

Interoperability and modernisation

A key capability issue exacerbated by enlargement is interoperability. For rapid response forces to be most effective, they will have to be highly interoperable to ensure swift deployment and effective engagement once in theatre. The NMS experience in NATO's operations in the Former Yugoslavia demonstrated some interoperability problems. In particular, there were problems with integrating and functioning in a multinational command: differing rules of engagement, rotating personnel on long-term deployments and limited language skills – principally the lack of English.[56] This issue will take several years, if not longer to rectify. NATO spent fifty years trying to standardise and rationalise equipment during the Cold War and was never entirely successful.

This problem may be further aggravated by competition between US and EU defence industries and the added burden of political pressure to 'buy European' or 'buy American'. An example of this was the competition between European and US defence manufacturers over a Polish order for fighter aircraft, eventually won by the US firm Lockheed Martin to supply F16s. However, on the positive side, the NMS have already been taking part in crisis management operations and are part of various multinational forces. This will have given them good experience in the doctrine, tactics and equipment of the EU fifteen, hopefully allowing the smooth development of ESDP operations involving all twenty-five states.

Leadership and decision making in an enlarged Europe

Regardless of efforts to converge policy, restructure armed forces, procure new equipment, adjust defence budgets and enhance interoperability, without clear leadership, such efforts may be futile. Clear leadership is needed to ensure decisions to launch operations are made swiftly and to ensure clear direction during operations. Yet, leadership and decision making are potentially the hardest issues to resolve, with an already extremely sensitive area further complicated by enlargement. In particular, the rise in the number of small states (all NMS except Poland) spells greater opposition to large state dominance in ESDP.

Leadership is required at three levels: the political drive to crystallise the idea of ESDP, the institutional responsibility within EU structures and the practical administration of EU policy at the military level. The lack of leadership at these levels makes it difficult to decide whether a crisis exists, to then determine the scale of a crisis and to achieve a consensus on the response. This failure was clearly illustrated by the arguments over Iraq. In addition, without leadership, it will be harder to achieve the defence reforms, capability improvements and increased defence spending required to close the capabilities–expectations gap. Finally, effective leadership is also vital to convince the public of ESDP's importance and utility. Without this, it will be difficult to gain the political and economic sacrifices and resources required to meet ESDP's objectives.

However, talk of leadership immediately raises concerns about the emergence of a *directoire*. This consists of a small number of states, usually the largest or most powerful, constituting the core decision-making body. The primary concern is that this will marginalise other smaller states. Yet, if it is the larger states that contribute most, in terms of personnel and equipment, it seems natural that they should take the lead. A *directoire* is not necessarily a bad way of getting decisions made. This is especially true if the *directoire* is not a permanent or fixed entity, but varying, dependent on the potential operation and on the states that are going to bear most of the burden. Nevertheless, this is a sensitive issue for many states and one the EU is unlikely to resolve swiftly.

Such sensitivities were evident in late 2001. UK Prime Minister Blair called an informal meeting with his French and German counterparts to discuss terrorism. When news of this meeting spread, several other EU states demanded to attend. Those that were not invited or found out too late took great offence at what they saw as a deliberate snub. They feared that the big three EU states were deciding policy without them and would then present them with a *fait accompli*. This helps demonstrate the improbability of such a fixed membership *directoire* becoming a permanent feature.

The NMS complicate the EU's political balance. Three states – France, Germany and the UK – continue to be crucial to ESDP. At the next level down, Italy and Spain will be joined by Poland as another 'large' state demanding 'a seat at the top table'. However, as the majority of states joining can be classified as 'small states', their sensitivities within ESDP decision making will become an even greater issue.[57] They will not want any form of *directoire* to emerge for ESDP decision making, regardless of what combination of large states that *directoire* may entail.

There is also the issue of veto politics, made more difficult by enlargement. The arguments in the European Convention between the medium-size states, such as Poland and Spain, and the largest states, particularly Germany, over the weighting of council votes and a double majority voting system exemplify the sensitivities of the issue. Despite ESDP decisions requiring unanimity, this argument illustrates how wary the NMS are about being dominated by the 'older' and larger states. The intergovernmental nature of ESDP decision making does not foster a sense of commonality. States may wield their veto whenever they disapprove, when the position taken is contrary to their interests, when external pressure is exerted upon them or when domestic opposition pressurises the government. The interesting aspect here is the relative influence of these interests and pressures. During the disputes over Iraq, opinion polling suggested that the majority of the populations of all the NMS were opposed to force being used in Iraq without an explicit UN mandate.[58] Yet these states continued to support the US, in part because of their desire to stay on the right side of the 'with us or against us' divide.

The Constitutional Treaty would have improved both leadership and decision making in this area. The introduction of a foreign minister, while initially controversial, may have improved leadership. Along with the external action service, it may also have increased coherence. Finally, the introduction of structured co-operation may have allowed a more flexible development of CFSP and ESDP. While not impossible, reopening negotiations may prove even more difficult in an enlarged EU, especially as some proposals will have been tarnished through association with the failed Constitutional Treaty.[59]

In the past, leadership has tended to come and go within ESDP, depending on institutional or state interest in a particular issue. The EU needs clearer leadership to generate the capabilities and budgets necessary for ESDP to be effective. However, overbearing leadership by a small minority may actually damage ESDP's development by creating more entrenched divisions. Without the necessary leadership, ESDP may flounder, yet overly strong leadership may divide ESDP.

Conclusion: a stronger or more divided ESDP?

This chapter has highlighted the three crucial areas in which the 2004 enlargement has crystallised both the risks and opportunities for ESDP. Firstly, the policies and priorities of the NMS bring risks in five key areas: Iraq, the US role, Russia, the nature of security, and their regional focus. In each area, the NMS, especially those CEE states, have already articulated their preferences and demonstrated that they are not the compliant states some in the EU may have wished for. Russia is now an even greater priority. Geo-politically, the regions around the Black Sea and Caspian are of increased importance. The 'new' security issues are even more pertinent after enlargement. Finally, the CEE states shift ESDP towards the 'Atlanticist' perspective. Nonetheless, the opportunity for a stronger EU voice on security matters is also apparent in the significant commonalities within the security strategies of all twenty-five states.

Secondly, enlargement has provided the opportunity to augment the pool of resources available for ESDP missions. On the military side, the NMS have shown the political will to commit capabilities, undertake defence reform, increase defence spending and participate in crisis management operations. However, while their political will is apparent, their actual resources are very limited. The resources are simply not available for simultaneous professionalisation and modernisation, meeting EU and NATO targets and contributing to operations. This risks entrenching a double capability gap within the EU. The NMS can, however, provide a new opportunity for

ESDP. Their shift towards role specialisation and capability pooling is a model that all EU states should adopt, as defence spending is insufficient to maintain a 'full spectrum' of forces. These solutions have political disadvantages, such as the guaranteed availability of those capabilities, but, economically, they may be the only way to realistically fulfil ESDP's objectives.

Finally, in the area of leadership and decision making, the risks inherent in enlargement are clear. The increase to twenty-five states complicates the issue of leadership in EU foreign, security and defence policies. The NMS are more fearful of being marginalised by overly strong leadership than some of the EU fifteen states were. Their fear of a *directoire* telling them what to do has the potential to leave ESDP leaderless and directionless. Yet, without a strong lead from within the EU institutions, a *directoire* may be necessary. This can, however, be flexible and, in some situations, the NMS may actually be part of it. Finally, the intergovernmental nature of ESDP means that an additional ten potential vetoes reduces the likelihood of swift decisions, a key requirement in crises management. Both decisive leadership and prompt decision making are vital to ESDP, yet they are the most problematic issues crystallised by enlargement.

As a result, the EU should use enlargement, and the failure of the Constitutional Treaty, as an opportunity to reassess the three fundamental questions identified earlier. What priorities and common interests shape ESDP? What capabilities does ESDP possess and what does it still need? What sort of leadership and decision making are needed for a cohesive ESDP? Enlargement also emphasises the need for greater political will to consolidate and complete ESDP. In particular, the ESS needs to be transformed from a framework of ideas into a true security strategy, the required civilian and military capabilities must be acquired and radical solutions must be embraced (such as flexible *directoires*, role specialisation and capability pooling).

Enlargement risks weakening ESDP by reducing further the coherence of EU security policy and capabilities. Yet, enlargement also provides opportunities for a greater exchange of ideas, policies, capabilities and means. If there is a process of reassessment and learning, then ESDP may become more convincing, more achievable and more effective. Enlargement should provide the opportunity to re-launch, refocus and realise ESDP. If it does, ESDP will enhance the EU's role in international security, allowing it to advance from being a Cold War security receiver to realising its long-held ambition to become a comprehensive security provider.

Notes

1 See Charlotte Bretherton and John Vogler, *The European Union as a Global Actor* (London: Routledge, 1999); D. Allen and M. Smith, 'Western Europe's presence in the contemporary international arena', *Review of International Studies*, 16:1 (1990), pp. 19–37; Karen Smith, *EU Foreign Policy in a Changing World* (London: Polity, 2003).
2 Simon Duke, *Beyond the Chapter: Enlargement Challenges for CFSP and ESDP* (Maastricht: EIPA, 2003), p. 11.
3 Council of the European Union, *Conclusions of the Helsinki European Council* (Brussels, December 1999).
4 See *Declaration by the Presidency on behalf of the European Union on the Situation in Georgia* (Brussels: 24 November 2003).

5   Anand Menon, 'From crisis to catharsis: ESDP after Iraq', *International Affairs*, 80:4 (2004), pp. 631–48.
6   'United we stand', Statement issued to newspapers by Jose Maria Anzar, Jose-Manuel Durao Barroso, Silvio Berlusconi, Tony Blair, Vaclav Havel, Peter Medgyessy, Leszek Miller and Anders Fogh Rasmussen (30 January 2003), www.useu.be/categories/global affairs/iraq/jan2003europeletteriraq.html.
7   Ibid.
8   'Statement of the Vilnius group of Countries in response to the presentation by the United States Secretary of State to the United Nations Security Council concerning Iraq', Statement by the Foreign Ministers of Albania, Bulgaria, Croatia, Estonia, Latvia, Lithuania, Macedonia, Romania, Slovakia, Slovenia (5 February 2003), www.bulgaria-embassy.org/!/02052003-01.htm.
9   Thomas Fuller, 'American lobbyist swayed Eastern Europe's Iraq response', *International Herald Tribune* (20 February 2003), www.iht.com.
10 Joschka Fischer, Speech by Federal Foreign Minister Fischer to the United Nations Security Council, (19 March 2003), www.auswaertiges-amt.de/www/en/archiv_print?archiv_id=4224.
11 Dominique De Villepin, Speech by Dominique de Villepin, Minister of Foreign Affairs, at the United Nations Security Council, (14 February 2003), www.diplomatie.gouv.fr/actu/bulletin.gb.asp?liste=20030219.gb.html#chapitre2.
12 Ian Traynor and Ian Black, 'Eastern Europe dismayed at Chirac snub', *The Guardian* (19 February 2003).
13 Council of the European Union, *Conclusions of Extraordinary European Council* (Brussels, February 2003).
14 Brian Crowe, 'A common European foreign policy after Iraq', *International Affairs*, 79:3 (2003), p. 535.
15 The National Security Strategy of the Republic of Hungary (2004), www.mfa.gov.hu/kum/en/bal/foreign_policy/security_policy.
16 Slovene Foreign Minster Dimitrij Rupel, speech: 'On the doorstep of EU and NATO: Slovenia's contribution to European integration and security' (Helsinki, 25 September 2002), www.gov.si.mzz/eng/speeches/default.html.
17 See North Atlantic Council, *Prague Summit Declaration* (Brussels, November 2002).
18 Council of the European Union, *EU–NATO Declaration on ESDP* (Copenhagen, December 2002) and Council of the European Union, *NATO/EU Consultation, Planning and Operations* (Brussels, December 2003).
19 Olaf Osica, 'A secure Poland in a better Union? The ESS as seen from Warsaw's perspective', in 'The European Security Strategy: paper tiger or catalyst for joint action? Part II', *German Foreign Policy in Dialogue*, 5:14(October 2004), p. 915, www.deutsche-aussenpolitik.de.
20 National Security Concept of the Republic of Estonia (6 March 2001), www.vm.ee/eng/kat_177/aken_prindi/838.html.
21 'National security concept of the Republic of Estonia' (2004), www.vm.ee/eng/kat_177.
22 This sample is taken from the 'Security strategy of the Czech Republic' (February 2004), www.mzv.cz/wwwo/mzv/default.asp?id=24118&ido=7567&idj=2.
23 *A Secure Europe in a Better World: European Security Strategy* (Brussels: European Union, 2003).
24 Ministry of Defence, *Delivering Security in a Changing World*, Defence White Paper (December 2003), p. 5 and Budesministerium der Verteidigung, *Defence Policy Guidelines* (May 2003), p. 4.
25 Krzysztof Wojtowicz, 'Non-military security issues in Central Europe', *International Relations*, 18:1 (2004), pp. 43–53.
26 *A Secure Europe in a Better World*, p. 4.
27 See Polish Ministry of Foreign Affairs, *National Security Strategy of the Republic of Poland* (22 July 2003).

IMPLICATIONS OF EU ENLARGEMENT

28 *A Secure Europe in a Better World*, pp. 7–8.
29 Ibid.
30 Ibid., p. 9.
31 Andrew Beatty, 'EU braced for first Middle East mission', *European Voice* (3–9 November 2005), p. 2.
32 See concerns in The National Security Strategies of Poland, Hungary, Romania(undated) Slovakia (2001).
33 *EU Strategy against the Proliferation of Weapons of Mass Destruction* (Brussels, December 2003) and *EU Plan of Action on Combating Terrorism* (Brussels, June 2004).
34 Osica, 'A secure Poland in a better Union?', p. 14.
35 See Pal Dunay, 'The half-hearted transformation of the Hungarian military', *European Security*, 14:1 (2005), pp. 17–32.
36 Andrew Cottey, Timothy Edmunds and Anthony Forster, 'Military matters beyond Prague', *NATO Review* (Autumn 2002).
37 Figures adapted from IISS, *The Military Balance 2004–2005* (Oxford: Oxford University Press, 2004).
38 Ibid., pp. 37–76 and Timothy Edmunds, 'NATO and its new members', *Survival*, 45:3 (Autumn 2003), p. 157.
39 Jeffrey Simon, *NATO Expeditionary Operations: Impacts upon New Members and Partners* (Washington, DC: NDU Press, March 2005), pp. 4–14.
40 Marcin Zaborowski, *From America's Protégé to Constructive European: Polish Security Policy in the Twenty-First Century* (Paris: EU-ISS, December 2004), p. 22.
41 See Hans-Christian Hagman, *European Crisis Management and Defence: The Search for Capabilities* (Oxford, Oxford University Press, 2002) and Gilles Andreani, Christoph Bertram and Charles Grant, *Europe's Military Revolution* (London: Centre for European Reform, 2001).
42 *Termination of the EU-led Military Operation Concordia and Launch of EU Police Mission Proxima* (Brussels: Council of the European Union General Secretariat Press Office, December 2003).
43 Press and Public Information EUPM, 'Weekly establishment of EUPM personnel by countries (non member states)' (21 November 2003), www.eupm.org/people/31/313-t.pdf.
44 EUPOL, 'EUPOL Proxima Staff', www.eupol-proxima.org.
45 EUFOR (August 2005).
46 EUPM (August 2005).
47 Gustav Lindstrom, *EU–US Burdensharing: Who Does What?* (Paris: EU Institute for Security Studies, 2005), pp. 96–7.
48 Ibid., p. 99.
49 Zaborowski, *From America's Protégé to Constructive European* and *Euobserver*, Further Steps taken on EU battle groups (23 May 2005), www.euibserver.com.
50 Gustav Lindstrom, *The Headline Goal* (Paris: EU-ISS, April 2005), p. 4.
51 Ibid., p. 30.
52 Figures adapted from IISS, *Military Balance 2004–05*, pp. 353–4.
53 Figures adapted from IISS, *Military Balance 2004–05*.
54 Council of the European Union, *Capability Improvement Chart II/2004* (Brussels, November 2004).
55 See Edmunds, 'NATO and its new members' for details.
56 Simon, *NATO Expeditionary Operations*, pp. 4–14.
57 Anders Wivel, 'The security challenge of small EU member states: interests, identity and the development of the EU as a security actor', *Journal of Common Market Studies*, 43:2 (2005), pp. 393–412.
58 For example see: BBC News, 'Polls find European oppose Iraq War' (11 February 2003) and BBC News 'New Europe US leanings', http://news.bbc.co.uk.
59 Richard Whitman, 'No and after: options for Europe', *International Affairs*, 81:4 (2005), pp. 673–87.

3

The impact of enlargement on the EU's counter-terrorist framework

David Brown[1]

Counter-terrorism has emerged from the shadows of the EU's Third Pillar, propelled into the limelight by the events of September 11 and maintained by terrorist incidents in Spain and the UK. In the same period, the organisation's most extensive enlargement, to embrace the eight CEE states, Malta and Cyprus, was undertaken. In fact, the two processes – widening the EU's geographical scope and deepening internal security co-operation – have proceeded along much the same time-line. For example, the Third Pillar was created as part of the 1991 TEU, while the initial membership requirements – the so-called Copenhagen criteria – were presented only two years later, in June 1993.[2] Over a decade later, as applicants became members in May 2004, the EU adopted a new five-year work programme for its internal security agenda, the so-called 'Hague Programme', agreed in November 2004.[3] The year 2004 is, however, not the culmination of either process. Enlargement is likely to dominate the wider EU agenda for the foreseeable future. Equally, terrorism will remain at the very top of the EU's internal – and increasingly external – security agenda.

Given the relative symmetry of the two processes, it is worth considering what bearing enlargement has had on the EU's counter-terrorist framework, in developing an 'area of freedom, security and justice'. In order to fully comprehend what impact it has had, it is first necessary to sketch out some of the key trends that have coloured the Third Pillar's first decade, before moving on to the post-enlargement phase. While it would be easier to make a simple comparison between the periods before and after May 2004, the impact of September 11 complicates matters a little. As the real driver of progress in this field, it in effect creates three phases of activity – pre- and post-September 11 and post-enlargement.

The primary focus will be on three noted elements within the overall field of internal security. Firstly, the relative prioritisation of counter-terrorism within the crowded internal security pillar will be considered. Initially relegated in importance at the outset of the Third Pillar arrangements, counter-terrorism has been propelled to the forefront of the EU's internal agenda, driven primarily by the demands of the 'War on Terror'. This has continued post-enlargement, as seen in the development of a second five-year programme of initiatives, the aforementioned Hague Programme. However, as will be demonstrated later, the proliferation of new initiatives, occasionally in areas which seem inappropriate for a European level, may be a step too far for the EU, which needs to ensure it is prioritising its efforts and ensuring 'added value' to arrangements at the national level. The fact that the Hague Programme was agreed post-enlargement suggests that the EU has not taken advantage of the opportunity offered by such a significant widening of its membership to more rigorously consider where its counter-terrorist efforts should be directed.

Secondly, the 'implementation gap' will be examined. There has been a tendency in the past for EU member states to seek out new initiatives and activities, rather than to ensure pre-existing commitments were fully implemented and enforced. This allowed a gap to develop between stated intentions and implemented policies. Such a gap was already causing concern regarding the EU fifteen. Their poor implementation record should not be forgotten, even as the focus naturally shifts to scrutinising the efforts of the new member states. In fact, given that they had to adopt a substantive legislative burden, as part of the wider *acquis communautaire*, their record stands up reasonably well in comparison with their more established counterparts, particularly in the wider UN arena. As such, it is to be hoped that, longer term, enlargement will herald a more rigorous inspection of the implementation gap, leading to its eventual closure. However, given the Hague Programme's wide-ranging scope, it seems that, even with the potential limitations of operating within a twenty-five state veto structure, the EU has yet to fully appreciate the importance of the implementation stage.

Finally, the labelling of such internal security competences, including counter-terrorism, as a 'matter of common concern', a nomenclature given to them as part of the Maastricht arrangements, will be placed under the spotlight, in terms of the commonality both of the problem facing the EU and the nature of their response. Using statistical data obtained from both EU and US sources,[4] the evolving nature of the terrorist threat over the last fifteen years will be documented, demonstrating an uneven pattern of activity across the EU, both pre- and post-enlargement. Given that states have to balance limited resources with extensive legislative priorities, the actual nature of the threat facing each of them will affect the nature of their response (and therefore helps explain the development of the 'implementation gap'). The widening of the membership base, bringing with it new challenges, differing priorities and competing agendas, will strain the sense of commonality still further. It is worth considering each of these areas separately – although, clearly, they impact upon each other – starting with the issue of prioritisation in the pre-enlargement phase.

Prioritisation

Counter-terrorism was not at the top of the Third Pillar agenda when the new institutional structures were created. In fact, it was not even included as one of nine separate 'common concerns', but was relegated to part of an overarching category of 'police co-operation', centred on the European Police Office (more commonly known as Europol). This was a somewhat ironic development, given that counter-terrorism was then excluded from Europol's initial remit. In fact, Europol had to wait until 1999 before including counter-terrorism in its remit. Such decisions, as well as demonstrating the occasionally chaotic EU decision-making processes, also highlight that counter-terrorism was not a priority, at least initially.

A more detailed study of the Third Pillar's legislative instruments in the pre-September 11 era reinforces this point. Between 1992 and 2000, of 509 registered legislative instruments – both binding and non-binding – only fourteen were dedicated primarily to counter-terrorism.[5] In fact, in one year – 1997 – there were no counter-terrorism instruments registered at all. Ironically, in the same year, the Treaty of Amsterdam made counter-terrorism a separate and distinct competency. Had events elsewhere not intervened, this situation may not have changed dramatically, as the Scoreboard indicates. The Scoreboard was an initiative intended to focus on the implementation process, by setting deadlines and allocating clearer lines of responsibility. As such, it gives a clear indication of the EU fifteen's planned counter-terrorist priorities. There was only one direct reference to counter-terrorism in any of the pre-September 11 iterations, namely a commitment to prepare 'common definitions and penalties' by the third quarter of 2001.[6]

As it turned out, that commitment was kept, accompanied by a far more extensive raft of initiatives agreed in the wake of September 11. For example, the EU fairly rapidly agreed two key measures, the Framework Decision on Combating Terrorism[7] and a similar measure establishing the European Arrest Warrant (EAW).[8] The latter has proved to be the more successful arrangement, reducing extradition times from an average of nine months to forty-three days between January and September 2004.[9] In the same period, 2,603 warrants were issued, leading to 653 arrests and a further 104 persons surrendered.[10] Yet, there was a slight sting in the tail. The speed of the decision-making process led to some noted errors, with the Commission pointing out that eleven of the twenty-five member states made mistakes in the national legislation ratifying the EAW.[11]

Two other developments are worthy of consideration to demonstrate this greater interest in counter-terrorism. Firstly, Europol was granted a new anti-terrorist task force, although only on a temporary mandate, renewable every six months. While this allowed the EU member states to decide whether such a development was a necessary permanent addition, it stood in stark contrast to the longer-term perspective adopted by US President George W. Bush. Rather than allowing it to bed in institutionally, the EU adopted a stop–start approach, allowing the task force to disband, only to have to enact the 'resuscitation of this system'[12] in the wake of the 2004 Madrid bombings. In the second development, Gijs de Vries was appointed as the EU's counter-terrorist co-ordinator in 2004, answerable to Javier Solana, the High Representative for the Common Foreign and Security Policy. This was a belated, but welcome, recognition that a greater level of co-ordination was required in this most sensitive of areas. As well as monitoring progress towards implementing agreed objectives, he was tasked with managing the myriad of different committees, institutions and agencies that make the EU's counter-terrorist framework an institutional reality. Once again, some caution is required. De Vries' institutional position is relatively weak, lacking the power to propose legislation or even call together the relevant national ministers in order to advance his agenda. In fact, de Vries has recognised these restrictions, noting that 'the role of the Union in the field of counter-terrorism is an important one, a growing one, but a limited one'.[13] Even in the post-September 11 world, where counter-terrorism dominated every agenda, there were noted limitations as to the steps the EU and its member states were prepared to take.

One step forward: the implementation gap

One noted limitation can be found in terms of the implementation stage of decision making. The enlargement process has rested, in part, on an element of legislative and institutional hypocrisy. The EU fifteen have been able to demand – at least in the pre-accession stage – complete acceptance of the *acquis communautaire*, while not always showing a similar level of commitment. As such, it is worth considering the record of the EU *before* enlargement took place. At the end of the day, the 'implementation gap' did not emerge, fully formed, in May 2004.

Pre-enlargement, the EU's record was unimpressive across the gamut of internal security arrangements. It is necessary to take a wider view, not only because the problem is endemic across the Third Pillar, but also because, in its initial years, the limited counter-terrorist measures tended to be non-binding in nature. Across the internal security spectrum, only one convention out of twenty-five has actually been fully ratified, let alone implemented in full.[14] While the Europol Convention has significant relevance for counter-terrorism, at least post-1999, it remains the exception to the general rule. In fact, partly as a result of such a poor ratification record, the EU has moved away from utilising conventions. The UN continues to do so, and it is worth considering the EU fifteen's record in this arena to further emphasise the scale of the problem. Pre-enlargement, only eleven of the fifteen had both signed and ratified all twelve UN Conventions.[15] For example, Ireland had still to sign even two Conventions, while Luxembourg had left four Conventions completely unsigned.[16] While this is a significant improvement on the pre-September 11 period, where only the UK had signed and ratified all twelve Conventions,[17] it is still problematic for a number of reasons. Firstly, as part of the principles underpinning the CFSP, member states were committed to harmonising their positions in other international organisations, such as the UN.[18] Secondly, their regular exhortations to other states to ensure they have fully ratified and implemented such Conventions are likely to fall on deaf ears, if the EU itself cannot fully meet the required standards. In addition, in the post-September 11 era, where all states were keen to demonstrate their counter-terrorist credentials, the failure to meet the UN's required legislative standards seems inexcusable.

The Commission has produced a number of reviews of legislation, passed in the wake of September 11, and they tell a similar story to the preceding phase. Even with the EAW, not all EU member states had completed the national ratification process by February 2005 (Italy only agreed to full ratification in April 2005). The situation with the Framework Decision on Combating Terrorism was even worse, as the Commission could not even get the necessary information to make assessments on the state of ratification. As the Commission – and de Vries, in his new role – are ultimately dependent on the member states' goodwill to even begin their monitoring responsibilities, the record here does not make for easy reading. When the initial deadline for ratification – 31 December 2002 – was reached, only five of the EU fifteen had supplied the Commission with information. After further exhortations and a new deadline, another seven states responded in some fashion, leaving only Greece (providing non-specific information), Luxembourg and the Netherlands (the latter two providing no information at all).[19] If they cannot even provide information when requested, the likelihood of achieving full ratification and subsequent implementation has to be called into question.

Recognising that a problem exists is one thing; rectifying it is another matter. Caroline Flint, UK Home Office Minister, argued that, unlike previous practice, 'as we develop initiatives, we think about monitoring and evaluation of any policy at the same time'.[20] Given that this should have been happening as a matter of course, calls for a culture change within the JHA Council may not be a sufficient guarantee. There is a world of difference between stating a case and actually carrying it out. Also, a senior UK official, Jonathon Faull, has accepted that the Scoreboard has proved to be, at best, a double-edged sword. It provides 'an enormously focused target' but also gives some member states a further opportunity for 'quibbling about details', which ends up with them having 'lost sight of the overall objective'.[21] There are informal levers of persuasion and a peer review process, providing another level of supervision. Yet, the overall process lacks enforcement. Amnesty International have argued that there is little point in setting deadlines or enhancing the ever-increasing monitoring sector, if there is no punishment to go along with it.[22] Yet, what level of 'punishment' would be possible to ensure compliance? Given the peer review process is carried out away from the public view, the EU is unlikely to adopt a public 'naming and shaming' for those states who are not fully co-operating in counter-terrorist efforts, the so-called 'passive sponsors'.[23] While Monar has suggested a benchmarking system as a more realistic alternative,[24] it remains to be seen whether the EU has the political will to even move in that direction. However, post-enlargement, where co-ordination will take place between twenty-five states, clarification of what might happen to those that do not fully meet their responsibilities would be welcome.

A question of commonality?

In the wake of the September 11 terrorist attacks, President Bush suggested, rightly or wrongly, that we lived in a Manichean world, where states were either 'with us or against us'.[25] Yet, the idea of shared counter-terrorist endeavour is nothing new. In the TEU, internal security concerns were labelled 'matters of common concern', yet there was little to denote what exactly made an issue one of 'common concern'.[26] While such phrases offer the comforting veneer of togetherness, the reality may be more complex, suggesting a surface level sense of solidarity at best. Within the EU, while problems and issues may be framed as regional concerns, success or failure tends to be measured in national terms. This stands in direct contrast to the assertions of Commissioner Frattini, responsible for the AFSJ, who claimed that 'one cannot divide, by region or country, the security of such a Union'.[27] Yet, how else can you explain the implicit process of 'burden shifting' rather than burden sharing that has taken place over illegal immigration and asylum? On several occasions, as with the Chinese winkle pickers in June 2000, states have effectively 'dumped' asylum seekers across national borders, effectively 'removing' them from their national responsibilities, while still locating them within a European or – in certain cases – a Schengen zone. As Bigo has noted, 'each state, national institution or service plays its hand according to its own interests'.[28] Politicians are ultimately answerable to national electorates and supervised by an occasionally voracious national media, who tend to portray issues as a zero sum game. As such, it is insufficient simply to accept the formal terminology of 'commonality'. There is a need to analyse the situation in more depth, particularly in relation to the nature and scale of the problem (as elements of the legislative and policing response have already been considered above).

During the period 1993–2000, eight of the fifteen member states registered a terrorist incident, with the remaining seven, thankfully, free of terrorist activity. In fact, when a qualitative element is added to what is essentially a fairly basic quantitative survey, the picture becomes even more muddied. For example, both France and Italy, during that period, had effectively tackled their left-wing threat, through either effective policing and legislative efforts or the fragmentation of the terrorist group from within. Also, Denmark, included within the eight, registered only one incident in the total reporting period.[29] As such, the actual level of commonality may be even lower, perhaps closer to Verbruggen's assessment, that, after the 1998 Good Friday Agreement, Spain remained 'the only EU member state with deeply entrenched domestic terrorist activity still as the prime concern of both politics and law enforcement'.[30] The only point of contention here would be in relation to his implicit suggestion that, prior to 1998, the UK – while facing a substantive terrorist threat in Northern Ireland – was committed to a European level of response, either in the Province or within the UK as a whole, a suggestion unsupported by the bulk of the evidence. It should also be remembered that the nature of the threat faced by each state will differ slightly, depending on the terrorists' ideological motivation, as this will affect the likely targeting and methodology selected.

In the post-September 11 era, there has been a much greater emphasis on the international dimension to the current terrorist threat, with Al Qaeda and Osama bin Laden displacing ETA and Action Directe in both the public and political eye. In the era of militant Islamist terror, the language and imagery is global. Such a global discourse is given some credence by the geographical range of terrorist incidents. Yet, as the Balkans example has demonstrated, such global imagery must be treated with caution. Claims regarding the level of Al Qaeda involvement on the ground, which was used to reframe Operation Allied Force and the ensuing international involvement in the region as part of the 'War on Terror', have been disputed.[31] As such, there is a need to more critically examine the nature of the post-September 11 threat within the EU.

In the 2002–03 Europol report, which notes that 'no major terrorist attacks occurred within the EU', there is a slight shift of balance within the EU fifteen, with eight states registering no incident.[32] The following year, the last before enlargement, there is a further shift, with only five states registering any form of incident. Additionally, three member states – Belgium, Finland and Portugal – did not even provide any information.[33] As such, the perceived level of commonality does not rest on substantive statistical foundations. There are also concerns regarding Europol's methodology. In the 2002 report, the claim is made that 'the risk of a serious attack with right-wing motivation committed by a single person still exists', without any supporting evidence offered.[34] In 2003, in relation to left-wing terrorism, the report noted that 'a dozen events have been reported so far, for 2003, but none considered a terrorist attack'.[35] This begs the question why such incidents have been included in the report. In addition, Europol's former Deputy Director, Willy Bruggeman, noted that 'almost every country was confronted with different forms of terrorism, or at least extremism',[36] which are not the same thing. There is a danger, if such anomalies are not corrected, that the credibility of Europol's assessment will be at risk. In addition, the seeming inappropriateness of the 'common concern' label, given the uneven nature and scale of the threat throughout the pre-enlargement period, helps explain the difficulties in sustaining a European level of response. As a result, it may lead to a move away from a formal, EU-wide response, such as Europol, towards less formal initiatives between concerned states. As Keohane has noted, 'governments do not need to wait for EU measures if they wish to co-operate more closely'.[37]

No more in common?

This seems to have been a lesson learned, at both the political and policing level, in the wake of enlargement. With a greater number of voices at the political level, bringing with them their own distinct interests, issues and initiatives, there has been an implicit recognition that a twenty-five state forum may not be the ideal vehicle for ensuring progress. It is within this context that the latest institutional grouping – the G5 meetings of the Home Affairs and Interior Ministers from France, Germany, Italy, Spain and the UK – and the latest Treaty development – the 2005 Treaty of Prum – have to be understood. In the latter case, in May 2005, seven states – the Benelux states, Austria, France, Germany and Spain – established new policing arrangements, forming new rules for DNA sharing, fingerprint data and airline security.[38] This is based on established precedents, such as the Schengen arrangements, which were initially organised outside the auspices of the EC/EU. As with Schengen, the Prum states hold out the prospect of others joining at a later stage, although there will be a three-year period before any widening takes place. While the Treaty arrangements may, like Schengen, act as a laboratory for eventual EU measures, equally it could be viewed as recognition that the European level may not be the most effective means to initiate progress in the wake of enlargement.

That is certainly the case with the G5. Rather than being linked by geography, as with the Baltic Task Force on Organised Crime, the G5 is a functional arrangement, 'a driver' for EU policy, by getting 'support and agreement from the five countries with the largest counter-terrorist capability in Europe'.[39] As a UK Home Office submission notes, the G5, with its smaller membership, enables 'a freer exchange of views . . . than would be possible at formal EU meetings involving all twenty-five member states'.[40] As such, it is difficult to view it as anything other than a response to enlargement. The issue of building and ensuring trust, essential for ensuring information exchange within the EU, has still to be reconciled within an enlarged EU. It was a problem faced by Interpol in the past, with one commentator noting that they would 'rather hand over operational information to Interflora as Interpol'.[41] It is also likely to dog the EU, at both the policing and the political levels, given the widening of membership. As a result, the tide may be turning slightly, away from formal EU-level responses and back towards more informal, bi- or multilateral arrangements.

Such developments are unsurprising, given the impact that widening membership has had on the scale and nature of the terrorist problem facing the EU. The 2004 Europol report notes only seven states as registering a terrorist incident, all of whom were pre-existing member states. Eleven states registered no incident, while a further seven – all of whom are new members – failed to provide any information at all.[42] In the case of Estonia, given that they only signed an agreement with Europol in 2005, this is less surprising,[43] but for the others – the remaining Baltic States, the Czech Republic, Malta, Poland and Slovenia – the failure to even submit information is less explicable. In fact, it has been suggested that some members of the Slovenian political elite are so unconcerned about terrorism as to suggest that the declared 'War on Terror' is not actually their fight.[44] This reinforces the doubts – noted earlier – regarding the scale of Islamist terrorism in the Balkan region. It also exacerbates the already questionable sense of commonality, with its knock-on effects in terms of organising and implementing a formal, EU-wide response. Furthermore, the threshold for inclusion in the report cannot have been substantial. There is some space given over to a brief discussion of Hungarian animal rights terrorism, despite the fact that the incidence was 'very low'.[45] This suggests that little evidence was actually required to ensure mention in the final report. Finally, looking beyond the 2004 enlargement process, the inclusion of both Romania and Bulgaria, EU members by 2007, will not reverse the trend, as neither state registered any terrorist incident in 2004.

An enlarged implementation gap?

This lack of commonality will, potentially, have consequences in terms of organising an EU-wide response. This raises the second theme of this chapter, namely the marked difficulty in implementing previously agreed commitments. As has been noted, the example set by the EU fifteen across the gamut of internal security, including counter-terrorism, was hardly inspiring. Post-accession, the rules have changed. The ensuing loss of direct institutional leverage when the ten accession states became full members, with commensurate status, voting rights and a greater ability to affect the agenda, effectively guarantees that, should calls to fully implement commitments be heard in the future, they do not have to be heeded.

As a result, in the short term at least, the widened EU finds itself in much the same situation as before, with a notable gap between agreed initiatives and implemented policies. A few selected examples will demonstrate this unsatisfactory note of continuity. The Framework Decision establishing Joint Investigative Teams has been ratified by only ten of the twenty-five potential participants.[46] The three additional Europol Protocols, important in fully establishing the Police Office as a significant player within the framework of different policing arrangements, have also suffered a similar fate. Agreed in 2000, 2002 and 2003 respectively, they have been ratified, on a sliding scale, by thirteen, eleven and seven states respectively.[47] It should be remembered that the tasks facing the new member states are even more daunting than those of the pre-existing members, who have had, in some cases, significantly longer to meet their expressed commitments. The ten new states have also had to accede to the *acquis communautaire* in its entirety, not just in the internal security sphere. Such matters help to place the post-enlargement 'implementation gap' into context.

While the 'implementation gap' remains, the pace of activity has not slowed down post enlargement. There has been a series of new initiatives, building up to and then centring on the 2004 Hague Programme. Ludford has collated those proposed both by individual member states and the European institutions between 2001 and 2004. She has noted fifty-one initiatives from the member states, supplemented by an additional thirty-eight proposals from the Commission. While this demonstrates that the pace of activity has not slowed down, even within the context of a substantively widened JHA Council, there is an issue of quality to consider. In her assessment, 'most of these initiatives were designed as press stunts, at the beginning of a Presidency, and have little value'.[48] While quality of legislation is important, the sheer weight of numbers, at a time when deadlines are being missed on pre-existing commitments, is worrying in itself.

There is, at least, some recognition that this situation has to be rectified. Commissioner Frattini has noted that there is little point in maintaining the pace of activity, if policies are not fully implemented or enforced: 'Adopting new legislation will not help, if existing legislation is not used to its full potential.'[49] Sweden is also on record as noting the need for a breathing space. It insisted that the 'starting point for the new programme should . . . be to finalise what remains undone on the Tampere scoreboard' and has called for a clear demonstration of the practical value of pre-existing commitments before advancing to the next set of initiatives.[50] The new members – generally, although not always accurately, lumped together with those perceived to be part of Donald Rumsfeld's so-called 'new Europe' – have yet to indicate clearly whether they will side with Finland and Sweden in this debate. However, there are some positive indicators worth bearing in mind, including the ten new states' record with regard to UN ratification, where their overall record is better than the EU fifteen. Of the ten new members, only Poland and the Czech Republic have yet to become full parties to all twelve Conventions, with Poland having one outstanding Convention to sign and the Czech Republic one to ratify.[51] Should they do so, and echo these calls for restraint, the widening gap may yet be closed.

A missed opportunity?

However, if actions speak louder than words, the case of the Hague Programme, agreed by all twenty-five member states, suggests that we should not be overly optimistic. The most common metaphor used when considering European integration – one that was even given the briefest physical manifestation during the 1997 Amsterdam European Council – is the bicycle ride. It is regularly called upon in defence of continued European integration; the member states must keep 'cycling' forward, in order to ensure that momentum is maintained. For example, in the wake of the French and Dutch referenda rejections of the European Constitution in 2005, a senior official insisted that life would go on, pointing out that, 'We'll all be turning up at the office the following week . . . There is a large programme of legislation that has to be enacted . . . the institutions are there to enact them and that will continue.'[52] It is this sort of response, suggesting that the process of European integration can somehow be hermetically sealed from even the most rigorous external shock, which helps to explain some of the increasing Euro disenchantment. Rather than pause and examine the nature of the message being sent by such expressions of public discontent, the EU simply gets back on its bike, to carry on the ride. However, there is a need to challenge this metaphor. Rather than simply carrying on, to ensure that momentum is not lost, perhaps it would be better to pause, consider what stage of the journey the EU is at and, more importantly, where it wants to go in the future. There is nothing to be lost by taking such a breathing space, in order to rationally consider the scale, pace and scope of integration. This would be in line with the EU's own expressed commitments to both subsidiarity and the guarantee that European internal security initiatives 'add value' to efforts undertaken by member states, either bilaterally or in smaller groups.

Instead, if the Hague process is anything to go by, the EU is still committed to cycling. With its 150 plus commitments, initiatives and plans, it constitutes another step-change in the process of JHA integration, with counter-terrorism at the forefront of a much wider agenda. This agenda embraces projects to tackle radicalisation, initiatives on the protection of witnesses and victims, confiscation orders, efforts to counter-terrorist financing and protection of key infrastructure, to name but a few. In fact, it is one that, if widely interpreted and fully implemented (although there is no guarantee of that, if past history is anything to go by), could alter the existing balance between regional and national levels in the provision of internal security. It is worth considering a number of examples, both in the legislative and policing field, to demonstrate its potential scope.

In the sphere of police co-operation, as part of an overall commitment to increase the level of information sharing, suggestions have been made that past convictions should be included as part of the mandatory information exchange. This has been suggested, despite the fact that a similar proposal was contained within the 1970 Council of Europe Convention on the international validity of criminal judgements, which, as of 2004, had only been ratified by four of the current EU membership.[53] As well as demonstrating a lack of appreciation for the past history of internal security co-operation, it also serves as an unnecessary duplication of effort.

Information exchange remains Europol's primary function, and, in the wake of the Hague Programme, two competing benchmarks have been suggested to reinvigorate such exchanges. The Netherlands requested 'equivalent access' to information, arguing that regional partners should have the same level of access as exists within the state.[54] This, of course, presupposes an effective level of information sharing within the state, which is not always the case. The alternative benchmark is the principle of 'availability'. In this case, 'information for law enforcement purposes needed ... by one state will be made available by the authorities of another ... subject to certain conditions'.[55] These would include the guaranteed integrity of the data, the protection of confidential sources and common standards for data access.[56] Yet, even accepting these principles, there is little the EU institutions and agencies can actually do to initiate higher levels of information exchange, beyond continued remonstration and exhortation to greater efforts. This is one of the potential obstacles inherent in establishing a formal level of co-operation. Yet, the Commission has continued to propose further formalisation, suggesting the establishment of a Law Enforcement Network, situated within Europol, as part of a wider proposal to formalise the existing network of bilateral exchanges.[57] This runs contrary to the advice of the UK Association of Chief of Police Officers (ACPO), which has accepted that 'bilateral exchange may be the best way forward'.[58]

As it stands, the process of information exchange remains voluntary, based on the nature of the problem at hand and the level of confidence expressed in the agencies of potential partners. However, veiled hints have been given that a more mandatory system might be worthy of consideration: 'In terms of addressing Europol's need for information and the poor information flow it still suffers, this could be overcome through the institution of a *formal* intelligence requirement, which member states would respond directly to' (emphasis added).[59] This was the view expressed by a representative of the UK's National Criminal Intelligence Service (NCIS). Their suggestion that a formal intelligence requirement should even be considered is all the more significant given the UK government's more limited formal position, which notes that, 'Europol has to be able to contribute properly within its existing remit of work.'[60] While it does not constitute a change in the UK's position, the fact that such an influential UK policing agency is prepared to even consider some sort of mandatory exchange is noteworthy.

There has also been a suggestion made that the EU, through Europol, should consider establishing the intelligence requirements for member states.[61] This seems wholly impractical. At the end of the day, it is difficult to imagine any member state,

THE IMPACT OF ENLARGEMENT

old or new, permitting that level of external supervision in a field as sensitive as national intelligence. However, that has not prevented the Commission at least moving in that direction. In December 2005, it proposed a Council Decision that would permit Europol to receive information on the activities of security and intelligence services.[62] While nothing may come from the proposal regarding Europol setting intelligence requirements for the twenty-five member states, the fact that such suggestions are even colouring the debate is suggestive that the cycle ride continues apace.

Policing is not the only area where The Hague Programme proposes further developing the EU level of counter-terrorist response. The field of civil protection, where efforts are taken to 'prepare ourselves, in a spirit of solidarity, to manage and minimise the consequences of a terrorist attack, by improving capabilities to deal with it: the aftermath; the co-ordination of the response; and the needs of victims',[63] is a further such example. While this may seem to be an area where the EU has little to offer to supplement national efforts, proposals have been made to create a more extensive European level, building on the 2001 Civil Protection Mechanism, with a Monitoring and Information Centre to link up national contact points.[64] It would do this by creating a Solidarity Fund, a Critical Infrastructure Warning Information Network and a raft of training plans and scenario exercises. Three of these have been related directly to managing a terrorist incident, although the emphasis has been placed on managing natural disasters.[65]

The EU's greater involvement is justified on the basis of the perceived inadequacies of organising bilateral assistance in this area, particularly in an enlarged EU. The Commission notes that bilateral assistance 'between twenty-five member states cannot guarantee coherence and cost-effectiveness and, moreover, places a considerable administrative burden on the affected state'.[66] However, it is difficult to see how this assertion can be sustained, for a number of reasons. Firstly, by definition, a bilateral relationship – such as the one that has proved so effective between France and Spain – would not involve all twenty-five states. Ironically, it is the Commission's desire to create an additional level of regional support that would involve all EU member states, even in situations where they did not possess a direct link to the crisis at hand. Secondly, in relation to cost effectiveness, for the Commission to be accurate there would have to be an absence of national planning. As states are likely to have prepared, at some level, for the management of both terrorist and natural emergencies, an additional budget line at the European level is, in effect, a duplication of costs, rather than a reduction. As such, while there may be a role for the regional level in terms of training and the sharing of best practice, it is questionable whether it will require the functioning administrative structure that is being suggested.

Conclusion

When assessing the impact that the enlargement process has had on the EU's counter-terrorist framework, it is worth recalling at the outset that the ten new states have only been members for a relatively short period of time, finally joining the EU in May 2004. While they may have been associated and involved in certain policy developments prior to accession, to ensure that their own national legislative efforts were in line with the way the *acquis communautaire* was developing, the widened EU is still in its relative infancy. For example, in relation to finding a balance between implementation and new initiatives, there is little clear evidence (at the time of writing) as to how the new member states will react, longer term, to Sweden's declared intentions to prioritise implementation of pre-existing initiatives over the search for new activities.

That said, the process of widening the membership has already begun to impact on the already unsteady EU counter-terrorist framework in a number of ways. Firstly, in relation to the process of commonality, increasing the diverse approaches and interests at the EU top table has stretched the sense of solidarity still further. In essence, as a direct result of enlargement, initiatives such as the G5 may herald the renaissance of the multilateral or even bilateral level, operating independently – and perhaps more effectively – than the formalised European level. Additionally, the widening of membership has been reflected in the 'implementation gap', which was already a problem of some significance before enlargement. The new members are, in no sense, the worst offenders here, but the gap remains and needs to be tackled before the EU caravan moves on to new destinations. There is a tendency within the EU to look to wider horizons, such as the next tranche of the on-going enlargement process, rather than deal with the nitty-gritty detail of implementation.

That trend can be seen with the 2004 Hague Programme and the additional proposals built on the back of it. Pre-accession, it was feared, at one stage, that enlargement would ultimately weaken the cohesiveness of the EU, particularly in areas operating under the unanimity rules, and would endanger the momentum of integration. This was part of the justification in the UK, at least, for supporting the proposed Constitution, as part of – in Peter Hain's memorable phrase – 'a tidying up exercise' before enlargement.[67] In the case of counter-terrorism, that has not happened. A tranche of new initiatives and potentially controversial proposals have emerged in the wake of the new five-year Hague agenda, maintaining the position of counter-terrorism at the front of the EU's internal security agenda. While many of these may remain at the initial stage of the decision-making process, never to actually be implemented, they are an unnecessary distraction and potential diversion of resources and time, away from pre-existing and unfinished commitments. This, in turn, impacts on the credibility of the EU in this important area. Rather than embrace the potential opportunity offered by an unprecedented widening of the EU's membership to pause and reflect on what actually can be done at the European level to 'add value', the enlarged EU has pushed on, carrying on with its lengthy cycle ride. As such, enlargement may yet prove to be an opportunity missed.

Notes

1 The views expressed here are personal and do not represent the opinions or views of the British Government, Ministry of Defence or the Royal Military Academy Sandhurst.

2 Council of the European Union, *Conclusions of the Copenhagen European Council* (Brussels, 1993).
3 See *The Hague Programme: Strengthening Freedom, Security and Justice in the European Union* (Brussels, November 2004).
4 US State Department data has to be used, particularly for the pre September 11 period, as the EU did not carry out any assessment at that time.
5 For details, see the Justice and Home Affairs Acquis 1993–2000 (2001), www.statewatch.org/semdoc/acquis.htm.
6 See, for example, European Commission, *Biannual Update of the Scoreboard to Review Progress on the Creation of an Area of Freedom, Security and Justice in the European Union* (Brussels, October 2001).
7 Justice and Home Affairs Council, *Framework Decision on Combating Terrorism* (Brussels, 2002).
8 Justice and Home Affairs Council, *Framework Decision on the European Arrest Warrant and the Surrender Procedures between Member States* (Brussels, 2002).
9 Daniel Keohane, *One Step Forward, Two Steps Back* (London: Centre for European Reform, 2005), p. 37.
10 *Report from the Commission on the European Arrest Warrant and the Surrender Procedures between Member States* (Brussels, February 2005), p. 4.
11 Hugo Brady and Daniel Keohane, *Fighting Terrorism: The EU Needs a Strategy not a Shopping List* (London: Centre for European Reform, 2005), p. 2.
12 Adrian Fortescue, *The Department of Homeland Security: A Partner but not necessarily a Model for the European Union* (Harvard, MA: Harvard University, 2004), p. 27.
13 House of Lords, *After Madrid: The EU's Response to Terrorism. Testimony of Gijs de Vries for Fifth Report, Taken before the Select Committee on the European Union on 3 November 2004* (London: HMSO, 2004), p. 3.
14 Joanna Apap and Sergio Carrera, 'Progress and obstacles in the area of freedom, security and justice in an enlarging Europe: an overview', in Joanna Apap (ed.), *Justice and Home Affairs in the European Union* (Northampton: Edward Elgar, 2004), p. 10.
15 *Country Reports on Terrorism 2004* (Washington, DC: US Department of State, 2005), pp. 17–26.
16 Ibid.
17 Edward Oakden, 'Combating transnational terrorism: views from Europe and the US', RUSI Conference, Transnational Terrorism: A Global Approach, London, 16 January 2006.
18 See Art. 19(1) TEU (consolidated text).
19 *Report from the Commission on the Council Framework Decision on Combating Terrorism* (Brussels, June 2004), p. 3.
20 House of Lords, *The Hague Programme. Testimony of Caroline Flint MP for Tenth Report, Taken before the Select Committee on the European Union on 26 January 2005* (London: HMSO, 2005), p. 29.
21 Jonathan Faull, interview, 'Our ambition should be that justice, freedom and security become as normal as possible a part of community business', www.europa.eu.int/comm/dgs/justice_home/director/dg_directorgeneral_en.htm.
22 Amnesty International cited House of Lords, *The Hague Programme*, p. 23.
23 Daniel Byman, 'Ending state sponsorship of terrorism', in *How to Win the War against Terrorism* (Washington, DC: The Saban Center for Middle East policy, 22 September 2004).
24 Jorg Monar, 'Maintaining the Justice and Home Affairs acquis in an enlarged Europe', in Apap (ed.), *Justice and Home Affairs in the European Union*, p. 49.
25 President George W. Bush, joint news conference with President Jacques Chirac (Washington, 6 November 2001), http://archives.cnn.com/2001/US/11/06/ret.bush.coalition/index.html.

26 Having conducted an extensive search of JHA documentation, and consulted with senior figures within the European institutions, I have been unable to ascertain a formal, agreed definition of 'common concern'.
27 Franco Frattini, speech, 'Presentation of the Commission Memorial Report dedicated to the victims of terrorism' (Strasbourg, 9 March 2005), http://europa.eu.int/comm/commission_barroso/frattini/doc/speech_09_03_05_en.pdf.
28 Didier Bigo, 'The European internal security field: stakes and rivalries in a newly developing field of police intervention', in Malcolm Anderson and Monica Den Boer (eds), *Policing Across National Boundaries* (London: Pinter Publishing, 1994), p. 167.
29 For full figures, see *Patterns of Global Terrorism 1994–2001* (Washington, DC: US Department of State, 1995–2002).
30 F. Verbruggen, 'Bull's eye? Two remarkable EU Framework Decisions in the fight against terrorism', in C. Fijnaut, J. Wouters and F. Naert (eds), *Legal Instruments in the Fight against International Terrorism: A Transatlantic Dialogue* (Leiden: Martinus Nijhoff, 2004), p. 300.
31 Rohan Gunaratna, *Inside Al Qaeda: Global Network of Terror* (London: Hurst & Company, 2002), pp. 131–4.
32 See *Terrorist Activity in the European Union: Situation and Trends Report – October 2002–15 October 2003* (The Hague: Europol, 2003).
33 Ibid.
34 *Terrorist Activity in the European Union: Situation and Trend Report – October 2001–Mid-October 2002* (The Hague: Europol, 2002), p. 19.
35 *Terrorist Activity in the European Union 2002–2003*, p. 21.
36 Willy Bruggeman, 'Countering the threat of terrorism in the EU in a broader organised crime perspective', in Fijnaut *et al.* (eds), *Legal Instruments in the Fight against International Terrorism*, p. 154.
37 Keohane, *One Step Forward*, p. 38.
38 Hugo Brady, 'An avante-garde for internal security', *Centre for European Reform Bulletin*, 44 (November 2005), p. 2.
39 Jonathan Faull cited House of Lords, *After Madrid*, pp. 37–53.
40 Home Office cited House of Lords, *After Madrid*, p. 129.
41 Rachel Woodward, 'Establishing Europol', *European Journal on Criminal Policy and Research*, 1:4 (1993), p. 24.
42 See *Terrorist Activity in the European Union: Situation and Trend Report – October 2003–17 October 2004* (The Hague: Europol, 2004).
43 *Europol Annual Report 2004* (The Hague: Europol, 2005), p. 6.
44 Steven Woehrel, 'Slovenia', in Paul Gallis (ed.), *European Counter-Terrorist Efforts: Political Will and Diverse Responses* (New York: Nova Publishing, 2004), p. 107.
45 *Terrorist Activity in the European Union 2003–2004*, p. 18.
46 *European Union Plan of Action on Combating Terrorism* (Brussels, June 2004), p. 26.
47 Ibid., p. 36.
48 Sarah Ludford, 'An EU Justice and Home Affairs policy: what should it comprise?', in Apap (ed.), *Justice and Home Affairs in the European Union*, p. 29.
49 Franco Frattini, Speech by the Justice and Home Affairs Commissioner to the Bundestag (Berlin, 14 February 2005) http://europa.eu.int/comm/commission_barroso/frattini/doc/speech_14_02_05_en.pdf.
50 For details, see 'Area of freedom, security and justice: assessment of the Tampere Programme and future orientations', Memorandum from the Swedish Ministry of Justice on the Commission Communication' (Stockholm, 8 September 2004).
51 *Country Reports on Terrorism 2004*, pp. 19 and 23.
52 Ambassador John Bruton, 'Where does Europe end?', in 'Europe's Global Role', The Brookings Centre on the United States and Europe Annual Conference (Washington, DC, 11 May 2005), p. 78.

53 European Commission, *Proposal for a Council Decision on the Exchange of Information and Cooperation regarding Terrorist Offences* (Brussels, March 2004).
54 House of Lords, *After Madrid*, pp. 12–18.
55 European Commission, *The Hague Programme: Ten Priorities for the Next Five Years* (Brussels, May 2005), p. 10.
56 *The Hague Programme* (2004), p. 27.
57 European Commission, *Enhancing Police and Customs Co-operation in the European Union* (Brussels, May 2005), p. 8.
58 ACPO cited House of Lords, *After Madrid*, p. 16.
59 NCIS cited House of Lords, *The Hague Programme*, p. 51.
60 Caroline Flint cited ibid., p. 20.
61 *Strengthening the EU Operational Police Co-operation* (Brussels, October 2004), p. 3.
62 European Commission, *Proposal for a Council Decision on the Transmission of Information Resulting from the Activities of Security and Intelligence Services with Respect to Terrorist Offences* (Brussels, December 2005).
63 Press Release of the Conclusions of the 2696th Justice and Home Affairs Council (Brussels, December 2005), http://ue.eu.int/uedocs/cmsupload/JHA,1-2.12.05.pdf.
64 European Commission, *Preparedness and Consequence Management in the Fight against Terrorism* (Brussels, October 2004), pp. 3–4.
65 Ibid., p. 5.
66 European Commission, *The Civil Protection Community Mechanism and the Solidarity Declaration Non-paper* (Brussels, April 2004), p. 51.
67 Peter Hain cited Ambrose Evans-Pritchard, 'Hain accuses press critics of lurid fantasy', *The Daily Telegraph* (16 May 2003).

4

The external shield of internal security: the EU's emerging common external border management

Jörg Monar

Introduction

Since the entry into force of the Treaty of Amsterdam in 1999, the creation of an 'area of freedom, security and justice' has become one of the fundamental treaty and integration objectives of the EU. The AFSJ's central rationale as a political project is to provide cross-border 'freedom, security and justice' within the external borders of this 'area'. Although some of the most serious forms of cross-border crime, such as terrorism and organised crime, often find ways to bypass external border controls, these controls are a relatively effective instrument regarding other challenges (such as illegal immigration and smuggling) and serve as a general deterrent. All of this makes external borders a core element of the entire AFSJ project. As the outer shield of the AFSJ, the EU's external borders are of crucial importance for at least two of the major functions of the AFSJ: to provide citizens with a 'high level of safety'[1] and to allow for a 'more efficient management of migration flows'.[2]

Border security also continues to be seen as an important internal security issue in some member states. Regardless of how effective border controls actually are as a security instrument, they have political salience and are of considerable sensitivity and visibility as an issue on the EU's agenda. Hardening external border controls also tends to be an easier option for collective action by EU governments than measures in the national context, which often are more vehemently contested by civil liberties groups and opposition parties.

The enlargement implications of this emphasis on external border security are obvious. For the sake of the effectiveness and credibility of the AFSJ, external borders must be managed in such a way that they can provide an effective shield for EU internal security, even under the conditions of the enlarged Union. There is no doubt that the 2004 EU enlargement has considerably increased the challenges for EU external border controls. Not only has it lengthened the external land and sea borders of the Union by several hundreds of kilometres, but many of the new member states – facing organisational, personnel, equipment and funding problems – still have to struggle to meet the standards of external border control and safety that current member states,

THE EXTERNAL SHIELD OF INTERNAL SECURITY 55

mostly in the context of the Schengen system, have been developing and implementing for more than a decade. The EU's response to these challenges has been to gradually develop an 'integrated border management' system, which could ultimately involve the establishment of a common European Border Guard, a quite revolutionary and still rather controversial answer to the challenges of border management in the enlarged Union.

After exploring the historical and political background of co-operation between EU member states on external border issues, this chapter will identify and analyse the core elements of the Union's emerging common external border management, with a particular focus on the creation of the EU's new External Borders Agency and the Schengen Borders Code. It will end with an evaluation of the progress made, including the limitations and the future prospects of 'integrated external border management' in the enlarged Union.

The Schengen system

Co-operation between member states regarding issues of external border security started in a systematic way in the second half of the 1980s within the Schengen context. Originally, the Schengen system only comprised five member states,[3] which – in contrast to the others – were willing to go ahead with the abolition of internal border controls and had to do so outside the framework of the EC Treaties. The objective of a full abolition of these controls, as laid down by the Schengen Agreement of 14 June 1985, was, to a large extent, based on the idea that common standards, procedures and certain common instruments at external borders – such as the Schengen Information System (SIS) – should compensate for the 'loss' of controlling possibilities at internal borders. The Schengen Convention finally entered fully into force on 26 March 1995. Since that time, checks and surveillance at the external borders of the EU member states party to the Convention have been governed by uniform common principles.[4] This created *de facto* a single internal security zone encompassing all Schengen members, in which the absence of any internal border controls meant that the external border parts of each individual Schengen member became a matter of common concern.

Yet, the Schengen internal security zone – often mockingly referred to as 'Schengen-Land' – is not identical with the EU territory, forming the most notable example of differentiation in the European construction thus far. Only thirteen of the fifteen old EU member states are integral parts of the Schengen zone, because Ireland and the UK have insisted on preserving their 'opt-outs' on the abolition of internal border controls, while accepting selected parts of the Schengen acquis. The ten new member states have had to fully accept the Schengen acquis as part of their accession obligations and have, since 2001, participated in the decision-making process. However, because of capability deficits, they have not yet been integrated into the operational parts of the Schengen system. As a result, the 'old' external borders of the

Schengen *vis-à-vis* the new member states are currently still in place. This will only change once the new member states are declared ready to assume all operational Schengen obligations, which is currently expected to happen by 2008 or 2009. To make matters even more complex, three non-member states – Iceland, Norway and (as a result of the positive outcome of the 2005 Swiss referendum) Switzerland – participate as 'associated' Schengen members in the system. The associates are expected to fully implement the acquis but – because of their non-EU member status – do not have formal decision-making rights.

Over the years, the Schengen members have not only extended the corpus of common standards and procedures, most of which were consolidated in April 2006 in the new 'Schengen Borders Code',[5] but have also increased the sharing of information on border security relevant issues, mainly, though not exclusively, through the SIS. This allows for the exchange of law enforcement relevant data on persons and certain types of property. They have also developed other forms of co-operation, such as the posting of liaison agents, common training projects and occasional co-ordinated or joint operations.

In the context of the completion of the Internal Market, there was also a move in the EC as a whole towards increased co-operation on external border security issues, involving Ireland and the UK, in spite of their non-participation in Schengen. This move suffered a major setback in 1991 (and again in 1993) when the proposed EC external frontiers convention failed to be adopted, mainly because of the British–Spanish differences over Gibraltar.[6] However, this did not prevent member states from developing further bilateral and multilateral co-operation on border security issues (such as, for instance, Franco-British co-operation on controls in the Channel area). Nor did it stop them agreeing on a number of common EU texts on external border issues, such as the 1997 recommendations on effective control practices at external borders for applicant countries. The launching of the Odysseus Programme in 1998, which allowed for common training measures, exchanges and studies in the area of external borders crossings and controls, marked a further step towards a common EU approach, involving all member states, not only Schengen members.

At the end of the 1990s, a number of factors created an even more favourable context for an EU-wide common approach to external border security. Of primary importance was the entry into force of the 1999 Treaty of Amsterdam, which finally led to the incorporation of the Schengen system into the EU, with a continuing opt-out for Ireland and the UK, but an obligation for all newly acceding member states to adopt the Schengen acquis in full. It also extended possibilities for the Union to act on external border issues. Yet, there were also other favourable factors. Firstly, from the 1999 Tampere European Council onwards, matters pertaining to the external border were increasingly included in EU strategies to combat cross-border crime and illegal immigration. This was done partly as a response to mounting concerns over security at the new, post-enlargement external frontier. Secondly, there was the British and Irish opt-in to parts of the Schengen acquis since 1999.

The European Border Guard project

With the big eastward enlargement approaching fast, it became more and more clear to EU member states during 2000–01 that the external border control capabilities of the future new member states were not going to fulfil EU/Schengen standards by the time of their accession. Substantial EU help would be needed well beyond 2004. There were also more general concerns about external border security as an important instrument in the fight against illegal immigration and the various forms of cross-border crime, later reinforced by the events of September 11. This emphasised the need to reduce risks of terrorist attacks through enhanced border controls. In spite of their common standards and agreed general procedures, the Schengen countries were also acutely aware that differences in national legislation and administrative implementation practices were causing security discrepancies between the sections of external borders controlled by different member states. For example, persisting differences in interpretation of the rules on SIS alerts, regarding the storage of information beyond the duration of alerts, affected both the efficiency and homogeneity of Schengen external border management.

This led several member states to give support to the idea of setting up a common European service for the safeguarding of EU external borders. This would provide an instrument of solidarity for sharing the burden of controlling external borders. Additionally, it allowed for better use of personnel and technical resources, as well as of available expertise, while, at the same time, marking a step forward for political integration. The idea of creating a European Border Police had been raised in the Council as a joint initiative of Germany and Italy at the beginning of 2001. Following this, a group of states, including Belgium, France, Germany, Italy and Spain embarked – under Italian leadership – on a feasibility study of a European Border Police. This was backed by the Commission and was financed on an 80 per cent basis under the Odysseus Programme.[7] Other member states, including the UK, shared the view that more co-operation on external border issues was needed, but expressed reservations about the idea of creating a European Border Police corps, considering it both impractical and potentially incompatible with national sovereignty.

The 2001 Laeken European Council arrived at a carefully worded compromise on co-operation on external border issues. It gave the Council and the Commission a mandate to work out 'arrangements for co-operation between services responsible for external border control and to examine the conditions in which a mechanism or common services to control external borders could be created'.[8] The terms 'European Border Police' or 'European Border Guard', although already used by some member states' governments, did not appear in the mandate. In response to the Laeken mandate, on 7 May 2002, the Commission presented a Communication on the way 'towards an integrated management of external borders' to the Council and the European Parliament.[8] Based on an analysis of the main challenges at external borders and the current state of co-operation between member states, it proposed a gradual move towards an 'integrated management' of external borders. This would start with a consolidation and codification of common rules and standards for external border controls and continue, *inter alia*, with the creation of an 'External borders practitioners common unit' and other co-operation mechanisms. This would lead to the creation of financial burdensharing mechanisms and, finally, a 'European Corps of Border Guards'.

The use of the term 'integrated management' appeared doubly justified, as the proposals were aiming at a progressive integration, both between the border security services of the different member states and between the different services in charge of external border security. The Commission placed a particular emphasis on enhancing operational synergies between services and on arriving at a more homogenous level of security at external borders. With its more long-term approach to the creation of a European Border Guard, the Commission clearly made an effort to satisfy both the advocates and the sceptics of such a project, placing a lot of emphasis on the practical progress that could be achieved in various fields in the meantime. As all the member states could find substantial elements in the Communication that they were able to support, its reception was broadly positive. That said, several member states did not agree with the Commission's view that integrated border management should ultimately lead to the creation of a European Border Guard Corps.

On 30 May 2002, the Italian-led feasibility study was presented at a Ministerial Conference in Rome.[10] The feasibility study was based on the input of a number of senior national experts from Belgium, France, Germany, Italy and Spain, most of whom tended to defend their national methods and organisational structures. This partially explains why the feasibility study, rather than coming out clearly for or against the creation of a European Border Police, advocated instead a complex network of national border police forces, which would be linked by a number of important common elements. These would include 'centres' in different member states, specialising in different areas of border security expertise and serving as 'knots' of the network. There would also be common units for special tasks, including a 'rapid response unit', a common risk assessment, a certain degree of financial burdensharing and a common training curriculum. While filled with detailed operational and organisational assessments and recommendations, the 'polycentric' network model proposed was lacking in clarity, providing a mosaic of proposed structures and individual measures, rather than a grand design. Even some of the participating states were not fully satisfied. Yet, in spite of its shortcomings, the feasibility study made it clear that there are indeed different possible models for a European Border Guard, ultimately based on different political concepts on how far integration should go in this area. These models can be summarised as follows:

1 The first model – which may be called the 'integrated force model' – would involve the creation, surely only in a longer-term perspective, of an integrated border guard force under Council authority. It would have a common command structure and common training and equipment standards. It would be financed through the EU budget and would be vested with full law enforcement powers at external borders, partially or (eventually) totally replacing national border police forces.

2 The second model – which may be called the 'network model' – would mean the creation of a European Border Guard as a network of national border guard units. According to this model, border guards would continue to exist as separate national forces, but would also be subject to common instructions issued by a new body within or attached to the Council and based on common training and equipment standards. Some of the national border guards could be trained and equipped to constitute a contingency reserve (or 'rapid response force'). This would consist of national units able to merge into joint units and capable of being deployed at particular 'hot spots' at external borders upon request and approval by the Council body.

The first model would clearly be the most straightforward and efficient from an organisational point of view and would go furthest with the creation of a comprehensive system of burdensharing and mutual trust building. Yet, it would also be the most difficult to implement. The example of the establishment of Europol – which, after nearly a decade of development, still does not have any operational powers – has shown how reluctant most member states are to create any supranational body in the law enforcement field and to confer law enforcement powers in their territory on officials from other member states. This also applies to those that would – in terms of burdensharing – benefit most from the creation of such a force, namely the CEE states. Having regained their full national sovereignty at the end of the Cold War, most of these states are wary of the creation of further supranational structures at the EU level. As Colonel Marian Kasinski, Deputy-Commander-in-Chief of the Polish Border Guard, noted, 'each one [i.e. country] should try to protect its own borders'.[11] In addition, it would necessitate substantial changes to national legislation in several countries, including France. The organisational difficulties would also be considerable. An integrated force would need to be created through the merger of national forces, which, up to now, are marked by major differences in terms of tasks, structures, training and equipment. The language problems in an integrated border guard force, consisting of officials from twenty-five different member states, could only be effectively resolved by agreement on one official language. This would be politically sensitive and would require an unprecedented effort in language training.

The second – 'network' – model would clearly be easier to implement, as it would leave national forces legally and structurally largely untouched, bringing them only gradually, and to a limited extent, under a common regime of standards and procedures. Under the 'network model', the creation of common structures is to be limited to a steering body at the European level, a number of joint 'centres' for common analysis and co-ordination purposes and the possibility of deploying specially earmarked units in joint operations, as part of a 'rapid response force'. Although some organisational problems would also need to be resolved under this model – especially as regards the creation, organisation, language regime and command of the 'rapid response force' – these would be on a much smaller scale, as most of the border guards would continue to operate in a purely national organisational context. The costs of change would, overall, be lower, as separate national forces would remain the core elements of the system and political resistance would, as a result, be much more limited.

There are, however, also a number of specific problems with the 'network model'. As separate national forces would continue to exist, the effectiveness of the network would heavily depend on these forces implementing external border control standards and procedures as uniformly as possible, in line with the issued common guidelines. The adoption of sufficiently precise, demanding and timely common standards could turn out to be a major challenge in an EU of twenty-five or more states. An even bigger challenge would be to secure a sufficiently effective and uniform implementation, with national forces still being organised on different principles, with different powers, political and legal contexts and cultures.

The June 2002 Action Plan and its implementation

Differences over both the need for a European Border Guard and the model to be selected ensured that the project lost some momentum after the feasibility study was presented. Yet, at the same time, the Council had come under serious pressure to act on external border security issues, as Prime Ministers Blair and Aznar jointly called for more measures at external borders in the fight against illegal immigration. On 13 June 2002, the Council of Ministers agreed on a 'Plan for the management of the external borders of the Member states', which endorsed most of the analysis and the proposals of the Commission Communication, merging it with some elements of the feasibility study, such as the idea of creating a network structure.[11] This Action Plan was different from the Commission Communication, in that it placed distinctly less emphasis on common legislation and common financing. It also referred only in rather vague terms to a later 'possible decision' on the setting up of a European Corps of Border Guards, which would support, but not replace, national border police forces.[12] Instead, the Plan – which is currently still in force – provides for a wide range of more immediate practical measures on 'integrated management'. These are aimed at reinforcing operational co-ordination, common integrated risk analysis, training measures, the adoption of common minimum standards and enhanced burdensharing. Overall, it is based on a comprehensive concept of common EU external border management, aimed at an increasing synergy between the member states border guard services on a broad range of issues. Quite distinctive is its focus on measures of an operational, rather than legal, nature, which gives the whole Plan a very 'pragmatic' orientation.

On this basis, significant progress has been made towards the 'integrated management' of external borders through enhanced operational co-operation and co-ordination between national border guard forces. Progress was also enhanced by the institutionalisation of the co-operation process regarding external borders and enhanced burdensharing. As regards *operational co-operation*, there have been a considerable number of joint operations and projects, such as 'Ulysses', 'Triton', 'Nettuno

I and II' and 'Semper Vigilia I and II' in 2003 and 2004, in which land and/or sea border guard services from several member states have participated. 'Nettuno II' and 'Semper Vigilia II', both carried out in 2004, contained the active involvement of the new member states in such operations. For example, 'Nettuno II' was targeted at illegal immigration by sea and involved units from Cyprus, Greece, France and the UK. In addition, Poland participated alongside Germany, Italy, Austria and the UK in the co-ordinated mixed team controls of 'Semper Vigilia II'. Although not always an unqualified success, because of communication and co-ordination difficulties, significant experience has been gained regarding interoperability and co-ordination problems. Not only that, but co-operation mechanisms have also been improved and the operations have helped to create new networks and better mutual understanding between participating forces. On the downside, in all of these operations, only some member states have participated, while non-participating member states have not always been kept effectively informed. Additionally, the reporting and evaluation procedures have often been ineffective.[14]

As regards *institutionalisation*, major steps forward have been taken, in particular the creation of the Risk Analysis Centre (RAC) in Helsinki and the Ad-hoc Centre for Border Guard Training (ACT) in Vienna. On the basis of a common integrated risk analysis model (CIRAM), the Helsinki centre has proven its value for both periodical reports on the border security risks situation – one under each Presidency – and the analysis of specific border security problems or border areas. Each month, the member states submit written information to the RAC regarding networks of human traffickers and the methods they are using, new routes used by traffickers and illegal immigrants, the use of fraudulent methods to obtain visas and the use of false documents. The training modules of the ACT have been instrumental in encouraging the approximation of control standards, especially customs and administrative standards. They have also provided specific organisational, legal and linguistic knowledge to border guards engaged in multinational operations. The other centres – including the Centre for Land Borders (CLB) in Berlin, the Air Borders Centre (ABC) in Rome and the Eastern Sea Borders Centre (ESBC) – have mainly played a planning, co-ordination and supporting role for joint operations, with full involvement of the new member states since accession. Co-ordination and information exchange between these different structures have, over time, improved. The centres have also started work on common rules and procedures for the carrying out of joint operations.[15] Yet, many shortcomings remain, such as the non-systematic application of the integrated risk analysis model and the fact that there is no uniformity in their membership.

As regards *burdensharing*, there has been a clear move towards financial solidarity. The first example was the 2002 introduction of the ARGO programme,[16] whose financial framework for measures regarding the management of external borders was upgraded in 2004. Secondly, there was the introduction of the €960m Schengen facility for the new member states (2004–06). The ARGO programme has, from the start, been used primarily as a funding instrument for measures regarding external borders.[17] It also provides much of the funding for the Centres. Yet, ARGO only provides for co-funding of 60 per cent (in exceptional cases 80 per cent), and, with an overall ceiling for 2005 of just under €6.7m,[18] its overall financial envelope remains a rather modest one.[19] This is hardly adequate for the training and equipment challenges of current and future new member states. As regards the Schengen facility, it is obviously only a temporary instrument. It was part of a special accession deal for new member states – especially Poland – with particularly heavy responsibilities at the new EU external borders.

Burden-sharing can, of course, take an operational form, with joint operations (see above) and the establishment of the new EU External Border Agency (see below) regarded as steps towards institutionalised solidarity. The Hague Programme on the strengthening of the area of freedom, security and justice, which was approved on 4 November 2004, rightly stresses the importance of financial solidarity. With the provision for the creation of a Community border management fund by the end of 2006, a further step is taken in this direction.[20] In May 2005, the Commission proposed a total of €2.152bn for this fund between 2007 and 2013.[20] This is an impressive amount, yet will be heavily dependent on the overall framework of the 2007–13 Financial Perspective, on which the European Council failed to reach agreement in June 2005.

Overall, the progress made with the implementation of the objectives set in the June 2002 Council Plan is quite impressive. Five years ago, few experts would have thought it likely that member states would, by now, have been carrying out joint patrolling operations in the Mediterranean or working on the basis of a common risk analysis model. Driven at least partially by the challenges of border security in the enlarged EU, the member states have gone quite some way towards regarding EU external border controls as a common challenge. Yet, at least four major problems have become apparent, which have, to some extent, limited progress.

Firstly, there is no uniform level of commitment from the states to joint projects. In most cases, only some member states have participated and, on occasions, even the participating states either have left it at a declaration of interest or have failed to fully deliver what they promised.[22] While this voluntary participation has the advantage of allowing different groups to explore different ways forward at the same time, it is clearly not optimal in terms of developing an EU common approach. Nor does it draw maximum benefits from each state's know-how, capabilities and geographical situation. The second issue is that projects have often been introduced and carried out on an *ad hoc* basis, without a strategic plan or effective co-ordination. More often than not, individual member states have taken the lead on a project and carried it out with interested partners, without paying much attention to overlaps or potential synergy effects with other projects.[23] The third problem is the absence of a proper legal framework for seconding border guard officers to other member states. In most cases, it has limited their role in common operations to observer status, without any executive powers. As a result, even in cases where multinational teams have been formally created at external frontiers, these have, in most cases, remained national teams from an operational perspective, with full command and law enforcement powers limited to the national border guards. Then there are funding difficulties. In many cases, the availability of EU funding for co-operation projects has a major impact on the degree of their success. Projects may not even take off at all, if no such funding is available. Currently, these funding possibilities are limited to a small number of EU programmes and their mobilisation is subject to rather restrictive conditions and cumbersome procedures.

Varying standards and practices in the implementation of border controls also continue to be a major challenge. The Schengen countries have introduced a system of mutual evaluations of member states on a rotating basis, which is based on questionnaires and multinational inspection missions. Yet, these so-called Schengen evaluations normally allow the evaluated administrations plenty of time 'to get things right' before inspection missions arrive. They are carried out at intervals of several years for the individual member states and normally result in reports that are drafted in a rather careful and diplomatic language.[24] The reports also have no judicial follow-up and are kept confidential, so that the pressure generated by this peer review process has tended be rather limited. The Hague Programme tries to address this deficit by providing for the supplementing of the existing Schengen evaluation system with a new supervisory mechanism, which will also include unannounced visits.[25]

The new EU External borders agency

Some of the above problems, especially those on the co-ordination side, are going to be addressed by a new institution, which has just been established at the time of writing. Driven forward by a strong initiative from the Greek Presidency at the European Council in Thessaloniki in June 2003, the member states agreed, on 16 October 2004, on the establishment of an Agency for the Management of Operational Co-operation at the External Borders.[26] The Agency – for which the acronym FRONTEX has been introduced – has a number of significant tasks. These include the co-ordination of operational co-operation in the field of external border controls, the provision of assistance in the training of national border guards (including the establishment of common training standards) and the carrying out of risk analyses. These will assist in the development of research relevant for the control and surveillance of external borders and help member states requiring increased technical and operational assistance. They will also provide necessary support in organising joint return operations of rejected asylum seekers and illegal immigrants.

The seat of the Agency, formally inaugurated on 30 June 2005, is in Warsaw, which can be taken as an indication of the importance attached to the responsibilities of the new member states as regards the control of EU external borders. On 25 May 2005, the Finnish Colonel Ilkka Laitinen was appointed as its first Executive Director. He had previously been the director of the Risk Analysis Centre (see above), whose functions will be taken over by the Agency. It has been allocated a budget of €6m for 2005 and €10m for 2006[27] and is currently expected to have fifty-seven members of staff.[28] It has been vested with quite substantial operational powers, which go distinctly beyond those of other JHA agencies, such as Europol and Eurojust. According to Article 2 of the Regulation, it shall not only evaluate but also approve and co-ordinate proposals for joint operations and pilot projects made by member states. It can also itself, and in agreement with the member state(s) concerned, launch initiatives for joint operations and pilot projects, in co-operation with member states. In cases in which individual member states are faced with particular difficulties at the external border, requiring increased technical and operational assistance, the Agency can organise this assistance, by co-ordinating support and deploying its own experts (Article 8). It can also decide to put its technical equipment at the disposal of member states participating in the joint operations or pilot projects.

A particular feature of the Agency is that it can, on the basis of a decision of its Management Board and subject to the consent of the member states concerned, decide upon the setting up of 'specialised branches'. Initially, these will be the operational and training centres already established (see above), specialising in their respective aspects of control and surveillance (Article 16). They will develop best practices with regard to the particular types of external borders for which they are responsible, and the Agency will ensure the coherence and uniformity of such best practices. The national 'branches' can also be used by the Agency for the practical organisation of joint operations and pilot projects. Finally, the Agency has been vested with an important monitoring and evaluation function. It will be responsible for evaluating the results of joint operations and pilot projects and making a comprehensive comparative analysis of those results. This should enhance the quality, coherence and efficiency of future operations and projects.

The establishment of the new Border Management Agency must be regarded as an important step towards a more integrated and 'institutionalised' management of external borders. An important element of progress is the solidarity dimension, introduced by the emergency support possibility in Article 8 of the Regulation (see above). The 'promotion of solidarity' is actually mentioned amongst the reasons for its establishment in Article 1. While the Agency clearly does not constitute a European Border Guard as such, it certainly creates some sort of co-ordinating command structure. Through the 'specialised branches', it gives the Agency a direct reach into national border guard forces, which could, at a later stage, considerably facilitate the build-up of European Border Guard structures. The member states may have found the Agency's operational functions, which are more substantial than Europol', quite acceptable for two reasons. Firstly, the principle of national border guard forces and their executive powers remains untouched. Secondly, they retain control of the Agency through its Management Board, which consists of national representatives.

The 'Schengen Borders Code'

For both the efficiency and the credibility of the EU's external border management, a common set of rules on how controls should be carried out is of crucial importance. The Commission has, therefore, placed significant emphasis on the need for the consolidation and further development of a 'common corpus' of legislation. In April 2004, it proposed a Regulation establishing a 'Community Code on the rules governing the movement of persons across borders', based on existing Schengen rules. As a result of the proliferation of different documents adopted over time, the Schengen rules had become rather complex and non-transparent. After intense negotiations, both in the Council and between the Council and the European Parliament,[29] a compromise text of this Code – commonly referred to as the Schengen Borders Code – was passed by the European Parliament on 23 June 2005.[30] The Code defines the conditions for crossing external borders and entry into member states. It also elucidates the principles governing the implementation of external borders controls, including surveillance between authorised border crossing points, co-operation between member states and the conditions for refusal of entry. It also establishes special rules for border checks for the different kinds of borders and specific procedures for certain categories of persons, such as aircraft pilots and diplomats.

The adoption of the Schengen Borders Code on the basis of co-decision by the European Parliament has been seen by some NGOs as a test case for the emergence of a potentially more liberal EU external border control regime.[31] The European Parliament made a significant contribution to the strengthening of the procedural rights of third country nationals, as regards checks and potential refusals of entry. However, it also tightened the border regime in other respects, such as the rights of border guards to consult national and EU databases, in order to ensure that a person does not represent a danger to internal security.[32] This suggests that the involvement of the Parliament as a co-legislator will not lead to any fundamental change to the strong security rationale of the EU's overall approach.

Conclusions

Since the 2002 Council Action Plan and, as a result of the border security challenges linked to EU enlargement, the Union has made significant progress towards an integrated management of its external borders. The main indicators of progress are enhanced operational co-operation, increased institutionalisation – most recently through the establishment of the External Borders Agency – and the moves towards financial solidarity, which are of particular importance to the new member states. The adoption of the Schengen Borders Code will, in addition, contribute to the strengthening of the regulatory basis of external border management.

Yet, the 'integrated' system clearly continues to have major limitations. There are still substantial co-ordination and evaluation deficits, as well as major constraints imposed by the absence of cross-border law enforcement powers for border guards. While the establishment of the External Borders Agency marks a substantial step forward, the Agency does not create any sort of integrated force structure. It will still have to struggle with largely independent national border guard forces, which are differently organised, differently trained and have different powers and priorities.

It also has to be remembered that 'integrated border management' does not even apply to the EU as a whole. As pointed out earlier, currently only thirteen of the twenty-five member states are fully operational parts of the Schengen system (Ireland and the UK maintain their 'opt-outs'). In addition, the ten new member states are still on the way towards 'Schengen maturity'[33] which commissioner Franco Frattini believes they are unlikely to reach before 2008. Further differentiation is generated by the participation of Norway, Iceland and Switzerland as non-member states. All this variable geometry certainly does not help with the development of a uniform EU-wide external border system and adds to the complexity of common policy making in this area.

As regards the future, a lot will depend, firstly, on the development of the financial solidarity mechanisms. These will be essential, both for completing the full integration of the current ten new member states and for enhancing the joint operation capabilities at external borders. In this context – and based on experiences with the last enlargement – the EU may also need to develop new instruments, which can ensure the effective integration of Bulgaria and Romania into the EU border management system from 2007 onwards. Secondly, the development of the Agency could have an important impact, especially if – as provided for by The Hague Programme – it is to be vested with additional tasks. Thirdly, and finally a lot will depend on the effective implementation of agreed objectives. Of particular importance will be the introduction of SIS II, now delayed until June 2008, which will upgrade SIS capabilities and is also a technical precondition for the integration of the new member states in the Schengen external border system (which may be further delayed until 2008 or 2009). The current SIS was designed for a maximum of eighteen states and is considered to be out-dated. The SIS II will be adapted to the needs of the enlarged EU and will also allow for the processing of a range of other law enforcement relevant data categories. It will also be open to a wider number of law enforcement agencies and provide for increased interoperability with other EU databases.[34] Of crucial importance from an implementation perspective, however, will be the improvement of the mutual evaluation procedures.

Contrary to some earlier negative expectations, the EU external border system has not been significantly weakened or even collapsed as a result of enlargement. What has happened instead is that the old member states – with the Schengen countries as their core – have extended their model of the external shield of EU internal security to the new member states. This move is likely to be completed during 2008–09 and to be repeated with the next round of enlargement in due course. This extension has certainly come at a price. As the EU border regime is manifestly driven by a security rationale, it is inevitably restrictive in nature, with negative implications for the position of asylum seekers and immigrants.[35] The new member states, in particular Poland, have made no secret about the economic, financial and human costs the 'forced' adoption of Schengen would mean to them, because of the hardening of the external borders towards their eastern neighbours. Yet, none of them really fought for longer-term or even permanent derogations, and, since accession, none of them has seriously questioned, let alone opposed, the 'integrated border management' objectives. On the contrary, some of the new developments, especially the establishment of the Border Agency, have received strong support among the new member states.

How can one explain this relatively smooth assimilation of the new member states? Both the EU 'stick' – linking the lifting of Schengen controls towards the new member states to effective implementation of the external border acquis – and the EU 'carrots' – financial sweeteners such as the 'Schengen facility' and other EU support measures – may have contributed to the adherence of the new member states to the EU's external border security rationale. Yet, it should be remembered that the new member states have an interest in effective external border security, with their citizens being at least as concerned by cross-border crime and illegal immigration as those in the old member states. Ultimately, therefore, old and new member states share common strategic objectives in this respect. This seems an essential precondition for the collective political will of the member states. This will be necessary to further develop integrated external border management, currently still very much an external shield in the making.

Notes

1 See Article 29 Treaty on European Union and Article 61(e) Treaty on the European Community.
2 Council of the European Union, *Conclusions of the Tampere European Council* (Brussels, October 1999), para. 22.
3 Belgium, France, Germany, Luxemburg and the Netherlands.
4 The basic principles of Schengen external border controls are established in Title II, Chapter 2 of the 'Convention implementing the Schengen Agreement' of 19 June 1990. For details, see www.zuwanderung.de/english/downloads/schengen.pdf. The detailed rules for applying them are laid down in the 'Common manual for external borders', http://eur-lex.europa.eu/LexUriServe/site/en/aj/2002/c_313/c_31320021216en00970335.pdf.
5 Regulation (EC) No 562/2006 of 15 March 2006 establishing a Community Code on the rules governing the movement of persons across borders, *Official Journal of the European Union*, no. L 105/1 (13 April 2006).
6 On the initial progress made in the Schengen context and the setbacks regarding the external frontiers convention see Wenceslas de Lobkowicz, *L'Europe et la sécurité intérieure* (Paris: La documentation française, 2002), pp. 23–32.
7 See Otto Schily, *Guter Start auf dem Weg zur Europäischen Grenzpolizei* (Berlin, Bundesministerium des Innern, 30 May 2002).
8 See Council of the European Union, *Conclusion of the Laeken European Council* (Brussels, December 2001).
9 See *Communication from the Commission to the Council and the European Parliament: Towards Integrated Management of the External Borders of the Member States of the European Union* (Brussels, 2002).
10 'Feasibility study for the setting up of a "European Border Police"' (30 May 2002), www.statewatch.org/news/2005/may/eba-feasibility-study.pdf.
11 House of Lords, *Proposals for a European Border Guard: Minutes of Evidence for Twenty-Ninth Report, Taken before the Select Committee on the European Union (Sub-Committee F) on 4 March 2003* (provisional transcript) (London HMSO, 2003), p. 14.
12 Council of the European Union, *Plan for the Management of the External Borders of the Member States* (Brussels, June 2002).
13 Ibid., see paras 118–20.
14 For details see *Report of the Greek Presidency on the Implementation of Programmes, Ad Hoc Centres, Pilot Projects and Joint Operations* (Brussels, June 2003).

15 For details on the activities of the Eastern Sea Borders Centre, see http://register.consilium.eu.int/pdf/en/04/st09/st09469.en04.pdf.
16 *Action Programme for Administrative Cooperation in the Fields of External Borders, Visas, Asylum and Immigration* (Brussels, 2002), http://ec.europa.eu/justice_home/funding/argo/funding_argo_en.htm.
17 In its First Annual Report on the implementation of the ARGO project (2002–2003) the Commission reported that eight out of ten projects were dealing with external border security issues. For details, see http://europa.eu.int/comm/justice_home/funding/argo/doc/annual_staff_working_argo_en.pdf.
18 See the Commission Work Programme for ARGO 2005, http://europa.eu.int/comm/justice_home/funding/argo/doc/annual_work_programme_2005_en.pdf.
19 See list of the projects funded in 2004, http://europa.eu.int/comm/justice_home/funding/argo/doc/list_grants_awarded_2004_01_en.pdf.
20 *The Hague Programme: Strengthening Freedom, Security and Justice in the European Union* (Brussels, December 2004).
21 'Hague Programme: ten priorities for the next five years', press release, http://europa.eu.int/rapid/pressReleasesAction.do?reference=MEMO/05/153&format=HTML&aged=0&language=en&guiLanguage=en.
22 See *Report of the Greek Presidency*.
23 Ibid.
24 *Report on the Proposal for a Regulation of the European Parliament and of the Council Establishing a Community Code on the Rules Governing the Movement of Persons Across Borders by the Committee on Civil Liberties, Justice and Home Affairs* (Brussels, June 2005), pp. 64–5.
25 See *Hague Programme*, p. 15; *Council and Commission Action Plan implementing the Hague Programme on Strengthening Freedom, Security and Justice in the European Union* (Brussels, June 2005), p. 10.
26 *Council Regulation Establishing a European Agency for the Management of Operational Cooperation at the External Borders of the Member States of the European Union* (Brussels, November 2004).
27 For details on the appointment, see http://hallitus.fi/vn/liston/base.lsp?r=94512&k=en&old=716&rapo=1628.
28 Basic facts about the External Borders Agency, http://europa.eu.int/rapid/pressReleases Action.do?reference=MEMO/05/230&format=HTML&aged=0&language=EN&guiLanguage=en.
29 Since 1 January 2005, the European Parliament has acquired legislative co-decision powers over border control issues (and other 'first pillar' areas of justice and home affairs).
30 *European Parliament Legislative Resolution on the Proposal for a Regulation of the European Parliament and of the Council Establishing a Community Code on the Rules Governing the Movement of Persons across Borders* (Brussels, June 2005).
31 See, in particular, Steve Peers, 'Revising EU Border Control Rules: a missed opportunity?', www.statewatch.org/news/2005/jul/eu-border-code-final.pdf.
32 *European Parliament Legislative Resolution*, Article 6(2).
33 Franco Frattini, 'EU newcomers partly to blame for delays in expansion of Schengen visa system', *International Herald Tribune* (Europe edition), 23 October 2006.
34 See *Council Regulation Concerning the Introduction of Some New Functions for the Schengen Information System, Including in the Fight Against Terrorism* (Brussels, April 2004).
35 See Marat Kengerlinsky, 'The EU's new external borders and restrictions in immigration and asylum policies', 'UACES European Studies on-line essays', 5, (March 2005), www.uaces.org/E53Kengerlinsky.pdf.

5

EU enlargement and organised crime: Transdniestria as a case study

Graeme P. Herd and Anne C. Aldis

Either the region takes control of its borders or the criminals will take control of the region.[1]

Introduction: soft and hard security and EU enlargement

The relationship between EU enlargement and the soft security threats posed by organised crime is complex and heavily contested. Enlargement and the opening of EU borders to new EU members from the east was understood as exporting a zone of peace and security to the east, as Schengen borders have the potential to filter out criminal activity. The Czech Republic, for example, has benefited greatly from undertaking reforms necessary to enter the Schengen zone. Indeed, serious crime has remained steady or decreased since EU entry, though police have registered a growth in organised prostitution.[2] However, Danish Justice Minister Lene Espersen has noted that organised crime is an increasing problem in the Balkans, with illegal trade accounting for more than 50 per cent of economic activity in some areas.[3] International criminal gangs are based mainly outside the EU, located in Russia, Eastern Europe, Central Asia, China, Nigeria and Brazil. Some terrorist groups use organised crime to finance their political activities – the Madrid bombers sold fake CDs and DVDs, for example. However, the core activities of organised criminals remain drugs (importing heroin from Afghanistan, cocaine from Colombia and ecstasy from Europe); counterfeit goods (including CDs, DVDs, jeans, perfumes, aircraft parts, medicines and baby-food); identity theft; currency counterfeiting; theft of luxury cars for sale in Eastern Europe; cigarette and alcohol smuggling and money-laundering.[4]

These activities destabilise the EU's new neighbourhood and delay progress in terms of European integration. Despite the French and Dutch failure to ratify the European Constitution, Romania and Bulgaria will join the EU in 2007. It is also likely that, within this same timeframe, both Serbia and Montenegro and the international protectorate of BiH will join NATO's Partnership for Peace (PfP) process. Moreover, the EU–Balkans Summit of June 2003 endorsed the belief and aspiration that the entire region could be integrated into the EU over the next decade.[5]

Alongside international terrorism, illegal migration and frozen conflicts, organised crime is one of the most serious security threats confronting the EU. It is also a significant challenge to the prospects of these states wishing to join the EU. This chapter provides an overview of organised crime in the Balkans and selects Transdniestria as a case study of a criminalised zone in the EU's new neighbourhood. The Transdniestria example focuses on identifying the links between organised crime and frozen conflicts and the policy implications this has for EU enlargement and foreign policy. It argues that the EU is not yet able to effectively address the destabilising role of organised crime and criminal groups, particularly when embedded in geo-economic and geo-political conflicts.

The EU, organised crime and the Balkans

The role of organised crime in CEE states is an issue of rising strategic importance for the EU. In 2001, the EU elaborated a 'Strategy to Prevent Organised Crime'[6] and, in its December 2003 Security Strategy, it identified organised crime as an issue of strategic security concern.[7] Organised crime also has a transatlantic dimension. The US rejection of the EU-supported International Criminal Court (ICC) resulted in the freezing of military aid programmes for key US allies in Europe and Latin America, over their refusal to sign bilateral agreements granting immunity to all US citizens from war crimes prosecution by the ICC. Waivers had been given to Albania, BiH, FYROM, Romania and Tajikistan, but diplomats and analysts were surprised that the US did not exempt the European countries that were due to join NATO in 2004 (Bulgaria, Estonia, Latvia, Lithuania, Slovakia and Slovenia), as well as the aspirant and existing PfP members.[8] Romania, in particular, supported the US position on the ICC, in the process straining its relations with the EU. The US position towards the ICC has not substantially changed since 2003. The issue of 'extraordinary renditions', which hit the headlines in late 2005, served, at best, to refocus attention on differing US and European legal interpretation and approaches to international law, at worst on US illegality and European hypocrisy.

Despite disputes over the ICC and other high-profile issues, the processes of EU and NATO integration and enlargement have continued. These processes are viewed as an important means to address and manage soft security threats in the region, such as organised crime, thereby stabilising the Balkans. The June 2003 EU–Balkan Summit reaffirmed the EU's desire to eventually integrate all Balkan states into the Union.[9] As Slovene Prime Minister, Anton Rop, stated: 'The EU has shown that the integration of the Balkan states is one of the priority tasks.'[10] There is a need for border controls to be strengthened, so that gaps between different border regimes, exploited by organised crime, can be closed and a key threat to regional stability reduced. The quotation at the head of this chapter highlights where today's security guarantees lie – not in a military alliance such as the old NATO, but in forces controlling and checking the flows of other kinds of potential threats across regional boundaries.

However, there are a number of challenges that must be overcome, particularly in the areas of security, crime and justice. Let us take the Stability Pact as an example: 'Initiated by the EU with strong US support and placed under the auspices of the OSCE, the Stability Pact aims to strengthen democracy, economic development and security throughout the region.'[11] In the founding document, signed in June 1999, more than forty partner countries and organisations undertook to strengthen the countries of South-eastern Europe 'in their efforts to foster peace, democracy, respect for human rights and economic prosperity in order to achieve stability in the whole region'.[12] Euro-Atlantic integration was promised to all the states in the region. Despite the enormous amount of governmental, institutional and volunteer activity being devoting to Stability Pact activities, its 2004 Annual Report noted that 'throughout the year, the key message of [Special Co-ordinator Erhard] Busek was that South-eastern Europe's governments needed to follow up their commitments with rigorous implementation'.[13] The signature tune of post-Cold War Europe, 'sign and celebrate', is still playing. According to the Stability Pact Core Objectives for 2005:

> Organised crime and corruption undermine the political, economic and social development prospects of the countries of SEE. Fighting organised crime is thus essential for the development of the region and requires sound judicial systems and efficient law enforcement institutions. Effective action against transnational crime requires cooperation between SEE governments and with the EU and other international partners, aiming at a comprehensive approach in combating organised crime, by facilitating regional cooperation between networks of public prosecutors, legislators, the judiciary and law enforcement officials.[14]

One of South-east Europe's own creations, the South-east European Co-operation Initiative's Regional Centre for Combating Trans-Border Crime based in Bucharest, was established largely to encourage an atmosphere of information sharing in policing across the region. In this it has been fairly successful, despite a lack of enthusiasm from Western European states, which have observer status. It plays a major role in the Pact's activities in the area of security, but there is still a long way to go.

Organised crime groups both contribute towards and benefit from weak governance in the Western Balkans. Enlargement has brought these states to the EU's borders, exacerbating EU security concerns and complicating its efforts to stabilise the region. BiH, for example, has low internal cohesion: thirteen prime ministers, 180 ministers and 760 legislators within three entities, led by nationalist leaders with a zero sum mentality.[15] Currently, BiH can only be governed through the international supervisory administration. The power and credibility of the international community, particularly of the EU, is weak. Security promises and actions by the EU have little credibility in BiH, more than ten years after the massacres at Srebrenica on 11 July 1995. Trust will be hard to rebuild. Serbia and Montenegro had to face the implementation of a huge reform process after the assassination of Prime Minister Djindjic in February 2003. Difficulties were compounded by the independence of Montenegro, following the election, in early 2003, of a pro-independence president and the result of a referendum in May 2006. Last, but not least, the final status of Kosovo has still to be decided. This also has the potential to destabilise the region.

Including these new states, the prevailing characteristics of government at both national and local levels in the Balkans and around the EU's borders are cronyism, corruption and lack of accountability and transparency in a culture where the political class and governing mechanisms (police, judiciary, etc.) are largely unreconstructed. The prevalence of violent crime amongst the business elite is more than just a crime statistic. The murder of Bulgarian businessman Emil Kyulev in October 2005 is a case in point. It is an indication of a business and political culture that is far removed from that to which EU states aspire. Indeed, that shooting took place the day after the Commission had 'warned Bulgaria that unless it acted to curb crime in the next six months, it would not be able to join the EU on time in January 2007'.[16] The delays, inefficiency and impenetrability of the legal processes do not inspire optimism.

Moldova and Transdniestria: a case study

The Western Balkan states are, albeit at a glacial pace, moving towards assimilation with European norms of behaviour, with interest and funding from Western Europe to help the process. However, outside the magic circle of current and prospective EU members – though on its very borders – the story is even more depressing. Here, organised crime is not just endemic and in league with governing elites, it is the very engine of separatist regions and frozen conflicts. Abkhazia, Chechnya, Nagorno-Karabak, South Ossetia and Transdniestria – or *Pridnestrovskaya Moldavskaya Respublika'* (PMR) – are typical examples. The case of Moldova and PMR illustrates this point in great detail.

The existence of PMR appears an insurmountable blockage to the consolidation and democratisation of the post-Soviet Moldovan state and to any aspirations of Moldova joining the EU. It corrupts political life within Moldova and frames the nature of Moldova's relations with its nearest neighbours Ukraine, Russia and Romania, as well as the EU. As an unresolved frozen conflict, it also poses serious 'credibility traps' for external actors, such as the OSCE or EU. Failure to negotiate a conflict settlement undermines the credibility of external actors, while failure to attempt or to achieve a resolution questions their legitimacy and utility. More than a decade after the introduction of an OSCE-sponsored conflict resolution process, PMR is still a diplomatically isolated haven for transnational criminals and possibly terrorists. Yet, it appears to be economically sustainable and its very survival and durability raises the possibility of its eventual emergence as an independent state. Equally, its survival makes Moldova's EU aspirations more problematic.

The Tiraspol elite, under the control of President Igor Smirnov, who holds a diplomatic passport issued by the Russian Federation, prefers the continuation of the status quo to settlement, and is using state-type institutions to consolidate power. He has advanced PMR's corporate interests 'through lobbying, economic opportunism, political posturing and creative negotiating'.[17] Grigori Marakutsa, Speaker of the Supreme Soviet in Tiraspol, stated on 26 December 2003: 'Every year we are getting closer to our international recognition.'[18] PMR has all of the symbolic and many of the actual attributes of an independent state: a Constitution, President, national bank and currency, judiciary, army, police and militia, strong internal security services, national anthem, coat of arms and a flag, not to mention the national football stadium. It also exhibits foreign policy pretensions. In combination, these defining characteristics raise the question: what occurs in PMR and who benefits?

Smirnov has stated that PMR 'is historically geared to the priority of ties with Russia and Ukraine'.[19] At the same time, it has maintained permanent contacts with leaders of the breakaway republics of South Ossetia and Abkhazia in Georgia. On 2 June 2004, for example, Vladimir Smirnov promised to aid South Ossetia, including the provision of military help, if Georgia resorted to the use of force: 'We [the Dniester region, Abkhazia and South Ossetia] have signed a treaty on mutual help in difficult times. If there is an act of aggression, we will not stand aside, we will provide our brothers with all-round help, including military help.'[20] The leaders of these unrecognised states have continued to meet regularly since then. On 4 October 2004, the three 'foreign ministers' of Abkhazia, South Ossetia and PMR accused the governments in Chisinau and Tbilisi of:

> violation of the existing security and stability system. Given these conditions, Russia continues to hold the key position in preventing sizeable armed conflicts. The attempts to discredit the Russian peace maintenance mission are determined by the will to revise and change the historical role of the Russian Federation, actions that could produce unpredictable and dangerous consequences spilling over the regional framework.[21]

These self-styled foreign ministers argued that only the Commonwealth of Independent States (CIS) could negotiate a resolution to the conflicts between Chisinau and Tiraspol, and between Tbilisi and Sukhumi and Tskhinvali.[22] According to Grigory Marakutsa, PMR planned to open diplomatic representations in Moscow and Kiev, with $250,000 earmarked in PMR's budget for this purpose.[23] This prospect is now highly unlikely, following the result of the 2004 Ukrainian presidential elections, and the inclusion of Ukraine as an EU ally in the fight against organised crime in the region is significant. A key manifestation of this is that the Ukraine–Moldova border regime is now supported by an EU-monitoring mission and is much more effectively controlled as a result, thereby undercutting PMR organised crime profits.

PMR can be considered a 'super-presidential republic', in that all political power resides with the presidency. Residents cannot elect their leaders democratically, and they are also unable to participate freely in Moldovan elections.[24] The president appoints and dismisses all heads of administration and ministers to the Cabinet of Ministers (which replaced the office of prime minister, and is chaired by the president). In addition, an indeterminate legal environment is maintained. The PMR Minister of National Security, Vladimir Antyufeyev, formerly headed an Interior Ministry special unit (OMON) in Latvia during the 'January events' of 1991 and is currently wanted by Interpol for the murder of Latvian journalists during this period.[25] He restored and reformed the Cossack forces in PMR, and is widely believed in Chisinau both to have very close links with Russian Federal Security service (FSB) personnel and to be the right hand of the Smirnov clan.

The relationship between Russia and PMR is difficult to characterise precisely. As one report noted: 'At its most mischievous, the Kremlin's strategy may view Transdniestria as a second version of Kaliningrad, the Russian enclave near Poland, in other words, a trouble-making outpost on the borders of NATO.'[26] Another analyst has argued: 'Moscow has tended to see the EU, US and OSCE as rivals for geopolitical influence in its "turf" rather than as partners in efforts to mediate the serious conflict between the legitimate government in Chisinau and [Transdniestria].'[27] Moldovan President Voronin has concluded that Russia's role is complete and decisive in shaping PMR policy. After the experience of the Kozak Memorandum process of late 2003 (Dmitry Kozak, a member of Putin's Presidential Administration, proposed that Moldova become a Federation in which PMR had a right to secession and a blocking veto over foreign treaties), Voronin concluded that President Putin has both the opportunity and capacity to influence the Tiraspol regime: 'I am convinced that, if Russia wants it, this Smirnov will not stay even two hours longer in Tiraspol.'[28] This is perhaps to overstate the case, though Russian influence is undoubtedly strong, underwritten as it is by $50m a year in energy subsidies, which, by 2004, were calculated to be the equivalent of $1bn with interest.[29]

Political and military levers of control in PMR are buttressed by a managed economic order, both legal and illegal. The Sherrif Company, a corporation under the control of the president's son, is PMR's largest business. The Russian firm ITERA controls the majority of shares in the Moldovan Metallurgical Plant (at Ribnita), which generates two-thirds of the region's tax revenues. The Cuciurgan power station and KVINT brandy factory also provide the PMR with 'state' revenues. Smirnov has stated that PMR has a $53m positive trade balance with the US, Germany, Poland and the Czech Republic, and 'Trade with CIS member countries totalled $639m in the first 11 months of 2004, of which import made up $440m.' Italy, the US, Portugal, Germany, Greece and Poland are among PMR's main trade partners in the West; Russia, Ukraine and Belarus are their equivalent in the CIS. In 2004, 'imports' from Moldova fell by 20 per cent and 'exports' by 15 per cent, after economic sanctions were imposed in August. In August–September 2004 alone, the losses from exports totalled $41.38m dollars, while another $32m worth of products failed to be exported.[30] Just over 50 per cent of PMR's officially registered exports are directed towards two key markets – Russia and Russian companies registered in North Cyprus.[31] From these figures, it is clear that many governments and influential economic elites in the region (and further afield) gain from the indeterminate legal environment and status of PMR, and so are prepared to turn a blind eye to less than transparent business deals.

The illegal economy is widely perceived to be dominant and is also fostered by PMR's indeterminate legal status. Then Romanian Foreign Minister Mircea Geoana, for example, characterized the PMR in 2002 as 'a black hole of trans-border organised crime, including drug smuggling, human trafficking, and arms smuggling'.[32] Trafficked humans, particularly women and children, are transported primarily to the Balkans, United Arab Emirates, Turkey and Western European 'markets'. President Voronin himself noted that 'foreign specialists' and analysts have 'calculated that about $2–3bn are being laundered in this black Dniestr zone annually'.[33]

Elements of the Soviet-era military–industrial complex, which was located in PMR during the Soviet period, are still active. Some arms factories, such as the Elektromash and Tochlitmash works, produce weapons for the Russian military. However, since the 1992 conclusion of the civil war to the present, there has been a steady stream of allegations that the PMR 'defence ministry' sells the products of secret military production lines and surplus materials on the black market. These have gone to states involved in regional conflicts or even to terrorist organisations, including Chechen rebels and the Abkhaz regime, which are well positioned to purchase such weapons.

For example, in 1993, seven Grad (rocket) units assembled in Tiraspol from Russian parts were sent to Abkhazia. According to expert analyst Oazu Nantoi: 'most probably, the equipment was loaded onto railway carriages and taken to [the Ukrainian cities of] Odessa, Ilychivsk and Mykolayiv, from where they were shipped to Abkhazia. This means that this is an international gunrunning network.'[34] In 1998, V. Nemkov (a Lieutenant Colonel in the PMR armed forces) admitted that he had sold Igla air-to-surface rockets from the Cobasna arms depot in 1996–97. In autumn 2000, Vasilyok mortars, which are manufactured only by factories located in PMR, were seized by the Russian armed forces from Chechen rebels.[35] More recently, in May 2004, three rocket launchers were allegedly sold to Chechen rebels for $150,000. The airport in Tiraspol is not part of the 'security zone' and so OSCE and other foreign observers are unable to monitor exports. The chairman of the Moldovan parliamentary committee for national security, Iurie Stoicov, stated that he had 'information from foreign secret services that certain criminal groups in the Dniester region are selling weapons. Any activities in the Dniester region related to selling armaments abroad are illegal. Any weapons being sold without a strict record may fall into the hands of terrorists, criminal groups or other structures.'[36] However, the OSCE mission spokesman, Claus Neukirch, cautioned, 'there is often talk about the sale of armaments from the Dniester region, but there is no convincing evidence'.[37] More recently still, *The Sunday Times* reported that three radioactive (strontium and caesium) Alazan rockets capable of contaminating a city centre were offered for sale for $500,000 (£263,000).[38]

The status and role of PMR in shaping Moldova's internal security politics and the wider region – particularly its relationship with Abkhazia and South Ossetia and associated informal criminal networks – has implications for Moldova's relations with the EU. It also has implications for economic and political elites in another aspiring EU candidate country, Ukraine. Not only does Ukraine share 460 kilometres of the PMR segment of the Moldovan–Ukrainian border (which is widely considered to be porous), but Russians and Ukrainians represent about 51 per cent (some 650,000) of the PMR population, evenly split between Ukrainian and Russian citizens.[39] Russian and Ukrainian oligarchs have taken part in the PMR privatisation process, profiting from and contributing to both the legal and illegal political economy. The five-sided conflict resolution format, consisting of the OSCE, Russia, Ukraine, PMR and Moldova, ideally suited the business interests of these companies, as well as corrupted military and security services, as it effectively freezes the conflict and upholds the profitable status quo. According to one analyst, 'with Moscow's open support, the Dniester region has fulfilled no agreements signed at the five-party talks since 1999'.[40] As the 2004 EU enlargement approached and EU's role in the Balkans grew, its short-sighted, hands-off approach to PMR became less sustainable.

Chisniau–Tiraspol–Moscow–Brussels relations since 2004

The certainties and absolutes that had characterised political calculations changed through 2004–05. The ongoing low-intensity frozen conflict between Chisinau and Tiraspol began to heat up as 2004 unfolded. The EU, which had hitherto stood aside as the OSCE focused on the conflict, began to take a much more proactive role, as the realisation dawned that PMR fell within the EU's new neighbourhood. In February 2004, the foreign ministers of EU member states decided to extend the one-year travel ban imposed in February 2003 on seventeen senior PMR leaders, including Igor Smirnov and his two sons. The ministers said the stance of the separatist leadership, which they said remained unwilling to engage in full efforts to reach a peaceful and comprehensive solution to the conflict with Moldova, was 'unacceptable'.[41]

The EU regime of visa sanctions against the PMR leadership was intensified in July 2004, in reaction to Tiraspol's harassment of six Moldovan language schools (that is, schools that use the Latin rather than Cyrillic alphabet), following the refusal of the boards of these schools to register with the PMR authorities. Following a discussion by member states of the EU in the Political and Security Committee (PSC), the EU called on the PMR leadership to halt the intimidation campaign that forced the closure of these Moldovan language schools, condemned the actions taken by PMR armed police and warned that it would consider 'appropriate measures' against those responsible, should the situation not improve.[42] Beyond words, however, the EU's involvement in the 2004 crisis was limited. The OSCE High Commissioner on National Minorities, Rolf Ekeus, was a little sterner in his criticism, characterising the closure as 'linguistic cleansing', while, on 22 July, the OSCE Permanent Council described the PMR actions as 'irresponsible and provocative'.[43]

In response to the schools crisis, on 1 August 2004 the Moldovan customs authorities suspended the customs service to PMR businesses that were not registered in Moldova (those that did not pay taxes to Moldova). Not only that, but the Chamber of Commerce and Industry ceased issuing origin certificates and Moldovan Railways withdrew the provision of carriages for companies based in PMR. All government privileges to PMR companies were suspended. Both Igor Smirnov and the Russian Foreign Ministry described the measure as an economic blockade.[44]

The Moldovan Ministry of Defence issued an official denial of supposed plans to attack PMR, indicating the extent to which the schools crisis and railway blockade had heightened tension between Chisinau and Tiraspol.[45] This tension was alleviated when PMR President, Igor Smirnov, met a delegation of the EU, led by the Director-General of the Council of the EU Common Foreign and Security Policy, Robert Cooper, in August 2004. Cooper noted that the visit took place at the personal request of Javier Solana and stated, 'Moldova will shortly become our neighbour, and we hope the crisis will be defused by the beginning of the new school year.' He suggested an OSCE draft protocol could become 'a solution to the problem'.[46] In response, Smirnov argued that Moldovan authorities had sought to exploit the schools issue for political capital ahead of the March 2005 parliamentary elections: 'The real problem is that an election campaign has started in Moldova. Therefore, if the schools weren't there, Messrs Communists (the Moldovan authorities) would have found some other pretext to put pressure. Their aim is obvious – to tarnish the Dniester Moldovan republic's international reputation'.[47]

Smirnov will not entertain the prospect of the integration of PMR into Moldova proper. PMR integration into Moldova would spell the end of his power base and raise the prospect of legal prosecution. Currently, a 'soft landing' option that would provide immunity from personal prosecution and the opportunity to export capital to some third destination does not appear to be in the offing. Yet PMR integration into Moldova is a necessary precondition for the integration of Moldova into the EU.

Increasingly, the PMR conflict has been viewed as an East–West geopolitical point of contention. Rationally, Russia will seek to use such influence it has as a bargaining chip in diplomacy with Western institutions, looking for a *quid pro quo* in return for supporting either a negotiated conflict settlement or by pressuring the PMR regime to comply with Russia's instructions. This could be achieved by, for example, cutting subsidies, collecting debts, or enforcing visa restrictions.

From President Voronin's perspective, in terms of moving the conflict resolution agenda to a format and process better suited to Chisinau's objectives, 2004–06 can be understood as a success. The status and implications of PMR are no longer viewed as an internal Moldovan security issue, but rather, in the words of one Moldovan newspaper: 'If so far Europe viewed the Dniester conflict as a scandal between two villages located on different banks of the Dniester river, now the international community admits that this conflict threatens regional and even continental security.'[48] Moldova's reintegration was increasingly supported by the EU and the US and was included in their working agendas, as well as that of the OSCE.[49] President Voronin's re-election in spring 2005 on an avowedly Euro-Atlantic platform signalled unequivocally Moldova's desire to solve the separatist problem, and also its recognition that it was unable to do so without assistance from Europe and beyond.

Moldova's strategic reorientation: rhetoric and reality

Given these new realities, what might EU policy makers do to help create and implement a policy that has a greater chance of success? The European Parliament resolution on Moldova, passed on 18 December 2003, characterised the state as having a weak administration that lacks effective democratic controls. It noted that 80 per cent of the market is informal, that little tax revenue is raised and charged that controls over the Eastern border were non-existent and that the social system was ineffective.[50] Moldova, for example, only accounts for a meagre 0.04 per cent of the EU's imports in 2004.[51] Ivan Borisavijevic, then the Commission's envoy to Moldova, noted in March 2004 that the main obstacles on the road to Moldova's integration with the EU are the Transdniestria conflict, organised crime and corruption, poverty and a lack of genuine reform. As a result, it will take Moldova at least ten to fifteen years to catch up with those former communist countries that have moved towards EU living standards in the last decade: 'The reason rests in a weak economy, an underdeveloped infrastructure, few investments, and much corruption.'[52]

However, there are compelling reasons as to why the PMR frozen conflict should be considered an issue of rising strategic importance. Firstly, by 2007, Romania will be an EU member state, and the soft security threats that emanate from PMR will have become more obvious and less easy to dismiss. This will be particularly the case, as similar soft security threats in the Balkans hopefully diminish as Balkan integration into the Euro-Atlantic security order gathers pace. Secondly, as EU third-echelon enlargement in the Black Sea region (Moldova, Ukraine, Georgia) will be unlikely, EU contributions to the unification of Moldova can be presented as a compensatory alternative to membership. Thirdly, as the Balkans stabilise and the ESDP gains operational confidence and strength, it will become harder to avoid the logic of the deployment of EU civilian and/or military instruments in PMR. Fourthly, a failure to uphold the credibility of the EU's wider partnership policies will be exposed by inaction.

The EU's ENP was launched in May 2004. The aim of ENP is to promote prosperity and stability through the promise of the extension of the 'four freedoms' (free movement of people, goods, services and capital) to the EU's neighbours. The ENP has buttressed the existing contractual framework – the 1998 PCA (Partnership and Co-operation Agreement) – which governs relations between the EU and Moldova. This policy needs support to become an effective instrument of stabilisation and Moldova provides both the challenge of earlier inaction and an opportunity to make significant gains. In early November 2004, Ambassador Ian Boag, the new chief of the Commission Delegation to Moldova, then based in Kiev, stated that the EU sought a more active role in the PMR settlement process, 'to develop practical actions aimed to create a favourable environment for settlement of the Transnistrian crisis'.[53]

At the same time, Moldovan officials at the OSCE Permanent Council in Vienna invited the US and EU to become more actively involved in the settlement of the conflict in PMR.[54] They also called on Russia, Ukraine and Romania to support the declaration of stability and security for Moldova, in order for Moldova to enter the Stability Pact during the OSCE Council of Ministers in Sofia on the 6–7 December 2004.[55] This initiative had the support of Javier Solana and signalled a very real alignment of the Republic of Moldova and the EU.[56] The OSCE Council of Ministers adopted a draft but, because of a lack of consensus, failed to adopt a final document at the end of the session. However, most OSCE member states said Russia remained under an obligation to withdraw its troops and weapons from Moldova and Georgia. The deputy head of the CIS department at the Russian Foreign Ministry, Nikolay Fomin, stated that, 'Russia will not sign the declaration on stability and security for Moldova. In the basic political accord, Russia admitted territorial integrity, sovereignty and independence of Moldova. This is enough for development of the relations between our states and it meets mutual interests.'[57] According to OSCE sources, the draft declaration reiterated the obligation on the Russian Federation to respect its commitments assumed at the 1999 Istanbul summit regarding the complete and unconditional withdrawal of troops and ammunition from Moldova. Moldovan Foreign Minister, Andrei Stratan, stated, 'the presence of Russian troops in Moldova is illegitimate, because it violates Moldovan laws and international treaties'.[58]

In January 2005, following a meeting at the inauguration ceremony of Ukrainian President Yushchenko, Ukraine and Moldova resumed talks on enhancing border controls between the two countries.[59] The newly appointed Ukrainian Minister of Foreign Affairs, Boris Tarasyuk, identified the Transnistria settlement efforts as 'one of the important-most tasks of the Ukraine's national security'. In a very strongly worded statement, he noted that Ukraine regards Transnistria as 'Europe's black hole, where very few get fabulously rich while hundreds of thousand eke out hand-to-mouth existence. I am convinced that the existence of the Transnistrian and other puppet regimes, impeding the building of a unified Europe, are strategically disadvantageous for the Russian Federation as well'.[60] He went on to declare: 'We must recognize also that the illegitimate, corrupt regimes of self-styled republics have nothing in common with the legitimate rights of the people living in such territories.' Signalling a new approach to PMR and a more active and independent role within the OSCE-sponsored five-sided format, he stated, 'Terms such as "sanitary cordons", "red lines", "spheres of influence" and the like ought to be withdrawn from European diplomats' vocabulary. Ukraine is not an exercise ground for geopolitical battles between the European Union, United States, and Russian Federation'.[61]

Since the 2004 Ukrainian presidential election, the prospects for the creation of effective Ukrainian–Moldovan border monitoring and agreement on customs stamps and exports from PMR are much better.[62] The EU recently proposed that Moldova and Ukraine implement a computerised system to exchange information between the customs services of both countries. The system is aimed at fighting organised crime, such as illegal trafficking, in the border areas. The EU signed an agreement on an unprecedented border assistance mission (BAM) on the Moldova–Ukraine border on 7 October 2005. Originally an OSCE initiative, the EU mission became fully operational on 1 December. It has an office-based core of fifteen full-time EU employees, and fifty mobile staff, seconded from EU member states.[63] The BAM is likely to be both effective and sustainable, as it trains and focuses Ukrainian Border Guards specifically on an effective PMR border-monitoring role.[64] According to Valdimir Socor, the EU's move shows some benefits but also many problems: 'On the plus side, the response is unusually quick by EU standards. As a further plus it minimises the OSCE's role, placing all responsibility firmly in EU hands'.[65] Prior to the EU role, the OSCE had claimed the BAM mission for itself, despite Moldova's lack of confidence in the OSCE and preference for the EU to be involved. Socor suggests that the EU stepped in, during the spring of 2005, after it saw how easily Russia had killed off the OSCE's Border Monitoring Mission in Georgia.[66]

The results of the presidential elections in Romania also reinforced the pressure for Moldova to consolidate its strategic reorientation westwards. The new President Traian Basescu declared Romania's willingness to participate in the negotiation process on the settlement of the Transnistrian conflict during a press conference in Moscow in mid February 2005: 'no matter what would be the final variant of the Transnistrian settlement, it must be based on the respect for the Republic of Moldova's sovereignty, independence and territorial integrity'. He also underscored Romania's support for the process of Moldovan–European integration: 'The European partnership with Moldova is not only a project, but a priority. In the first place, we shall support Chisinau's steps, aimed at the implementation of the [Moldova]–EU Plan of Actions'.[67]

President Voronin of Moldova also hardened his attacks against Smirnov and Russian support for PMR. In January 2005, Voronin prevented Russian and Ukrainian ambassadors from entering Tiraspol, leading Smirnov to respond: 'Moldovan authorities' decision to ban the entrance to the Dniester region by Russian and Ukrainian diplomats . . . pursues far-reaching aims.' In his view, 'attempts are made to put an end to Russia's presence in the Dniester region and replace Russian peace-keepers with foreign ones. In addition, this is made to change the format of the talks – with the involvement of the US, the EU and Romania. Moldova is trying to exclude the Dniester region as a participant in the talks'.[68] Despite US and EU participation, this impasse persisted to the end of 2006.

The re-election of President Voronin on 6 March 2005 maintained a degree of domestic stability and predictability in Moldovan security politics, and the trends that characterised the post-2003 era are being consolidated, but within a changing strategic context. Continuity is maintained by the persistence of the same issues which block conflict resolution, namely the division of competencies between local and federal authorities; Russia's failure to fulfil the 1999 Istanbul commitments; and the pervasive and corrupting influence of organised crime groups on Moldova. Change is introduced through the process of strategic reorientation and engagement westwards, which President Voronin has pursued through 2005–06. In June 2006, Moldova advanced its PfP commitments to include an Individual Partnership Action Plan.[69] The Council of the EU appointed Adriaan Jacobivts de Szeged as its special representative in Moldova in March 2005 and, in the summer of 2005, the Commission delegation established an office in Chisinau, headed by Cesare de Montis.

While the May 2005 Russia–EU Summit in Moscow produced agreement on the Road Map for the Common Space on External Security, the continued deterioration in Russia–Moldova relations point to the obstacle that any potential EU–Russia brokered agreement would first have to overcome.[70] The continued deterioration of the Russia–Moldova relationship is largely exhibited in the context of the PMR issue. Although Russia had initially high hopes of close relations with President Voronin (because of his communist party affiliation), by the end of his first term Voronin was convinced he could not do business with the Russians in good faith, a realisation reinforced by the Kozak memorandum fiasco of late 2003.[71]

Nevertheless, a number of resurrected settlement plans have since been proposed. In April 2005, Ukraine's National Security and Defence Council advocated the 'Towards settlement – through diplomacy' plan, the so-called 'Yushchenko Plan', and, in July of the same year, the OSCE and Russian Federation advanced a Yushchenko–Kozak hybrid variant settlement proposal.[72] Each of these variants essentially stuck to the traditional five-sided format and would limit the foreign and security policy-making ability of a centralised authority based around Chisinau. They were thus completely unacceptable to the Moldovan authorities. In July 2005, the OSCE, Russian and Ukrainian mediators delivered a proposal to Moldova/PMR entitled 'Arms Control – Confidence and Security Building Measures in Moldova'. However, this appeared to be largely of rhetorical value.

On 20 June 2005, Modest Kolerov, the head of the newly created Division for Inter-Regional and Cultural Relations with Foreign Countries, stated that Russia is deeply interested in the security and success, both political and economic, of PMR. Like Russia, the main task of PMR and its 'compatriots', he suggested, was to preserve its sovereignty. This suggested quasi-recognition of PMR sovereignty by a high-ranking Russian official.[73] Also, in June 2005, President Putin appointed Vladimir Titov to be a special representative on PMR. This suggested a hardening of Russia's support to PMR, which, in policy terms, might be understood as a calibrated attempt to balance the increasing EU presence in the region.

The five-sided talks resumed at the end of October 2005, this time with an important change: the EU and the US were admitted as observers. Whilst this is in keeping with the EU's belated but nonetheless welcome recognition that the problems of states on its borders demand EU involvement, the talks are unlikely to result in a breakthrough. The EU would only seek to impose a settlement with a UN mandate, which Russia would veto. Even acting as a full partner in the talks would demand PMR and Russian consent, hardly a likely outcome. Observer status gave the EU the greatest leverage and influence it could have expected, but did not allow it to be particularly effective.

The 2003 OSCE–Russia–Ukraine moves to federalise Moldova, thereby giving greater legitimacy to PMR, revived in late 2006 under the Finnish Presidency of the EU, are not in the longer-term interests of the EU or Moldova. However, while there are compelling reasons why the EU should focus on Moldova, it is not clear if this process can occur in a decisive manner. The PMR elite remain intransigent and, as highlighted in the gas crisis of January 2006, the EU is 60 per cent energy dependent on the Russian Federation. Hence, the EU may well become a key external actor, but Russia will maintain its block on conflict resolution. In the words of Mikhail Margelov, chair of the Foreign Relations Committee in Russia's Federation Council: 'Given

Moscow's influence on the region and the degree to which the Moldovan economy depends on it at the present time, any unilateral settlement attempt in Transdniestria in circumvention of Moscow is doomed'.[74]

Conclusions

The EU's belated recognition that problems on its borders are reflected inside its member states, and therefore must be dealt with, is encouraging. That it took more than a decade to do so is little short of scandalous. In the case of Moldova, where cries for help had been regular and the need great, the damage to the EU's credibility as a provider of soft security will take many years to repair, with or without a settlement to the Transdniestria problem. That around half of Moldova's population had worked legally or illegally inside the EU during that period should have lent greater urgency to the formulation of an EU policy.[75] That the same traffickers in people were also dealing with weapons, drugs and other forms of criminal trade should have given the EU police and border structures the ability to act, even in the absence of any neighbourhood policy.

This chapter has concentrated on a case study from outside the EU's borders, because it highlights both the scale of the problem and the EU's limitations in dealing with it at a political and operational level. There is a great deal more co-operation and co-ordination in respect of cross-border crime than there was even a decade ago. However, it is still nowhere near enough, and is beset by bureaucratic obstacles, by institutional inertia, and by a residual reluctance to take the crime-fighting and other efforts of foreigners seriously. Indeed, lack of staff and funding has limited the effectiveness of the EU Crime Prevention Network (EUCPN), according to its own 2004 annual report.[76] Given the prevailing atmosphere of corruptibility and ineffectiveness that stalks the internal security apparatus of many countries, this may be understandable. However, given the international agility of organised crime, it is inexcusable.

Notes

1 Lord Robertson, Agence France Press (22 May 2003), www.afp.com/english/home/.
2 'Rising crime not among problems brought by EU entry', CTK Czech News Agency (19 April 2005), www.ctk.cz/english/page/?id=1966.
3 'EU/Balkans: fight against organised crime must be stepped up, say Ministers', *European Report* (1 March 2003).
4 'Crime: harmonised sanctions for organised gangs backed by Parliament', *European Report* (28 October 2005).
5 'Declaration EU–Western Balkans Summit' (Thessaloniki, 21 June 2003), www.eu2003.gr/en/articles/2003/6/23/3131/.
6 'EU issues report on strategy to prevent organised crime', *Transnational Organised Crime*, 17:9 (September 2001).
7 *A Secure Europe in a Better World, European Security Strategy* (Brussels: European Union, December 2003).

8 Ronald H. Linden, 'Twin peaks: Romania and Bulgaria between the EU and the United States', *Problems of Post-Communism*, 51:5 (September/October, 2004), pp. 45–55.
9 'Declaration EU–Western Balkans Summit'.
10 'STA News Agency', (Ljulbjana, 21 June 2003).
11 'About the Stability Pact' (2004), www.stabilitypact.org/about/default.asp.
12 Ibid.
13 Ibid.
14 'Core objectives of the Stability Pact and respective achievables for 2005', www.stabilitypact.org/about/TF2005SPforweb.pdf.
15 Graeme P. Herd and Tom Tracy, 'Democratic civil–military relations in Bosnia Herzegovina: a new paradigm for protectorates?', *Armed Forces and Society*, 32:1 (Winter 2005), pp. 1–17.
16 'Where killing is a habit', *Economist* (29 October 2005); 'EU/Bulgaria: need for financial control and anti-fraud efforts stressed by Commissioner', *European Report* (19 May 2005).
17 Nicolas Whyte, *Moldova: Regional Tensions over Transdniestria* (International Crisis Group, 17 June 2004).
18 'No End in Sight', *IWPR'S Balkan Crisis Report*, 524 (5 November 2004).
19 *Rossiyskaya Gazeta* (Moscow, 31 March 2004).
20 'Moldovan breakaway region pledges to help South Ossetia in dispute with Georgia', Interfax News Agency (2 June 2004), www.interfax.com.
21 'Transnistria, Abkhazia and South Ossetia claim that Moldova and Georgia would like to use force', Basa-Press (5 October, 2004), www.basa.md/.
22 Ibid.
23 Infotag News Agency (21 December 2004), www.infotag.md/.
24 Freedom House, 'Country Report on Transnistria (Moldova)' (2004), www.freedomhouse.org/research/freeworld/2004/countryratings/moldova-transnistria.htm; 'Severe violations of human rights in the Transdnistrian region of Moldova', Statement by the International Helsinki Federation for Human Rights and the Moldovan Helsinki Committee (11 August 2004), www.ihf-hr.org/documents/doc_summary.php?sec_id= 3&d_id=3955.
25 International Crisis Group, 'Moldova: no quick fix', *Europe Report*, 147 (Brussels/Chisinau, 12 August 2003), www.unhcr.ch/cgi-bin/texis/vtx/home/opendoc.pdf?tbl=RSDCOI&id=3f5219924.
26 'The hazards of a long, hard freeze', *The Economist* (19 August 2004), www.economist.com/world/europe/displaystory.cfm?story_id=3110979.
27 Nicolas Whyte, 'Moldova: regional tensions over Transdniestria'.
28 ProTV (1 December 2004), www.protv.md/.
29 Tod Lindberg, 'Turmoil in Transdnistria', *The Washington Times* (1 June 2004).
30 Infotag News Agency (28 December 2004), www.infotag.md/news_en_2/.
31 Vladimir Socor, 'Western diplomacy unmoved by "linguistic cleansing" in TransDniestr', *Eurasia Daily Monitor* (3 August 2004).
32 George Jahn, 'Soviet weapons cache, arms dealing, dirty bomb cause concern in Moldova's separatist enclave', *AP Investigations* (12 January 2004).
33 ProTV (1 December 2004), www.protv.md/.
34 Dumitru Lazur, 'Tiraspol rockets for Chechens', *Journal de Chisinau* (Chisinau, 28 May 2004).
35 Ibid.
36 Ibid.
37 Ibid.
38 Brian Johnson Thomas and Mark Franchetti, 'Radiation rockets on sale to "terrorists"', *The Sunday Times* (8 May 2005).
39 Dov Lynch, 'Crisis in Moldova', *ISS–EU Newsletter*, No. 2 (May 2002).
40 Corneliu Mihalache, 'Government paper defends Moldova's "pro-Western" stance', *Moldova Suverana* (Chisinau, 21 October 2004), p. 1.

41 World of Information, *Moldova Country Report* (18 May 2004), www.worldinformation.com/woi/.
42 European Commission, 'Common foreign and security policy (18/26), Moldova', *Bulletin of the EU* (July/August 2004), http://europa.eu.int/abc/doc/off/bull/en/200407/p105018.htm.
43 Europe Information Service, *European Report* (31 July 2004), http://eisnet.eis.be/Content/Default.asp.
44 Nicholas Whyte, 'In search of a solution', *IWPR'S Balkan Crisis Report*, No. 524 (5 November, 2004); 'Moldovan–Dniester railway war enters second day', ProTV (3 August 2004), www.protv.md/.
45 Moldovan Radio (4 August 2004), www.trm.md/radio/.
46 Nicu Popescu, 'Special representative of the EU for Moldova: from opportunity to actions', *Moldova Azi* (18 February 2005), www.azi.md/investigation?ID=33112.
47 Olvia-press (10 August 2004), www.olvia.idknet.com/.
48 *Moldova Suverana* (21 October 2004), www.moldova-suverana.md/.
49 Ibid.
50 European Commission, 'Relations with the countries of Eastern Europe, the Caucasus and Central Asia (9/12) Moldova', *Bulletin of the EU* (December 2003), www.europa.eu.int/abc/doc/off/bull/en/200312/p106114.htm.
51 European Commission, 'Moldova: EU bilateral trade with the World' (17 June 2005), http://trade-info.cec.eu.int/doclib/docs/2005/july/tradoc_113419.pdf.
52 'European Commission official outlines obstacles to Moldova's EU integration', www.hri.org/news/balkans/rferl/2004/04-03-12.rferl.html#56.
53 'EU to play more active role in the Transnistrian conflict settlement', Basa Press (8 November 2004), www.peacebuilding.md/monitor.htm?lang=en&idm=418f20f 17ef52.
54 'Moldova wants to alter format of Transdniestria settlement talks', Interfax (12 November 2004), www.interfax.com/com?item=Mold&pg=0&id=5769803&req=.
55 'OSCE foreign ministers pledge to enhance counter-terrorism efforts, protect human rights', www.osce.org/mc/item_1_8792.html.
56 'Javier Solana thinks Declaration signature is possible', Infotag News Agency (29 October 2004), www.azi.md/news?ID=31517.
57 Infotag News Agency (6 December 2004), www.infotag.md/news_en_2/.
58 'OSCE Ministerial council closes, no document adopted' (7 December 2004), www.osce.org.
59 Valery Demidetsky, 'Moldova to resume talks to enhance border control', ITAR-TASS News Agency (26 January 2005), http://www.itar-tass.com/eng/.
60 'New Ukrainian Foreign Minster speaks on Transnistria', Infotag News Agency (14 February 2005), www.azi.md/news?ID=33033.
61 Ibid.
62 George Dura, 'Prospects for the establishment of an international monitoring mission on the Ukraine–Moldova border' (April 2005), Eurojournal.org.
63 Vladimir Socor, 'EU launches unprecedented mission on Ukraine–Moldova border', *Eurasia Daily Monitor* (14 October 2005), www.jamestown.org/publications_details.php?volume_id=407&issue_id=3490&article_id=2370332.
64 Ibid.
65 Ibid.
66 Ibid.
67 'Romania is ready to participate in the negotiation process on the settlement of the Transnistrian conflict' (15 February 2005), www.azi.md/news?ID=33053.
68 Yelena Volkova and Andrei Popov, 'Chisinau actions show probable final break-up with Tiraspol', ITAR-TASS News Agency (26 January 2005); Olvia-press (24 January 2005), www.olvia.idknet.com/.
69 www.nato.int/docu/speech/2006/s060622a.htm.
70 Dov Lynch, 'EU–Russia: prospects for the common space' (June 2005), Eurojournal.org.

71 'President Voronin claims Russia influenced election returns in Moldova', http://politicom.moldova.org/stiri/eng/6471/.
72 Vladimir Socor, 'Kozak Plan resurfaces under OSCE colors', *Eurasia Daily Monitor*, 2:136 (14 July 2005); Vladimir Socor, 'Moldova elegantly disposes of the Poroshenko–Yushchenko Plan', *Eurasia Daily Monitor*, 2:120 (21 June 2005).
73 'Kremlin to Force Dnestr', *Kommersant* (23 June 2005).
74 *RIA Novosti* (8 June 2005), http://en.rian.ru/; 'Statement by Alexander Yakovenko, the spokesman of Russia's Ministry of Foreign Affairs, regarding the recent decisions of the Parliament of the Republic of Moldova' (11 July 2005), www.ln.mid.ru/brp_4.nsf/e78a48070f128a7b43256999005bcbb3/7015979b7d7.
75 M. Sander-Lindstrom, International Organization for Migration, 'Presentation at NATO Workshop' (Chisinau, March 2004).
76 'EU crime prevention network under-resourced, annual report shows', *European Report* (19 October 2005). Only has one person based in the European Commission and €182,700 per year. Commissioned four studies, only one of which was delivered on time.

6

Enlargement and human rights law: norms and realities

Karim A.A. Khan and Anna Kotzeva[1]

The Union is founded on the principles of liberty, democracy, respect for human rights and fundamental freedoms, and the rule of law, principles which are common to Member States. TEU Article 6(1)[2]

Introduction

The logic of respect for human rights and democratic values contributing to the political and economic stability of current and prospective EU member states is irresistible. Yet, what is the European driving force in the promotion of human rights? And are the means employed to encourage countries aspiring for membership consistent with the EU's internal standards for human rights protection? In the fight against terrorism, has Europe learnt any lessons on human rights protection? Looking towards the sixth and subsequent waves of European enlargement, in particular the prospective membership of Turkey, further and unusual challenges await. In that context, is a truly universal, or even European, approach to human rights possible?

Human rights: building blocks to conflict prevention and security

Within the framework of the EU programme for the Prevention of Violent Conflicts, the Commission has developed a Checklist for the Root Causes of Conflict, which serves as a list of early warning indicators of potential conflict and instability.[3] Although the primary use relates to monitoring danger spots outside the borders of the EU, the criteria are a useful reminder of the elements needed to enhance security, just as applicable within as outwith the EU. The Checklist comprises eight criteria, beginning with perhaps the most fundamental of all – the legitimacy of the state. Its components include proper checks and balances in the political system, respect for the Constitution, the ability of the judiciary and Parliament to check on the executive and the inclusiveness of the political and administrative power. The second criterion, the rule of law, requires an independent and effective judiciary, equality of citizens before the law and the possibility of taking legal action against state decisions. The third requirement in the Checklist is respect for fundamental rights, comprising civil and political freedoms, religious, cultural and other basic human rights.[4] As can be seen from these first three criteria, security and stability are intrinsically linked to constitutional protection of basic human rights and their effective enforcement through the rule of law.

In the context of the most recent enlargement by the ten new member states and the forthcoming entry of Bulgaria and Romania into the EU, the particular focus has been on the fight against corruption and organised crime, strengthening the independence and efficiency of judicial institutions and the protection of minorities. In the case of accession negotiations with Turkey, which started on 3 October 2005, the focus can be expected to shift to even more fundamental questions – the level of respect for national authorities in the context of the problems in Turkey's south-east, the use of unlawful state violence, the relationship between government and the security forces, particularly with regard to political control, to name but a few. The remaining early warning indicators in the Checklist also focus to a large degree on human rights. They relate, respectively, to civil society and independent media (4), relations between communities and dispute resolution mechanisms (5), sound economic management (6), social and regional (in)equalities (7) and the wider geopolitical situation (8).[5]

So, how does the EU seek to foster human rights outside its borders, particularly within states aspiring to membership? The list of available measures is extensive. Firstly, since the early 1990s, the EU has included 'human rights' clauses in its bilateral trade and co-operation agreements with third countries, including association agreements. The latter typically provide tariff-free access to several or all EU markets and financial or technical assistance, in exchange for political, economic and human rights reform. Association agreements are covered by two EU policies – the Stabilisation and Association Agreements (SAA) and the ENP, as administered by the Enlargement Directorate and the External Relations Directorate respectively. The key difference lies in the fact that the SAA will explicitly include provisions for future EU membership. In the Western Balkans, SAAs were signed with Croatia and FYROM in 2001 and they have now entered into force. Negotiations towards the adoption of SAAs have also been started with Albania, Serbia and Montenegro and BiH.

The practice of including 'human rights' clauses within association agreements has not been without its problems. Drafting of the agreements has had to take into account the Vienna Convention on the Law of Treaties, Article 60 of which prohibits suspension or termination of an agreement unless one of the parties has violated an 'essential clause'.[6] Arguably, for a human rights clause to be considered as an 'essential clause', it has to additionally display a reasonable connection to the object or aim of the agreement. Only if such a connection is made can non-compliance with human rights standards by the particular state lead to the suspension or termination of the agreement.[7]

Secondly, in the enlargement context, all candidate states have to satisfy the Copenhagen criteria developed in 1993. The 'political criteria' for accession require candidate countries to demonstrate 'stability of institutions guaranteeing democracy, the rule of law, human rights and respect for and protection of minorities'.[8] Furthermore, the candidate country must have been certified by the EU as a functioning market economy, capable of coping with the market forces and competition within the Union. Finally, the capacity to take on the obligations of full membership must be demonstrated, including adherence to the aims of political, economic and monetary union.[9] All prospective members of the EU must enact legislation in order to align themselves with the common European legal framework, known as the *acquis communautaire*. Hence, a further membership criterion mandates that the revised national legislation must be implemented effectively through appropriate administrative and judicial structures. Countries' progress towards accession is monitored by the Commission through regular reports to the European Council, which take into account the achievement of specific objectives set within Partnership documents specifically formulated for each particular candidate country.

EU internal standards and human rights

A key question to consider is whether the means employed to encourage states aspiring for membership are consistent with the EU's internal standards for human rights protection. The requirement to satisfy human rights and democratic norms as a precondition to accession, often referred to as 'conditionality', is, to a certain extent, controversial, as it does not mirror any similar requirement applied previously to acceding member states. Further, the Copenhagen political criteria have been applied to candidate states for a much longer period than the principles corresponding to these criteria as they apply to EU member states through Article 6(1) TEU, which was inserted by the Treaty of Amsterdam in 1999. A significant distinction in the methods of internal and external enforcement of these principles, and their potential deterrent force also has to be noted. The rights of member states can be suspended under the provisions of Article 7 TEU, if they breach the principles contained in Article 6(1).[10] However, this is, arguably, much more difficult to achieve than the simple refusal of entry to the EU.[11]

Additionally, the correspondence between Article 6(1) as regulating and binding countries within the EU on the one hand and the Copenhagen political criteria as applied to candidate states on the other, is not exact. For example, the requirement for institutional provisions guaranteeing 'respect for and protection of minorities' is not found in Article 6. This particular anomaly was not addressed in the Charter of Fundamental Rights of the European Union (the Charter). That was despite the representatives of Slovenia, a then applicant country, having suggested that the draft Charter include 'rights "pertaining to the *protection of national minorities*, and rights *protecting vulnerable groups*, in particular *children* and *disabled persons*"'.[12] The protection offered to minorities by the Charter extends solely to the prohibition on discrimination on the basis of membership of a national minority (Article 21(1)) and, indirectly, through the provisions of Articles 24 and 26, to requiring the protection of cultural, religious and linguistic diversity.[13]

It has been noted by certain commentators that France has not signed the Council of Europe's Framework Convention for the Protection of National Minorities.[14] Its ability to satisfy the Copenhagen criteria on minority rights protection, were they to be applied to it, would be questionable. In contrast, candidate countries' records regarding minorities are assessed on a yearly basis, in reports presented by the Commission to the European Parliament and Council. The monitoring has focused, in particular, on the treatment of the Roma communities, who comprise minorities in certain CEE countries, including some of the ten new member states, and total around six million in number. Significant progress in this field has been achieved through EU financing of a range of initiatives, aimed at increasing both the protection of minorities and capacity building, not only within the state structures, but also within NGOs and minorities communities. The total spending in favour of the Roma communities in 1999 totalled €10m, increasing to €13m in 2000.[15]

The European Constitution and the EU Charter of Fundamental Rights

Despite currently being stalled, the drafting of the European Constitutional Treaty raises a number of significant questions. In particular, what practical difference would the European Constitution have made to the protection of human rights within the EU and in candidate states? Additionally, is protection afforded by other European, though not Union, institutions greater than that provided by the EU Charter of Fundamental Rights?

Currently, the Charter of Fundamental Rights of the European Union is not a treaty or legal constitutional document. It is a 'solemn proclamation' by the three most important institutions of the EU – the Council, European Parliament and Commission. It does not, however, have legal force, as it was not incorporated into the Treaties establishing the EU. The Charter has been included as the second part of the draft European Constitution, which itself requires ratification by all twenty-five member states of the EU. As the process of ratification has stalled, following the double rejection of the Constitution in referenda in France (on 29 May 2005) and the Netherlands (on 1 June 2005), at the present time, the prospects of the Charter gaining legal force through the Constitution seem remote.

However, the practical effect of the lack of strict binding force in the Charter is somewhat limited, as it does not establish new rights, but seeks to raise existing rights to the status of fundamental rights. In fact, the main reason for having the Charter, given that the rights provided for in its Articles already exist, is 'to make these rights visible for citizens'.[16] The foundation for the rights in the Charter are to be found in other charters, conventions, treaties or jurisprudence, the most important of which is the European Convention on Human Rights (ECHR).[17]

The ECHR is one of the main successes of another international organisation – the Council of Europe. This is not to be confused with the European Council, with the latter being an EU institution. Membership to the Council of Europe is open to all

European states that accept the principles of the rule of law and guarantee fundamental human rights and freedoms to their citizens. Discussions, familiar in the context of EU enlargement as to how far 'Europe' extends, have not featured in the Council of Europe, with Turkey, Iceland, Russia, Armenia and Azerbaijan having been admitted as members. The Council of Europe is the oldest institutional watchdog of human rights and democratic principles in Europe. The European Court of Human Rights (ECtHR) in Strasbourg, as set up by the ECHR, provides a unique method of human rights enforcement – the possibility for individuals to bring cases directly to the Court. In terms of deterrent effects in the sphere of human rights abuses, the major impact of the ECtHR has been in rendering public judgements for human rights breaches against states that are members of the Council of Europe. The weaknesses derive partly from the relatively small monetary compensation to successful applicants before the ECtHR, with such sums insignificant in terms of having any deterrent value against a state. Additionally, by definition, the Court only deals with *ex post facto* determination of past breaches.

There is a high degree of co-operation between the EU and the Council of Europe, the legal basis of which, from the EU perspective, lies in Article 303 TEU. Historically, following an exchange of letters, yearly reports were submitted in both directions regarding matters of common interest. Since 1987, co-operation has become more structured, through high-level meetings, in particular quadripartite meetings between the EU Presidency and Commission on the one hand and the Council of Europe Chairmanship and the Secretary General, on the other. The EU wish to sign up to the ECHR was frustrated, as the European Court of Justice (ECJ) ruled[18] that the founding treaties of the EC did not empower it to accede, despite all its member states also being signatories to the ECHR.[19] The European Constitution, if adopted, would provide the basis for the EU's accession to the ECHR.

In the meantime, on 3 April 2001, there was a further declaration between the Commission and the Council of Europe, which set up the framework for drawing up objectives, planning activities and monitoring and evaluating joint programmes.[20] Joint programmes, co-financed by the Commission and the Council of Europe, have supported the efforts of CEE states towards achieving democracy and respect for human rights, since the changes in the regional political situation in 1989. Such efforts help to stabilise these states and develop a sense of security, both internally and across the European institutions. Current country-specific programmes, aimed at institutional reform and support for the legal system, were launched in Albania, Ukraine, Russia and Moldova in the period 1993–97. More recent beneficiaries include Armenia, Azerbaijan and Georgia since January 1999, Serbia and Montenegro and Turkey since 2001 and BiH since 2003. The cost of sixteen Joint Programmes and activities completed by April 2003 amounted to a total of €12.7m.[21] The most recent and future prospective waves of EU enlargement have dictated the focus of the new areas of co-operation between the EU and the Council of Europe, such as combating money laundering, trafficking in human beings and enhancing the protection of minorities.[22]

Therefore, despite the Charter lacking legal force and the absence of an EU enforcement body, in practice respect for human rights is enhanced throughout

EU member states by their being signatories to the ECHR and the policing of the system by the ECtHR. With specific reference to EU enlargement, the ECHR and other treaties, such as the European Convention for the Prevention of Torture and Inhuman or Degrading Treatment or Punishment, are considered to be part of the EU *acquis*. Therefore, states applying for EU membership are required to have acceded to them. Even with regard to the drafting of post-communist constitutions and charters of rights, expert bodies of the Council of Europe, such as the Venice Commission, have been judged to exert more influence than the co-operation agreements, 'which are more to do with the promotion of free-market ideals than of human rights and constitutionalism'.[23]

Challenges to human rights protection in the fight against terrorism

In the context of EU enlargement, the dominating theme is of candidate states striving towards and achieving the Copenhagen political criteria for membership. This focus on 'getting over the hurdle' carries with it the risk of assuming that, once inside the EU, the challenges of upholding human rights disappear. This could not be further from the truth, as very recent experiences of EU member states grappling with the problems thrown up by terrorism show.

In the UK, issues relating to the detention of foreign terrorist suspects have reached the House of Lords twice in as many years. Analysis of the UK domestic experience in attempting to uphold human rights in the context of the fight against terrorism affords some interesting perspectives on the impact of human rights on security issues. In this particular setting, the logic seems to be reversed. Allowing the suspects certain procedural and substantive rights seems to work against the security of the state, for example by restricting the methods of interrogation, as well as the type of evidence that might be used in a court of law when seeking to secure a conviction. The problems of simultaneously ensuring human rights and securing the 'homeland' have been common to all EU states in the wake of September 11. The case of the UK serves here to highlight the difficulties governments have in reconciling the two objectives. It also illustrates the importance of strong judicial and constitutional frameworks, something that is still relatively new to many of the new and would-be EU member states. The issues raised here are an example of a broader clash of priorities apparent across the EU, between the concepts of security and freedom.

The background to the House of Lords hearings is worth briefly sketching out. In response to the September 11 attacks in New York and Washington DC, the UK legislature passed the Anti-Terrorism, Crime and Security Act 2001, in order to implement measures to deal with this new grave threat. This Act established a new regime, which applied to non-British citizens whose presence in the UK the Secretary of State reasonably believed to be a risk to national security and whom he reasonably suspected of being terrorists, as defined in the Act ('foreign suspected terrorists').[24] The problem facing the authorities was that evidence against such persons was inadmissible, or insufficient, for a conviction in trial in a court of law, yet the risks to national security were assessed to be too great for those individuals to remain at liberty. The UK, as a signatory to the ECHR, was bound by Article 5(1) (f) of the ECHR, which mandates that:

> 5 Everyone has the right to liberty and security of person. No one shall be deprived of his liberty save in the following cases and in accordance with a procedure prescribed by law:
>
> ...
>
> (f) the lawful arrest or detention of a person to prevent his effecting an unauthorised entry into the country or of a person against whom action is being taken with a view to deportation or extradition.[25]

None of the other qualifications to Article 5 applied, such as detention after conviction by a competent court (Article 5(1) (a)). The UK government recognised that it may not be possible to rely on the only potentially applicable exception – the one established by Article 5(1) (f), as deportation of foreign suspected terrorists was unlikely to take place. This was largely due to concerns that they would be tortured in the states to which they could be returned. Therefore, a different way of ensuring public security was required. The solution adopted by the UK was to derogate from Article 5(1) of the ECHR, thus allowing for detention of foreign terrorist suspects without trial, including detention for an indeterminate period. The circumstances when derogation from the provisions of the ECHR is permissible are strictly limited by Article 15. Derogation is only possible 'in time of war or other public emergency threatening the life of the nation'.[26]

The validity of the Derogation Order was the issue before the House of Lords in the first appeal, *A and others* v *Secretary of State for Home Department*,[27] an issue on which the government ultimately lost. The House of Lords afforded a wide margin of discretion to the Secretary of State in making the decision that there was a state of public emergency, which threatened the life of the nation. This was in line with ECtHR jurisprudence and with the legal principle that purely political decisions are less appropriate for judicial ruling. Weight was also placed on the fact that the Special Immigration Appeals Commission (SIAC), which was the first-instance judicial body, had seen confidential material not seen by the House of Lords. It had been satisfied that the government had been right to declare that there was a public emergency. However, the measures adopted, which authorised potentially indefinite detention of foreign international terrorist suspects without trial, were judged not to be strictly required within the test of Article 15. Thus, there were more proportionate ways of achieving the national security aims sought.

Before proceeding further, it is important to note several points. Firstly, the executive had proposed and the legislature had passed measures, which the House of Lords had ruled to be contrary to the UK's international obligations and, in effect, were unconstitutional. The UK, as one of the founding members of the Council of Europe and having joined the EC as part of its first enlargement, was not beyond error in the field of human rights protection. Being a member of the Council of Europe, and having incorporated the ECHR in domestic law, also did not ensure complete protection of human rights. If such an 'error' could occur in a long-established political and judicial system as the UK, the possibility for human rights violations in less well-established systems may be even greater.

Secondly, the strength and independence of judicial institutions had made such a judgement possible, and the adherence to the rule of law had ensured that both the government and Parliament accepted the result. In implementing the judgement, the executive proposed and the legislature adopted a new package of powers, which allowed for various restrictions on the liberty of suspects through control orders, up to the most draconian measure of essentially house arrest. This aspect of human rights implementation, following judicial pronouncements, be they by domestic courts or the ECtHR, is often not articulated, as it is presumed in the case of older EU member states. However, in the context of enlargement, institution building and the fostering of a human rights culture and the rule of law, as well as developing judicial independence, have been very much at the fore. In the context of further enlargement, in particular with regard to the future potential membership of Turkey, the most valid concerns relate not to the adoption of human rights norms and other *acquis* provisions, but to their effective implementation and continued enforcement.

Thirdly, part of the rationale for the existence of the problem facing the UK authorities was that the most immediately obvious way of resolving it, through deporting the suspects abroad, was not available, due to the UK's adherence to the fundamental right that no one should be subjected to torture or inhuman or degrading treatment. This right, as enshrined in Article 3 of the ECHR, does not permit exception and cannot be qualified. Further, the international prohibition on the use of torture enjoys the enhanced status of *jus cogens*, or peremptory norm of general international law. Respecting the rights of suspects in respect of ECHR Article 3, however, could not be argued to permit or justify the withdrawal of their right to liberty of the person, protected under ECHR Article 5.

Fourthly, when considering any future potential human rights standards setting by the EU in the context of further integration, another interesting question arises. Is there some advantage to having a multiplicity of legal orders within the EU? The House of Lords, in this first case, considered as one of the relevant factors the fact that none of the other state signatories to the ECHR had thought it appropriate or possible to derogate from ECHR Article 5(1). Such comparisons, and indeed any lessons from comparative jurisprudence, would be lost if the human rights competency in a much more highly integrated EU passes to, say, the Commission. For the purposes of the current example, it would then be empowered to decide whether the EU, as a signatory to the ECHR, should derogate from one of its provisions. The power to derogate is, in one sense, an emergency power. As a result, its exercise should be entrusted to a political body, which is able to take effective and swift action. In addition, the democratic imperative also dictates that such important decisions with regard to human rights protection should be taken by a more representative body, such as the European Parliament in the above example.

The second time the same group of cases of *A and others*[28] reached the House of Lords was on the issue of whether the SIAC may receive evidence which has or may have been procured by torture, inflicted to obtain evidence by officials of a foreign state, without the complicity of the British authorities. Such evidence could have been potentially used in appeal hearings before SIAC. The Anti-Terrorism, Crime and Security Act 2001 allowed for those certified by the Secretary of State as 'international terrorists' to challenge such certification and, hence, their detention in an appeal in front of SIAC. As these provisions of the 2001 Act were repealed following the first judgement of the House of Lords, the application was of direct relevance to a reasonably small number of cases. However, the principles set out by their Lordships would be of the most persuasive authority in any other analogous situation, should it arise in the future. In the UK, where there is no written constitution, with the role of elaborating fundamental rights performed by the common law,[29] the House of Lords pronouncement on the issue of the use of torture evidence can be seen as the formulation of a fundamental constitutional right.

The Secretary of State had stated that, as a matter of policy, it was not his intention to rely on evidence which he knows or believes to have been obtained by torture in a third country. However, the use of such evidence was not precluded by law, it was argued, whereas the prohibition existed in the case of evidence obtained under torture in the UK. The Secretary of State relied on a concession by the appellants that he was not prohibited from using foreign torture evidence for operational reasons. For example, if a man tortured abroad revealed the whereabouts of a bomb planted by a terrorist in the Houses of Parliament, the authorities could (and must) remove the bomb and arrest the terrorist, if possible, thereby acting operationally on torture evidence.

In delivering their opinions, Their Lordships spoke with one voice on the condemnation of torture in English common law, as well as in the ECHR, which the UK had adopted. Torture, like genocide, were crimes against international law, which every state was obliged to punish, wherever they may have been committed. The unanimous conclusion of the House of Lords was that there was a deeply embedded exclusionary principle, which compelled the exclusion of 'third party' 'foreign' torture evidence as, in the words of Lord Bingham, 'unreliable, unfair, offensive to the ordinary standards of humanity and decency and incompatible with the principles which should animate a tribunal seeing to administer justice'. The House of Lords took into account the fact that development of the common law (i.e. domestic law) should be in harmony with the UK's international obligations. The latter included compliance with the Torture Convention, Article 15 of which mandated that:

> Each State Party shall ensure that any statement which is established to have been made as a result of torture shall not be invoked as evidence in any proceedings, except against a person accused of torture as evidence that the statement was made.[30]

Further, it was noted that the Council of Europe Convention on the Prevention of Terrorism of 16 May 2005 and UN Security Council Resolution 1566 of 8 October 2004 called for measures in combating terrorism to be in accordance with international law, in particular human rights law and humanitarian law.[31]

The concession that the Secretary of State was allowed to take into account, namely to act on foreign torture evidence operationally to prevent terrorist attacks and arrest perpetrators, although accepted as correct by their Lordships, did not make such evidence admissible before SIAC. Lord Bingham, delivering the leading speech in the House of Lords, stated that the lack of prohibition on the use of foreign torture evidence operationally 'may be seen as an anomaly, but . . . it springs from the tension between practical common sense and the need to protect the individual against unfair incrimination. The common law is not intolerant of an anomaly'.[32] However, it could not be extended further, to allow admissibility of the evidence in judicial proceedings.

Given the tension between human rights and increased security identified in the context of the fight against terrorism, thus far the conclusions of the House of Lords appear to fall overwhelmingly on the side of human rights protection. This indeed is what made the headlines: The House of Lords rules that torture evidence is not admissible in British Courts. This was even the case with courts such as SIAC, which, according to its rules, 'may receive evidence that would not be admissible in a court of law'.[33] However, as always, the substance of the right is more important than its pronouncement. Perhaps the most important issue was on whom lies the burden of showing that evidence was obtained under torture, and to what standard must he prove it?

On this central issue, which would define how effectively the right could be enforced, the House of Lords was split. The majority recognised that it was unrealistic to expect the detainee to prove anything, given that he is denied access to so much of the information to be used against him. All that could be reasonably expected of him was to raise the point about whether evidence against him was obtained from third parties under torture abroad. It was then up to SIAC to decide. The majority held that 'SIAC should refuse to admit the evidence if it concludes that the evidence was obtained by torture'.[34] In applying this test, SIAC should apply the standard of proof 'on the balance of probabilities', rather than the higher criminal standard of 'beyond reasonable doubt'. Therefore, evidence would be excluded if SIAC concludes that it is more likely than not to have been obtained by torture abroad. However, 'if SIAC is left in doubt as to whether the evidence was obtained in this way, it should admit it. But it must bear its doubt in mind when it is evaluating the evidence'.[35] In reaching this conclusion, the majority relied on the wording of Article 15 of the Torture Convention (quoted above), which sets out the exclusionary principle as extending to any statement that 'is established' to have been made under torture.

Thus, in the opinion of the majority, even if the detained person were able to introduce a reasonable doubt in the minds of the SIAC judges, this would not be sufficient to exclude the evidence under the exclusionary rule applicable to torture evidence. In reality, this practical application of the human rights principle does pay silent respect to the operational imperatives of maintaining national security at a cost slightly higher than the idealised absolute respect for human rights. To put it another way, in the fight against terrorism, where the human rights imperatives against the admission of torture evidence are pitched squarely against the security interests of the state, the proclaimed absoluteness of the human rights principle does yield, to some extent, in its application, on the grounds of the opposing security interest.

The minority, Lords Bingham, Nicholls and Hoffmann, in a House of Lords constituted of seven Law Lords, dissented on this very important issue. The test adopted by the majority was said to 'undermine the practical efficacy of the Torture Convention and deny detainees the standard of fairness to which they are entitled under Article 5(4) and 6(1) of the European Convention'.[36] The alternative test proposed by the minority would have seen appellants adducing some plausible reason why evidence may have been procured under torture, which could be shown by pointing to the fact that the evidence is likely to have originated from a state that is known to practice torture. The SIAC enquiry thereafter would focus on 'whether the evidence has, or whether there is a real risk that it may have been, obtained by torture'. Put another way, 'If SIAC is unable to conclude that there is not a real risk that the evidence has been obtained by torture, it should refuse to admit the evidence.'[37] Proof on the balance of probabilities was not required.

On analysis, bearing in mind the grave concerns of the minority with regard to the practical application of the fundamental norm of excluding torture evidence, it could be argued that the right (as implemented by the majority) is essentially empty. Potentially, this is even more starkly the case with fundamental rights enshrined in constitutions, which are formulated with a higher level of generality. A good example can be taken from a study published in September 2002 on the Charter and European enlargement. Sadurski cites Poland's new constitution as an example of 'consolidation of constitutional rules in the minds of the main political players who come to accept the rules – even if, at the beginning, grudgingly – as useful parameters for their strategies and behaviour'.[38] He elaborates in relation to Poland:

> When the centre-right coalition won the parliamentary election in 1997, the very same year when this coalition had earlier condemned the new Constitution as an act of betrayal of Poland, they soon learned that the Constitution was no obstacle to any important aspect of their political and ideological goals . . . Within the area of constitutional rights, the centre-right political forces soon realised that the constitutional catalogue of rights earlier condemned as liberal, left-wing, secularist, anti-religious, etc, was no obstacle to any of the pet projects of the Right. For example, the principle of religious impartiality of the State did not preclude a privileged position of the Catholic Church (including teaching religion in public schools, protection of 'Christian values' in public broadcasting, etc.) and the absence of the mention of protection of human life from the moment of conception did not preclude the quasi-absolute prohibition of abortion.[39]

If fundamental rights and constitutional principles by their generality afford such wide and diverging interpretations,[40] then how far can they be stretched? Should Turkey become a fundamentalist Islamic state, the stretch would be beyond breaking point. Yet, as a potential future member of the EU, Turkey is often criticised for failing to allow greater freedom of religious expression. Curiously, though, it is Turkey's secularism that has enabled its candidacy to the EU. Most voices against its future membership focus on Islam and its size, as well as its human rights record. As one scholar has put it: 'Human rights thinking is often based on the idea of universally valid rights as "only by locating human rights beyond society and history can it be assumed that such rights are not just a clever attempt at imposing someone's – the Europeans' – values on everybody else" . . . Universal and European do not appear as equivalent.'[41]

If the conception of human rights norms is not universal, then Turkey faces a clear choice – adopt an interpretation of human rights palatable to European tastes or be refused membership.

Conclusion

It is hoped that some of the issues raised in this chapter would inform discussion in the sphere of developing and future European security initiatives. Respect for human rights should be guaranteed, and enforced. This is even more important as the EU initiatives move from co-operation between member states in criminal matters, such as sharing of intelligence through Europol and the SIS and expedited extradition procedures, to a common security policy, including the creation of an ERRF for peacekeeping, an EU military staff and EU satellite centre for intelligence purposes. With the creation of such supranational structures, the best way to achieve consistent enforcement of human rights is by enabling the EU to become a signatory to the ECHR. A final illustration: The wars in the former Yugoslavia in the 1990s and the EU member states' acknowledged failure to respond sufficiently coherently and quickly to those wars, served as the foundation of the ESDP. EUFOR, or the European Union Force, is an international military force, supervised by the European Council. In December 2004, as part of Operation Althea, EUFOR replaced the NATO-led SFOR in BiH, overseeing the military implementation of the Dayton Peace Agreement. As Javier Solana described it, 'the [ESDP] missions' purposes are now evolving from crisis management and conflict prevention to institution building – assisting the countries of this region as they reform their institutions and prepare for closer integration and eventual membership in the EU.'[42] In doing so, however, the EU must itself be bound by the same human rights standards it espouses – in other words, it must lead by example.

Notes

1 The views expressed in this chapter are the authors' own and are not attributable to any organisation.
2 *European Union Consolidated Version of Treaty on European Union* (Brussels, 1997).
3 *EU Programme for Prevention of Violent Conflicts* (Göteborg, June 2001).
4 Ibid.
5 Ibid.
6 C. Pinelli, 'Conditionality and enlargement in light of EU constitutional developments', *European Law Journal*, 10:3 (May 2004), p. 357.
7 Ibid.
8 For details, see http://europa.eu.int/comm/enlargement/intro/criteria.htm.
9 Ibid.
10 *Treaty on European Union*.
11 The difficulties in the application of Article 7 have been illustrated in the case of Austria, whom other member states sanctioned, whereas the Commission found that the political aspect of the dispute to be outside its remit. See C. Pinelli, 'Conditionality and enlargement', p. 358.
12 W. Sadurski, 'Charter and enlargement', *European Law Journal*, 8:3 (September 2002), p. 347.

13 *Charter of Fundamental Rights of the European Union* (Brussels, December 2000).
14 See Sadurski, 'Charter and enlargement'.
15 'The EU's human rights and democratisation policy', www.europa.eu.int/comm/external_relations/human_rights/rm.
16 'The Charter of Fundamental Rights: frequently asked questions', www.europa.eu.int/comm/justice_home/unit/chare/en/faqs.html.
17 The less familiar and newer-sounding rights in the Charter in relation to bioethics and the protection of personal data are also derived from Council of Europe conventions.
18 See Opinion 2/94, 'Accession by the Community to the European Convention for the Protection of Human Rights and Fundamental Freedoms' (28 March 1996).
19 The first convention to which the EC became a party was the European Agreement on the Exchange of Therapeutic Substances of Human Origin.
20 The Joint Declaration on Co-operation and Partnership was signed by Secretary General Schwimmer for the Council of Europe and Chris Patten for the Commission.
21 'The EU's relations with the Council of Europe', http://europa.eu.int/comm/external_relations/coe/.
22 See the joint EC/CoE project on the promotion of the status of Roma – Roma under the Stability Pact.
23 Sadurski, 'Charter and enlargement', p. 343.
24 *Anti-Terrorism, Crime and Security Act 2001* (London: HMSO, 2001), www.opsi.gov.uk/acts/acts2001/20010024.htm.
25 Council of Europe, *European Convention on Human Rights* (Strasbourg: Council of Europe, 1950), http://conventions.coe.int/treaty/en/Treaties/Html/005.htm.
26 Ibid.
27 *A and others v Secretary of State for the Home Department*, UKHL 56 (2004); 2 AC 68 (2005).
28 *A and others v Secretary of State for the Home Department*, UKHL 71 (2005).
29 It should be noted, however, that the international legal obligations of the UK under the European Convention on Human Rights were transposed into domestic law in the Human Rights Act 1998.
30 *Convention against Torture and Other Cruel, Inhuman or Degrading Treatment or Punishment* (New York: UN, 1985), www.hrweb.org/legal/cat.html.
31 Council of Europe, *Convention on the Prevention of Terrorism* (Strasbourg: Council of Europe, 2005), http://conventions.coe.int/Treaty/EN/Treaties/Word/196.doc; UNSC, Security Council Resolution 1566, http://daccessdds.un.org/doc/UNDOC/GEN/N04/542/82/PDF/N0454282.pdf?OpenElement.
32 UKHL (House of Lords, UK Parliament) 71 (2005), Lord Bingham, para. 48.
33 UKHL 71(2005).
34 UKHL 71 (2005), per Lord Hope, para. 118.
35 Ibid.
36 UKHL 71 (2005), per Lord Bingham, para. 62.
37 UKHL 71 (2005), per Lord Bingham, para. 56.
38 Sadurski, 'Charter and enlargement', p. 349.
39 Ibid.
40 See the striking comparative example of the differing approaches of EU member states to the right to life (Article 2 of the ECHR) in their legal approaches to abortion and euthanasia in Paivi Leino, 'A European approach to human rights? Universality explored', *Nordic Journal of International Law*, 71 (2002).
41 Ibid., p. 460, citing M. Koskenniemi, 'The preamble of the Universal Declaration of Human Rights', in G. Alfredsson, and A. Eide (eds), *The Universal Declaration of Human Rights* (Dordrecht: Kluwer, 1999), p. 32.
42 Javier Solana, *The EU's Security Agenda and the Western Balkans G17 Institute/EU ISS seminar*, 7–8 April 2005.

7

An assessment of the Baltic States contribution to EU efforts to prevent proliferation and combat illicit arms trafficking

Paul Holtom

> Illicit arms trafficking cannot be effectively tackled through a narrowly focused regime to prevent or combat arms smuggling by criminals. A more comprehensive approach is needed . . . International co-operation . . . needs to be embedded in broader efforts to combat transnational criminal networks and to prevent and reduce excessive accumulation and spread of small arms and light weapons.[1]

Phythian has persuasively argued that the nature of the post-Cold War illicit arms trade is qualitatively different to the Cold War era.[2] Across Europe, a number of factors have impacted upon thinking about the arms trade in general, and the illicit arms trade in particular, including the increased Europeanisation of arms and defence industries, changes in the significance and functions of borders, Schengen, the blurring of the categories of conflict and crime, and a significant increase in international trade. It is also assumed that the black market in arms has been boosted by the influx of military equipment from the stockpiles and near bankrupt arms companies of post-communist Europe.[3] These arms are then trafficked and covertly supplied to undesirable end users, including embargoed regimes in regions of conflict, criminal gangs, insurgents and/or terrorist groups.

By the late 1990s, a considerable number of measures had been adopted to attempt to tackle the proliferation and trafficking of illicit arms. Recognised 'holes' in the international system for controlling shipments of arms and strategic goods began to gain more attention, with new initiatives developed regarding arms brokering and the strengthening of controls at transit and trans-shipment hubs.[4] Therefore, while the Cold War presented a complex set of challenges, it also 'helped to create the space required to begin to tackle the trade'.[5]

A number of EU initiatives, in particular the 1998 Code of Conduct on Arms Exports, have been launched since the late 1990s, accompanied by a number of innovations in EU member state border, customs and law enforcement agencies. However, with the 2004 EU enlargement, concerns are being voiced that 'the large number of new states having joined the EU at the same time has increased the risk that future interpretation and implementation of relevant EU mechanisms will be watered down'.[6] This has led to fears that there will be 'purely rhetorical' moves by new members in relation to calls for increased stringency in controls on arms and anti-trafficking initiatives, in part because their administrative capacities fail to meet the requirements of national legislation and established EU norms.

Estonia, Latvia and Lithuania have subjected shipments of arms, strategic and dual-use goods to export, import and transit controls since the early 1990s, with their current laws and directives all explicitly referencing their compliance with EU, OSCE and UN actions. Unfortunately, well-meant legislation does not implement and enforce itself and there are concerns about the abilities of all three states to prevent diversions taking place via their airports, ports or land border crossings. Assessments by the Commission and the Council of Europe's Group of States against Corruption (GRECO) have not reported favourably upon the performance of their judiciary, law enforcement, border and customs services. They have highlighted a number of general concerns with corruption, experience and resources, which could impact upon their ability to uncover attempted diversions and arms brokering activities. Indeed, individuals from the Baltic States have been involved in several well-known cases of diversion to illicit end users. They have also been unable to divest themselves of their reputations as gateways for illicit trafficking in drugs, stolen vehicles, people, arms and other dangerous materials. These concerns pose potential problems for those now charged with guarding the EU's external frontier and contributing to its overall security.

This chapter will focus upon the Baltic States' alignment with EU initiatives relating to controlling legal and combating illegal transfers of arms and military equipment. It begins by briefly commenting upon the challenges posed by the illicit arms trade in the post-Cold War era. A summary of the EU's main efforts to harmonise export control legislation and co-ordinate responses to the illicit arms trade will be critically appraised, followed by an assessment of the Baltic States' support for EU-led initiatives and other efforts in this sphere. A number of examples will demonstrate that their law enforcement, border and customs services have been able to apprehend individuals and groups involved in attempts to divert licit arms transfers to illicit end users and illicit trafficking through the Baltic States. The ability of these agencies to enforce legislation and successfully combat illicit trafficking will also be assessed. It is feared that, as the Baltic States transform from gateways to EU gatekeepers, they may struggle to overcome a number of challenges, including problems with interagency and transnational communication, lack of resources, corruption and containerised security threats.[7]

Challenges for researchers of diversions and illicit arms trafficking

Gillard has questioned the idea that '"illicit" arms transfers are commonly held to mean those that occur outside the control, or against the wishes, of exporting states', arguing that references to international humanitarian and human rights law, embargoes, aspects of the UN Charter and related declarations also need to be taken into consideration.[8] A number of analysts acknowledge that there has been a problem in clearly defining the differences between illicit, illegal and licit arms transfers. However, a consensus appears to have emerged regarding using the UN as a useful starting point when considering such questions. For example, Greene and Wezeman both suggest that the UN has been moving towards a relatively inclusive international definition since agreeing on the 1991 Guidelines for International Arms Transfers. These guidelines define illicit arms trafficking as the 'international trade in conventional arms, which is contrary to the laws of states and/or international law'.[9] They note that the definition has been expanded by the 2001 UN Protocol against the Illicit Manufacturing of and Trafficking in Firearms, Their Parts and Components and Ammunition, to cover the import, export, acquisition, sale, delivery and movement of arms, their parts and ammunition from one state to another, without the explicit authorisation of both importing and exporting state. In their opinion, transfers of military equipment to armed groups, criminal organisations, terrorists, individual criminals, private security services, mercenaries and private citizens should also be considered illegal. Of course, this still leaves room for disagreement, as one government's insurgent or terrorist is another's freedom fighter and worthy ally.

Such issues were not clarified by the UN Panel of Experts on Small Arms, which recognised that transfers carried out secretly by governments to insurgents were 'not necessarily illicit'. However, if the transfer was not approved by the recipient state's competent authorities, it *could* 'be classified by that state as interferences in its internal affairs and therefore illegal'.[10] Of course, national legislation and export control regimes differ, so that a transfer of military equipment to Sudan may be refused by Sweden, but regarded as worthy of an export licence by Russia. Within the EU, it is hoped that the Code of Conduct's eight criteria on arms exports can help to overcome such differences. However, member states can still have different assessments of the receiving state's human rights situation (criteria 2), technical and economic situation (criteria 8), potential for diversion (criteria 7), behaviour within the international community and its region (criteria 4, 5 and 6) and the potential for fuelling or prolonging conflict within the recipient or its region (criteria 3 and 4). Therefore, different assessments of end users and the granting of export licences can still occur within the EU.

While defining the key concepts remain open to debate, some baselines have been established. Assessing the size of the global black market in arms, however, is generally recognised as impossible, in part because it is extremely difficult to estimate the size of the legal market, due to 'commercial confidentiality' clauses and the opacity of reporting on the arms trade. Those wishing to make recommendations for combating illicit arms trafficking are, therefore, left to construct partial pictures, based upon court proceedings of cases launched against arms traffickers, reports of interceptions of diversions, smuggling attempts, thefts from arms dealers and military, police and security force stores and other anecdotal evidence.[11] Bearing that in mind, there are four broad means for diverting arms to illicit end users:

1 individuals or small firms undertaking small-scale transactions, in which they knowingly break the law by illegally transferring arms to 'undesirable' or illicit recipients;

2 higher value and more complex transfers that may involve defence companies, corrupt officials, arms brokers, shipping agents and other enterprises that try to conceal illicit sales by using forged documents, short-ordering, well-established networks and channels for smuggling;
3 governments covertly supplying insurgents through proxies, with the weapons later moving onto the black market.[12]
4 battlefield recoveries, the reselling of arms legally purchased and the theft of equipment from military or state arsenals.[13]

It should, therefore, come as no surprise that most of the arms currently circulating in the black market, or in the hands of 'undesirable' end users, were legally manufactured and held at some point in their lifetime. This helps explain why many of the recent efforts to combat illicit arms trafficking at all levels have stressed the importance of tightening export controls for licit transfers of military, dual-use goods and firearms. Research into arms transfers from licit to illicit markets has tended to find arms brokers at the centre of these diversions. In fact, many governments and reputable arms manufacturing companies rely on arms brokers for marketing their weapons and helping to facilitate sales.[14] However, unscrupulous arms brokers are suspected of supplying arms to states subject to UN, OSCE and EU embargoes and other 'undesirable' end users. They play a key role in moving arms shipments from the licit to the illicit markets, aid governments with their covert or 'grey' arms transfers and make available weapons that are not permitted for sale on the international arms market.[15] They can be highly skilled, making it difficult to stop a diversion or even spot at which point on its journey the arms were diverted to an undesignated end use: 'shipping agents and arms brokers go to considerable lengths to establish intricate international webs involving multiple subcontractors, front companies and circuitous transport routes'.[16] Research into arms brokering suggests that shipping agents, freight forwarders, financiers, insurers and even government officials wittingly and unwittingly help provide a mountain of paperwork to help conceal diversions.

Therefore, while the interception of a shipment that is illicit or in the process of being diverted helps to reveal information about arms brokering and illicit trafficking practices and networks, the likelihood of discovering such a shipment is not necessarily very high. Falsified or forged documents, mislabelling and other means of concealment can be used successfully, if the route chosen has a high volume of traffic and/or ill-equipped, poorly trained and undermanned controls. For example, research carried out pre-enlargement found a comparatively high number of diversions and trafficking attempts in areas with high volumes of trade, such as Amsterdam and the border areas of Austria, Italy and Germany.[17] One should not assume that the situation will dramatically improve at the EU's enlarged borders. Additionally, if border, customs and law enforcement agents have low salaries, poor working conditions and a proclivity towards corruption, their susceptibility to accepting bribes or acquiescing with the demands of those threatening violence or intimidation is high, further complicating efforts to combat illicit trafficking.[18]

EU efforts to prevent proliferation and combat illicit trafficking

Although illicit arms trafficking has attracted considerable attention since the end of the Cold War, Karp is extremely sceptical about recent global diplomatic efforts and meetings.[19] He is particularly scathing about the 2001 UN Conference on the Illicit Trade in Small Arms and Light Weapons (SALW), which he regards as a lost opportunity for establishing an effective global regime, as it left too many responsibilities to the endeavours and whims of individual states. However, it should be noted that many states around the world have recently increased the stringency of their export controls on arms and strategic goods. For example, more states now require end-use/end-user certification, post-shipment checks, delivery verification certificates and assessments of the seller and recipient's international reputation, reliability and the contents of particular shipments before issuing export or import licenses. These changes are considered to be vital, because 'without the creation and implementation of effective national controls, little meaningful action to curtail trafficking can occur'.[20] Yet, an international or regional dimension is still necessary, as it can enable better compliance with global commitments and is considered more responsive to the concerns of particular regions. Individual states can only have partial information on the many buyers and sellers of military equipment located around the world.[21] Therefore, one can observe moves towards 'postmodern arms control',[22] a process which expands upon the general principles for controlling non-proliferation by calling upon groups of states to exchange information regarding their export controls, export denials and suspicions. Yet, greater transparency with neighbours and potential competitors in the licit arms market in these areas is only part of the process.

The EU is, quite rightly, lauded as the leading example of regional co-operation in this sphere, due to its efforts to harmonise export control legislation, co-ordinate responses to the licit and illicit arms trade between member states, associates and 'like-minded' neighbours and other third countries. In the late 1990s, the EU adopted a number of key initiatives in this area:

- Programme on Preventing and Combating the Illicit Trafficking of Conventional Arms (June 1997);
- Code of Conduct on Arms Exports (8 June 1998);
- Joint Action on the EU's Contribution to Combating the Destabilising Accumulation and Spread of SALW (17 December 1998);
- Plan of Action to Prevent, Combat and Eradicate the Illicit Trade in SALW in all its Aspects (14 December 2000).[23]

Taken together, these share the same basic principles:

- to stringently control exports, imports and transits of licit arms transfers, with 'minimum common standards' for an enlarged EU;
- to stop diversions of arms to undesirable end users, regions of instability and transfers regarded as contributing to proliferation;

- to combat illicit trafficking through greater international co-operation, co-ordinated activities and capacity building between customs and law enforcement agencies within and beyond the EU;
- to increase transparency in the licit arms trade, with details of denials and sales being shared between EU member states.

Although these measures contain a mixture of suggestions to control the demand and supply side of the arms trade, to prevent diversions and a willingness to assist with the implementation of stricter export controls and anti-trafficking measures, they have been criticised for not going far enough. The claim that the Code is 'the most comprehensive international arms export control regime'[24] is probably true. However, this is due to a lack of competition, rather than to it necessarily achieving its objective, to make a significant impact on combating diversions, the risks of diversions and proliferation.[25] For example, the Code still only calls for 'common *minimum* standards', permitting a considerable degree of heterogeneity and a lack of clarity on key terms, such as 'essentially identical transfers' (EIT),[26] thereby providing loopholes for exploitation. It also fails to provide clear guidelines on the minimum requirements for accurate, comprehensive, timely and comparable reporting on licensed arms transfers. As such, it is relatively useless for researchers interested in monitoring licit transfers for possibilities of diversions and supplies to undesirable end users. It has also done little to make it easier to scrutinise arms exports or to introduce more measures to combat the corruption that plagues the arms trade.[27]

It is clear that there were problems building consensus for this politically, but crucially not legally, binding agreement on arms export controls. However, gradual improvements have been made to the Code's content, and certain aspects have been adopted by many EU member states, both old and new.[28] To its credit, the EU's Conventional Arms Exports Working Group (COARM) has recognised a number of deficiencies in the Code's scope and implementation, and has worked towards achieving clear definitions and common positions, including on EITs and common lists of military and non-military equipment to be subjected to export controls and arms brokering.

Analysts are concerned that even these modest improvements could be weakened with the 2004 enlargement.[29] There are fears that diplomatic and political rhetoric in the ten new member states will not be matched with the necessary implementation. They worry that denial notifications and consultations will lead to more, not less, undercutting and the continued supply of arms to undesirable end users. Such shortcomings appear to have been acknowledged, as recent COARM priorities include increasing co-operation with associate countries and offering the possibility of technical assistance – if requested.[30] Brown has drawn attention to the fact that the Commission's assessments of the new member states' border, customs and law enforcement agencies have applauded achievements made in recent years. However, he also notes that a great deal needs to be accomplished before anti-trafficking and export control systems are comparable with those of the older EU members.[31] The rest of this chapter will explore some of these concerns with regard to the Baltic States.

The Baltic States: suppliers and trafficking/diversion route for arms

Although Estonia, Latvia and Lithuania are not significant producers of arms, military equipment or other strategic goods, there are a number of reasons why the Baltic States are regarded as a source of concern in this area. Firstly, unauthorised sales and thefts of remaining Soviet army hardware took place in the early 1990s. These legally held arms were diverted into the black market, helping to arm criminal gangs that sought to establish control over the trade flows in contraband goods moving into, out of and through the Baltic States.[32] For many of the former Soviet troops, stationed in the Baltic States until the mid 1990s, illegal sales of arms and other items were a means of providing additional money. This benefited not only the soldiers, as the cost for the purchaser was only a fraction of the price for which the item would retail on the licit market (although some items purchased would not have been made available on the licit market). These sales also helped several cities in the region acquire reputations for violent crime and illegal firearms ownership, including the Estonian cities of Narva and Tallinn, the Latvian capital Riga and Vilnius in Lithuania. Yet, according to Estonian authorities, reporting in 2001, 'illegal arms trading is practically non-existent in comparison to the mid-1990s'.[33] Only 250 illegal arms were seized in 2000. In Latvia, around 800 illegally owned SALW, including automatic weapons, were reportedly still being seized annually in the late 1990s.[34] The number of Lithuanian seizures is contained in table 7.1.

Secondly, it was not only former Soviet military personnel who were accused of diverting arms to illicit end users. In the early 1990s, Estonian and Latvian military and para-military personnel were involved in diverting arms and military equipment. For example, in 2001, several members of the Estonian Defence Forces General Staff received suspended sentences for their part in diverting over 1,000 handguns, rifles, shotguns and ammunition during 1994–95. These weapons, supposedly destined for the Estonian civil guard, were given to criminal gangs in Estonia, Russia and beyond. Various Russian media outlets have also accused the Kaitseliit of serving as a front for selling arms to criminal groups in Estonia and Russia and the Irish Republican Army (IRA).[35] In Latvia, a former Latvian Colonel is suspected of diverting millions of US dollars worth of arms to the UN-embargoed states of Somalia and Croatia and organised crime groups in the early 1990s.[36] Concerns have also been raised about the surplus stocks of the new NATO members, including the Baltic States, as they re-equip.[37]

Thirdly, despite the occasionally bitter political relations between the Baltic States and Russia, the volume of exports and imports that passed from east to west

Table 7.1 **Seizures of illegally held firearms in Lithuania**

Year	1996	1997	1998	1999	2000	2001	2002	2003	2004
No. of seizures	479	428	482	487	497	374	349	375	395

Source: Figures taken from the Centre for Crime Prevention in Lithuana, www.npic.it/stat/nus24.htm.

and vice versa 'was one of the seemingly few stable and income bringing activities that many in the Baltic Sea region adhered to'.[38] 'Gateway ports', with a high cargo turnover, irrespective of the state in which they reside, are likely to have illicit shipments in their turnover.[39] It would, therefore, have been an unbelievable success story if the Baltic ports had been immune. The fact that these ports compete for container trade is also a potential concern, as they are moved in such quantities that they 'can be easily housed in *mislabelled freight containers*, flown to non-official landing strips on private aircraft, sent via small ships, or on trucks' (emphasis added).[40] Freight containers provide an excellent means of shipping illicit arms and other goods. Not only are they infrequently screened, but the complexity of transactions, involving a number of different actors, can also leave a paper chain that helps cover the tracks of unscrupulous brokers and traffickers. In addition, state customs authorities often have inadequate equipment or experience for screening and checking containers. For example, Estonia garnered a reputation in the 1990s as a transit route for illicit shipments of arms and other goods between buyers and sellers in western countries, Russia and other parts of the former Soviet space.[41] There have been a number of interceptions in recent years of mislabelled cargoes of components for aviation weapons and defence systems, in transit from Russia to Latvian ports and airports, with Iran one of the suspected destinations.[42] For Rawlinson, Lithuania is 'particularly sensitive to illegal transit routes, bordering as it does Belarus and the Russian exclave of Kaliningrad. Not surprisingly, the proximity of Kaliningrad accounted for the high percentage of Lithuanian-based organised crime groups involved in the illegal weapons trade, estimated at one time to number more than forty'.[43]

Thus, Kaliningrad is the fourth reason for regarding the Baltic States as a source of concern. During the Soviet period, Kaliningrad 'became one of the most militarised regions in the Soviet Union'.[44] After the USSR collapsed, there was a massive reduction in the number of troops and equipment stationed there, going some way towards assuaging their neighbours' military security concerns. However, there has been a shift in the security discourses on Kaliningrad. In 2001, a Commission Communication described Kaliningrad thus: 'as in many parts of Russia, crime is widespread in Kaliningrad, thriving on weak institutions. Organised crime, trafficking in human beings, drugs and stolen vehicles and illegal migration are present.'[45] Although there is 'scant information' regarding weapons smuggling involving the military in Kaliningrad, Main argues that 'there is little doubt that it does occur and does involve members of the armed forces'.[46] One commentator has argued that, 'with such a high concentration of military equipment inadequately guarded by demoralised poorly paid troops, Kaliningrad soon developed a reputation' as the 'centre for the smuggling of a wide range of illegal arms across Northern Europe'.[47] According to one report, around $800,000 worth of spares were allegedly stolen and sold off by a group of Baltic Fleet officers between 1995 and 2000. A number of other reports have discussed the way in which serving and former military personnel use seemingly legitimate businesses as 'shell companies' for smuggling mislabelled military equipment from Kaliningrad's military stores to buyers in other parts of Russia and overseas, often transiting Lithuania.[48]

It has also been argued that those soldiers involved in illicit trafficking have established links to criminal gangs and corrupt local politicians, particularly during the period when Leonid Gorebnko was Kaliningrad's governor.[49] In addition to unauthorised sales and thefts from military stores, it is believed that arms and munitions from the Second World War have also been used in and smuggled from Kaliningrad. Figures have also been made available to the author relating to seizures of illegally held arms, ammunition and explosive materials and devices in Kaliningrad, between 2000 and 2003 (see table 7.2).[50] While the totals seem fairly impressive, it is unlikely that the Russian authorities in Kaliningrad have a 100 per cent success rate for discovering illegally held firearms and military equipment in the region. For example, the increased detection rate for pistols and revolvers may indicate that more of these weapons are held in Kaliningrad or are being trafficked, rather than suggesting that detection mechanisms are discovering a greater percentage of illegally held arms.

Finally, there are the concerns that the Baltic States are not yet ready for the full transition from gateways to EU gatekeepers. Various analysts, NGOs and the Commission have repeatedly stressed that they fear that the Baltic States lack the experience, resources and abilities in their border, customs and law enforcement agencies to combat trafficking in general, and arms trafficking and diversions in particular. Reports of interceptions of smuggling attempts and diversions in these states may just be the tip of the iceberg. Phythian has spoken of the increasing 'amateurisation' of the illicit arms trade, and it may well be that those caught were just the

Table 7.2 **Quantities of illegally held weapons, ammunition and explosive materials and devices discovered in the Kaliningrad region**

Weapon, ammunition and explosive materials and devices	2000	2001	2002	First five months of 2003
Hunting and sporting weapons	278	468	622	271
Hunting and sporting rifles	58	76	132	37
Automatic weapons	3	16	4	0
Carbines and rifles	41	76	69	1
Pistols and revolvers	23	24	187	13
Homemade weapons	12	18	12	3
Weapons from Second World War	59	63	71	13
Gas weapons	41	63	265	9
Ammunition	29,952 rounds	42,163 rounds	58,417 rounds	1,360 rounds
Grenades	75	242	43	3
Explosive materials (in kilograms)	353,098	212,630	87,780	14,637

Source: Figures taken from: 'The state of work on the struggle with the illegal circulation of firearms, ammunition, explosive materials and explosive devices for 2000 – the first five months of 2003', a paper prepared by the Department for Internal Affairs of the Kaliningrad region.

'amateurs',[51] with experienced traffickers and brokers still seemingly able to evade controls and trial. Particularly worrying is the way in which a number of cases have involved corrupt state officials. The access that corrupt arms dealers have to state officials has been demonstrated admirably by Wood and Peleman. Their account of Lithuanian arms brokers caught in a US sting operation trying to sell nuclear weapons to a Columbian drug cartel in 1995, backed up with documentation obtained from the Lithuanian Ministry of Defence helping them to divert their shipments, highlights such links.[52]

The Baltic States' efforts to prevent proliferation and combat illicit trafficking

The EU's comprehensive monitoring reports on the Baltic States' preparations for membership noted that they have made numerous and significant legislative changes in recent years, with earlier reports also highlighting their support for the principles of 'non-binding' initiatives, such as the EU Code of Conduct on Arms Exports.[53] Their most recent control laws on arms and strategic and dual-use goods all explicitly refer to their compliance with EU Joint Actions, directives and the EU Code of Conduct on Arms Exports.[54] In addition, they have publicly supported the OSCE and UN initiatives, although they have been slow to sign the UN Protocol against the Illicit Manufacturing of and Trafficking in Firearms, Their Parts and Components and Ammunition. Since the mid 1990s, Estonian, Latvian and Lithuanian export controls have required licences for certain transit shipments, unlike many older EU member states. The most recently adopted laws contain provisions for registering and licensing nationals and residents involved in arms brokering activities, therefore putting a control system for brokering in place before 'older' EU member states, such as Greece, Luxembourg and the UK.

However, concerns remain regarding the ability of their border, customs and law enforcement agencies to fulfil their obligations and effectively implement controls laid down to combat trafficking. Improving border infrastructure and training have been prioritised by PHARE (Pologne, Hongrie Assistance à la Reconstruction Economique) funding programmes in the region, yet the capacities of these new member states to monitor and enforce controls at the enlarged EU's eastern border are still generally considered to be insufficient. In addition, GRECO's reports have highlighted a number of general concerns with corruption, experience and resources, which could have an impact upon the ability of these states to uncover attempted diversions and illicit arms trafficking.[55]

The first GRECO evaluation reports noted that bribery and corruption were a cause for concern, as were the small fines and lack of custodial sentences for those found guilty.[56] Despite launching a number of 'anti-corruption' drives and programmes, a 2002 report on corruption in the Baltic Sea Region reported that, in Latvia, 'the perceived level of corruption in Latvia continues to be relatively high'.[57] Further, an EU-employed expert on corruption, responsible for improving Latvia's anti-corruption measures, highlighted the lack of political will to tackle corruption.[58] In the light of such withering assessments, one could also ask whether the development of legislation in line with international norms is worth the paper that it is written on.

Some of the reported shortcomings are being actively addressed with international assistance from both EU funds and bi-lateral and multi-lateral projects for training and best practice with EU member states, the US, Norway and others. For example, Latvia has received financial and technical assistance from the US in establishing a computerised database on export control licenses issued and denied over the past few years, in addition to a number of international briefings and seminars. Lithuania has participated in an EU twinning project with Finland, dedicated to implementing the EU directives on firearms and explosives, and established a dialogue with the Swedish National Inspectorate of Strategic Goods on end-use verification measures.[59] However, a number of NGOs still consider that insufficient attention was given to the export control systems and anti-trafficking measures of those states acceding to the EU in 2004.[60]

Of course, due to their very nature, combating illicit trafficking and preventing the diversion of arms and strategic goods to the international illicit arms trade requires multi-lateral co-operation and degrees of transparency. International non-proliferation regimes have been established to more effectively counter proliferation by providing forums for information exchanges on materials, goods and dubious end users. Membership of such regimes has traditionally been reserved for states that house manufacturers and suppliers of certain controlled goods and materials. Therefore, the Baltic States did not appear to have sufficient grounds on which to join these regimes. Yet, they are challenging the twentieth-century non-proliferation regimes to reform to meet the challenges of the twenty-first century, and include them amongst their number, with some success. For example, Estonia and Lithuania were admitted to the Nuclear Suppliers Group in May 2004.

While the Baltic States already co-operate and exchange information with members of these regimes, for example through Baltic Sea Region and EU structures, this is insufficient to ensure that the Baltic States can effectively prevent dangerous goods and materials being delivered or diverted to undesirable end users. Small states have limited human, financial and intelligence resources to monitor end users and end uses, and therefore co-operation with other states is essential for pre-shipment controls and post-shipment monitoring.[61] Regional co-operation forums, such as the *ad hoc* Baltic/Nordic States meetings, provide an opportunity for information sharing to enhance controls and awareness of potential diversions. They also enable the forging of good personal relations, developing trust, goodwill and like mindedness. Raba argues that these are essential 'cornerstones' for effective information sharing relating to pre- and post-shipment controls on end users and trans-border co-operative actions and operations. Regional arrangements for exchanging information in relation to arms controls and trafficking offer a foundation to build on at the global level. For example, the EU has already successfully exported its Code of Conduct to associate states and beyond.

Concluding remarks

If assessed in terms of political rhetoric and legislation, the Baltic States could serve as 'models' for small European transit states with regard to their export, transit and import controls for military equipment, firearms and other dual-use goods. Estonian, Latvian and Lithuanian legislation stipulates that the EU Code of Conduct's eight criteria should be applied to exports, transits and imports of arms transfers, with various developments in the Code's operative provisions also being incorporated into national laws. However, the levels of transparency and accountability of the military and other state agencies involved in the process still need to be increased and exposed to enhanced parliamentary and public scrutiny.[62] It is, therefore, interesting to note that a number of media reports in Latvia and Lithuania have recently called for increased transparency in exports and imports of arms, and the threats posed by arms brokers.[63] Hopefully, this will lead to more pressure being put on governments to seriously consider the future application of the EU Code of Conduct.

In addition, greater efforts are still required to change the culture of the customs, border and law enforcement agencies to make officers aware that bribes are not a 'perk' of the job, but need to be eradicated. The EU has already recommended improved pay levels, better working conditions and the provision of resources for detecting and prosecuting corruption. By establishing and defining specific projects or groups to be responsible for combating trafficking and organised crime, lines of funding can be ensured, thereby facilitating the development of pockets of expertise that are cohesive and knowledgeable.[64] Of course, this will require breaking down the traditional divisions of law enforcement, border controls and state security services in these states. These divisions have to be softer, as information sharing and co-ordination are necessary if arms controls and anti-trafficking operations are to be effective. Many of the intercepted diversions noted above were the results of co-ordinated and inter-agency actions. Finnish border management practices have been the subject of considerable praise and lauded as 'best practice' for the enlarged EU–Russian borders, and are worthy of further exploration by the Baltic States. Of course, the development of an EU Border Corps could also have a significant impact in this sphere.

One of the most challenging suggestions calls for far more than political rhetoric and legislating: a Baltic State should instigate a test case against an unscrupulous arms broker or smuggler, based on their newly improved national legislation. This may be particularly difficult, as it requires the discovery of an attempted diversion or smuggled shipment and a considerable amount of political will to bring to trial and hear the testimonies of individuals who could implicate a number of government officials.

On the international level, the Baltic States should continue to challenge traditional non-proliferation regimes and models and support regional and global efforts to combat illicit arms trafficking and diversions. For example, they 'should actively support a process to develop a legally binding international arms trade treaty', currently being proposed by a number of international NGOs.[65] They are pushing for a global arms trade framework, which would require commitments to greater transparency and accountability, the licensing of overseas arms production, the registration and monitoring of arms brokers and brokering-related services, better stockpile management and destruction programmes, clearer and more stringent transit and trans-shipment controls and improved mechanisms for monitoring end use.[66]

Finally, a role could be found for the Baltic States to explore the possibilities of building 'trust' and 'a sense of like-mindedness', through information exchanges on export controls and combating illicit trafficking, with their neighbours to the east. The Baltic States have already co-operated with Russian anti-organised crime units during the past decade, through bi- and multi-lateral forums, such as the Baltic Sea Task Force on Organised Crime. Therefore, it is not unreasonable to expect enhanced co-operation along the EU–Russian border. Kaliningrad offers itself as a site for enhanced co-operation, and has already served as a location for joint operations between Russian and neighbouring border, customs and law enforcement agencies to combat the trafficking of stolen cars. Significant political and legislative markers have been laid down by the Baltic States with regard to curbing arms proliferation and illicit trafficking. It remains to be seen whether they can effectively meet these high standards.

Notes

1. Owen Greene, 'Examining international responses to illicit arms trafficking', *Crime, Law and Social Change*, 33 (2000), p. 152.
2. Mark Phythian, 'The illicit arms trade: Cold War and post-Cold War', *Crime, Law and Social Change*, 33 (2000), p. 18.
3. See Lora Lumpe (ed.), *Running Guns: The Global Black Market in Small Arms* (London: Zed Books, 2000); Andrew J. Pierre (ed.), *Cascade of Arms: Managing Conventional Weapons Proliferation* (Washington, DC: Brookings Institution Press, 1997).
4. See: 'Emerging issue: transit and transshipment controls', *NIS Export Control Observer*, 4, (2003), p. 18.
5. Phythian, 'The illicit arms trade', p. 21.
6. *Undermining Global Security: The European Union's Arms Exports* (London: Amnesty International, 2004), p. 93.
7. Paul Holtom, 'The gatekeeper "hinge" concept and the promotion of Estonian, Latvian and Lithuanian new/postmodern security agendas', in David J. Smith (ed.), *The Baltic States and Their Region: New Europe or Old?* (Amsterdam/New York: Rodopi, 2005), pp. 292–312.
8. Emanuela-Chiara Gillard, 'What's legal? What's illegal?', in Lumpe (ed.), *Running Guns*, p. 27.
9. Quoted in Pieter D Wezeman, *Conflicts and Transfers of Small Arms* (Stockholm: SIPRI, 2003), pp. 6–7.
10. *Report of the Panel of Government Experts on Small Arms* (New York: UN, 1997), para. 51.
11. Michael T. Klare, 'The subterranean arms trade: black market sales, covert operations and ethnic warfare', in Pierre (ed.), *Cascade of Arms*, pp. 43–7.
12. Ibid., pp. 52–4; Greene, 'Examining international responses', p. 154.
13. Nicholas Marsh, 'Two sides of the same coin? The legal and illegal trade in small arms', *The Brown Journal of World Affairs*, 9:1 (2002), pp. 221–5.
14. Kathis Austin, 'Illicit arms brokers: aiding and abetting atrocities', *The Brown Journal of World Affairs*, 9:11 (2002), p. 205.

15 Marsh, 'Two sides of the same coin?', pp. 221–3; Lucy Mathiak and Lora Lumpe, 'Government gun-running to guerrillas', in Lumpe (ed.), *Running Guns*, pp. 55–80.
16 Brian Wood and Johan Peleman, 'Making the deal and moving the goods: the role of brokers and shippers', in Lumpe (ed.), *Running Guns*, p. 130.
17 See Ian Davis (*et al.*), Organised Crime, Corruption and Illicit Arms Trafficking in an Enlarged EU: Challenges and Perspectives (London: Saferworld, 2001).
18 Anton Bebler, 'Corruption among security personnel in Central and Eastern Europe', *Journal of Communist Studies and Transition Politics*, 17:1 (2001), pp. 129–45.
19 Aaron Karp, 'Small arms: back to the future', *The Brown Journal of World Affairs*, 9:1 (2002), pp. 179–80.
20 Sarah Meek, 'Combating arms trafficking: progress and prospects', in Lumpe (ed.), *Running Guns*, p. 186.
21 For example, the sub-regional Economic Community of West African States (ECOWAS) has been particularly active in this sphere. For details, see: Alhaji Bah, 'Implementing the ECOWAS Small Arms Moratorium in post-war Sierra Leone', Project Ploughshares Working Paper, 4:1 (May 2004).
22 Pertti Joenniemi, 'Prologue: towards post-modern arms control?', in Pertti Joenniemi (ed.), *Confidence-Building and Arms Control: Challenges around the Baltic Rim* (Aland: The Aland Islands Peace Institute, 1999), pp. 127–46.
23 'Security-related export controls', http://ue.eu.int/cms3_fo/showpage.asp?id=408& lang=en&mode=g.
24 *Fourth Annual Report on EU Arms Exports* (Brussels, 2002).
25 *Taking Control: The Case for a more Effective European Union Code of Conduct on Arms Exports* (London: Saferworld, 2004), p. 2.
26 'Essentially identical transfers' refer to instances where the contents of two proposed transfers are not the same, but are virtually the same. This becomes an issue when an export licence application for one shipment of military equipment is denied, but an 'essentially identical' shipment is granted an export licence.
27 See, for example, Maria Haug (*et al.*), 'Shining a light on small arms exports: the record of state transparency', *The Small Arms Survey and Norwegian Initiative on Small Arms Transfers*, 4 (2002).
28 Sibylle Bauer, 'The EU Code of Conduct on Arms Exports – enhancing the accountability of arms export policies?', *European Security*, 12:3–4 (2003), pp. 129–47.
29 See, for example, Davis (*et al.*), *Organised Crime*.
30 This issue has been attracting more attention since 2001, with the *Sixth Annual Report on EU Arms Exports* (Brussels, 2004) stating that technical and practical assistance will be rendered if requested.
31 David Brown, 'Defending the fortress? Assessing the European Union's response to trafficking', *European Security*, 13:1–2 (2003), pp. 95–116.
32 For example see: John Berryman, 'Russia and the illicit arms trade', *Crime, Law and Social Change*, 33 (2000), pp. 85–104; Paddy Rawlinson, 'Russian organised crime and the Baltic States: assessing the threat', ESRC 'One Europe or several', Programme Working Paper, 38:1 (2001); Ernesto U. Savona, 'Illicit trafficking in arms, nuclear material, people and motor vehicles: the most important things we have learnt and priorities for future study and research', Transcrime Working Paper, 23 (1998).
33 Council of Europe, *Organised Crime Situation Report 2001* (Strasbourg, 2002), pp. 35–6.
34 See *The Baltic Times* 171 (19 August 1999), http://archives.baltictimes.com/.
35 For more details on these cases see Paul Holtom, *Arms Transit Trade in the Baltic Region* (London: Saferworld, 2003), pp. 30–2.
36 Ibid., pp. 64–8.
37 'Arms trade, human rights, and European Union enlargement: the record of candidate countries', Human Rights Watch Briefing Paper (2002), http://www.hrw.org/backgrounder/arms/eu_briefing.htm.

38 Claes G. Alvstam and Alf Brodin, 'An introduction to Russian transit trade', in Alf Brodin (ed.), *Russian Transit Trade in the Baltic Sea Region* (Centre for European Research, Goteborg University, 2002), p. 25.
39 Hong Kong and Singapore were singled out for attention in this regard. 'Emerging issue: Transit and transshipment controls', *NIS Export Control Observer*, 4 (2003), p. 18.
40 Phythian, 'The illicit arms trade', p. 21.
41 Police in Finland and Estonia have identified twenty-three people involved in arms smuggling, with ex-Soviet arms moving from east to west and modern arms moving from west to east, see: Mika Junninen and Kauko Aromaa, 'Crime across the border Finnish professional criminals taking advantage of Estonian crime opportunities', in Petrus C. van Duyne et al. (eds), *Cross-border Crime in a changing Europe* (New York: Nova Science, 2001), pp. 98–9.
42 Holtom, *Arms Transit Trade in the Baltic Region*, pp. 41–2.
43 See Rawlinson, *Russian Organised Crime and the Baltic States*.
44 Ingmar Oldberg, 'The emergence of a regional identity in the Kaliningrad oblast', *Cooperation and Conflict*, 35:3 (2000), pp. 11–12.
45 *Communication from the Commission to the Council: The EU and Kaliningrad*, (Brussels, 2001). The Communication did not explicitly mention arms trafficking.
46 Steven J. Main, 'Kaliningrad 1997', Conflict Studies Research Centre Paper, 30 (May 1997), p. 12; Mark Galeotti, 'Russia's criminal army', *Jane's Intelligence Review*, 11:6 (1999), pp. 8–10; Mark Galeotti, 'The challenge of "soft security": crime, corruption and chaos', in Andrew Cottey and Derek Averre (eds), *New Security Challenges in Postcommunist Europe: Securing Europe's East* (Manchester: Manchester University Press, 2002), pp. 151–71.
47 Berryman, 'Russia and the illicit arms trade', p. 93.
48 See Holtom, *Arms Transit Trade in the Baltic Region*, pp. 78–80.
49 Galeotti, 'Russia's criminal army', pp. 8–10; Galeotti, 'The challenge of "soft security"', pp. 151–71.
50 Amongst these discoveries were a number of arms produced outside Russia.
51 Phythian, 'The illicit arms trade', p. 2.
52 See Brian Wood and Johan Peleman, *The Arms Fixers: Controlling the Borders and Shipping Agents* (Oslo: International Peace Research Institute, 1999).
53 For further details, see http://europa.eu.int/pol/enlarg/index_en.htm.
54 For Estonia see: 'Strategic Goods Act of the Republic of Estonia', in force since 5 February 2004, www.upcw.org/docs/la_natimpleg/Estonia-StrategicGoodsAct-2004.pdf. For Latvia see: 'Law on Arms Circulation', in force since 1 January 2003; 'Law on the Circulation of Strategic Goods', in force since 1 May 2004 – www.iem.gov.lv. For Lithuania see: 'Law on Arms Circulation', in force since 1 January 2003; 'Law on the Circulation of Strategic Goods', in force since 1 May 2004 – www.vrm.lt/index.php?id=124&lang=2.
55 *Group of States against Corruption: First Evaluation Round Evaluation Report on Estonia* (Strasbourg, GRECO, 2001); *Group of States Against Corruption: First Evaluation Round Evaluation Report on Latvia* (Strasbourg: GRECO, 2002); *Group of States against Corruption: First Evaluation round Evaluation Report on Lithuania* (Strasbourg: GRECO, 2002).
56 Ibid.
57 *Situation Report on Corruption in the Baltic Sea Region* (Warsaw: Task Force Clearing House on Corruption, 2002), p. 75.
58 David Wallis worked on the EU experiment to tackle corruption in the applicant state of Latvia from 1999–2001, and was reported to have expressed extreme disappointment at the lack of progress made in Latvia during his two years in the country according to 'EU report blasts Latvia on corruption', *RFE/RL Crime, Corruption and Terrorism Watch*, 2:2 (2002), www.rferl.org/corruptionwatch/2002/01/2-170102.asp.
59 *Undermining Global Security*, p. 94.
60 Ibid., p. 95.

61 Toomas Raba, 'Enhancing export controls in transit states', *The Monitor: International Perspectives in Nonproliferation*, 8:2 (2002), pp. 19–21.
62 Algiras Gricius and Kestutis Paulaskas, 'Democratic control over the armed forces in Lithuania', *Lithuanian Strategic Review* (2003), pp. 233–54.
63 See the Latvian Daily newspaper *Diena* for items carried on 24 February 2004, 10 June 2004 and 9 September 2004, www.diena.lv.
64 One can point to the experiences of NCIS in the UK or the Anti-Mafia Directorate (DIA) in Italy as examples of where national agencies have been created to combat the specific challenges posed by organised crime networks. See: Davis et al., *Organised Crime*, pp. 28–9.
65 *Undermining Global Security*, p. 98.
66 Ibid.

8

Russia–EU relations: opportunities for a security dialogue

Dmitry Polikanov

Despite the pomp of the 2003 St Petersburg summit and the breathtaking decision to start the elaboration of the 'roadmaps', Russia–EU relations have been stagnating in recent years. They were characterised by a significant lack of substance and a growing gap between Brussels and Moscow on a variety of issues, from the economic consequences of enlargement to the notorious Yukos case. Hence, the parties reached a certain impasse in their relations and had to consider the advisability of adapting their strategies to a new reality. Along with intra-EU problems, such as the complicated process of post-enlargement adaptation, the situation is further aggravated by the ambiguity of Russia's foreign policy during Vladimir Putin's second term. The praised predictability of Moscow gave way to conflicting signals and substantial contradictions between declarations and deeds. Russia–EU relations can be characterised by a classical four-cluster matrix (see table 8.1).

While the first two – declarative partnership and declarative negativism – seemingly have little impact on actual foreign policy, they do affect both elite and public opinion and, therefore, reinforce the growing skepticism about the possibility of good neighbourly relations with the EU. The last two reflect the struggle between pragmatism (driven by economic or political reasons) and Soviet-style suspicion of Western

Table 8.1 **Figures matrix of EU–Russia relations**

	Partnership	*Negativism*
Declarative	See Putin's statements on Russia as a major European power, willing to be part of the European family, sharing European values.	A campaign in the Russian media about the EU's meddling in Ukraine or support of the Belarussian opposition.
Real	See the developing energy dialogue. Some economic security matters are well tackled, e.g. customs compatibility with EU standards.	See the growing number of statements that the EU is over-regulated, highly bureaucratic and isolating Russia, ending the need for EU membership.[a]

Note: [a] European Forum, Legitimacy, Democracy and Sovereignty in the Post-Soviet Space (Moscow, June–July 2005), pp. 44–6.

bureaucrats or, more precisely, between two major groupings within the Presidential entourage, which have different views on Russia's future development.

The security dialogue is no exception, leaving one of the most prospective areas of Russian–EU co-operation a hostage of fierce bureaucratic rivalry. This is further complicated by the subdivision of the single security space into domestic and external 'routes', as reflected in the 2005 'roadmaps'. While this runs contrary to any coherent concept of comprehensive security – terrorism, for instance, is mentioned in both agreed documents[1] – it fits quite well with the existing division of labour between the Presidential administration and the Foreign Ministry. Assistant to the President, Victor Ivanov, has responsibility for domestic security, due to his 'siloviki' past, while Sergey Lavrov, Minister for Foreign Affairs, is responsible for external security and backs the other wing.

Unfortunately, during the decade of Russia–EU co-operation, security matters have tended not to be the major item on the agenda. The parties focused more on economic co-operation and on wider political issues. The Commission has always been keen on promoting European business interests (e.g. over fees for flying over Russia, with the Commission backing European airlines) and tended to be more focused on this agenda, believing it could achieve more than in other areas.[2] Moscow, for its part, preferred to concentrate on political and, hence, less tangible matters, which did not require substantial commitments. Moreover, this strategy facilitates Russia's efforts to consolidate its position in global decision-making and demonstrate its involvement in major world processes. Therefore, over twelve years after the signature of the framework PCA, there are few substantial achievements to be reported in the security sphere. What are the major reasons for that?

Stumbling blocks for the security dialogue

Firstly, one of the fundamental reasons is that the EU is not taken seriously as a security actor, with many in Moscow, both elite and public, still considering it an economic giant and security dwarf.[3] The EU is regarded as a player in strengthening world peace (according to 54 per cent of the sample), able to stimulate economic growth (49 per cent) and protect environmental standards (48 per cent).[4] However, only 22 per cent believe that Russia should co-operate with the EU in combating international terrorism and only 4 per cent favoured joint action against illegal migration.[5]

In fact, 2004 was an exceptional year in this respect, which nearly shook Russia's confidence in the EU's 'toothless' policy. The adoption of the ESS, combined with the launch of the European Constitution, a successful enlargement and intensified foreign policy activities in the former Soviet Union,[6] nearly forced Russia's elite to rethink the EU's importance in the security sphere. However, the referenda failure in France and the Netherlands in 2005 raised a new wave of criticism and skepticism about the CFSP's long-term effectiveness. As a result, many in the expert community returned to praising (or intimidating) the public with talk about possible NATO expansion as a security anchor, compensating for the EU's perceived impotence.[7]

Actually, Russians have reasons to think so. Before 2001, Russia was quite willing to promote ESDP development, believing that the EU could develop into a security actor. This was accounted for by the desire to counterweigh the EU (at that time, 'good partner') to the might of NATO (at that time, 'suspicious foe') and its enlargement eastwards. Moreover, Moscow was seeking new military–industrial contracts and could benefit from lending Europe airlift or satellites. These ambitions soon dissipated. The 'divide and rule' strategy turned out to be counterproductive and the EU did not manage to convince Moscow of its significance as a power center. By 2005, the Kremlin again viewed the EU as a 'toothless giant' and the ESDP as a 'paper project'. The prospects for substantial military–technical co-operation did not materialise, even though Russia and France, for instance, are advancing in aircraft production and have, since 2002, had the Council for Security Cooperation, which meets twice a year. And, after the withdrawal of Russian peacekeepers from the Balkans, Moscow had few further areas within which to co-operate with the EU and NATO or to test interoperability. There was no desire to let either organisation work in the post-Soviet space, nor any willingness to be engaged in Afghanistan or Iraq, let alone some far away places, such as the Democratic Republic of Congo (DRC). Russia has sent a military liaison officer to Brussels, dispatched some troops to the EU mission in BiH and contributed to the Darfur operation, yet this nearly completes the list of practical steps. Much more advanced interaction takes place at the bilateral level with France, Germany, Italy and even the UK, since most security matters still fall within the competence of national governments.

Secondly, there is an evident gap between the notions of security shared by the parties. The baseline for such dialogue is a common, or, at least, not contradictory, vision of primary challenges and threats. All major Russian conceptual documents were approved in the pre-September 11 era, before the global 'War on Terror' and the controversy in Iraq. As a result, the perceptions in the 2000 doctrines are partly outdated, containing thin touches of Cold War thinking. The Security Council is (at the time of writing) still preparing the National Security Strategy to replace the 2000 document. It was initiated after the Dubrovka events in Moscow in October 2002, so that Russia's doctrines might more adequately meet the challenges of the modern world. However, after nearly three years, only a draft is ready, which is being reviewed by selected experts. This lengthy process indicates bureaucratic inertia and the shortage of strategic thinking and new approaches.

Meanwhile, the effective National Security Concept, Military Doctrine, Foreign Policy Concept and even the 2003 White Book of the Defense Ministry are oriented towards repelling traditional hard security threats. The National Security Concept, in its international section, prioritises the following matters:

- the attempts of some states to diminish the role of international institutions, including the UN and OSCE;

- Russia's political, economic and military influence in the world continues to decrease;
- the strengthening of military blocs and NATO's eastward enlargement;
- foreign military bases and large contingents near the Russian borders;
- weakening integration processes in the CIS;
- escalation of conflicts near Russian borders and CIS external borders;
- territorial claims;
- continued resistance to 'Russia's strengthening its positions' in various parts of the world;
- WMD proliferation;
- terrorism, especially international terrorist activities;
- domination of some states in global information space and development of information warfare techniques.[8]

Among the military challenges mentioned, one can find:

- NATO and coalitions of the willing, expanding the scope of their operations beyond traditional areas of responsibility and without UN Security Council resolutions;
- the increasing technological gap in the military sphere, with Russia falling behind in the modernisation of its armed forces;
- intensified activities of the foreign intelligence services.

This is further consolidated by the 'border' problems:

- the economic, demographic and cultural expansion of neighbouring states;
- cross-border organised crime;
- activities of foreign terrorist organisations.[9]

The 2003 Actual Tasks of the Armed Forces[10] did not go far beyond the list of threats mentioned in the 2000 Military Doctrine; it seems that many of them were just copy-pasted from previous documents, with a changed list of priorities. This presents a good mixture of views within the Russian establishment and the eclectic vision of threats. On the one hand, the White Book recognises the growing role of WMD proliferation, terrorism, ethnic and religious radical movements, the drugs trade and organised crime. But it also refers to exclusion from military planning, the probability of global nuclear war or large-scale conventional wars with NATO or US-led coalitions. The 'western direction' and 'far eastern direction' are mentioned more specifically from the point of potential operations, which suggests that the General Staff is still looking for adversaries in the wrong places. Russia's obsession with maintaining nuclear might – nearly 50 per cent of the defense budget[11] – and building super-weapons[12] is further proof of the existence of this mentality. As part of the 2003 'Actual Tasks', the Defense Ministry claims a central role in co-ordinating the state's security activities. This reflects the political ambitions and bureaucratic resources of Sergey Ivanov, one of Putin's close friends.

Key external threats include the interference of foreign states and coalitions into internal affairs (lessons learned from Kosovo and Iraq), instability in neighbouring states (caused by the weakness of central governments) and the development of WMD programmes. There is a more assertive approach with respect to the deployment of foreign troops in the territory of friendly states, emphasising the need for UNSC sanction and also Russia's approval. More attention is paid to the protection of rights and freedoms of Russian citizens abroad. In recent years, this issue has become highly sensitive, exploited by the entire political spectrum. Its importance will further increase, with the situation in Latvia and Estonia normally promoted by Moscow in discussions with the EU. The military also added the threat of hampering Russia's access to strategically important communications, particularly the Caspian and Black Sea routes, as Russia is very sensitive about keeping control over these water basins and not opening them to NATO warships, for example.

The list of internal threats did not undergo significant changes. Violent change of the constitutional government and territorial integrity, the training and equipping of illegal armed formations and illicit arms trafficking were all considered priorities. This list was supplemented by the growing threat of organised crime, particularly when it threatens the security of a constituent entity of the Russian Federation (although it is particularly difficult to identify any quantitative threshold for that). Finally, the Russian military prepare to face cross-border threats, predicted to increase in importance. The cross-border challenges, external by nature and internal by form, include international terrorist structures on Russian territory, as well as their training and equipping on the territory of other states. Moscow also draws particular attention to cross-border crime, including smuggling, which requires military enforcement and support to the Border Guards (this runs counter to the EU approach). Hostile information activities and drug trafficking were moved to this sphere as well.

One cannot blame Russian analysts for shaping the general list of threats in this way, as many of them come from Russia's history and her traditional concerns. However, some security challenges are far less important and realistic than others, which are not at the top of the list and to which the armed forces and other security agencies should be ready to respond. There are clear discrepancies in the hierarchy of threats, as far as political leadership and the military are concerned. While the President and his team are more willing to focus on more realistic tasks, such as soft security matters (organised crime, corruption, drug trafficking)[13] and co-operative approaches, the military remain quite obstinate in promoting the hard security agenda (the Conventional Forces in Europe (CFE) Treaty is a good example). In the Russian case, it is not a matter of leadership (the President is the chief arbiter in security matters), but implementation, where executors try to impose their own agenda on decision-makers.

The EU prefers to deal with present-day threats (some of which are 'post-modernistic') and has a slightly different order of priorities. These are terrorism linked with violent religious extremism, WMD proliferation, regional conflicts, state failure associated with corruption and abuse of power, organised crime and overall privatisation of force.[14] While the list is nearly the same, the priorities are slightly shifted. It is also noteworthy that the parties do not mention demographic challenges, which are quite topical for both. As their populations are aging and decreasing, it will be more and more difficult to confront external pressures, including the regulation of migration and integration of newcomers. Russia, for instance, loses between 500,000 and 750,000 citizens per year, due to alcoholism, drugs, suicides, murders and emergency situations.[15]

What unites both is the US-prompted recognition of terrorism as a top-level priority. This is typical of both official Brussels and Moscow political and military circles and the Russian public. However, their concepts of terrorism are different. It is clear that, for Moscow, it is mostly confined to the Chechen issue and the threat of radical Islamism. The Kremlin is quite harsh in its suggested set of counter-measures, including the possibility of extraterritorial pre-emptive strikes and physical elimination of terrorists.[16] As for the international aspects, Russians believe that world terrorism is nourished by global competition for natural resources and expanding US influence in the world.[17] Thus, it is considered by Russia to be an inherent element of world rivalry necessary to resist Washington's hegemony. Meanwhile, the EU is more likely to view terrorism as a social phenomenon, caused by a number of complex reasons, above all resistance to modernisation and the growing global gap between rich and poor. Hence, terrorism is regarded as an asymmetric response to the missionary spread of democracy and the consumer society. These, in parallel, serve as shock absorbers, tools to prevent violence through sustainable and fair development. Many Europeans and their governments condemn any attempts at unilateral action with dubious legitimacy. Their view is that terrorism should be confronted with greater respect for human rights and democratic procedures.[18]

Another discrepancy in their security visions lies in the risk orientation. The EU admits that 'with the new threats, the first line of defense will often be abroad. The new threats are dynamic'.[19] Thus, it is keener on protection from external threats and, hence, projecting soft influence in its neighborhood, to ensure its overall stability. The EU, as with any technocratic institution, is trying to achieve this goal via integration. Enlargement required internal attention and was driven from inside (economy) but had external implications (partly performing the aforementioned soft security task). As a matter of fact, the EU's dominating strategy in recent years has not been confined to maintaining the 'Bastion of Europe', but rather wrapping the world with a cobweb of multilateral institutions, cultural and economic links and various legal regimes, ensuring greater engagement with the potential *enfants terribles*. The most eloquent examples are the Balkans, China, Iran or even the US, with its sense of transatlantic solidarity.

Russia is acting more like a snail, looking inwards. It fears that the Russian state may well collapse, the worst manifestation of which is terrorism connected with separatism, notably in the Caucasus.[20] Another challenge is the lack of concord within the ruling elite and clashes among the power groupings around the President. They are normally denied,[21] but as 2008 is approaching – a crucial year of Presidential elections, when, under the Constitution, Vladimir Putin has no more right to stay in power and has to think of a successor – they will intensify.[22] Finally, Moscow is obsessed with the idea of promoting stability at any price, above all through further centralisation of power and the prevention of any 'velvet revolution' scenario. This results in the consolidation of a revised version of the 'Iron Curtain', as seen in the 'anti-orange' preparations of the administration. Pressure on NGOs and their external donors is another illustration, with Russian officials obsessed with the idea that NGOs should avoid politicisation or receive money for political activities, even though politicisation may mean little more than criticism of the practices of the authorities. This 'Iron Curtain' approach is supported by the increasing isolationism of the Russian public.

Such an isolationist mood and the syndrome of the besieged fortress run counter even to some Kremlin initiatives undertaken in the former Soviet Union area. Polls indicate that 51 per cent of respondents would like to live in their own country rather than in any alliance – be it CIS, Single Economic Space (SES) or the EU. Russians tend to be totally indifferent to major conflicts in adjacent territories. They prefer a policy of non-interference, whether towards Abkhazia, South Ossetia, Transdniestria or any of the 'velvet' republics. They oppose most of the economic measures envisaged within the SES of Russia, Ukraine, Belarus and Kazakhstan.[23]

Even the potentially dangerous regions are defined differently. In terms of *realpolitik*, Moscow is more concerned about Central Asia and the Caucasus, along with some distant threat of possible Chinese 'soft occupation' or outright military clashes with their eastern neighbour. Suspicion of the 'genuine intentions' of the West[24] does not help promote co-operation, but can rather be considered as a risk, mainly to the current political regime, rather than a threat to the state as a whole. At the same time, for the EU, the eastern neighbourhood is an important, but not a crucial element, of the security architecture. Within the logic of enlargement, the stability of the 'new neighbours' was important to prevent any massive exodus of refugees, environmental catastrophes or existence of 'gray zones', which encourage smuggling, drug trafficking and organised crime. However, now that the 2004 enlargement process has been completed, it is time that Brussels turned its face to more hazardous regions, which have always been a higher priority for security professionals. The EU should be and is preoccupied with the Middle East, North Africa and even Sub-Saharan Africa – all of which represent real challenges, compared with remote areas of Central Asia or 'civilised' Eastern Europe. After all, when it comes to China or the Afghan drug trade, the EU has Russia, Turkey or Ukraine as buffer zones to mitigate the damage. With all the neighbours living across the Mediterranean, there are no such geopolitical filters.

Thirdly, common security should be based on common values and philosophy. These are also lacking. Moreover, there is a certain gap within Russia, between the declarative aspirations of the President and public sentiments. During his first and second terms, Putin has repeatedly emphasized Russia's belonging to the common European legacy. In 2001, he told the German Bundestag that 'Russia is a friendly European country'.[25] By late 2003, it became clear that the Russian–Western partnership had reached a certain threshold that required qualitative changes, including the acceptance of European values and substantial transformation of the society. As a result, Russia stopped at the phase of mutually beneficial and pragmatic co-operation and did not want to move further. This was camouflaged by the proclamations of Russia's 'self-sufficiency' in defense and security issues, as well as mocking about some EU regulations and 'double standards'.

The wave of Western criticism after the 2004 Beslan tragedy and notorious elections in Ukraine has pushed the President back onto the European course, to prevent the emergence of 'new dividing lines' on the continent. In his 2005 address to the Federal Assembly, he eloquently pointed out that 'above all, Russia was, is and certainly will be the largest European nation. The ideals of freedom, human rights, justice and democracy gained through suffering and hard-won by the European culture have been the determining value reference point for our society.'[26] This idea was further developed during the Victory Day celebrations and at the 2005 Russia–EU summit.

Do the elite share the President's ideals in this respect? One would say 'hardly'. The Russian military and security officers are difficult partners for the EU in negotiations and are quite tough in their estimates of the situation. As such, they have learned how to circumvent Presidential decisions. Additionally, their bureaucratic culture is totally different from approaches typical of multilateral institutions, with their practice of consensus, compromises, long debate and ability to come to terms. The politicians, who mostly believe in Russia's 'special mission in the world' and the necessity of restoring Great Power status, are also far from sharing 'common values' with Europe.

Will the population share this rapprochement? One notices a growing split among the Russians. While 40 per cent of respondents are ready to back political forces standing for Russia's quick integration into the West, 46 per cent assume that there is no need to hurry.[27] Following Western criticism of Russia's response to the Beslan attack and Putin's programme of strengthening the 'power vertical', by making the system more centralised, the response is almost the same – 37 per cent believe the criticism to be fair, while 46 per cent do not.[28] Other polls indicate that the Russian public's vision of democracy, their understanding of security – and of the means to meet these – their idea of corruption and law abidance, all differ substantially from European concepts. Evidently, some of the differences are the product of stereotypes and myths. However, it is difficult to deny that elements of the Russian armed forces and the police are, to a large extent, corrupt[29] and have some 'specific' notion of human rights, which does not easily facilitate interaction with their European colleagues.

Fourthly, both parties are so obsessed with their internal processes that they have no time for getting closer on external issues and ensuring further rapprochement. While Moscow has to solve many domestic problems, including the economic slowdown and public unrest, the EU faces a deep inner crisis connected with the competition of the French and UK models of the future,[30] the need to keep to enlargement promises and to push forward the constitutional process. Obviously, under these circumstances, given the absence of any common Russia–EU strategy in the security sphere, Moscow and Brussels can hardly be expected to focus vigorously on security issues. This is why many experts are calling for the adoption of a comprehensive document[31] and for the launching of negotiations on the new framework agreement by 2007, when the current PCA expires, a move implicitly supported by President Putin.[32]

Fifthly, there are numerous technical issues preventing the parties from deepening interaction. Russia, for example, lacks co-ordination and the Foreign Ministry not only fails, but does not want to play such a role.[33] Unlike in Ukraine or Moldova, there is no specially designated officer with ministerial powers who would take responsibility for co-ordination. It is a positive sign that the Presidential Administration has taken the lead and Sergey Yastrzhembsky, as well as Victor Ivanov, are trying to become contact points. There is even a department for EU relations within one directorate, but its status is low. However, there is still much to be done to ensure that the structure of EU co-operation is streamlined. The Commission faces a similar problem, carrying out the arduous task of enhancing the coherent position of various member states, who often have totally different views on EU–Russia relations (e.g. 'old Europe' v. 'new Europe').[34] New EU members remember the Soviet legacy and are suspicious of Russia. They possess many unresolved problems with Moscow, including Latvia and Estonia over borders and the Russian-speaking population, or Poland over the North European Gas Pipeline. Their approaches differ from those of large states, such as Germany, France or Italy, which seem to take balanced or even more pro-Russian positions.

The poor state of the Russian armed and security forces, which are permanently under-financed or suffer from financial abuses, is also worth mentioning. The shortage of equipment and relevant IT skills also impedes interoperability and co-operation. For example, even if Russia has signed the readmission agreement with the EU, it is practically impossible to ensure strong border controls in the vast and sparsely populated areas of Central Asia.

Russia–EU: ongoing activities in the security sphere

Taking all of this into account, one may regretfully assume that any co-operation is impossible. Yet, this is not completely true. The rapprochement is declarative, the interaction is slow and low scale, but it takes place. A network of regular meetings has been established, at the level of the relatively newly born Permanent Partnership Council, or ambassadorial and expert discussions. Efforts to persuade Moscow to join various international legal regimes are undertaken and, hence, the harmonisation of legislature is ensured. As far as JHA is concerned, the 2003 Europol agreement seems extremely important, even though information sharing could be more efficient and extradition practices are yet to be improved on both sides. Seminars and exchange of experts are organised, as provided for in the EU Common Strategy on Russia[35] and the Technical Aid to the Commonwealth of Independent States (TACIS) framework.

Finally, in May 2005, the parties have agreed on the 'roadmaps', three years after the ideas of closer co-operation and common spaces were first proclaimed. According to the parties, these documents were the outcome of extremely tough negotiations[36] and were, by definition, a compromise. Most experts criticised the documents for their lack of specific commitments,[37] which were initially envisaged to fill the 'roadmaps' with concrete projects, in order to build up common spaces. They should serve as a provisional framework for developing a new PCA. Two of the roadmaps are devoted to security issues and, in general, they contain quite accurate definitions of the problems, although they are based on ideal patterns of smooth co-operation among the parties.

Within the JHA Roadmap, they managed, at least on paper, to formulate 'common values' (which does not necessarily mean that Russia will not follow them in its own 'special way' as usual, as the concept of truly Russian 'sovereign democracy' becomes more and more popular). They agreed to maintain the balance between security and freedom. The latter implied the commitment on further talks concerning the no-visa regime for Russian citizens and simultaneous conclusion of the readmission agreement. Moscow has already reached facilitated travel regimes with Germany, France and Italy and is seeking the same pledge from the EU, in exchange for strengthening Russia's southern borders. Most of the bilateral plans in this sphere are quite feasible, even though they are not free from sudden interruptions and even false orientations (i.e. protecting Russia's western borders and developing a 'security buffer' there, as was decided in October 2005, instead of thinking about the less manageable and more vulnerable southern frontiers of the Russian Federation). A good example of aforementioned interruptions was when Russia denounced its border treaty with Estonia and showed an unwillingness to conclude a similar treaty with Latvia, over the situation of the Russian-speaking population in both countries and its irritation over their smooth membership of NATO.

Improvements on the Russia–EU border may consolidate dividing lines, rather than combat illegal migration. After all, Russia is said to have the best border with Finland, but an open steppe with Kazakhstan. The parties have failed to fix any specific commitments stipulating, for example, EU technical and financial assistance in equipping Russia's frontiers with Asia. Such assistance could be a leap forward, if the EU was really interested in building a shield against illegal immigrants and drug trafficking. Training programmes for border guards and exchange of information on migration are necessary, but cannot substitute for the more decisive steps of tightening controls. One cannot expect a miracle, but, if more input is received from the EU, the situation will slowly change, with fewer black holes on the Russian southern and eastern borders. Some hopes can be rested on biometric passports, which the Russian Federation is eager to introduce, probably faster than some EU members, but this process may face substantial financial and organisational difficulties. Exchange of information in this sphere is impeded by Russia's ratification of the Council of Europe Convention on personal data protection only in late 2005.[38]

In the sphere of domestic security, the parties promised to counter terrorism and all forms of organised crime. A positive sign is the desire to boost joint work on enhancing the international legal norms, which should be further stimulated after the 2005 attacks on the London underground. As with other provisions, their chances of full implementation seem quite dubious. As for their joint obsession with combating illegal terrorist financing, one may note that the amount of finance required for the organisation of attacks in today's world is normally extremely low. Moreover, despite titanic efforts in this area, aimed at filtering millions of financial transactions, there are few cases reaching the court or ending up with the real freezing of assets. Russia is no exception in this respect. The 2005 explosions in London have indicated, once again, that European terrorism has certain socio-cultural roots and requires further actions to ensure Muslim integration in Western society. Russia, with its experience of peaceful coexistence with Islam (about 20 per cent of the population are Muslims and radical Wahhabis in the Caucasus are an exception rather than a rule in the Russian tradition) could help the EU. An exchange of experience in this sphere would be more beneficial than costly searches for small money transfers. Another disputable issue is extradition, which, in the Russia–EU case as a rule, stumbles over the aforementioned difference in the visions of terrorism. The most notorious example is the case of Akhmed Zakaev, who keeps travelling around Europe.

As far as organised crime is concerned, it is good that the parties are trying to concentrate on interoperability issues, including information and communication technologies and invitations to 'participate in bilateral law enforcement operations'.[39] A matter of particular importance is drug trafficking, the bulk of which comes from Afghanistan. Russia and the EU not only discuss blocking the transportation routes, but would also like to deal with prevention issues, such as co-operation in treating drug addicts. The same relates to illicit human trafficking, which also requires some very specific measures. Most of the 'roadmap's steps are likely to be realised, bearing in mind the significance of the issues and the political will of the parties. However, such zeal may be hampered by the Russian police's lack of skills, including languages, as well as high levels of corruption. The document is weak in combating corruption, suggesting mainly legislative measures.

It will be even more difficult to make the Russian judicial system transparent, independent and more efficient. Seminars and training programmes may be an incentive, but, upon returning to everyday Russian practice, judges and officers of the Prosecutor General will hardly follow the EU's advice, since the circumstances will force them to behave differently. However controversial were the cases of Mikhail Khodorkovsky and Yukos, it was a success in terms of demonstrating the incompetence and weak points of the Russian system of selective justice. The growing number of cases won by Russian citizens in the ECHR is further proof.

The roadmap for external security is full of diplomatic stock phrases, which do not reflect reality. The parties start by reiterating their commitment to multilateral regimes, including the UN, the OSCE and the Council of Europe. The UN is in deep crisis and failed to rescue itself during the September 2005 General Assembly session, while the other two enjoy little or no respect in Moscow. The Kremlin called the OSCE obsolete,[40] blocking its decisions,[41] while it views the Council of Europe as a platform for empty discussions, even suggesting reducing its contribution to the Council's budget.[42] The parties' declared desire to intensify their dialogue in the international arena, especially in the regions adjacent to Russia–EU borders, including respect for democratic principles and human rights, runs counter to Moscow's fear of 'velvet revolutions'. As such, it is quite difficult to expect breakthroughs in this sphere, as some influential forces in Moscow continue to look at the ex-USSR space as an area for 'zero sum' games. Russia will, one day, have to accept the presence of international forces in Moldova, Georgia or Nagorny Karabakh, but, so far, Moscow opposes them. Despite its allegedly friendly approach to the Yushchenko plan for a peaceful settlement in Transdniestria, Russia does not demonstrate significant rapprochement with Moldova.[43]

More promising in this respect is the co-operation in the non-proliferation sphere. Both parties have a genuine interest in strengthening existing regimes, such as the Non-Proliferation Treaty (NPT), the IAEA and export controls, since, at the current stage of development of missile technologies in potentially dangerous countries (India, Pakistan, Iran or North Korea), Moscow and Brussels may become the first casualties, due to accidental launches or radiological terrorism. Their policy of soft pressure and bargaining has already born some fruit with respect to the Tehran nuclear programmes. Besides, both parties would like to restrain the arms race in outer space, notably US efforts to deploy laser weapons and some aggressive elements of the National Missile Defense system. If they fail to resist this, their falling behind US capabilities may become non-recoverable. Military-to-military contacts are important, especially as the EU has established the European Defense Agency and turned to the concept of rapidly deployable Battlegroups.[44] However, here again the co-operation will be quite modest, concentrating on small-scale steps, such as 'naval forces co-operation in the sphere of navigation and hydrography, underwater exploration with a view of ensuring navigation safety, hydrometeorology and early warning of disasters, co-operation of the EU Satellite Center with Russia'.[45]

Conclusions

Thus, one may conclude that Russia–EU co-operation in the security sphere will continue to be mostly declarative and substantially dependent on the political climate. It will be limited to intense consultations on various international and regional issues, but will hardly go beyond the talking shop. Russia is likely to apply the same pattern that it uses with NATO. Imitation of activities makes both partners happy, but is not really helpful in times of real crises or in response to emerging challenges.

Much more active contacts can be expected at the bilateral level, unless the change of generations of leaders in France, Germany, Italy and eventually the UK smashes the well-established inter-personal dialogue between 'friend Vladimir' and his counterparts. After all, the Russia–EU security dialogue is not different from other areas of the interaction and is not free from the strategic impediments of a higher and more fundamental character. Unless these contradictions are resolved, one cannot expect deepening and further rapprochement between the parties, who are yet to decide whether they are true partners. The situation is aggravated by the fact that security issues are mostly decided on the margins (except visa matters), while major battles go on around economics. Enlargement brings the EU closer to the Russian borders, but does not eliminate the trust problem. On the contrary, there are fears of further isolation of Russia by the EU.[46]

However, this should not be a reason for pessimism. The Russia–EU security dialogue should not pose ambitious goals; the parties should rather specify some small-scale projects and start their implementation. This could be EU assistance in equipping the Russian southern border, joint training for police forces (not simple exchanges, which normally imply flows of specialists in the European direction), or the elaboration of common databases, in order to facilitate information flows. Such small steps may eventually lead to the Marxist formula of 'quantity transformed into quality', which sounds familiar to the ears of the Russian bureaucrats. Combined with EU efforts to promote cultural and educational exchanges, targeted at bringing up a new generation of Russians, Russia–EU interaction in the security sphere may eventually turn into a real dialogue.

Notes

1. See the texts of Russia–EU roadmaps, approved on 10 May 2005, http://europa.eu.int/comm/external_relations/russia/summit_05_05/finalroadmaps.pdf.
2. Dmitry Suslov, 'Za Evropu gosudarstv, a ne burokratii', *Nezavisimaya Gazeta* (7 July 2005).
3. Dmitry Polikanow, 'Europäische Sicherheitspolitik als Herausforderung für Russland', in Raimund Krämer and Hans Arnold (eds), *Sicherheit für das größere Europa: Politische Optionen im globalen Spannungsfeld* (Bonn, Dietz, 2002).
4. *Kak my dumali v 2004 godu: Rossiya na pereputye* (Moscow, EKSMO-Algoritm, 2005), p. 306.
5. Ibid., p. 305.
6. For example, the appointment of the EU Special Representative for the South Caucasus, greater involvement in the settlement of the Transdniestrian conflict and intense shuttle diplomacy during the 2004 political crisis in Ukraine.
7. Nikolai Poroskov, 'V poiskah protivnika', *Vremya Novostei* (14 July 2005).
8. *Concept of National Security of the Russian Federation: Approved by Presidential Decree No. 24* (Moscow, January 2000), www.fas.org/nuke/guide/russia/doctrine/gazeta012400.htm.
9. Ibid.
10. *Aktualnye zadachi vooruzhennykh sil Rossiiskoi Federatsii* (Moscow, 2 October 2003).
11. About 50 per cent of Russian defense contracts (out of 187bn rubles) will be spent on maintenance and upgrading of the nuclear triad. *RIA Novosti* (30 December 2004).
12. The Russian President and the military keep talking about secret supersonic missiles, capable of penetrating any missile defense system, allegedly operational in the foreseeable future. It is clear, however, that only the US is progressing in this area. See Dmitry Polikanov, 'Russia's Secret Weapon: Myth or Reality', *BASIC Reports*, 85 (March 2004).
13. They are also named as priorities in the Partnership and Cooperation Agreement Title VII and VIII.
14. *A Secure Europe in a Better World. European Security Strategy* (Brussels: European Union, 2003), pp. 5–6.
15. This should be compared with terrorist casualties, 852 people in 2003–04. Alexander Torshin, 'Den smerti i doroga zhizni', *Strategiya Rossii*, 6 (June 2005), p. 10.
16. For example, the assassination of Zelimkhan Yandarbiev in Qatar in February 2004 and Aslan Maskhadov in Chechnya in spring 2005. As of April 2005, 79 per cent of respondents supported 'preemptive strikes' for the physical elimination of terrorists and their bases abroad.
17. Viktor Levashov, 'Chuvstvuyut li sebya rossiyane v bezopasnosti?', *Monitoring obshchestvennogo mneniya: ekonomicheskie i sotsialnye peremeny*, 4 (October–December 2004), pp. 30–1.

18. *G-8 Statement on Counter-Terrorism* (London, July 2005), www.fco.gov.uk/Files/kfile/PostG8_Gleneagles_CounterTerrorism.pdf.
19. *A Secure Europe in a Better World*, p. 8.
20. Vladislav Surkov, speech 'Davat vlast "liberalnym druzyam" opasno i vredno dlya strany', on 17 May 2005, *Polit.ru* (12 July 2005), www.polit.ru.
21. Valery Fadeev, 'Sokhranit effektivnoe gosudarstvo v sushchestvuyushchikh granitsakh', Interview with Head of the Presidential Administration Dmitry Medvedev, *Expert* (4 April 2005).
22. Kaha Kahiani and Dmitry Slobodyanyuk, 'Dokole Putin budet terpet?', *Politichesky zhurnal*, 24 (4 July 2005), pp. 4–5.
23. According to Eurasian Monitor's third wave, conducted by VCIOM jointly with Ukraine, Belarus and Kazakhstan, the Russian public seem to oppose economic liberalisation. Between 43 and 45 per cent were opposed to the movement of goods and investments to and from Russia, while 71 per cent do not want businesses from neighboring states to buy Russian land and property.
24. Elena Ovcharenko, 'Zamestitel glavy administratsii presidenta RF Vladislav Surkov: Putin ukreplyaet gosudarstvo, a ne sebya', *Komsomolskaya Pravda* (29 September 2004).
25. Vladimir Putin, Speech to the German Parliament (25 September 2001), www.pegmusic.com/putin-in-germany.html.
26. Vladimir Putin, Presidential Address to the Federal Assembly of the Russian Federation (Moscow, April 2005), www.kremlin.ru/eng/speeches/2005/04/25/2031_type70029_87086.shtml.
27. VCIOM poll results, March 2004.
28. VCIOM poll results, October 2004.
29. See, for example, the comments of Prosecutor General Vladimir Ustinov on the work of police and other law enforcement agencies, *Interfax* (21 January 2005), www.interfax-news.com.
30. Ruslan Khestanov, 'Elektoralnaya revolutsia', *Politichesky zhurnal*, 24 (July 2005), p. 50.
31. Dmitry Danilov, 'Rossiya-ES: na puty k obshchemu prostranstvu bezopasnosti – ili na perepute', *Evropeiskaya bezopasnost: sobytia, otsenki, prognozy*, 12 (2004).
32. Dmitry Suslov, 'Koloniya Evropy ili ee chast', *Nezavisimaya Gazeta* (23 May 2005).
33. Katinka Barysch, *The EU and Russia: Strategic Partners or Squabbling Neighbours?* (London, Centre for European Reform, 2004), pp. 58–9.
34. Konstantin Kosachev, 'Sila malykh', *Nezavisimaya Gazeta* (15 July 2005).
35. *Common Strategy of the European Union of 4 June 1999 on Russia* (Brussels, June 1999).
36. *ITAR-TASS* (10 May 2005), www.itar-tass.com.
37. Dmitry Danilov, 'Dorozhnye karty vedushchie v nikuda', *Nezavisimaya Gazeta* (24 May 2005).
38. *Russia and the Enlarged European Union: The Arduous Path toward Rapprochement* (Russia in United Europe, Moscow, 2004), p. 51.
39. Ibid., p. 28.
40. 'Strany SNG v svoem zayavlenii "razgromili" deyatelnost OBSE', *Izvestia* (9 July 2004).
41. Natalia Ratiani, 'Rossiya predlozhit OBSE novuyu "dobavochnuyu stoimost"', *Izvestia* (7 December 2004).
42. *Polit.ru* (17 May 2005), www.polit.ru.
43. Alexei Makarkin, 'Geopoliticheskaya borba za Pridnestrovye vyshla na finishnuyu pryamuyu', *Nezavisimaya Gazeta* (19 July 2005).
44. IISS, *Europe: Soft Power, Hard Choices: Strategic Survey 2004–2005* (London: Routledge, 2005), p. 139.
45. For details on the Road Maps, see http://europa.eu.int/comm/external_relations/russia/summit_05_05/finalroadmaps.pdf.
46. European Forum, *Legitimacy, Democracy and Sovereignty in the Post-Soviet Space*, p. 46.

9

Russia–EU relations and the Chechen issue

Tracey C. German

Introduction

As the EU borders edge eastwards and progress is made in developing the CFSP, the EU has to focus on conflict resolution on its periphery, where the presence of undemocratic or unstable areas could pose a threat to its stability. A stable, democratic Russia is vital to European security, even more so post-enlargement. Javier Solana has described the development of a partnership with Russia as 'the most important, the most urgent and most challenging task that the EU faces at the beginning of the 21st century'.[1]

What is so important, urgent or challenging about developing a relationship with Russia, which, whilst still a key actor, both regionally and globally, is no longer a superpower? Russia is the EU's largest neighbour and, post-enlargement, they share a 1500km common border. Although the prospects of Russian membership are minimal, it is too large to ignore. For its part, Russia views a relationship with the EU as key to developing its role on the world stage. The relationship is mutually beneficial, with the EU serving as a major source of investment and trade for Russia, which has considerable potential for economic growth. The EU is Russia's principal trading partner, accounting for over half its total trade. Enlargement has only increased the EU's importance in this respect. In 2004, their total trade amounted to over €125bn, the bulk of which was Russian energy imports. The EU currently obtains 44 per cent of its oil and a quarter of its natural gas from Russia and the International Energy Agency (IEA) estimates that this will rise to 94 per cent and 81 per cent respectively within twenty-five years, as indigenous reserves dwindle.[2]

However, there is a major challenge in the development of a closer partnership – Chechnya. The protracted Chechen crisis has proved to be a significant benchmark in the development of Russian democracy.[3] It is crucial to an understanding of post-Soviet politics and the development of the Russian Federation, as well as its relations with other countries, notably Georgia.[4] It also affects the leadership's attitude towards democratic values, human rights and the rule of law, all of which are guiding principles of the EU. Thus, it could be expected that the well-documented violations of human rights, committed by both sides in Chechnya since 1994, would be a focus of the EU–Russia discourse. However, the Chechen conflict is not an area of specific dialogue between the EU and Russia, nor is it a key driver of the relationship. It only represents a very small component of the relationship, yet colours all aspects of interaction and remains a fundamental impediment to the development of a strategic partnership.

The two actors take very different approaches towards the Chechen issue, demonstrating the considerable gulf that remains between them. The EU continues to insist on a political resolution to the conflict, while Moscow believes that military action is the only solution, resenting any criticism of what it perceives to be an internal counter-terrorist operation. This resentment was underscored in a statement by then Foreign Minister Ivanov in 2000. Claiming that Russia was 'defending the borders of Europe against a barbaric offensive from international terrorism', he questioned the aim of those who 'wish to exploit our current problems in order to criticise Russia'.[5]

This chapter will explore the impact that the ongoing Chechen conflict has had on the evolution of the Russia–EU strategic partnership, investigating key periods of tension, which have tended to coincide with an escalation of events in Chechnya. The relationship can be traced with an analysis of when either the EU, or individual member states, have criticised Russian action, making Chechnya a 'political barometer' of relations.[6] This chapter will examine the approach of both the EU and its member states towards Russian actions and assess the efficacy of the approach it has taken to date, together with the impact of enlargement. What impact will the addition of ten new member states have on this lack of coherence? Is engagement always preferable to isolation? Should the EU have done more to enforce the guiding principles of the documents that form the basis of its relationship with Moscow? Furthermore, Russian actions in Chechnya have highlighted the lack of a coherent and consistent approach amongst EU member states towards the issue and Russia's democratic transition in general. Thus, what conclusions can be drawn about the development of CFSP and the EU's relations with non-member states?

Building a relationship

Post-Cold War EU–Russia relations got off to a tentative start, gradually gathering momentum as the decade progressed. During the 1990s, the key mechanisms that would provide a framework for the relationship were put into place: the PCA, the Common Strategy of the European Union on Russia (CSR) and the Medium-term Strategy for Development of Relations between the Russian Federation and the European Union (MTS). The PCA forms the core of the relationship, with its principal focus on trade and economic co-operation. It also asserts that the EU, its member states and Russia share 'common values', although it does not define what these common values are.[7] EU ratification of the PCA was delayed by the first Russian military operation in Chechnya in December 1994, triggering the first public crisis in relations and demonstrating that, whilst Chechnya may not be on the agenda as a specific item for discussion, it nevertheless impacts upon all aspects of the partnership. Signed on 24 June 1994, the PCA did not actually come into effect until 1 December 1997, after the signing of the 1996 Khasavyurt peace accords, which ended the first post-Soviet conflict between Moscow and Grozny.[8]

The Kremlin justified the military invasion on the basis of protecting 'the unity of Russia', stating that the longer the situation was allowed to continue, 'the more destructive an influence it has on stability in Russia'.[9] The EU supported the principle of Russia's territorial integrity, concerned about the prospect of its disintegration and the impact this could have on European security. It was also keen to provide support for Yeltsin's regime as it continued with the process of democratic transition. Whilst the EU supported Russia's territorial integrity, it sought to remind it of its PCA commitments and to persuade it to return to the negotiating table, consistently calling for a political resolution to the conflict and condemning human rights violations by both sides.[10] Such condemnations had little effect on the Russian military operation and merely served to underline the EU's lack of influence. In addition, the suspension of the implementation of the PCA was conducted in a very lackadaisical manner, further highlighting the EU's lack of resolve. Bilateral programmes remained in force and TACIS funds were not frozen. Thus, Moscow surmised that Chechnya was not a major obstacle to the development of closer relations, an assumption that was reinforced both by the adoption of a 1996 interim agreement, which enabled trade clauses to come into effect, and the continuation of bilateral relations with EU member states.

The lack of clear and decisive EU action at this early stage laid the foundations for persistent mutual misunderstanding and misperceptions. It also undermined the value of human rights in the relationship, emphasising the EU's ultimately pragmatic approach to Chechnya. Timmins has argued that Russian military intervention in Chechnya demonstrated the political limitations of the PCA as a way of influencing Russian behaviour.[11] It certainly demonstrated to EU member states that the PCA alone was insufficient to guarantee strategic guidance and flexibility of EU action. Thus, the CSR was born.[12]

The EU unveiled the CSR at the Cologne Summit in June 1999. The CSR was the EU's earliest attempt to articulate a common vision, as part of its embryonic CFSP, and Russia was the first state to receive such a strategy, highlighting its importance to the organisation. The EU's vision affirmed the necessity of a 'stable, democratic and prosperous Russia' for lasting European peace. It also welcomed 'Russia's return to its rightful place in the European family in a spirit of friendship, cooperation, fair accommodation of interests and on the foundations of shared values enshrined in the common heritage of European civilisation'.[13] Interestingly, the CSR referred to 'shared' as opposed to 'common values': the idealism of the PCA was gradually giving way to a more realistic approach. The CSR declared that one of its principal goals was the development of Russia as a stable, open and pluralistic democracy based on the rule of law and underpinning a prosperous market economy benefiting both Russia and the EU.

Russia's response was the 'Medium-Term Strategy for the Development of Relations between the Russian Federation and the European Union (2000–10)', presented at the

EU–Russia summit in October 1999. Unfortunately, this important document was overshadowed by the Chechen issue, which had risen to the top of the agenda once again with the renewal of Russia's military campaign. Primarily aimed at 'ensuring national interests and enhancing the role and image of Russia in Europe and in the world', the MTS emphasised that, 'as a world power situated on two continents, Russia should retain its freedom to determine and implement its domestic and foreign policies'.[14] There is also no mention of 'common' or even 'shared' values, so prominent in both the CSR and PCA. Rather, the MTS talked of 'common interests' and made it clear that Russia's approach to EU relations was based on pragmatic notions of national interest and gain, rather than adopting its guiding values. A wide gulf between the two was becoming very apparent.

Isolation, not partnership

Far from bringing them closer together and establishing a more in-depth dialogue, the CSR was published at a time when relations were at an all-time low, shaken by reverberations from the NATO operation against Serbia.[15] 1999 was a pivotal moment in Russia–EU relations, as the former found itself increasingly isolated, both as a result of tension over NATO's Kosovo campaign and the renewed military operation in Chechnya. Furthermore, the EU was increasingly preoccupied with enlargement issues, drawing up a constitutional treaty and developing its ESDP, as opposed to developing its strategic partnership with Russia. The beginning of Russia's counter-terrorist operation in Chechnya in the autumn of 1999 raised doubts within the EU about the development of Russia as a liberal democracy and also tested the EU's commitment to the CSR, with its proclamations of 'closer co-operation', 'shared democratic values' and 'strategic interest'.

The EU was much more vocal in its criticism of the Kremlin's decision to launch a second military operation, describing Russian actions as disproportionate and indiscriminate.[16] It declared that Russia's methods in Chechnya were incompatible with the principles of democracy, the rule of law and human rights. The Presidency Conclusions of the December 1999 Helsinki European Council included a separate Declaration on Chechnya, which condemned the military action, although it did not question Russia's right to preserve its territorial integrity or its right to combat terrorism. It stressed that Russia is considered to be a 'major partner for the European Union', but that it 'must live up to its obligations if the strategic partnership is to be developed. The European Union does not want Russia to isolate herself from Europe.'[17]

The declaration called upon Russia to end the bombing, to begin political negotiations with the Chechens and to allow humanitarian aid to be delivered. It also emphasised that Russian military action contradicted both its OSCE commitments and its obligations as a Council of Europe member, an organisation to which it had been admitted in 1996, after its request for membership was delayed by the 1994 invasion. The Council of Europe's Parliamentary Assembly adopted a resolution in

January 2000 that censured Russia for violating 'some of her most important obligations under both the European Convention on Human Rights and international humanitarian law, as well as the commitments she entered into upon accession to the Council of Europe'.[18] In addition, in April 2000, the Council of Europe suspended Russian's full voting rights and did not restore them until January 2001. Both organisations provide norms and values for Europe, which, as Emerson reasons, the EU regards as fundamental to its own system of values.[19] Thus, it felt duty-bound to censure apparent violations, particularly as Russia had so recently acceded to the Council of Europe.

Russian commentators were highly critical of what were perceived to be the West's double standards over Chechnya, saying that the EU had no moral or legal right to interfere in Russia's internal affairs, particularly after its support for the NATO bombing of Serbia. It was also pointed out that, while the EU had not supported Milosevic's determination to uphold the territorial integrity of Serbia–Montenegro and prevent the secession of Kosovo, it was taking the opposite position over Chechnya.[20] EU criticism was seen as an attempt to interfere in the domestic affairs of a sovereign state, rather than an attempt to uphold certain norms and values, and the Russian reaction accentuated the Kremlin's sensitivity to any such interference. Moscow was surprised by the lack of support it received from states it had considered 'key partners', notably France, Germany and Finland, who all advocated a severe approach in the light of events in Chechnya. The Chechen crisis has been described as the 'moment of truth' in Russia's relations with the EU, demonstrating that Russia had no allies in Europe. This led to questions being raised about the efficacy of Russia's European policy, one of the cornerstones of which had been the creation of a Paris–Berlin–Moscow axis to counteract US influence.[21]

As a result of the military operation, there were calls for a review of the CSR, the suspension of certain provisions within the PCA and for the limiting of TACIS funds in 2000 to 'priority areas', such as human rights, the rule of law and support for civil society. The EU General Affairs Council implemented limited sanctions in February 2000, but these were lifted four months later, despite there being no change in the Chechen situation, as the EU sought to cement good relations with the new Russian President, Vladimir Putin. A European Parliament report published later in the year on the implementation of the CSR (the Oostlander report) highlighted the minimal impact that these sanctions actually had. Noting that the EU had reacted to the conflict by drastically reducing TACIS aid to Russia and limiting it to projects promoting democratic values, as well as delaying a scientific and technological co-operation agreement, the report concluded that no ongoing projects had been disrupted and the partial freeze of aid had had little impact on Russian policy.[22] Once again, the EU was sending out mixed messages: it was highly critical of Russian action, but only implemented sanctions in a very half-hearted manner. The failure of sanctions led to the implementation of a 'twin-track' approach, whereby the EU continues to criticise human rights violations in Chechnya, whilst seeking to develop co-operation with Moscow, confident that engagement is more likely to enable it to influence Russian policy than isolation.

The Oostlander report also denounced the EU member states' lack of coherence and consistency towards the Chechen issue. While the EU was more vocal in its criticism of the renewed Russian intervention in Chechnya, it was not completely united and the beginning of the second operation once again highlighted the lack of a coherent approach by individual member states. In spite of the imposition of sanctions, individual leaders maintained bilateral relations. France and Germany were very critical of Russian action in the North Caucasus republic, whilst supporting Russia's territorial integrity. Together with Italy, they issued a declaration expressing concern about the deteriorating situation in Chechnya and the risk of the conflict escalating.[23] However, UK Prime Minister, Tony Blair, took a different approach, citing his belief that engagement was better than isolation, and was the first European leader to ring Putin and congratulate him on his March 2000 election victory. Blair arrived in Russia on an official visit shortly afterwards, swiftly followed by an invite from then German Chancellor, Gerhard Schröder, for Putin to visit Berlin. These actions indicated to Moscow that there was a lack of unity within the EU and that member states gave priority to the development of bilateral relations over a coherent European foreign policy. They also revealed weaknesses within the organisation itself.

Relations were less tense again by the summer of 2000, with the EU taking a more pragmatic attitude towards the Chechen issue. As Haukkala argues, the EU and its member states had concluded that the Chechen problem was not going to go away and, as there was little the EU could do to solve the problem, it was preferable to look at the bigger picture and build a constructive, co-operative relationship, rather than focus on one issue.[24] In addition, Putin's arrival had a positive impact on the partnership. He has sought to engage with the West, as part of a 'pragmatic' foreign policy that will enable Russia to once more become a leading player on the global stage.[25] The fifth EU–Russia summit, held in May 2000, was hailed as a success, shifting the focus from the Chechen conflict to developing economic ties and EU enlargement. Russia's prevailing view was that, in terms of Chechnya, EU leaders had decided to attempt to resolve the issue by economic means.[26] Moscow reiterated its desire to be a 'constructive, reliable and responsible partner in working towards a new multipolar system of international relations, based on strict implementation of international law'.[27]

In June 2000, the Santa Maria da Feira European Council welcomed the outcome of the Moscow summit and affirmed the necessity of a 'strong and healthy partnership . . . based on common values, notably respect for human rights and fundamental freedoms'. The change in tone did not go unnoticed in Russia, with the EU moving from 'criticism to praise'.[28] However, this was tempered by a warning that a strong partnership 'implies the holding of an open dialogue based on trust', urging Russia to meet its commitments and obligations with regard to Chechnya and stating that 'only a political solution can put at end to this crisis'.[29] The impasse remained, as the EU continued to call for a political resolution to the conflict, although not in such vociferous terms, and Moscow continued to resist. During a meeting of the EU–Russia Partnership Council held in Luxembourg in April 2001, in response to concern expressed regarding human rights violations in Chechnya, the Russian delegation stated that a resolution of the Chechen issue was only possible once reforms had been conducted there, such as the establishment of a financial base, drafting an effective budget and creating effective authorities.[30]

The impact of September 11

The terrorist attacks against the US on September 11 had a significant impact on Russia's relations with both the EU and the wider international community. The Kremlin has constantly justified its second military operation on the grounds that it is defending itself against the threat from extreme Islamist terrorists, a claim lent considerable credence by the US attacks. Putin was able to reiterate his conviction that Russia had been fighting international terrorism for a long time and that the international community needed to broaden their co-operation. At the 2001 EU–Russia summit, Putin expressed his satisfaction that Europe had finally recognised the need to join forces in the fight against terrorism.[31] Russian officials were optimistic about the summit, which, in their view, was the beginning of a 'qualitatively new phase' in the development of a strategic partnership.[32] This opinion had been reinforced by then Chancellor Gerhard Schröder's statement during a visit by Putin to Germany at the end of September 2001 that, 'regarding Chechnya there will be and must be a more differentiated evaluation of world opinion', once again drawing attention to the lack of coherence amongst EU member states over this issue.[33]

This concurrence on the need to fight international terrorism did not mean that the EU ceased its calls for Moscow to seek a negotiated end to the Chechen crisis. The Country Strategy Paper (CSP) for the Russian Federation 2002–06, adopted by the Commission on 27 December 2001, affirmed that the human rights situation in Chechnya was a 'central issue of EU–Russia relations' and, once more, called for a political solution to the conflict.[34] The fact that a large gulf remained between the two became apparent in the wake of the October 2002 Dubrovka theatre siege and, on the eve of the tenth EU–Russia summit, relations again plunged to a new low. While the EU expressed its solidarity with Russia and condemned all forms of terrorism, there was a wide divergence in the conclusions that each actor drew from the attack: Russia believed that it demonstrated, once again, that it was fighting international terrorism, while the EU was reluctant to accept the Russian view that the Chechen problem was simply part of a wider struggle. The increased tension must also be viewed against the background of the EU's decision to invite former Soviet states to become members and the issue of Kaliningrad, which was a major stumbling block in relations at the time.

As Russian policy towards Chechnya hardened in the aftermath of the siege, so too did Russian policy towards European states deemed to be sympathetic to the Chechen cause. Denmark, which held the EU presidency at the time, was considered to be too supportive of the Chechens, due to it hosting the World Chechen Congress. As a result, the EU–Russia summit, scheduled to be held in Copenhagen in November 2002, had to be transferred to Brussels. The Chechen issue also tainted relations with France and the UK. Moscow was heavily critical of France for failing to prevent a meeting in Paris of a group purported to back Chechen 'terrorists'.[35] Relations between Russia and the UK were damaged in 2003 when a London court granted political asylum to Ahmed Zakayev, the deputy of former Chechen leader Aslan Maskhadov, wanted in Russia on charges of involvement in terrorist activities. The Zakayev case is a prime example of the divergence in views between Russia and EU member states on issues such as human rights and fundamental freedoms. It was also viewed by Moscow as an example of the West's hypocrisy and double standards in the fight against terrorism.[36]

The issue remained centre-stage throughout 2003, as the Chechens approved, by referendum, a new regional constitution keeping the republic within the Russian Federation, and then, in presidential elections, confirming the *de facto* president (and Russian-backed candidate) Akhmad Kadyrov as leader. There was widespread condemnation of both the referendum and elections, with the EU expressing 'serious concerns' about the conditions in which the elections were held.[37] The subject ignited considerable controversy at the EU–Russia summit held in November in Rome. Silvio Berlusconi, then Prime Minister of Italy, which held the EU presidency at that time, angered many of the fifteen member states and also the ten accession countries, by appearing to be too soft on Russian human rights violations. There was no mention of Chechnya (or the arrest of Yukos boss Mikhail Khodorkovsky) in a post-summit statement and Berlusconi offered a robust defence of Putin's human rights record. The incident soured relations between Italy and other EU member states, and once again demonstrated the lack of a coherent stance towards Russia, a problem that has only been exacerbated by the accession of ten new member states in 2004.

Self-criticism

As a direct result of this internal turmoil, Brussels turned a critical eye onto itself and its relationship with Russia. In February 2004, a European Parliament report (the Belder report) called for a reassessment of the EU's Russia policy, in light of the fact that Russia had not developed in the way foreseen in 1994. Noting Russia's increasing importance for the EU, as a result of enlargement, it acknowledged that the policies of the EU and its member states had been unable to prevent the weakening of democracy and the rule of law in Russia. It condemned the 'spectacular statements on Chechnya' that 'went straight against well-established and fully motivated EU positions', describing the lack of dialogue on Chechnya as 'morally and politically indefensible'.[38]

A week later, the Commission issued a communiqué, advising all member states that they needed to take a consistent, united approach and accentuating the 'need for increased EU coordination and coherence across all areas of EU activity – sending clear, unambiguous messages to Russia'.[39] The communiqué recommended 'respect for the values on which it [the partnership] is based'.[40] It called for the drafting of objectives' papers for future Summits, which should draw clear policy 'red lines' for the EU and its member states, beyond which they would not go. This upset Putin and the Kremlin, who were frustrated at being presented with a united front from the EU, reducing their ability to capitalise on good relations with certain EU member states and consequently exploit divisions within the EU. It has been argued that Russia should seek to influence the positions of individual member states, rather than trying to influence the EU as a single entity, recognising the divergence in the views and approaches of the various member states, together with the fact that they often fail to speak with one voice.[41]

The communiqué exacerbated tensions further, by questioning Russia's ability to support the values to which it is committed, or to even continue with democratic reforms: 'despite common interests, growing economic interdependence and certain steps forwards, there has been insufficient progress on substance'.[42] It was critical of the apparent lack of progress in building a genuine strategic partnership that had more substance to it than just 'grand political declarations' and maintained that the EU could influence developments in Russia only if it was willing to bring up difficult issues such as Chechnya in a 'clear and forthright manner'. They should discuss 'frankly Russian practices that run counter to universal and European values, such as democracy, human rights in Chechnya'.[43] It noted that relations between Brussels and Moscow had become increasingly strained and divergent on a number of issues, including ratification of the Kyoto Protocol (an issue that has subsequently been resolved), combined with a more assertive Russian position towards former Soviet states, such as Georgia and Ukraine, as seen in its reaction to the 2004 Orange Revolution.

The significance of this communiqué should not be underestimated. It accentuated the growing divergence in the perceptions and objectives of the two actors with regard to their partnership, as well as the EU's recognition of its own limitations and weaknesses to date. The communiqué, together with the Belder report, marked the beginning of a tougher line towards Russia and recognition that five years of increased co-operation under the CSR had not produced the results hoped for, either in terms of democratic development or their strategic partnership. A persistent discrepancy between the two actors had been highlighted time and again by their differing attitudes to the Chechen issue and the EU had finally recognised the need to establish a more coherent, strategic approach.

Ripples from Beslan

The Kremlin's sensitivity to any perceived criticism or interference in its internal affairs was once again demonstrated in the wake of the increasing wave of terrorist attacks throughout Russia in 2004, which culminated in the Beslan school siege in September. While EU leaders were quick to sympathise with Moscow and condemn terrorism, a row broke out when Bernard Bot, the Dutch Foreign Minister, apparently asked the Kremlin 'how this tragedy could have happened'.[44] Despite claims that Bot had been misinterpreted, Russian officials reacted furiously, with Foreign Minister

Lavrov calling it 'inappropriate and blasphemous'.[45] In order to understand the Russian reaction, it is important to appreciate the impact of both Beslan and the 2002 Moscow theatre siege (as well as a series of terrorist attacks against Russian cities) on the Russian people. The attacks struck at the heart of Russia, taking the war to the wider population, which had been largely unaffected by the protracted conflict in Chechnya up to that point. Putin has used very emotive language when referring to Beslan, describing it as an attack against Russia and declaring that the country was engaged in a 'cruel and full-scale war'. As Bobo Lo has pointed out, the last time a Russian leader used such language was when Stalin addressed the Soviet people following the 1941 German invasion.[46] Such feelings were perhaps misunderstood or underestimated in Brussels.

Post-Beslan, Putin concentrated on consolidating his position and strengthening the Kremlin's grip on power. The Chechen issue dropped back down the agenda, although, in October 2004, the Commission approved a €10m package of humanitarian aid for the victims of the ongoing conflict. The EU is the largest donor of aid to victims of the Chechen conflict, allocating approximately €137m in aid to the North Caucasus region since the beginning of the second military operation in 1999.[47]

At the May 2005 summit held in Moscow, the leaders of the EU and Russia adopted a single package of roadmaps for the creation of four Common Spaces, setting out shared objectives for the development of relations, as well as what was needed to make these objectives a reality. In an article published in a Russian newspaper days after the summit, Javier Solana gave an insight into the state of relations between the EU and Russia. He called for both sides to move 'from theory to practice', expressing his belief that 'sometimes . . . we spend more time making plans for our cooperation than actually cooperating'. With reference to Chechnya, Solana underlined the EU's concern about respect for human rights, but stressed that it was not about 'teaching lessons, it is about finding solutions'.[48]

The issue of values was central to a resolution on EU–Russia relations, adopted by the European Parliament at the end of May 2005. The resolution emphasised that relations 'must be based on common values . . . encompassing human rights, the market economy, the rule of law and democracy' and described the situation in Chechnya as 'out of control'. Acknowledging that steps had been taken over the past year to tackle 'major flaws' in the EU's policy-making procedures *vis-à-vis* Russia, it nevertheless stated that these measures had not resulted in sufficient improvement and further action was necessary.[49] Over a decade after the EU and Russia had begun to establish a strategic partnership, there are still significant challenges to be overcome, most notably the wide gap between rhetoric and reality.

Conclusions: common values, shared interests or self-interest?

The thorny issue of Chechnya has amply tested and revealed the limits of the relationship between the EU and Russia, accentuating the fact that the two are very different actors, pursuing different objectives in the development of their strategic partnership. The EU is an international organisation comprised of various member states, who have ceded a certain degree of sovereignty in the belief that a system of co-operation and interdependence will boost their security. Such a system is based upon the conviction that those involved share certain values and norms, and naturally relies upon a certain level of external 'interference' in the internal affairs of each member state. As an organisation that espouses 'the shared ideals of democratic institutions, human rights, the protection of minorities and the rule of law',[50] the EU will obviously seek to promote these ideals, both in its internal and external relations.

By contrast, Russia is a sovereign state that will seek to protect and further its own national interest, hence the divergence in the approaches of the two actors. It is incomprehensible and perplexing to Russia that a state would willingly cede sovereignty over certain issues to an external authority and encourage interference in its domestic affairs. This is incongruous at a time when Moscow is seeking to retain its influence over former Soviet states such as Moldova and Belarus, having 'lost' Georgia and Ukraine to the West.[51] Russia views its relationship with the EU as key to developing its own role on the global stage and shaping the international environment to assist its domestic development. In a speech delivered in July 2002, Putin affirmed that Russia needed to seek partners and allies who recognised the state's national interests. Referring to relations with the EU, he declared that compromise and the co-ordination of positions would not be made at the expense of the national interest.[52]

Chechnya is a very sensitive issue for Moscow and any criticism of Russian action there only serves to upset the political leadership. When the EU makes reference to human rights violations in Chechnya, it is perceived to be a cynical, anti-Russian move, rather than an intercession on the grounds of humanitarian and democratic values. Criticism from the EU must be constructive and based on specific, justifiable facts, something that the EU Commission in Moscow is very aware of.[53] Criticism should also be accompanied by recognition that progress is being made, as there is a perception in Russia that the EU merely seeks to highlight the instability and problems in the North Caucasus, without reference to any positive steps forward. Russia does not understand why Brussels is so concerned with events in Chechnya: it views the crisis as an internal matter and therefore of little relevance to its relations with external actors, such as the EU. This highlights a fundamental distinction in the development of the relationship: while Russia views human rights as a domestic issue, the EU views respect for human rights as one of the common values on which their partnership is based. The EU wants to believe that Russia is keen to integrate so-called 'European standards and values'[54], something which Russia is unlikely to embrace. Pavel Baev believes that the core problem demonstrated by the ongoing Chechen conflict is that Russia is trying to 'join Europe', without making any serious effort to 'Europeanise' itself by accepting standards of democratic governance or human rights.[55] Russia likes the benefits that accompany alignment with the EU, such as a seat at the table and a voice, but it does not want the obligations and is certainly not willing to permit itself to be influenced by an external actor.

The Chechen issue has raised the question of influence within the partnership and where the balance lies. The EU lacks any form of leverage by which it can seek to influence Russian behaviour – it cannot offer the potential of membership, as the prospects of Russia ever joining (or ever wanting to join) the EU are minimal. Conversely, Russia appears to have considerable leverage, in the form of its hydrocarbons. Tretyakov has argued that Russia should be treated as a European power without having to work for this status. He has proposed that Russia should enjoy all the privileges extended to EU member states, or it will not offer concessions on its oil and gas, essentially holding the EU to ransom.[56] It could perhaps be argued that Russia overestimates its own importance to the EU, believing that the organisation needs Russia in order to become a truly great power. For example, Vladimir Chizhov has argued that the future of Europe is impossible without Russia.[57] Facing this kind of attitude, and lacking any serious leverage of its own, the EU faces an uphill struggle in attempting to influence the actions of Russia, particularly in such a sensitive area as Chechnya.

As the 2004 Belder report noted, engagement is preferable to isolation and the EU is much more likely to hold some form of influence over Russian policy if it continues to pursue its twin-track approach of criticism and co-operation, rather than cutting Russia off entirely. Whilst EU member states clearly do not want to alienate Russia again, there is uncertainty about the form that closer integration should take. Russia is an important source of hydrocarbons for EU member states and the organisation cannot afford to upset one of its key suppliers, particularly as gas consumption in the region is set to grow dramatically over the coming decades as indigenous oil reserves decline.[58] Furthermore, Brussels and Moscow need to co-operate to tackle the numerous 'soft' security challenges facing the wider European continent as the EU expands further eastwards. The EU needs co-operation and dialogue with Russia. Whilst it is good to have high ideals and values to protect, sometimes these have to give way to a more pragmatic, realistic stance.

The issue of Chechnya has demonstrated that EU member states are prepared to disregard notions of common European values, pursuing bilateral relations with Russia when it is in their national interest. Consequently, the issue has revealed fundamental flaws in the concept of CFSP, as well as the lack of a coherent, consistent approach from the EU and its member states, a problem that has been exacerbated by enlargement. One of the principal arguments for CFSP is that the European view of world affairs is likely sometimes to diverge from that of the US. Chechnya has demonstrated that the views of individual member states are also likely to diverge at times. It is not just individual member states who fail to take a united approach; different organs of the EU have very different approaches to the Chechen issue. The European Parliament has tended to be openly critical of Russian actions in Chechnya, adopting eleven resolutions on the situation there during the 1999–2004 session. Then External Relations Commissioner, Chris Patten, also took a very critical line towards Russian attempts to impose a military solution, while other organs have been less outspoken.[59] The addition of ten new voices to the EU in 2004 only serves to strengthen the need for coherence and a common approach. In order to progress its partnership with Moscow, the EU first needs to overcome its own internal divisions and inconsistencies. Russia will not take the organisation seriously while its member states continue to pursue their own agendas, regardless of the official EU position.

While the EU continues to advocate a political resolution to the Chechen conflict and Moscow continues to stand by its military action, the Chechen issue will remain a major challenge in the development of an effective strategic partnership, a challenge that is likely to prevent the development of further integration. There have been a considerable number of political declarations, as well as the establishment of numerous negotiating mechanisms, but these have been unable to bridge the gap between the differing approaches of the two. While the relationship is important to both actors, particularly in economic and security terms, and is unlikely to be permanently derailed by the Chechen issue, it does raise questions as to whether they are capable of progressing their partnership further, in order to diminish the wide disparity that currently exists between rhetoric and reality.

Notes

1 Javier Solana, speech, 'The EU-Russia strategic partnership' (13 October 1999), www.ue.eu.int.
2 *Noviye Izvestiya* (6 December 2004), www.newizv.ru.
3 For further analysis of the background to the conflict see Anatol Lieven, *Chechnya: Tombstone of Russian Power* (London: Yale University Press, 1998); Carlotta Gall and Thomas de Waal, *Chechnya: Calamity in the Caucasus* (New York: New York University Press, 2000); Robert Seely, *Russo-Chechen Conflict, 1800–2000: A Deadly Embrace* (London: Frank Cass, 2000).
4 Notable areas of contention include Georgia's separatist regions of Abkhazia and South Ossetia, the presence of Russian military bases on Georgian territory, transit routes for hydrocarbons from the Caspian Sea region and the Pankiski Gorge in northern Georgia.
5 I.S. Ivanov, Speech by Minister for Foreign Affairs to the Parliamentary Assembly of the Council of Europe (27 January 2000), www.ln.mid.ru.
6 *Nezavisimaya Gazeta* (16 December 1999), www.ng.ru/english/.
7 For detailed analysis of the PCA, see Hiski Haukkala and Sergei Medvedev (eds), *The EU Common Strategy on Russia: Learning the Grammar of the CFSP* (Helsinki and Berlin: Finnish Institute of International Affairs and Institut für Europäische Politik, 2001); Thomas Gomart, 'Enlargement tests the partnership between the EU and Russia', *Conflict Studies Research Centre* (August 2004).
8 Smith has argued that the delay in ratification was more to do with the EU's external policies and Russian concerns about the agreement rather than the Chechen conflict. See Hanna Smith, 'Chechnya in Russian foreign policy', in Hanna Smith (ed.), *Russia and its Foreign Policy* (Saarijärvi: Kikimora Publishing, 2005), p. 102.
9 *Rossiiskaya Gazeta* (28 December 1994).
10 The EU issued numerous declarations on the Chechen situation throughout 1995. See, for example, *Declaration on Chechnya made by the Presidency on behalf of the European Union* (Brussels, January 1995); *Declaration on Chechnya made by the Presidency on behalf of the European Union* (Brussels, April 1995), www.ue.eu.int.
11 Graham Timmins, 'Strategic or pragmatic partnership? The European Union's policy towards Russia since the end of the Cold War', *European Security*, 11:4 (Winter 2002), p. 82.
12 Haukkala and Medvedev (eds), *The EU Common Strategy on Russia*, p. 29.
13 *Common Strategy of the European Union on Russia* (Brussels, June 1999), p. 1.

14 For details of the medium-term strategy for development of relations between the Russian Federation and the European Union (2000–10), see *Diplomaticheskii Vestnik*, 11 (November 1999), pp. 20–8.
15 Malashenko and Trenin have described the Kosovo crisis as the start of a 'short, but painful period of geopolitical isolation' for Moscow, which reached a peak at the Helsinki EU–Russia summit and Istanbul OSCE summit. Aleksei Malashenko and Dmitry Trenin, *Vremya Yuga: Rossiya v Chechnye, Chechnya v Rossii* (Moscow: Gandalf, 2002), p. 213.
16 Council of the European Union, *Conclusions of the Helsinki European Council* (Brussels, December 1999).
17 Ibid.
18 Parliamentary Assembly of the Council of Europe, *Recommendation 1444 (2000): The Conflict in Chechnya*, http://assembly/coe/int/Documents/AdoptedText/TA00/EREC 1444.htm.
19 Michael Emerson, *The Elephant and the Bear: The European Union, Russia and their Near Abroads* (Brussels: Centre for European Policy Studies, 2001), p. 14.
20 *Nezavisimaya Gazeta* (17 December 1999), www.ng.ru/english/.
21 *Izvestiya* (15 December 1999), www.izvestia.ru/.
22 Committee on Foreign Affairs, Human Rights, Common Security and Defence Policy, *European Parliament Report on the Implementation of the Common Strategy of the European Union on Russia: Rapporteur: Arie M Oostlander* (Brussels, November 2000). Moscow was fairly dismissive of the sanctions, branding them 'almost sanctions'. *Nezavisimaya Gazeta* (26 January 2000), www.ng.ru/english/.
23 *Nezavisimaya Gazeta* (1 October 1999), www.ng.ru/english/.
24 See Hiski Haukkala, 'The making of the EU's common strategy on Russia', in Haukkala and Medvedev (eds), *The EU Common Strategy on Russia*, p. 62.
25 See Vladimir Putin, 'Key tasks of Russian diplomacy', *International Affairs (Moscow)* (October 2004), pp. 1–6; Sergei Medvedev, 'Rethinking the national interest: Putin's turn in Russian foreign policy', *Marshall Center Papers*, 6 (August 2004).
26 *Nezavisimaya Gazeta* (31 May 2000), www.ng.ru/english/.
27 *Joint Statement by the President of the European Council A. Guterres assisted by the Secretary-General of the Council/High Representative for Foreign and Security Policy of the EU J. Solana, the President of the Commission of the European Communities R. Prodi, the President of the Russian Federation, V.V. Putin* (Moscow, May 2000), www.delrus.cec.eu.int/en/images/pText_pict/241/sum11.doc.
28 *Nezavisimaya Gazeta* (21 June 2000), www.ng.ru/english/.
29 Council of the European Union, *Conclusions of the Santa Maria da Feira European Council* (Brussels, June 2000).
30 *Nezavisimaya Gazeta* (12 April 2001), www.ng.ru/english/.
31 *Nezavisimaya Gazeta* (4 October 2001), www.ng.ru/english/.
32 'Rossiya-Evropeiskii soyuz', *Diplomaticheskii Vestnik*, 11 (November 2001), p. 19.
33 Quoted in Matthew Evangelista, *The Chechen Wars: Will Russia Go the Way of the Soviet Union?* (Washington, DC: Brookings Institution Press, 2002), p. 180.
34 European Commission, *Country Strategy Paper 2002–2006: National Indicative Programme 2002–2003 – Russian Federation* (Brussels, December 2001), p. 4.
35 *Nezavisimaya Gazeta* (29 October 2002), www.ng.ru/english/.
36 This view was reinforced in February 2005, when the British Channel Four News broadcast an interview with Shamil Basayev, the alleged mastermind behind the 2002 Moscow theatre-siege and Beslan, in spite of protests from Moscow.
37 *Declaration by the Presidency on behalf of the European Union on the presidential elections in Chechnya* (Brussels, October 2003), www.ue.eu.int.
38 Committee on Foreign Affairs, Human Rights, Common Security and Defence Policy, *Report with a proposal for a European Parliament recommendation to the Council on EU–Russia relations: Rapporteur, Bastiaan Belder* (Brussels, February 2004), pp. 8–11.

39 *Communication from the Commission to the Council and the European Parliament on Relations with Russia* (Brussels, February 2004), p. 3.
40 Ibid., p. 1.
41 Vasily Likhachev, 'Rossiya i Evropeiskii soyuz', *Mezhdunarodnaya zhizn*, 12 (2002), pp. 30–7. Nikolai Kaveshnikov believes that Moscow should seek to cultivate better relationships with individual European states, rather than the EU as a single entity, as individual states are likely to be more supportive. Author interview with Nikolai Kaveshnikov, Institute of Europe RAN, Moscow, 26 January 2005.
42 *Communication from the Commission to the Council and the European Parliament on Relations with Russia*, p. 3.
43 Ibid., p. 6.
44 Bot's remarks were published on the Dutch presidency's website, but changed to quote the Foreign Minister as saying '[i]n order to better understand what happened in the school, we would like to learn more details from the Russian authorities so we can help each other to combat terrorism', www.eu2004.nl.
45 *Izvestiya* (9 September 2004), www.izvestia.ru/.
46 Bobo Lo, 'Beslan: a people's trauma', *The World Today*, 6:10 (October 2004), p. 5.
47 This aid has not just been allocated to Chechnya, but also to internally displaced persons living in neighbouring Ingushetia and Dagestan. For details, see 'Northern Caucasus: Commission allocates Ä10m for victims of conflict in Chechnya', www.europa.eu.int/comm/external_relations/ceeca/news/ip04_1286.htm.
48 *Nezavisimaya Gazeta* (23 May 2005), www.ng.ru/english/.
49 *European Parliament Resolution on EU–Russia relations* (Brussels, May 2005).
50 Romano Prodi, speech, 'Russia and the European Union – enduring ties, widening horizons', 23 April 2004, www.europa.eu.int/comm/external_relations/news.prodi/sp04_198. htm.
51 Vladimir Putin, speech, 'Annual Address to the Federal Assembly', 25 April 2005, www.kremlin.ru.
52 Vladimir Putin, 'Speech to the Enlarged Conference, with Participation of Russian Federation Ambassadors at the Ministry of Foreign Affairs', 12 July 2002, www.ln.mid.ru.
53 Author interview with Political Officer at the EU Commission, Moscow, Russia, 25 January 2005.
54 Thomas Gomart, 'Enlargement Tests the Partnership Between the EU and Russia', Conflict Studies Research Centre, August 2004, p. 3.
55 Pavel Baev, 'Putin's Western choice', *European Security*, 12 (Spring 2003), p. 8.
56 Vitaly Tretyakov, 'Pragmatizm vneshnyei politiki V Putina', *Mezhdunarodnaya zhizn*, 5 (2002), pp. 19–25.
57 Vladimir Chizhov, 'Rossiya–ES. Strategiya partnerstva', *Mezhdunarodnaya zhizn*, 9 (2004), p. 25.
58 By 2020, it is estimated that two-thirds of EU's energy requirements will be imported. The consumption of natural gas in particular is forecast to rise dramatically. In 2003, 32 per cent of EU natural gas imports came from Russia and this figure is set to rise dramatically as indigenous reserves dwindle. See *European Union Energy Outlook to 2020* (Luxembourg, 1999).
59 Chris Patten, 'Declaration by the External Affairs Commissioner at the European Parliament Development Committee', 12 November 2002, http://europa.eu.int/comm/external_relations/news/patten/ip02_1655.htm.

10

A leap forward to Europe: the impact of the 'Orange Revolution' on EU–Ukraine relations

Rosaria Puglisi [1]

Introduction

Amidst the generally positive reactions generated by the 2005 EU–Ukraine Summit, one Ukrainian commentator went as far as to call the occasion 'a leap forward to Europe'.[2] The 'new' Ukrainian leadership, which had come to power following the 'Orange Revolution' roughly a year before, had been eager to stage a public event that would catch the imagination of its pro-European electorate. The EU had happily obliged.[3] In the presence of UK Prime Minister and then President of the European Council, Tony Blair, President of the European Commission, Jose Manuel Barroso, External Relations Commissioner, Benita Ferrero-Waldner, and the Secretary-General/High Representative for CFSP, Javier Solana, it was announced that Ukraine would finally be granted the long-awaited market economy status. Consultations for an enhanced agreement, which would replace the PCA, talks on visa facilitation and negotiations for the establishment of a Free Trade Area, following Ukraine's entry into the WTO, were also promised. More importantly, however, a Memorandum of Understanding was signed on co-operation in the field of energy, aiming, amongst other things, at progressively integrating the Ukrainian energy market into the EU, thereby enhancing the state's energy security.

Standing in the freezing cold, waving their orange banners, Ukrainians demonstrating against the rigged Presidential elections in the autumn of 2004 could have hardly imagined that their exasperated reaction to years of corruption and abuse of power would contribute to that 'leap forward'. Struggling to protect values they considered inherently 'European', such as free and fair elections, democracy and freedom of expression, protesters sent the signal that Ukraine was also part of the European common home. Their European vocation now had to be reckoned with by the EU institutions. In the Summit's final statement, EU representatives attempted to do just that. They were adamant that the 'Orange Revolution' had had a significant impact on the further development of EU–Ukraine relations:

> Leaders welcomed the fact that commitment to democracy and reform had opened new prospects for Ukraine and EU–Ukraine relations. Leaders welcomed that EU–Ukraine

relations were now deeper and stronger as a result of the significant progress achieved in the implementation of the EU–Ukraine Action Plan . . . The EU welcomed Ukraine's firm commitment to shared values of democracy, rule of law and respect for human rights; and recognised the progress made in promoting economic reforms.[4]

As a result, in the period between President Yushchenko's inauguration in January 2005 and the aforementioned summit in December 2005, EU–Ukraine relations have gone through something of a major U-turn, shifting from a cautious, often mutually mistrustful rapport to an atmosphere of open, hopeful co-operation. While the EU was still unable to satisfy Ukraine's membership aspirations, expectations on both sides remained high. An exceptionally large number of high-ranking EU political visits throughout the year testified to Brussels's willingness to move towards an enhanced level of co-operation.

In the wider academic debate on the emergence and consolidation of the EU as a foreign policy actor, relations with Ukraine represent an interesting case study. They provide the opportunity to observe how EU foreign policy was shaped by the interaction of what Bretherton and Vogler call 'presence', 'opportunity' and 'capacity'.[5] While the EU provided a constructive point of reference for Ukraine, because of its positive public connotations and through an articulated set of agreements and programmes (presence), Brussels' policy line was significantly reviewed, as a result of a transformed political environment in Ukraine (opportunity). The 'Revolution' changed not only expectations among Ukrainians, making ordinary citizens as well as the new leadership more self-aware of their European identity, but also the whole Ukrainian discourse on European integration. At least in the first few months of the new administration, the coming to power of a political elite genuinely committed to European values and dismissive of their predecessors' unfounded demands provided the EU with a more trustworthy partner. Reliability in Kyiv created the conditions for heightened interest and increased engagement on the EU side, with each European institution – be it the Council, Commission or Parliament – interacting in this joint field of action according to their respective capabilities, functions and policy orientations (capacity).

Waking the sleeping elephant

In the whirlwind tour that took him to Moscow, Warsaw, Strasbourg and Davos in the immediate aftermath of his inauguration, President Yushchenko repeatedly referred to Ukraine as a 'sleeping elephant', whose huge potential he and his associates sought to wake up: 'My country has long been a wise, strong but sleeping elephant. It is waking today – democracy opens the way to implementing its potential to achieving its goals'.[6] Speaking in front of friendly audiences, he reassured the international community that his country was in for great changes:

> The end of the presidential election in Ukraine is only the beginning of a healing process, which will continue until restitution of full health, immune to the viruses of

corruption, autocracy, censorship and any violation of human rights. This is the beginning of a confident movement towards economic prosperity, social guarantees and a dignified life for each Ukrainian.[7]

In his relations with the West, the newly elected President made skilful use of the international limelight the 'Orange Revolution' had cast on Ukraine and drew sympathetic support for the achievement of what he defined as his country's 'strategic goal', namely European integration. Under no illusions that Ukraine could become an EU member any time soon, Yushchenko emphasised that the political and economic reforms suggested by Brussels would be undertaken anyway, for the sake of Ukraine's longer-term development: 'We will make Ukraine a European country in terms of values and standards and then we will see Europe knocking on our door'.[8]

Continuous reference to European integration went well beyond a sleek electoral slogan. References to Europe in general – and the EU in particular – had mainly positive connotations for Ukrainians.[9] According to a July 2003 survey, almost 65 per cent of Ukrainians were in favour of European integration, with only 15 per cent against.[10] In the imagination of most ordinary people, the EU represented so much progress, wealth and well-being that the prefix *evro* in the Russian and Ukrainian language had come to characterise anything state of the art, whether it be newly refurbished flats, water-tight window-frames or even effective dental care. Joining the European institutions was seen as a return to a common European home for Ukraine and a move away from the dark legacy of Soviet repression.[11] The positive character of the European model in Ukraine also reverberated through the lens of the CEE states' accession process. At least within progressive cultural and political circles, familiar with the Polish experience in particular, there was a feeling that the reform path created by EU enlargement would strengthen both statehood and the capacity to act in the states opting for it. The numerous hurdles imposed by a string of tight deadlines and often unpopular transformations were seen as prices worth paying for the sake of consolidation and modernisation.[12]

Unsurprisingly then, the date of accession for the ten new EU member states – 1 May 2004 – was perceived by many in Kyiv as a missed opportunity for Ukraine. Many Ukrainian commentators felt that Ukraine and its CEE neighbours had embarked upon the post-socialist phase of their economic and political development at an equal level. Had Ukraine's leadership been more consistent in its reform course and transparent in its relations with Brussels, it could have rightly aspired to European membership in 2004, or shortly afterwards.[13] Yet, for a host of reasons that will be considered in more depth later, relations between Kyiv and Brussels under President Yushchenko's predecessor, Leonid Kuchma, had been bumpy. Before considering the Kuchma period in more depth, it is worth sketching out the framework of relations between the EU and Ukraine.

The Commission had set up an office in Kyiv in 1994 and signed a PCA, the first with a former Soviet country, in the same year. Ratified by the Verkhovna Rada (the Ukrainian Parliament) in 1998, the PCA represents, to this day, the cornerstone of EU–Ukraine relations. Providing a framework for political dialogue, it identifies harmonious economic relations, sustainable development, co-operation in a number of specific areas (for example, energy, the environment and cross-border co-operation) and support for Ukraine's democratic transformation as the common objectives of bilateral interaction. At the same time, the PCA was meant as an important instrument to bring Ukraine in line with the legal structure of the single European market and the WTO system. In order to operationalise these objectives, a number of high-level political venues were created to discuss and enhance bilateral relations: a co-operation council at ministerial level, including the EU Presidency, the Commission, the High Representative and the Ukrainian government; a co-operation committee, including senior civil servants from both the Commission and the Ukrainian government; sub-committees, taking place at expert level and, finally, annual summits.[14] In addition, between 1994 and 2004, the EU, primarily through the Commission, granted more than €2bn in assistance to Ukraine, becoming its largest donor in 2004.[15]

In anticipation of enlargement and to pre-empt any potential negative consequences, the Commission launched its Wider Europe initiative in March 2003, followed, in July of the same year, by the ENP. Designed to avoid the risk of 'drawing new dividing lines in Europe' and 'to promote stability and prosperity on both sides of the new borders', the new policy line was meant to set up what then Commission President Prodi had called a 'circle of friends'.[16] Through these initiatives, the Commission intended to offer those neighbours to the east and to the south that lacked any formal membership process the possibility to participate in an 'enlarged area of peace, stability and prosperity'. In return for concrete progress and effective implementation of political, economic and institutional reforms, the EU's neighbourhood was promised that it would benefit from the prospect of closer economic and political links with the EU. A 'differentiated, progressive, and benchmarked approach' in implementing the initiative would be guaranteed, through the adoption of individually negotiated action plans.[17] These would cover areas such as political dialogue, trade and economic reforms, JHA, energy, transport, the information society, environment, research and innovation, social policy and people-to-people contact.[18]

Wider Europe and the ENP were met with little enthusiasm in Kyiv. In the run-up to Presidential elections, anything short of a date for membership or an association agreement was considered a defeat for incumbent President Kuchma and his chosen candidate, Prime Minister Yanukovich. Significantly, pro-European circles in Ukraine also lamented that the ENP had failed to address Ukraine's European vocation. Former Foreign Minister and Chairman of the Parliamentary Committee for European Integration, Borys Tarasyuk, was angry that the Ukraine had been considered alongside the likes of Algeria and Tunisia, as they had no membership aspiration and no obvious European identity.[19] The pro-European critics accused the Commission of a 'lack of imagination', having drafted a strategy too 'timid' to satisfy the growing demands of relations with the largest of its new eastern neighbours: 'The European Union currently has a unique opportunity to shape the political configuration in an important country east of its borders. But unfortunately it looks like it will let this chance simply slip away'.[20]

The ENP, admittedly, did not recognise any membership perspective for Ukraine. However, while clearly charting the course of EU–Ukraine co-operation in the short term – over a two to three year period – it left the door open for possible future changes in their 'contractual relation'. The new strategy proposed a new pattern of joint ownership and responsibility, where problematic areas could be tackled and progress rewarded. As timid as the ENP might have seemed, it was the best offer the EU could table at that stage, given the difficulties created, on the one hand, by the EU's need for post-enlargement internal consolidation and, on the other, by Ukraine's domestic instability. It is to Ukrainian domestic political circumstances that we now turn, to help explain why membership was not an option at the time of the ENP.

A bull-fight with Brussels

President Yushchenko's predecessor, Leonid Kuchma, was in office for two terms, with his administration marked by an erratic domestic and foreign policy course. In the period 1994–2004, Ukraine often found itself at odds with, and sometimes isolated from, the wider international community, as a result of decisions taken to protect the interests of the President and those close to his inner circle.[21] Having set up a system of personal rule, which developed into a form of soft authoritarianism, President Kuchma made international headlines for his suspected role in the murder of journalist Heorhy Gongadze in September 2000,[22] the alleged sale of the Kolchuga radar station to embargoed Iraq and his determination to stay in power, even in the face of massive popular protests to oust him.

Despite having embarked upon a pro-European course, formalised in the 2003 'European Choice' and in the 2004 Strategy 'Towards European Integration', the Kuchma administration paid little more than lip service to its European commitments.[23] This was especially true in relation to the promotion of democratic values and the undertaking of necessary economic and administrative reforms.[24] In the name of what the President defined as 'multivector foreign policy', Ukraine kept swinging between a pro-Moscow and a pro-Western orientation, depending, in part, on the President's fortunes in his on-going domestic political struggle.

The October 2004 Presidential elections were supposed to be a watershed in Ukrainian politics. With Kuchma officially leaving office, the old leadership was preoccupied with ensuring continuity, through the appointment of a suitable candidate, who would protect the interests of the economic clans that had developed over the previous eight years. The weight of the state administration was fully thrown behind Prime Minister, Victor Yanukovich, and against the opposition candidate, former Governor of the Central Bank and former Prime Minister, Victor Yushchenko. In what started to be called the 'war of the two Victors', Ukraine witnessed its dirtiest electoral campaign to date.[25]

European integration featured highly as a foreign policy issue, even before the official beginning of the campaign. Striving to counter the negative publicity deriving from a tangible lack of progress in Ukraine's European integration efforts, Presidential spin-doctors developed a twin approach.[26] On the one hand, they blamed Brussels for making unreasonable demands and showing scarce interest in Ukrainian concerns. On the other hand, they played the eastern card, claiming that Ukraine had to strengthen its economic capacity with the help of its eastern neighbours, namely Russia, before it could become a fully fledged member of the EU. The habit of blaming the EU, while leaning to the east, was not new. Following the launch of 'Wider Europe' and the ENP, the 2003 EU–Ukraine Summit had been preceded by President Kuchma's controversial statement that, even if offered, Ukraine would refuse EU membership.[27] Even with this backdrop, the event was presented as a great victory for Ukrainian diplomacy, with claims that Kyiv had snatched promises of additional assistance from a reluctant EU. Such promises were, in fact, already foreseen in both the 'Wider Europe' and New Neighbourhood instruments.[28]

This was followed by a lengthy Ministry of Foreign Affairs inspired debate to consider the so-called negative consequences of enlargement. Estimates flooded in regarding how much Ukraine would lose from the extension of EU trade tariffs to former socialist countries, who were key Ukrainian trading partners. The argument deliberately ignored the fact that the overall external trade tariff would go down, rather than up, as a result of enlargement.[29]

In addition, reflecting a perception of geopolitics as a zero-sum game, the Ukrainian discussion over EU membership was intertwined with recurrent plans to tighten up political and economic relations in the former Soviet arena. To counteract what was seen by the Kremlin as a European intrusion in its own backyard, Russia proposed the establishment of an SES, including Russia, Ukraine, Belarus and Kazakhstan, in the spring of 2003. The SES was ostensibly meant to be a free trade area, eventually developing into a customs, economic and monetary union. While the EU accepted that a simple free trade area would not obstruct potential future plans to deepen EU–Ukraine trade relations, incompatibilities were likely to arise in the future, as a result of a customs, economic and monetary union. Firstly, the creation of an EU–Ukraine free trade area would be impaired by the existence of a joint custom union with third countries that the EU might not be willing to consider as economic partners, such as Belarus and Kazakhstan. Secondly, the proposed 'unification' of legislation or the establishment of common principles of regulation within the SES would, eventually, clash with the process of regulatory convergence with EU legislation that was required to establish an EU–Ukraine free trade area.[30] The SES agreement, signed by President Kuchma in 2003 and endorsed by some of his closest political allies, including Governor of the Central Bank Serhiy Tyhypko and Prime Minister Yanukovich, sparked great controversy. Arguing that the SES project was incompatible with the aim of European integration, then Economic Minister, Valery Khoroshkovsky, and Deputy Minister of Foreign Affairs in charge of European Integration, Oleksandr Chalyi, resigned. In a last-ditch effort to save Ukraine from itself, the latter blamed SES advancement on the EU's failure to grant his state a membership perspective.[31]

The discussion and final parliamentary ratification of the agreement in April 2004 went hand in hand with a sustained Presidential campaign to weaken pro-European expectations.[32] In his 2004 State of the Nation speech, President Kuchma noted that Ukraine's course toward European integration was an 'internal issue', arguing that Ukraine should not take into account the experiences of the CEE states as they prepared for accession. Crucial for Ukraine would be to avoid a situation whereby, in a further enlarged Europe, it would occupy a junior position vis-à-vis richer EU member states. A month later, the President announced that Ukraine would postpone indefinitely its integration into the EU, until it had developed its own internal strength and increased its economic growth by 140 per cent.[33] Exchanging SES ratification documents with President Putin a few days later, Kuchma added that 'only dreamers could hope for a quick entry into the EU', while Russia and Ukraine were already moving closer to Europe, in terms of their standards of living and democratic values.[34] Imaginatively, on the eve of enlargement, President Kuchma again pointed the finger at the EU, comparing EU–Ukraine relations to a bull-fight: 'This whole thing reminds me of a corrida, where Ukraine is a young bull running after the red cloth while [the EU] is standing still . . . and the arrows keep flying at us. They don't care about closer economic ties [that] they just keep teaching us about.'[35] Furthermore, in July 2004, Kuchma decided to strike off NATO and EU membership as priority goals from Ukraine's military doctrine.[36]

Kuchma's more hostile intentions towards the EU formed only part of the environment in which negotiations over the drafting of the Action Plan took place.[37] Other potential obstacles included the intensification of electoral irregularities, protests from the international community and the ever-increasing interference from Russia, in support of Prime Minister Yanukovich's campaign. In the ten months of consultations, during which the Action Plan became the primary target of Kyiv public criticism, the Ukrainian demands centred on the provision of an association agreement, the creation of an EU–Ukraine free trade area and the granting of market economic status. In return, Brussels resolutely excluded any promise of association, postponed the establishment of a free trade area until Ukraine's entry into the WTO and made market economy status dependent on the satisfaction of a number of technical requirements. A final text was eventually agreed and approved at expert level in September 2004. Significantly, it was never signed by the Kuchma administration.

The keys of Europe's heart

The 'Orange Revolution' changed the discourse concerning European integration and, more generally, regarding Ukraine's foreign policy orientation. With the appointment of Foreign Minister Tarsyuk, observers could see, for the first time in eight years, the outline of a coherent foreign policy strategy. While confirming EU membership as its primary objective, Ukraine also tried to position itself firmly as a regional power. Determined to make good use of the strength derived from a leadership position earned on the ground, Ukraine took centre stage, both within GUAM (the organisation bringing together Georgia, Ukraine, Azerbaijan and Moldova) and the Black Sea Organisation. Through frequent bilateral visits, it signalled its willingness to tighten up relations with both Baltic and Eastern European countries. It promoted an initiative for the settlement of one of the many frozen conflicts in the post-Soviet space, namely the conflict affecting Transdniestria.

Foreign Minister Tarasyuk reassured European audiences that Ukraine was not facing a choice and that there was no dichotomy between good relations with Russia and European integration. Both orientations were, in fact, underpinned by shared values, such as justice, security and prosperity.[38] Ukrainian leaders portrayed EU integration as an instrument to bring prosperity to their people and participation in regional organisations as an opportunity to share experiences within a common European perspective. In this context, there were frequent references to the mutually supportive role played by the Visegrad Four in the enlargement process. After years of international isolation under the previous regime, Ukraine was now keen to present itself as a stable and reliable partner.[39]

The focus shifted from the expectation of EU concessions to the delivery of Ukraine's commitments. In this respect, acceptance and promotion of the Action Plan became one of the new government's first moves. While still calling for the renegotiations of a document that had been preliminarily agreed under a different administration, Foreign Ministry representatives started emphasising its positive points. The Action Plan was now depicted as a good short-term tool, which, if correctly implemented, could bring Ukraine into the EU.[40] Significantly, when Deputy Prime Minister for European Integration, Oleh Rybachuk, signed the EU–Ukraine Action Plan in February 2005, he was careful not to press on the issue of membership and stayed clear of any reference to a possible timeframe for accession.[41] By softening the tone of its demands to Brussels and promising to fulfil its obligations, the new leadership succeeded in finding, as then Prime Minister Yulia Tymoshenko put it, 'the keys to Europe's heart'.[42]

The 'Orange Revolution' and its promising aftermath had undoubtedly rallied European public opinion around Ukraine and made its quest for inclusion into the European system difficult to ignore.[43] It had also attracted increased attention within the EU institutions and prompted an extraordinary display of public sympathy. In discussions on possible further EU enlargement, the case of Ukraine remained the most controversial accession, after possible Turkish membership. Struggling to find its own internal balance following the accession of ten new countries, and engaged in a process of institutional reforms that culminated in the publication of the ill-fated Constitution, both EU member states and institutions appeared reluctant to make any promises. As a result, the question of Ukrainian membership was kept off the agenda.

Nonetheless, in the multilayered structure of European politics, Ukraine had managed to find allies. Against stronger resistance from the likes of Spain and Italy, who were preoccupied that a new wave of enlargement would lead to Europe's geo-strategic centre shifting east, certain northern and central states, including the UK, Sweden and Austria, encouraged Ukrainian aspirations. However, their strongest support came from the new CEE member states. Even before the 'Revolution', Lithuanian Acting President Paulauskas pledged that Lithuania would 'seek to secure greater European and transatlantic support for political, economic, social and institutional reforms in Ukraine'.[44] Slovakian President Schuster stated that Slovakia saw Ukraine as part of a united Europe and would back its integration efforts.[45] Polish President Kwasniewski went as far as criticising the EU for failing to support Ukraine's European aspirations, by imposing reforms as a precondition for integration.[46] Together with Javier Solana, Kwasniewski and Lithuanian President Adamkus played an important intermediary role in the 2004 electoral crisis.

The 'Revolution' also earned Ukraine the emotional support of the European Parliament, with the EU–Ukraine Parliamentary Co-operation Committee particularly active. Some MEPs had expressed positions favourable to Ukraine's integration as far back as 2002.[47] However, the 2004 presidential campaign and the subsequent street protests caught the imagination of European parliamentarians more than any other previous event. Members of the EU–Ukraine Parliamentary Committee travelled to Kyiv no less that four times in the aftermath of the elections. They mingled with the crowd. They spoke from the stage in Maidan, expressing their support for the demonstrators. Back in Brussels, they staged an all-orange parliamentary debate, during which they called upon the Council, the Commission and the member states to 'consider . . . giving a clear European perspective for the country and responding to the demonstrated aspirations of the vast majority of the Ukrainian people, possibly leading in the end to the country's accession to the EU'.[48] Despite its political significance, the Parliament's resolution had little direct impact. It testified, however, to a symbolic gear shift within the institutions and anticipated the eleven point letter Javier Solana and Benita Ferrero-Waldner addressed to the Council, proposing specific measures to enhance EU assistance to Ukraine. The eleven points were as follows:

1 A promise of early consultations on an enhanced agreement between the EU and Ukraine, to replace the PCA, as soon as the political priorities of the ENP Action Plan had been addressed.
2 Possibilities for closer co-operation in the area of foreign and security policy.
3 The deepening of trade and economic relations, in particular through intensified efforts to bring about the conclusion of steel and textile agreements, the acceleration of a feasibility study on the establishment of a Free Trade Area and an acknowledgement to start negotiations following Ukraine's accession into the WTO.
4 Provisions for further support to Ukraine's WTO accession
5 The granting of market economy status, following Ukraine's satisfactory resolution of the remaining technical requirement.
6 Preliminary analysis on the possibility of granting visa facilitations.
7 Enhanced co-operation in key sectors, including energy, transport, environment and health, as well as in private sector development.
8 Increased support to the process of legislative approximation.
9 Increased people-to-people contacts, particularly in the areas of youth and education.
10 Maximum access to European Investment Bank funding, with up to €250m to be made available after Action Plan endorsement.
11 Increased assistance to Ukraine's reform efforts.[49]

Without promising anything substantially new, the eleven points crystallised existing EU commitments towards Ukraine and made public a number of suggestions already expressed in expert-level bilateral talks. Approving the eleven points in February 2005, the General Affairs and External Relation Council reiterated EU support:

> The Council underlined the EU's commitment to support Ukraine at this crucial moment. It looked forward to the final endorsement of the EU–Ukraine Action Plan at the Co-operation Council and for work on its implementation to begin immediately. The Council underlined that the EU is prepared to move quickly ahead with all aspects of the Action Plan. While the pace of progress in the ENP Action Plan will depend on the quality of efforts undertaken by the Ukrainian authorities, the EU is strongly committed to responding in a timely manner on its side. The Council agreed to consider a first review of the implementation of the Action Plan already in the beginning of 2006, provided that significant progress has been made.[50]

What next?

The EU's inability to utter the m-word (membership) and Ukraine's lack of domestic political consolidation are the in-built shortcomings of their relationship. With a parliamentary campaign under way (elections in March 2006), issues of membership and association status have resurfaced.[51] The atmosphere in Kyiv is one of mild dissatisfaction for what Ukrainian commentators see as the EU's unwillingness to offer a helping hand. In the aftermath of the gas stand-off with Moscow in late December 2005–January 2006, with a gradual increase in popular support for President Yushchenko's opponent, Victor Yanukovich, the perception in Kyiv is that a signal from Brussels would play an important role. Recognition that Ukraine does indeed have a membership perspective, even one that is relatively long term, would help redress the balance of power in the eternal 'pro-Russian–pro-Western' contest of Ukraine politics and thus provide additional ammunition for reformist and democratic forces.

Admittedly, the Yushchenko administration has performed less well than was initially hoped. Throughout a year lived dangerously, Ukraine witnessed the ousting of Yulia Tymoshenko's government, brought down by a stream of corruption scandals, leading to the fragmentation of the orange coalition that brought Yushchenko to power. The Parliament voted down a package of reforms aimed at ensuring Ukraine's WTO accession, while foreign policy decisions seemed, once again, to be hostages of Russian energy deliveries. Not always well thought-out administrative reforms were followed by patchy implementation and economic indicators registered a halt in the country's growth. The systemic changes promised by President Yushchenko have indeed failed to materialise. Yet, declaring the death of the 'Orange Revolution' would be unfair. Post-revolution Ukraine is learning the difficult art of democratic pluralism. Freedom of expression has flourished. A noisy participative democracy, complete with impromptu demonstrations springing up everywhere, has given the population the feeling of being part of political processes.

At pains to pacify a domestic electorate scared by the potential costs of further enlargement, the EU has chosen the ostrich's strategy and postponed discussions on membership and association *ad infinitum*. Yet, what Brussels (and many of the member states) fail to recognise is that keeping Kyiv close to its sphere of influence is not only possible, but also in the EU's interest. A state of forty-eight million people, characterised by a rapidly changing society and an economy with substantive potential for growth, Ukraine could become a fully reliable political and economic partner for the EU. In the face of Russia's unabated imperialistic ambitions and continuous pressures on Ukraine, a membership perspective would help in this effort.

Notes

1 The opinions expressed are the author's only and cannot be ascribed to any of the EU institutions she has been engaged with.
2 See Novyny–UT1 (3 December 2005), www.ukrainatv.com/eng/catalogue/News/4585.html.
3 The Summit was originally scheduled to take place in London. On the insistence of the Ukrainian leadership, particularly First Deputy Prime Minister in charge of European Integration, Oleh Rybachuk, the decision was made to hold it in Kyiv.
4 *Joint Statement from the EU–Ukraine Summit* (Kyiv, December 2005), www.delukr.cec.eu.int/site.php/page47.html?lang=en&SESSID=ae54ef91efd0fd4f088e02005a74f5a9.
5 Charlotte Bretherton and John Vogler, *The European Union as a Global Actor* (London: Routledge, 1999), p. 5.
6 Anthony Browne and Robert Thomson, 'How I am going to wake this great sleeping elephant and ride into the EU: interview with Victor Yushchenko', *The Times* (31 January 2005).
7 Victor Yushchenko, 'Address by the President of Ukraine's on the occasion of the first part of the 2005 Ordinary Session of the Council of Europe Parliamentary Assembly', (25 January 2005), http://ww2.yuschenko.com.ua/eng/Press_centre/168/2197/.
8 Lynne Berry, 'Ukraine's President takes the stage', *Moscow Times* (31 January 2005).
9 While Ukrainians would hardly see the difference between the two, President Yushchenko started reclaiming a European identity disconnected from EU membership: 'I don't feel comfortable striving to join Europe, I feel like I am a European. I live in a European country and possess European values.' Ibid.
10 Interfax (2 July 2003), www.interfax-news.com.
11 Journalist Tataian Selina expressed this feeling quite effectively: 'The choice we are to make is not geopolitical in nature. It is a choice of civilisation. It is not about whom to be with – Russia, the EU or NATO – because we can cooperate with all of them. It is about what we will be like. It is about the principles and standards of life.' Tataian Selina, 'Ukrainians' National Pride', *Zerkalo Nedeli*, 44:519 (30 October–5 November 2004).
12 Several interviews with author in Kyiv throughout 2004.
13 Tataian Selina, 'The adjustment of virtual reality', *Zerkalo Nedeli*, 17:492 (30 April–15 May 2004).
14 For more information, see the Delegation of the European Commission to Ukraine, www.delukr.cec.eu.int/site/page36480.html.
15 Estimate of the Delegation of the European Commission to Ukraine, unpublished data.
16 Romano Prodi cited Roman Kupchinsky, 'On the border between Europe and Asia', *The Ukrainian Weekly*, 20 (16 May 2004), www.ukrweekly.com/Archive/2004/200404.shtml.
17 European Commission, *Wider Europe – Neighbourhood: A New Framework for Relations with our Eastern and Southern Neighbours* (Brussels, 2003).
18 European Commission, *European Neighbourhood Policy: Strategy Paper* (Brussels, 2004).
19 Borys Tarasyuk, 'Perspectives after ten years of the PCA', Speech at the Round Table, Kyiv (15 June 2004).

20 See, for example, Taras Kuzio, *EU and Ukraine: A Turning Point in 2004?* (Paris: Institute for Security Studies, 2003).
21 I have discussed these elements in 'The rise of the Ukrainian oligarchs', *Democratization*, 11:3 (Autumn 2003), pp. 99–123 and 'Clashing agendas? Economic interests, elite coalitions and prospects for cooperation between Russia and Ukraine', *Europe–Asia Studies*, 55:6 (2003), pp. 827–45.
22 Steven Boyd Saum, 'Orange Revolution: the rapping sound of democracy's arrival in Ukraine', *WorldView Magazine*, 18:1 (Spring 2005), www.worldviewmagazine.com/issues/article.cfm?id=154&issue=37.
23 Leonid Kuchma, *European Choice Conceptual Grounds of the Strategy of Economic and Social Development of Ukraine for 2002–2011: Address of the President of Ukraine to the Verkhovna Rada of Ukraine* (31 May 2002), www.infoukes.com/ukremb/kuchma-verkhovna.shtml; *Strategy of the Economic and Social Development of Ukraine (2004–2015) – Towards European Integration*' (Kyiv: Ministry of Economy and European Integration, 2004).
24 See *Joint Report on the Implementation of the Partnership and Co-operation Agreement between the EU and Ukraine* (Brussels, March 2003), www.delukr.cec.eu.int/data/doc/pca_report_0303_eng.pdf.
25 See Office for Democratic Institutions and Human Rights, *Final Report on the 2004 Presidential Elections in Ukraine* (OSCE, Warsaw: 2005).
26 During the last years of the Kuchma Presidency, Ukrainian information policy was dictated by the so-called *temniki*. These were instructions drafted within the Presidential Administration for newspaper and TV editorial boards concerning how news was to be covered, to ensure consistency across the whole media spectrum. See Marta Dyczok, 'Was Kuchma's censorship effective? Mass media in Ukraine before 2004', *Europe–Asia Studies*, forthcoming (2006).
27 Interfax (1 October 2003), www.interfax.com/.
28 Tataian Selina, 'It is important to hear each other', *Zerkalo Nedeli*, 39:464 (11–17 October 2003).
29 One such estimate, prepared by the Ministry of Economy and presented at the EU–Ukraine Co-operation Committee, put the figure at between $250–350m. See Ukrnews, (10 December 2003), www.ukrnews.net. For an EU response, see Tataian Selina 'EU Trade Commissioner Pascal Lamy: the first priority for Ukraine should be accession to the World Trade Organisation', *Zerkalo Nedeli*, 20:495 (22–8 May 2004).
30 European Commission, *Reactions to Draft Agreement establishing a Single Economic Space by Russia, Ukraine, Belarus and Kazakhstan', Information to the Press circulated by the Delegation of the European Commission to Ukraine* (Kyiv, September 2003).
31 Tataian Selina, 'A pearl casting game', *Zerkalo Nedeli*, 20:495 (22–8 May 2004).
32 The Delegation of the European Commission to Ukraine gathered evidence of *temniki* instructing media outlets to censor some EU statements.
33 Interfax (21 April 2004), www.interfax-news.com.
34 Interfax (26 April 2004), www.interfax-news.com.
35 UT1 (28 April 2004), www.ukrainatv.com/eng/catalogue/News/4585.html.
36 Ukrnews (16 July 2004), www.ukrnews.net/.
37 The EU, US, Norway, Turkey, and Japan established a working group for the monitoring of the electoral process. It was active from January to December 2004. With regard to Russian interference in the electoral campaign see, Olga Dmitricheva, 'Russia endorses Yanukovich's Presidential bid', *Zerkalo Nedeli*, 42:517 (16–22 October 2004).
38 These arguments were expressed by leaders across the pro-Yushchenko coalition. For more details see *Ukraine, EU, Russia: Challenges and Opportunities for new Relations Conference, East–West Institute, Kyiv* (10–11 February 2005), www.ewi.info/pdf/TRANSCRIPTS_Kyiv_10–11February2005.pdf.
39 Ibid.

40 This position was expressed, for example, by Igor Dir, Head of the Foreign Ministry Department for European Integration. Ibid.
41 For details of *The EU–Ukraine Action Plan* (Brussels, February 2005), http://delukr.cec.eu.int/files/Action%20Plan%20Text-final-website.pdf.
42 Ukrainska Pravda (6 February 2005), www2.pravda.com.ua/en/.
43 According to a survey published in March 2003, of 1,000 people questioned in France, Germany, Italy, Poland, Spain and the UK, 55 per cent said they would support a Ukrainian bid for membership. EUbusiness (24 March 2005), www.eubusiness.com/.
44 Ukranews (26 May 2004), www.ukranews.com.
45 Interfax (8 June 2004), www.interfax-news.com.
46 Ukrnews (2 September 2004), www.ukrnews.net.
47 For example, see the comments of UK MEP Charles Tannock, Ukrnews (3 September 2002), www.ukrnews.net.
48 *European Parliament Resolution on the Results of the Ukraine Elections* (Strasbourg, January 2005).
49 Press release of the 2641 meeting of the General Affairs and External Relations Council (Brussels, February 2005), pp. 14–16.
50 Ibid.
51 Meeting MEPs in January 2006, Foreign Minister Tarasyuk hinted that Ukraine is seeking to sign an agreement on association with the EU, which would give it a membership perspective. Ukranews (1 February 2006), www.ukrnews.net.

11

The EU and Turkey: bridge or barrier?

Bill Park

Introduction

Turkey's future relationship to the EU will have a significant impact on both the role Turkey plays in Europe's future security architecture and on Europe's security agenda. Yet, and notwithstanding the October 2005 decision by the EU to commence accession negotiations with Turkey, full Turkish membership is not a foregone conclusion, at least within the projected ten to fifteen years time scale. The reasons for this element of uncertainty are three-fold. Firstly, the rejection of the EU's Constitution by the French and Dutch electorates has thrown the European project into turmoil. Given the widespread view that these negative votes were partially related to the economic burdens and immigration 'threat' of Turkey's projected accession, it is possible that Turkey's entry could be put on hold by EU governing elites unwilling to provoke their unhappy electorates still further.

Secondly, there are persistent rumblings of unease with the very idea of Turkish accession, both amongst Europe's populations and governing elites. In addition to its population size – on current trends Turkey's population would be larger than that of any EU member state by 2014 – and relative poverty, Turkey's Islamic character renders it non-European in the eyes of many, especially Christian Democrat, Europeans. Germany's Christian Democrats have proposed a 'privileged partnership' rather than full membership for Turkey, whilst France, Austria and others are likely to hold referenda before Turkey's accession is finally granted. Opinion polls repeatedly suggest a positive vote would be unlikely.[1]

Thirdly, Turkey itself has many hurdles to overcome before it would be sufficiently regarded as ready for full membership. The Justice and Development Party (AKP), elected to government in November 2002, has made great strides in passing the requisite laws and in amending the constitution, but question marks continue to hover over both the will and the capacity of Ankara to fully implement these changes. Furthermore, Turkey's Kemalist establishment, although traditionally seeking Turkey's 'Westernisation', remains jealous of the country's sovereignty and of its somewhat authoritarian and incompletely democratic political culture and institutions. Even out of elected office, this state establishment possesses formidable scope to obstruct the elected government's efforts. In any case, Turkey's political future, and the fortunes of its AKP government, cannot be safely predicted.

The uncertainty that surrounds Turkey's EU future is not the only independent variable that renders any discussion of the security implications of Turkey's EU membership problematic. The framework within which Europe's security needs will be addressed in the future is itself unresolved. In the wake of the fall-out over the deposing of Saddam's regime, which split the EU's membership down the middle, the future cohesion of the Atlantic Alliance remains uncertain. The Bush administration's inclination towards unilateralism, and the shift in its security focus away from Europe towards the Middle East and Asia, adds to the sense that some of NATO's earlier certainties have been eroded. The majority of EU members are also NATO members, as is Turkey, and these fissures in perspective and behaviour are bound to impact on the security implications of Turkey's EU accession (or, indeed, of its non-accession), in ways that are hard to foretell.

The prospects of the EU's own endeavours to firm up a CFSP and associated ESDP are similarly uncertain. The 1998 Anglo-French St Malo agreement indicated that London and Paris were and are the primary engines behind any progress in ESDP. However, these states are yet to fully repair their differences in the wake of the debacle over Iraq. Only time will tell whether this state of affairs is temporary or not, but there is something in the view that the St Malo agreement papered over, rather than repaired, the cracks between the UK's Atlanticism and French Europeanism. European consensus on future security challenges is not assured. Declining defence budgets throughout much of the EU, and a marked tardiness in reforming European armed forces to take account of post-Cold War changes and the requirements of ESDP, encourage a scepticism concerning ESDP's prospects. The ESDP's Petersberg tasks, namely humanitarian missions, crisis management and peace support operations, and the Headline Force Goals agreed in 1999 for the creation of an ERRF, are quite modest. The material progress made by the EU has been similarly modest. While the EU took over responsibility for military peace-keeping in Bosnia at the end of 2004 and has also been able to launch a long-range – and largely French – mission in the Eastern Congo, this does not alter the essential modesty both of the EU's aspirations and its achievements.

Blending Turkey's distinctive security culture and geopolitical circumstances and outlook into some common European theme will be a far from straightforward exercise. Turkey's EU accession is itself emerging as a source of division between the EU's extant members. The security implications of Turkey's EU accession are especially uncertain and contested. As a consequence, this chapter contains some inevitable speculation. Too much is uncertain to permit over-definitive conclusions. Turkey's domestic evolution, events in its neighbourhood (especially Iraq), the path its accession negotiations will take (including the impact that the Cyprus issue has on them), the EU's future as well as that of the Atlantic alliance – all are subject to debate, difference and uncertainty. The intertwining of these themes will suffuse the analysis of this chapter.

Turkey, Europe and security

Turkey's association with the EU has been a long, and frequently tortuous, one.[2] The twists and turns of Turkey's bid to accede to the EU, which dates back at least to the Ankara agreement of 1963, suggest that the road ahead could be full of pitfalls and interruptions. Fresh doubts were cast over Turkey's accession bid in the wake of the French and Dutch referenda that 'rejected' the EU constitution. Subsequently, talk of a further delay in Turkish accession, or even its exclusion from EU membership, has intensified.

Although Turkey became a WEU associate member in 1991, explicit security considerations have generally been absent during the long saga of Turkey–EU relations. Even when present, they have rarely been paramount. Yet, as a consequence of its geo-strategically compelling location, security considerations are rarely far from any broader commentary on Turkey. Turkey straddles many cultural and political fault lines, such that it has been designated a 'pivotal' state in terms of regional and global security.[3] Turkey is simultaneously part of, or borders, Europe, the Middle East, the Caucasus and the Mediterranean, Balkan, Black Sea and even Caspian regions. It is geographically Eurasian, Islamic by faith but officially secular, and Turkey's political, social and economic elite and population are broadly 'European' in aspiration. Turkey shares a linguistic and cultural root, if not much recent history, with a Turkic world that embraces the former Soviet Central Asian states, Azerbaijan and a number of minorities in the Middle East, the Balkans and the FSU. Since the collapse of the USSR, Turkey has increasingly provided an outlet for the people, trade and energy resources of the former Soviet space. It is fast becoming an energy highway, with pipelines from Iraq and Iran, as well as from various locations in the FSU, most notably the Baku-Ceyhan pipeline.

Evidently, Turkish accession would entail a profound shift in the EU's geopolitical and geo-strategic circumstances. Elements within the EU are arguably more repelled by Turkey's proximity to troubled and turbulent regions than they are attracted by Turkey's pivotal geopolitical location. The EU may have neither the capacity nor the desire to cope with the problems such a dangerous 'neighbourhood' might bring. Some have argued that the EU's interests would be better served by preserving Turkey's role as Europe's security 'insulator' from the problems of the Middle East[4] – or, to put it another way, to keep it as a 'barrier' rather than as a 'bridge' to some of the globe's worst trouble spots.[5] Ankara and Washington have frequently failed to appreciate this when they have sought to impress the EU by highlighting Turkey's strategic significance.[6]

Much hinges on whether the EU has or can develop sufficient will or capacity to engage actively with trouble spots beyond its own borders. The EU's adoption of the ESS in December 2003,[7] expressing concern about global terrorism, WMD proliferation and the problems generated by failed states, together with the EU's Neighbourhood Policy,[8] suggest a growing EU interest in active engagement in areas of salience to Ankara, such as the Middle East, North Africa, the Caucasus and the

Black Sea region. The emphasis in these initiatives is on multilateral diplomacy and conflict resolution, but it remains unclear whether they genuinely herald either a greater foreign policy consensus or readiness to act more collectively than hitherto, let alone any enhanced European willingness to contemplate the use of force.[9]

In any case, and in addition to a general reluctance to focus on hard security issues, Europeans have not always sympathised with Turkey in its regional difficulties. This has served to reinforce a historical and instinctive mistrust of European diplomacy in Ankara that dates back to Ottoman times. There is no sound reason to assume that an enhanced European activism and foreign policy consensus would overlap with Ankara's preferences. Until the April 2004 referenda on Cyprus, in which the Greek side of the island voted against the UN settlement plan and the Turkish side voted for it, European sympathies with respect to Cyprus were generally with the Greek side. Indeed, (Greek) Cyprus acceded to the Union in May 2004, regardless of the island's continued division. In contrast, and notwithstanding greater sympathy for the plight of Turkish Cypriots in the north of the island, the EU remains unwilling to countenance Turkish membership in the absence of Ankara's recognition of the Nicosia government. At the time of writing, a settlement of Cyprus continues to look distant, and the issue retains the capacity to derail Turkey's EU accession bid.[10]

Iraq too has often been a source of difference. European arms deliveries to Turkey were held up in protest at Turkey's military incursions into Iraq during the 1990s in pursuit of Kurdish Workers Party (PKK) activists. On the eve of the US-led attack on Iraq in 2003, Germany, France and Belgium refused to sanction a transfer of NATO AWACS, chemical and biological detection teams and Patriot missiles to Turkey, confirming Turkish doubts as to the reliability of their European NATO allies. So serious was this crisis that the then US Secretary of State, Colin Powell, raised the spectre of NATO 'breaking up' as a consequence.[11] In addition, some European states are less impressed than Washington with Turkey's relationship with Israel, but share with Washington an influential Armenian (and Kurdish) lobby, whose activities often serve to undermine sympathy with Turkey.

On the other hand, although Turkey's location might suggest that it could constitute a security burden to the EU, Turkey can equally be seen as a security 'provider'. Since the Cold War in particular, Ankara's diplomacy has increasingly reflected the complexity and diversity of Turkey's geopolitical circumstances. For example, Turkey took the lead role in the establishment of the Black Sea Economic Cooperation Organisation (BSEC) in 1992, and the Black Sea Naval Cooperation Task Group (BlackSeaFor) in 2001. In late 2002, Ankara initiated the formation of the loose group of Regional Countries bordering Iraq that have since been co-opted by the UN in the search for a viable future for post-Saddam Iraq.[12] Turkey belongs to the Mediterranean Forum, formed in 1994, and has played a leading role in the multiplicity of groupings concerned with the Balkans – the Stability Pact, the South-East European Cooperation Process, the Multinational Peace-keeping Force for South-Eastern Europe (SEEBRIG) established in 1999, and so on. In addition to its intense bilateral relations with Azerbaijan and Georgia, Ankara forms part of the Minsk Group set up to mediate the conflict over Nagorno-Karabakh between Armenia and

Azerbaijan, and works hard to cultivate the Turkic countries of Central Asia. However, diplomatic relations with Armenia are frozen, chiefly as a consequence of the Nagorno-Karabakh conflict, and this too could be a problem, given the EU requirement that candidate members resolve differences with neighbouring states (an obligation not imposed on Greek Cyprus, or Greece).

Turkey has generally played a constructive NATO role, engaging actively in PfP training missions and agreeing to the establishment on Turkish territory of an anti-terrorist training centre and a tactical air training centre. Turkish troops are also amongst the most utilised in NATO, or anywhere else for that matter. Since 1993, Turkey has been a regular contributor to peace-keeping and other multilateral military missions, including Somalia, former Yugoslavia, Albania, Georgia, Kuwait, Hebron, East Timor and Afghanistan, where Turkey took over command of ISAF from the UK in 2002, and again in February 2005. In November 2003, a Turkish offer of 10,000 troops to assist the US-led coalition in peace-keeping duties in Iraq was withdrawn only in the face of Iraqi, and particularly Kurdish, opposition. In addition to its membership of NATO and other Western institutions, Turkey has long been a member of the Organisation of the Islamic Conference (OIC) and the essentially Islamic Economic Cooperation Organisation (ECO).

The EU's recognition and appreciation of Turkey's constructive diplomacy can be variable. For example, the EU's ESDP initiative failed to take account either of Turkey's utility or its security concerns. For the EU, the formal launch of the ESDP in 1999 was both an expression of the EU's aspiration to achieve greater political union and 'actorness' in its external dealings, and a means to address low-key threats to stability around its periphery or within its reach. Yet Ankara's initial reaction to its exclusion from the ESDP initiative was fierce, inspired both by an assumption that the EU was seeking to challenge NATO as Europe's pre-eminent security institution and by the consequence that Turkey would thereby be excluded from a key component of Europe's emerging security architecture. Given that thirteen of the sixteen 'hot spots' identified by NATO were located broadly within Turkey's vicinity, Ankara argued that the EU might engage itself in crises in which Turkey had a stake, but no right to be consulted.

The affair offered an indication of Ankara's perennial mistrust of its European allies. Ankara's outburst prompted a bout of intense diplomatic activity by London and Washington, in an endeavour to square Turkey's position with the EU's plans.[13] In the event, they were eventually able to satisfy Turkish grievances with the so-called 'Ankara document' agreed in December 2001. This incorporated mechanisms for more inclusive consultation with non-EU NATO allies, a commitment to exclude Cyprus as a non-NATO and non-PfP state from the ESDP's agenda, recognition of Turkey's right to a say and to participation in any ESDP activities in its region and an undertaking that ESDP missions would not come into conflict with any NATO ally. However, Greek objections to these arrangements meant that the issue was not finally 'resolved' until a year later.

As a carrot and as a reminder of the material contribution Turkey could make, Ankara had declared at Nice its willingness to commit to the EU's proposed ERRF a minimum of 5,000 troops, thirty-six F-16s and air transport and maritime vessels, in the event of the EU devising more inclusive mechanisms for non-EU participation in ESDP decision making.[14] On the other hand, the ESDP episode also demonstrated the scope for increased EU–Turkish tension should Ankara's endeavour to join the EU fail. It also confirmed many in their suspicion that Turkey would function as an Atlanticist 'Trojan horse' inside the EU, if it were ever allowed to join.

Turkey and the West during the Cold War and beyond

Turkey's aspiration to join the EU is part of a broader post-1945 integration into the Western world. From the west's perspective, Turkey's Cold War value derived largely from a location that offered a southern flank in the containment of an expansionist communist ideology from Moscow.[15] In addition to base facilities, Turkey was valued for the contribution of its armed forces which, with US help, were impressively modernised and currently stand at almost 500,000 strong, constituting the second largest in NATO. Turkey is also proximate to a Middle East region that became a recipient of Moscow's increased attentions and whose oil featured ever larger in the security interests of the world's industrialised states.

However, Turkey's NATO membership has largely taken the form of a Turkish–US bilateral strategic alliance, and has had hard security considerations at it heart. Europeans generally acquiesced to Turkey's membership of the alliance in the interests of containment of the Soviet Union in Europe and at the behest of Washington.[16] During the Cold War, only the UK and France consistently engaged with security issues beyond Europe itself. It is also worth recalling that the UK's initial post-Second World War preference, and that of many senior figures in the US too, was that Turkey should become part of a Middle Eastern, rather than European, security architecture. Turkey was not considered as unambiguously European geographically, geostrategically or politically.[17]

With the Cold War's demise, many anticipated a decline in Turkey's strategic utility. However, US preoccupation with Iraq, from the 1990 annexation of Kuwait until the 2003 removal of the Ba'athist regime in Baghdad, combined with its Iranian concerns to maintain Turkey's geostrategic value to Washington. During the crisis over the Iraqi annexation of Kuwait, Ankara closed the pipeline carrying Iraqi oil through Turkey to the Mediterranean, permitted the use of bases on Turkish territory for US bombing raids against Iraq, co-operated with the trade sanctions policy against Iraq and deployed a substantial military force on the Iraqi border. Then President Turgut Ozal's single-minded determination ensured that Turkey would be regarded as pivotal in Washington's approach to Iraq specifically and the Middle East generally.[18]

Subsequent to the liberation of Kuwait, access to the NATO base at Incirlik enabled the establishment of a 'no-fly-zone' over northern Iraq by US and UK (and initially French) forces. In the wake of the overthrow of Saddam Hussein's regime in 2003, Incirlik has again been useful in supplying and rotating US troops deployed in

Iraq. The post-September 11 'War on Terror', in which the November 2003 Istanbul bombings made Turkey a 'front-line' state, Washington's suspicion of Iran and Syria, general regional instability and Turkey's emergence as a conduit for gas and oil pipelines have also helped sustain Turkey's post-Cold War pivotal status in US eyes. Turkey's proximity to the troubled Caucasus, and its linguistic and cultural affinities with Central Asia, similarly add value.

A shift in Turkey–US relations?

Europe's strategic perspective on Turkey has not invariably brought comfort to Ankara and has frequently differed from that of the US. Although both have an interest in a stable and democratic Turkey, differences over how to prioritise and conduct relations with Turkey nevertheless add to transatlantic differences.[19] However, with the removal of Saddam Hussein and thus the need to contain him, there has also been cause for Washington to question the strategic utility of Turkey's geographical location. The 1 March 2003 vote in Turkey's National Assembly that refused US access to Turkish territory as a launch pad for an invasion of northern Iraq reminded Washington that Turkey could obstruct as well as enable its access to this vital region.[20] The vote also hinted at a possible weakening of the Turkish General Staff's (TGS) domestic political role, which would constitute a significant development, given the role the TGS has frequently played as the main conduit of Washington's policy preferences. The realisation that Washington and Ankara do not necessarily share perspectives on the Middle East has been reinforced by subsequent developments. Ankara remains unhappy with the US-led adventure in Iraq, and angry and frustrated at the perceived failure to reign in Iraq's Kurds and to quell the activities of those remnants of the PKK based in northern Iraq's mountains. Furthermore, Turkey's relations with Syria have warmed substantially, and its contacts with Iran are at least businesslike and respectful. These flirtations have met with Washington's ardent disapproval.[21]

In the future, it appears less likely that Ankara will be able to 'punch above its weight' in Washington. Although Turkey will surely remain a valued ally, the US–Turkish relationship looks set to alter its parameters, and acquire a less exclusively military dimension.[22] Former US Assistant Defence Secretary, Paul Wolfowitz, has speculated on how US–Turkish relations might, in future, be based more on their shared commitment to the development of a democratic, modernising Islamic world.[23] Indeed, this approach reinforces Washington's support for Turkey's EU membership. At the NATO summit in Istanbul in June 2004, US President George W. Bush remarked to the Turks that their country's EU membership would 'be a crucial advance in relations between the Muslim world and the west, because you are part of both'. It would 'prove that Europe is not the exclusive club of a single religion, and it would expose the "clash of civilisations" as a passing myth of history'.[24]

To some degree, the AKP government concurs with aspects of current US thinking about the political and economic failings of the Islamic world.[25] Turkish Foreign

Minister in the AKP government, Abdullah Gul, first outlined what he has dubbed 'the Turkish vision' for the Middle East region at the Islamic Foreign Ministers conference in May 2003. He called on the Muslim world to strive for good governance, transparency, accountability, gender equality and the upholding of rights and freedoms, so as to engender a 'sense of ownership on the part of the people of the systems they live in'. He also highlighted the need to reduce the corruption, economic irrationality and instability in the Islamic world, in order that progress could be made.[26] Furthermore, Gul has repeatedly argued that Turkey's fusion of traditional (Islamic) values with modernity proves they are not incompatible, and that the Middle East region as a whole could combine human and economic development with a maintenance of its cultural and religious values. He has asserted that 'Turkey is living proof that a Muslim society can be governed in a democratic, accountable and transparent manner in accordance with European norms . . . Turkey testifies to the fact that European values indeed transcend geography, religion and cultures.'[27] In the post-September 11, post-Saddam world, and with the AKP in office, Turkey might, for once, be genuinely positioned to bring together the values and interests of the west and the Middle East.

In short, and in the context of Washington's Greater Middle East Initiative, Turkey might, at last, begin to serve as the model of a democratised, Westernised but Islamic state that Washington has longed for it to be.[28] Paradoxically, however, this might partly come as a consequence, and be reinforced by, a less close US–Turkish relationship. Whether it would enhance Turkey–EU relations, or Ankara's prospects of EU accession, remains unclear. For some Europeans, such as German Chancellor, Angela Merkel, and former French President, Giscard D'Estaing, handing Turkey a 'privileged partnership', in effect rendering Turkey a key element in the ENP, would constitute sufficient recognition of Turkey's efforts and importance.

Turkey, Europe and identity

Notwithstanding the NATO-wide Cold War consensus on the need to contain the Soviet threat, the EU's security culture is at odds with that traditionally associated with Turkey and the US. After the Second World War, Western Europe set out to construct relationships between its constituent states such that the rivalry and wars that had bedevilled modern European history might be avoided in future. The key to achieving this goal was to 'de-securitise' relationships in Europe, and instead to base future relations on transparency, social and cultural interpenetration, economic integration, good governance, civilian control of the military, political consensus building and the adoption of common values. Ultimately, a measure of political union might even be achieved, implying a readiness to dilute national sovereignty. As a 'civil power', reliant far more on its economic and political influence and appeal than on its military prowess, and still unproven as an effective security actor externally, the EU is perhaps best seen as a security 'community' than as a security 'actor'.[29]

In 1993, the EU adopted the so-called 'Copenhagen criteria', outlining the conditions aspirant states were required to meet before membership could be granted. They emphasise political criteria, such as respect for human and minority rights, the rule of law, and stable democratic institutions, as well as economic criteria, such as a functioning market economy. They also reflected Western Europe's consensus that the extension of democratisation, transparency, the rule of law and integration eastwards would itself help guarantee the security and stability of the 'new' Europe. For the former communist CEE states, keen to throw off the residues of communism and 'return' to a Europe to which they rightfully and naturally belonged, the Copenhagen criteria – and partnership agreements with NATO that similarly constituted the pathway to expanded membership – offered a clarifying road-map. The Copenhagen criteria offered both guidance and incentive regarding the direction their internal transformations should take.

Unlike post-communist Europe, however, Turkey in the 1990s did not experience a critical juncture. Rather, in the Turkish case, the Copenhagen criteria confronted a fully formed, long-standing and entrenched political culture and system that, many Turks believed, had served them well in their endeavours to modernise and democratise their country. Nor was Turkey seeking to 'return' to a Europe to which it was seen to properly belong. Turkey had not been isolated from Western Europe during the Cold War. Notwithstanding Turkish claims that they had been part of Europe since Ottoman times, Turkey's aspirations were rather to be accepted as part of, rather than 'return' to, a Europe that, in civilisation terms, had long held it at arms length. Turkey had never been regarded as part of that centuries-old definition of Europe as something akin to 'Christendom', and its Cold War Western affiliations had not fully dispelled the impact of this.[30] Put another way, there was a sense in which, for at least some EU states, 'Turkey, rather than being a "natural insider", was an "important outsider".'[31]

Turkey's security culture

Turkey's distinctive security culture is one reason why Europeans can sometimes perceive Turkey as 'different'. Turkish political culture notes a strong attachment to the utility of military force and a tendency to adopt a hard security approach to domestic issues, such as Kurdish identity politics and the role of political Islam.[32] Ankara is also intensely jealous of its territorial integrity, a phenomenon sometimes referred to as the 'Sevres complex', and is sensitive to what it perceives as external 'interference' in its domestic affairs. This can appear somewhat at odds with the political culture of Western Europe.[33] Ankara's ready resort to the threat or use of military force – in Cyprus in 1974, Iraq on a number of occasions in the 1990s, against Syria in 1998 and during the crisis over the planned deployment of Russian S300 missiles in Cyprus in the same year – offer expressions of this distinctive security culture. Ankara's approach to Kurdish identity politics has also been almost exclusively military and repressive.[34] Recognition of (Kurdish) minority rights and a willingness to embrace diversity have been notable more by their absence. Although many would argue that Ankara's hard approach to security is primarily a consequence of its problematic neighbourhood, tendencies such as these nevertheless indicate how divergent the political and security cultures of the EU and Turkey can appear to be. The high profile of the TGS, both in domestic politics and in the determination of Turkey's external policies, both explains and exhibits some of Turkey's peculiarities.[35]

Turkish changes

On the other hand, the impact on Turkish domestic politics of the prospect of EU accession has been profound. The reform programme, introduced by the AKP government and by the coalition government that preceded it, has been impressive in scope.[36] Most notably, the military-dominated National Security Council (NSC) has been converted from an executive into a purely advisory body. Defence spending has been opened up to parliamentary scrutiny. The military-dominated State Security courts have been abolished. The state of emergency has been lifted throughout the entire south east of the country. Military representation on the country's media and educational boards has ended. Laws easing the restrictions on Kurdish language broadcasting and education have also been introduced. In short, Turkey's political and security culture has been subjected to something of a legislative assault.

Few doubt the impact that the AKP government, in particular, has had on the tenor of Turkish politics. In addition to lobbying strongly to achieve a settlement of the Cyprus problem, EU accession has been its top policy priority. Its calculation appears to have been that the obligations of EU accession offer the best opportunity to entrench political rights and to build the 'good governance' that the AKP leadership hopes will emerge from its EU-related reform programme. Its remarkably successful management of the economy and its anti-corruption campaign might similarly help marginalise the traditional political and bureaucratic establishment, and thus reinforce the AKP's domestic popularity, as well as meet the EU's requirements.[37] Paradoxically, these developments have cast elements of Turkey's 'Westernising' Kemalist establishment in the role of critics of the AKP government's success in Europe.[38]

Should the AKP remain in office, and if Turkey continues along its recent reformist path, the country might eventually evolve into a 'normal' modern European state. Given that the future EU–Turkey security nexus will hinge considerably on Turkey's domestic development, there are good reasons to suppose that, on present trends, Ankara's security policy might more and more align with the EU's mainstream. This will, in part, stem from a process of 'socialisation' into the EU's security culture, in which Ankara might increasingly adopt the 'security community' approach. Ankara's foreign policy dilemma has been characterised as that of a state located on a fault-line between the European co-operative, consensus-building, Kantian 'security community', on the one hand, and the Hobbesian political turmoil, violence, mistrust and zero-sum approach to security issues of Turkey's immediate region, on the other.[39]

One could argue that the current government, partly inspired by the prospect of EU membership, is seeking to apply, where it can, the diplomatic approach of the former to the more atavistic Middle Eastern arena. Examples might include its opening to Syria, the rest of the Arab world and Iran; its open embrace of the Islamic heritage it shares with its neighbours and beyond; its détente with Greece and its more constructive approach to the Cyprus issue; and its active and generally co-operative diplomacy towards the Black Sea and Caspian regions, Central Asia and much of the Balkans and Caucasus regions.

There are grounds for pessimism too, however. Much of Turkey's secular political elite remains wedded to the 'Sevres complex', a prickly brand of nationalism, security consciousness and paranoia that frequently elides into anti-European sentiment. Should these elements regain political power in the near future, a successful outcome to the EU accession negotiations would appear less likely. For example, the military's domestic political influence has traditionally relied on more than constitutional provision and its former capacity to dominate the NSC. It has also been expressed less formally, through a combination of threats, civilian self-censorship, legal and constitutional interpretation, a fragmented political culture and genuine domestic popularity.[40] Even in the wake of recent reforms, laws and constitutional clauses that place limits on freedom of speech and political activity remain in place. There is, too, an unsettling tension between the Islamic-inspired AKP government and the Kemalist establishment concerning, amongst other things, the nature and extent of Turkey's secularity.

The Kurdish issue, now inextricably bound up with developments in Iraq, also offers grounds for pessimism. The threat posed by Turkey's Kurdish separatists was substantially reduced in the wake of PKK leader Abdullah Ocalan's incarceration in 1999. However, there has been a marked increase in violent incidents since the PKK lifted its unilateral ceasefire in June 2004. In any case, it is not certain that the EU-inspired reforms, aimed at liberalising the laws governing political activity or cultural and linguistic expression, either go far enough or will be sufficiently implemented to encourage disaffected Kurds into the mainstream of Turkish society. Kurdish ethnic identity and a sense of grievance remain intact, and a continuation of the conflict in its more violent manifestations could set back both Turkey's democratisation, and EU accession, prospects.[41]

Should Turkey's neighbourhood implode as a consequence of continued chaos in Iraq, other possibilities emerge. The future of Iraq, and particularly its Kurdish north, looms large as a security concern in Ankara.[42] Ankara continues to fear that Iraq and the entire region could unravel, and is concerned at the prospect of a more or less sovereign Kurdish entity emerging in northern Iraq.[43] It is even conceivable that Turkey and other regional powers might feel they have no option but to intervene militarily in Iraq, in unison or competitively, to forestall the emergence of a *de facto* Kurdish state or in some way establish control over events.[44] For the time being, the hope of EU accession and US strategic sponsorship function as inhibitors on Turkish adventurism. Should Iraq descend into further chaos, particularly within the context of a US withdrawal, and should Ankara fail to get satisfaction from the EU, such constraints would be reduced. Intense regional turbulence could prompt a return of 'traditional' forces and politics in Turkey, putting back the prospect of EU accession. Domestically, the military would once again return to the forefront of Turkish politics, positive developments in the handling of Turkey's domestic Kurdish dilemmas could be reversed and Turkey might once again exhibit a more nationalistic and militaristic face. In such circumstances, Ankara might seek to develop its regional relationships more broadly, in the Middle East, perhaps in the wider Islamic world, the Caucasus, Central Asia, Russia and Ukraine. Alternatively, it could find itself pushed back into Washington's arms, particularly were Iran to emerge as a (WMD-armed) rival to Turkey for influence and control in Iraq. Turkish external policy could incorporate elements of each of these options.

Transatlantic relations and Ankara's dilemmas

The security implications of EU enlargement to include Turkey also hinge on the future of transatlantic relationships. US–European relations will suffer the more the latter seek to become counterweights rather than partners to Washington.[45] This in turn is more likely should US policy continue along the somewhat unilateralist and relatively unconstrained path associated with the Bush administration. The end of the Cold War, and the US post-September 11 sensation that their homeland is now vulnerable and that the 'War on Terror' is a vital national interest, make it unlikely that Europe could reasonably expect to continue as 'both the locus and the focus'[46] of US security policy. However, this shift in geo-strategic focus, combined with US unilateralism, might appear to leave the EU with little more than a supporting role to play. This could be an uncomfortable position to be in. At the minimum, such a predicament could lead many Europeans to the conclusion that a better course might be to keep a safe distance from at least the more controversial or risky US adventures. Differences of perspective and interest, and the sheer risks of too closely aligning with an adventurous and unconstrained US, might lead Europeans to adopt positions that are more explicitly distinctive.

The record to date, however, suggests that European unity is hardly more likely to be forthcoming than transatlantic consensus. Thus, some European states supported and others opposed the US-led military action against Iraq. The result was an EU whose internal differences appeared more brutally exposed than ever. This too could have an enduring impact. For example, it has been plausibly argued that progress with respect to ESDP relies on relatively tight Anglo-French co-operation. This is now less likely, given the profound differences between these two leading European states that the Iraq crisis revealed.[47] A longer historical perspective will tend to support the view that such differences concerning the importance of transatlantic relations and how best to preserve them will outlast changes in government, and not only in France and the UK. Furthermore, Robert Kagan's well-known thesis offers reinforcement to the view that transatlantic differences are here to stay.[48]

Where and how might Turkey fit into this blurred picture? We might begin addressing this question with the observation that Turkey's future role and place in European security arrangements will depend at least as much on the future of transatlantic relations as it will on Turkey's own internal evolution. The EU 'green light' in December 2004 might ordinarily have been expected to encourage a trend towards a 'Europeanisation' of Ankara's approach to foreign and security policy issues, as well as in its domestic arrangements. However, in the absence of European consensus on major issues, it is hard to see what such a shift might consist of in practice. Weakened transatlantic bonds might generate sensitive policy dilemmas for Ankara and force Turkey into an intensified internal debate concerning its foreign policy orientation. The outcome of any such debate might itself depend on how Turkey's domestic politics evolves. Past form might suggest that Turkey would continue to be located at the Atlanticist end of the European spectrum, but this too might be difficult to sustain in the event of US hegemonic behaviour, particularly on issues of direct and local concern to Ankara.[49] This could also encourage a cementing of EU–Turkish relations. Furthermore, future US requests for Turkish support, and Turkish readiness to offer it, is likely to be on a more case-by-case basis, not least as US forces now have regional basing alternatives, including Iraq, Afghanistan, the Caucasus, Central Asia and in South-eastern Europe.

At the same time, it need not necessarily be the case that a Turkey moving inexorably towards EU membership would be wise to anticipate greater sympathy from its European partners than from Washington. This has rarely been the case in the past, and need not be the case in the future. It is far from self-evident that a pacific and relatively secure Europe would embrace Turkish sensitivities and support conceivable Turkish reactions to the conflicts, terrorism and WMD proliferation that plague the Middle East region. One possible outcome could be that only one of Ankara's feet will be planted within the European security community. The other will remain planted in Turkey's crisis-prone Balkan, Caucasus, eastern Mediterranean and Middle Eastern neighbourhood. Thus, Ankara's future security relationship with Europe hinges too on US policy, on NATO's future and on regional developments. Paradoxically, Turkey's path towards the EU in security terms could be eased considerably were the recent bleak state of transatlantic relations to show signs of improvement.[50]

Conclusion

Were Turkey to remain excluded from the EU, its external policy stance could oscillate between a regional activism that sometimes contributes to friction with Washington and that, at other times, generates overlapping US–Turkish perspectives and interests. However, over 50 per cent of Turkey's trade is with the EU. It also enjoys a customs union with the EU and the bulk of its inward investment also comes from there. These are facts of Turkey's existence. Furthermore, Turkey's relationship with the EU is one in which the more dynamic elements of Turkey's society and economy will continue to have a stake. Following a period of anger and reflection, any difficulties with the EU would, in all probability, be papered over by a drift back towards the pursuit of Turkey's European 'destiny'. We should also note that the EU too has begun to think more creatively about the scope for establishing zones of stability and friendship around its periphery that fall short of membership, but which extend the benefits of the EU's stable security community and its economic might. Even in this context, the 'privileged partnership' with Turkey of which some of Europe's Christian Democrats are so enamoured could emerge as a viable alternative to Turkey's complete estrangement. Turkey could conceivably, if reluctantly, come to occupy a half way house in its relationship with the EU for some time into the future.

Predicting the future of Turkish security policy, even in the relatively short term, is an especially fraught activity. The one given in Turkey's security landscape is its geopolitical location. This does not determine Turkey's security policy in any particular direction, but it does ensure the state's vulnerability to developments around its borders. Furthermore, a Turkey bereft of strategic utility to Washington, or remaining outside the EU's 'security community', might find the safety net against its own economic mismanagement withdrawn. Its domestic political stability might be more vulnerable, its military less well armed and its behaviour in Cyprus, Iraq or with respect to its own Kurds – or, in the Middle East its relationship with Israel – less tolerated.

Turkish security policy must avoid the country's isolation, but this is not entirely in Ankara's hands. Turkey generally wishes to be on the Western side of any bridge. Others wish it to constitute a barrier to unwanted external threats and trends. Should the country's predicament be mishandled, or become worsened by circumstances, Turkey could find itself an island isolated between worlds, or as more of a problem than an asset to an EU seeking its own security.

Notes

1 See, for example, the Eurobarometer poll, May/June 2005, www.europa.eu.int/comm/public_opinion/archives/eb/eb63/eb63.4_en_.
2 See Gamze Avci, 'Turkey's slow EU candidacy: insurmountable hurdles to membership, or simple Euro-scepticism?', *Turkish Studies*, 4:1 (2003), pp. 149–70; Kramer Heinz, 'Turkey and the European Union: a multidimensional relationship with hazy perspectives', in Vojtech Mastny and R. Craig Nation (eds), *Turkey between East and West: New Challenges for a Rising Regional Power* (Boulder, CO: Westview, 1996), pp. 203–32; Meltem Muftuler-Bac, 'The never-ending story: Turkey and the European Union', in S. Kedourie (ed.), *Turkey before and after Ataturk: Internal and External Affairs* (London: Frank Cass, 1999), pp. 240–58; Ziya Onis, 'An awkward partnership: Turkey's relations with the European Union in comparative-historical perspective', *Journal of European Integration History*, 7:1 (2001), pp. 105–19.
3 Robert Chase, Emily Hill, and Paul Kennedy (eds), *The Pivotal States: A New Framework for US Foreign Policy in the Developing World* (London: Norton & Co., 1998); Stephen F. Larrabee and Ian O. Lesser, *Turkish Foreign Policy in an Age of Uncertainty* (Santa Monica: RAND publications, 2003).
4 See Barry Buzan, and Thomas Diez, 'The European Union and Turkey', *Survival*, 41:1 (Spring 1999), p. 47.
5 For the genesis of the 'bridge' and 'barrier' analogies as applied to Turkey, see Ian O. Lesser, *Bridge or Barrier? Turkey and the West after the Cold War* (Santa Monica: RAND, 1992); for

a later revision, see his 'Beyond bridge or barrier: Turkey's evolving security relationships with the West', in Alan Makovsky and Sabri Sariyer (eds), *Turkey's New World: Changing Dynamics in Turkish Foreign Policy* (Washington, DC: The Washington Institute for Near East Policy, 2000), pp. 859–74.

6 Bruce Kuniholm, 'Turkey's accession to the European Union: differences in European and US attitudes, and challenges for Turkey', *Turkish Studies*, 2:1 (Spring 2001), pp. 25–53.

7 *A Secure Europe in a Better World: European Security Strategy* (Brussels: European Union, 2003).

8 For details on the European Neighbourhood Policy, see http://europa.eu.int/comm/world/enp/index_en.htm.

9 For a comparison of the ESS and the US National Security Strategy, see Felix Sebastian Berenskoetter, 'Mapping the mind gap: a comparison of US and European security strategies', *Security Dialogue*, 36:1 (March 2005), pp. 71–92.

10 See Semin Suvarierol, 'The Cyprus obstacle on Turkey's road to membership in the European Union', *Turkish Studies*, 4:1 (2003), pp. 55–78; and Nathalie Tocci, 'Cyprus and the European Union accession process: inspiration for peace or incentive for crisis?', *Turkish Studies*, 3:2 (2002), pp. 104–38.

11 Quoted in Ivo H. Daalder, 'The end of Atlanticism', *Survival*, 45:2 (Summer 2003), p. 147.

12 See Abdullah Gul, 'Kuwait Address', 14 February 2004, www.mfa.gov.tr/MFA/PressInformation/Speeches?Speecges2004/StatementByGul_14February2004.

13 For accounts of Turkey–EU differences over ESDP, see Bill Park, 'Turkey, Europe, and ESDI: inclusion or exclusion?', *Defense Analysis*, 16:3 (December 2000), pp. 315–28; Antonio Missiroli, 'EU–NATO cooperation in crisis management: no Turkish delight for ESDP', *Security Dialogue*, 3:1 (March 2002), pp. 9–26; Sebnem Udum, 'Turkey and the emerging European security framework', *Turkish Studies*, 3:2 (Autumn 2002), pp. 69–103; Huseyin Bagci, 'Turkey and Europe: security issues', in Michael S. Radu (ed.), *Dangerous neighbourhood* (New Brunswick and London: Transaction Publishers, 2003), pp. 49–76.

14 Ibid.

15 See Bruce Kuniholm, 'Turkey and the West since World War II', in Mastny and Nation (eds), *Turkey's New World*, pp. 45–69.

16 For this observation see Buzan and Diez, 'The European Union and Turkey', pp. 41–57.

17 See, for example, Cihat Goktepe, *British Foreign Policy towards Turkey 1959–1965* (London: Frank Cass, 2003), pp. 7–25.

18 William Hale, 'Turkey, the Middle East and the Gulf crisis', *International Affairs*, 68:4 (October 1992), pp. 679–92.

19 James B. Steinberg, 'An elective partnership: salvaging transatlantic relations', *Survival*, 45:2 (Summer 2003), p. 124.

20 For an account of events leading up to the vote, see Bill Park, 'Strategic location, political dislocation: Turkey, the United States, and Northern Iraq', *Middle East Review of International Affairs (MERIA)*, 7:2 (June 2003), pp. 11–23.

21 'State of the Union Address', White House, Washington DC, 2002, www.whitehouse.gov/news/releases/2002/01/20020129-11.html.

22 For considerations of US–Turkish relationships in the context of differences over Iraq, see Barak A. Salmoni, 'Strategic partners or estranged allies: Turkey, the United States, and Operation Iraqi Freedom', *Strategic Insights*, 2:7 (July 2003); and Soner Cagaptay, 'Where goes the US–Turkish relationship?', *Middle East Quarterly*, 11:4 (Fall 2004), pp. 43–52.

23 For details, see www.dod.mil/transcripts/2004/tr20040129.

24 For details, see www.whitehouse.gov/news/releases/2004/06/20040629.4.html.

25 See Abdullah Gul, 'Turkey's role in a changing Middle East environment', *Mediterranean Quarterly*, 15:1 (Winter 2004), p. 5.

26 For details, see www.mfa.gov.tr/grupa/ai/islamicconference.1.htm.

27 For details, see www.mfa.gov.tr/ai/Gul12December2003.htm.

28 Graham E. Fuller, 'Turkey's strategic model: myths and realities', *The Washington Quarterly*, 27:3 (Summer 2004), pp. 51–64; and Mohammed Ayoob, 'Turkey's multiple paradoxes', *Orbis*, 48:3 (Summer 2004), pp. 451–63.
29 Paul Cornish and Geoffrey Edwards, 'Beyond the EU/NATO dichotomy: the beginnings of a European security culture', *International Affairs*, 77:3 (July 2001), pp. 584–603; Paul Cornish and Geoffrey Edwards, 'The strategic culture of the European Union: a progress report', *International Affairs*, 81:4 (July 2005), pp. 801–20; Francois Heisbourg, 'Europe's strategic ambitions: the limits of ambiguity', *Survival*, 42:2 (Summer 2000), pp. 5–15.
30 Bulent Aras, 'Turkey's insecure identity from the perspective of nationalism', *Mediterranean Quarterly*, 8:1 (1997), pp. 77–91; Ziya Onis, 'Turkey, Europe and the paradoxes of identity', *Mediterranean Quarterly*, 10:3 (1999), pp. 107–36; S. Pesmazoglu, 'Turkey and Europe, reflections and refractions: towards a contrapuntal approach', *South European Society and Politics*, 2:1 (1997), pp. 138–59.
31 Ziya Onis and Suhnaz Yilmaz, 'The Turkey–EU–US triangle in perspective: transformation or continuity?', *Middle East Journal*, 59:2 (Spring 2005), p. 267.
32 For thoughts on Turkey's security culture, see Umit Cizre, 'Demythologising the National Security Concept: the case of Turkey', *Middle East Journal*, 57:2 (Spring 2003), pp. 213–29; Dietrich Jung and Wolfgang Piccoli, *Turkey at the Crossroads: Ottoman Legacies and a Greater Middle East* (London: Zed Books, 2001); Ali L. Karaosmanoglu, 'The evolution of national security culture and the military in Turkey', *Journal of International Affairs*, 54:1 (2000), pp. 199–216.
33 Buzan and Diez, 'The European Union and Turkey'; H. Tarik Oguzlu, 'The clash of security identities: the question of Turkey's membership in the European Union', *International Journal*, 57:4 (Autumn 2002), pp. 579–603; Gulner Aybet and Meltem Muftuler-Bac, 'Transformations in security and identity after the Cold War', *International Journal*, 55:4 (Autumn 2000), pp. 567–82.
34 Henri J. Barkey and Graham E. Fuller, *Turkey's Kurdish Question* (Oxford: Rowman & Littlefield, 1998); Murat Somer, 'Turkey's Kurdish conflict: changing context, and domestic and regional implications', *Middle East Journal*, 58:2 (Spring 2004), pp. 235–53; Kemal Kirisci and Gareth M. Winrow, *The Kurdish Question and Turkey: An Example of a Trans-state Ethnic Conflict* (London: Frank Cass, 1997); Robert Olsen (ed.), *The Kurdish Nationalist Movement in the 1990s: Its Impact on Turkey and the Middle East* (Lexington: Kentucky University Press, 1996).
35 Gareth Jenkins, 'Context and circumstance: the Turkish military and politics', *Adelphi Papers*, 337 (2001); Nilufer Narli, 'Civil–military relations in Turkey', *Turkish Studies*, 1:1 (2000), pp. 107–27.
36 Turkish Foreign Ministry, www.mfa.gov.tr.
37 Gareth Jenkins, 'Muslim democrats in Turkey?', *Survival*, 45:1 (2003), pp. 45–66; R. Quinn Mecham, 'From the ashes of virtue, a promise of light: the transformation of political Islam in Turkey', *Third World Quarterly*, 25:2 (2004), pp. 339–58.
38 Ziya Onis, 'Domestic politics, international norms and challenges to the state: Turkey–EU relations in the post-Helsinki era', *Turkish Studies*, 4:1 (2003), pp. 9–35.
39 Kemal Kirisci, 'Between Europe and the Middle East: the transformation of Turkish policy', *Middle East Review of International Affairs (MERIA)*, 8:1 (March 2004).
40 See Jenkins, *Context and Circumstance*.
41 For alternative approaches to Turkish–Kurdish relations, see Somer, 'Turkey's Kurdish conflict'.
42 Bill Park, 'Turkish policy towards northern Iraq: problems and perspectives', *Adelphi Papers*, 374 (2005).
43 For speculation on possible Iraqi futures: 'Iraq in transition: vortex or catalyst?', *Middle East Briefing Paper*, 4:2 (September 2004).
44 On Turkey's future options with respect to Iraqi Kurdistan, see Michael Gunter, 'The consequences of a failed Iraqi state: an independent Kurdish state in northern Iraq?', *Journal*

of South Asian and Middle Eastern Studies, 27:3 (Spring 2004), pp. 1–11; Bill Park, 'Iraq's Kurds and Turkey: challenges for US policy', *Parameters*, 34:3 (Autumn 2004), pp. 18–30.
45 Steinberg, 'An elective partnership', p. 139.
46 Daalder, 'The end of Atlanticism', p. 149.
47 Jolyon Howorth, 'France, Britain and the Euro-Atlantic crisis', *Survival*, 45:4 (Winter 2003–04), pp. 173–92.
48 Robert Kagan, *Of Paradise and Power: America and Europe in the New World Order* (New York: Alfred A. Knopf, 2003).
49 Fuller, 'Turkey's strategic model; myths and realities', p. 63.
50 See Daalder, 'The end of Atlanticism', pp. 147–66; Steinberg, 'An elective partnership', pp. 113–246; and James Thomson, 'US interests and the fate of the Alliance', *Survival*, 45:4 (Winter 2003–04), pp. 207–20.

12

EU Enlargement and security in the Mediterranean region

Roderick Pace

The EU's fifth enlargement, comprising eight CEE countries and the two Mediterranean island states of Cyprus and Malta, extended the Union's frontiers southwards towards North Africa and further eastwards towards Russia. While, in theory, an enlarged Union has more resources at its disposal to deal with its security challenges, in practice, the larger number of member states makes consensus more difficult. Member states also tend to prioritise issues closer to them geographically, which, in turn, influences the manner in which they view the Union's security challenges. As such enlargement produced an increased preponderance of CEE states in the EU, thus shifting the Union's internal balance and raising the possibility of the EU becoming more focused on the problems of Eastern Europe, at the expense of the Mediterranean region.

However, there is no compelling evidence that the EU is neglecting the Mediterranean region. In fact, it is practically impossible for the EU to do so. Firstly, the EU has a long Mediterranean coastline. Seven of the current EU member states – Cyprus, France, Greece, Italy, Malta, Spain and Slovenia – are situated on the Mediterranean Littoral. Portugal, whose coastline lies entirely on the Atlantic seaboard, is included, due to its cultural affinities with and geographic location in the Iberian Peninsula. Secondly, since the region is an important source of petroleum and gas supplies, it is of strategic importance to the EU and helps the EU counter the possibility of becoming overly dependent on Russian supplies. Thirdly, unresolved problems in the region, particularly the Middle East question, raise tensions that threaten the EU's own stability and its policies in the region. Last but not least, threats such as illegal immigration, terrorism and WMD proliferation, evident in the wider Mediterranean area, constitute direct and immediate challenges, which the EU has no option but to face up to.

The EU's main policy instrument in the Mediterranean region is the Euro-Mediterranean Partnership (EMP), launched in Barcelona in 1995.[1] In fact, enlargement also changed the internal equilibrium within the EMP. Before enlargement, the EMP consisted of fifteen EU states and twelve Mediterranean partners. Now it consists of twenty-five EU states and ten partners, eleven if Libya eventually accepts the full EMP *acquis*.[2] Cast into the 'EU Civilian Power' mode, it aims to create a Euro-Mediterranean area of shared prosperity by establishing a Euro-Mediterranean Free Trade Area (EMFTA) by 2010, by establishing a common area of peace and security, by developing human resources, by enhancing the understanding between cultures and by promoting exchanges between civil societies. The original aim was to achieve parallel progress in all three baskets – economic, political and cultural – which would be mutually reinforcing.

It is worth exploring these baskets in a little more depth. In the economic area, the establishment of the EMFTA requires bilateral free trade accords between the EU and each of the Mediterranean states and free trading arrangements amongst the non-EU Mediterranean states. These should be accompanied by the uniform application of the Community's competition rules, a common system of rules of origin and the application of the principle of cumulative rules of origin to facilitate trade and encourage further south–south integration. The bilateral EU accords are almost complete, with only the Association Agreement with Syria outstanding. The Agadir Free Trade Area (AFTA), involving Egypt, Morocco, Tunisia and Jordan, has led to a limited amount of south–south economic integration. Officials in the four countries are optimistic that ratification will soon be completed and it will go into effect at the beginning of 2007. In addition, there are no visible signs that this initiative can be extended to the remaining EMP non-EU partners before 2010, when the EMTFA is supposed to be completed.

The political and security goals in the Barcelona Declaration included strengthening the rule of law and democracy, respect for human rights and fundamental freedoms, the right to self-determination, non-interference in internal affairs, the peaceful settlement of disputes, the preventing and combating of terrorism and the fight against organised crime. The 'hard' security issues identified were WMD proliferation, arms control and disarmament, accompanied by verification methods to ensure compliance. The EU and its partners agreed to establish weapon-free zones, particularly an 'effectively verifiable Middle East Zone free of WMD'.[3] Finally, Euro-Mediterranean partners agreed to consider any confidence and security-building measures to create a Mediterranean area of peace and stability. The EMP's third basket focused on social, cultural and human affairs. A central component was cultural and religious dialogue, incorporating elements of civil society. Social and migratory issues also fell under this heading, as did the Euro-Mediterranean Parliamentary Forum. In 2005, this developed into a Euro-Mediterranean Parliamentary Assembly, composed of national parliamentary representatives from the EU member states and their Mediterranean partners, as well as the European Parliament.

The EMP is connected to the ENP, launched in March 2003 on the initiative of then Commission President, Romano Prodi.[4] The ENP is a global strategy framework, offering advantages in the longer term to Russia, the western FSU and the states of the southern Mediterranean. Its objectives are 'to share the benefits of an enlarged EU with neighbouring countries in order to contribute to increased stability, security and prosperity of the EU and its neighbours' and to offer the EU's neighbours 'the prospect of an increasing close relationship . . . involving a significant degree of economic integration and a deepening of political cooperation'.[5] It is based on the 'shared values' of liberty, democracy, respect for human rights and fundamental freedoms and the rule of law.[6] The EU has also created a single Neighbourhood Financial Instrument to replace the existing financial instruments extending aid to the neighbouring states. However, is the ENP subsuming the EMP? In reality, the EMP is still operational but, for the more ambitious Mediterranean partners, there is the prospect of a deeper bilateral relationship with the EU on the basis of Action Plans, negotiated bilaterally under the ENP. These Action Plans, tailor-made to each partner's particular needs, can lead to increased access to the Single Market and to wider economic benefits, should the partner achieve all its agreed aims. Thus, the ENP can act as a driving force for the EMP.

The manner in which the ENP and the EMP help the EU attain its security aims in the Mediterranean region are analysed further in this chapter. In addition, it is worth keeping in mind that the EU is not the only major actor in the Mediterranean region. It should be remembered that the US, the Union's Mediterranean partners and some of the larger EU member states themselves pursue their own national objectives in this region, while NATO established its Mediterranean Dialogue in 1994. This chapter will address the main security challenges faced by the EU in the Mediterranean region and the effectiveness of EU policies in dealing with them. Mindful of the array of threats the EU faces in the region, this chapter narrows the focus to a select few. These are security of energy supplies, illegal immigration, terrorism and the Middle East conflict and WMD proliferation. It also deals with the advantages and pitfalls of the Union's soft or 'civil' power approach. The EU has traditionally behaved as a 'civilian power' in the Mediterranean region, but its policies have tended to suffer from the divided attention of the EU member states, their often conflicting interests, the weak involvement of the EU's Mediterranean partners in the decision-making structures, their reluctance to adopt a self-help mentality and their lack of enthusiasm to fully implement agreed measures. However, to begin with, it is necessary to briefly sketch out some of the major security concerns facing the EU in this area, as noted above.

EU energy dependence

The EU's priorities in the region have changed in line with changing geo-political situations but, in recent years, it is terrorism and the security of energy supplies which have become the dominant issues. In the energy field, the EU is heavily dependent upon fossil fuels, over half of which are imported. About 46 per cent of oil imports originate in Russia and Norway, while slightly less than a third come from the Arab World.[7] According to the 2000 Green Paper, 'Towards a European strategy for security of energy supply', the EU imports 30 per cent of its gas from Algeria and a quarter from Norway.[8] Relations with the Gulf States and the wider Mediterranean are thus as crucial as the EU's relations with Russia and the oil rich republics around the Caspian Sea. The Arab states' importance is expected to grow as the EU's external dependence on energy supplies increases. The Green Paper estimates that if, by 2030, no marked shift to alternative energy sources occurs, the EU's external dependence will reach 90 per cent for oil and 80 per cent for gas. The geo-political implications of these developments explain the Union's eagerness to maintain strong relations with the Arab world and secure a lasting solution to the Middle East conflict, given its destabilising effect on the wider region. Algeria's gas supplies are also crucial in lessening the EU's dependence on Russia, as demonstrated in the January 2006 gas crisis. Gas and oil exports constitute more than 90 per cent of Algeria's exports to the EU. Algerian low sulphur oil is also crucially important to European refineries eager to observe strict EU environmental rules.[9]

Illegal immigration

Another major security challenge is that posed by illegal immigration. The phenomenon comprises different categories of people requiring responses that straddle traditional security policy divisions. It involves economic refugees and genuine political refugees fleeing instability, mostly from sub-Saharan Africa. Europol claims that organised crime organisations have taken over migration flows in the Mediterranean region, raising the possibility that such networks could combine with traditional criminal activities, such as illicit arms and drug trafficking or terrorist penetration of the EU.[10] Europol stresses that many of the traditional transit countries that joined the EU in 2004 are now, more than before, targeted as destination countries by the facilitators of illegal immigrants. These facilitators, already well established in those states, utilise the fact that the new control systems in the enlarged EU are not yet running smoothly. Furthermore, the EU's borders are now closer to many key source and transit countries.

The complexity of moving large volumes of people across long distances requires a degree of organisation, specialisation and sophistication that can only be met by organised crime groups.[11] A number of examples demonstrated the scale of the potential problem. For example, the EU's southern member states, particularly Spain, Portugal, France, Italy, Malta, Greece and Cyprus, are in the forefront of the 'Mediterranean Boat People' crisis.[12] This raises a number of issues, such as the humanitarian treatment of migrants, the maintenance costs incurred until they are re-settled or repatriated and the level of co-operation, or lack of it, shown by the countries of origin, which have little incentive to stop the illegal flows or to readmit illegal immigrants. In addition, in the wake of incidents in Cueta and Mellila in September 2005, when dozens of illegal immigrants were killed or injured as they tried to storm the barriers separating the two Spanish enclaves from Moroccan territory, Spain called for a Euro-African Summit, a call endorsed by France at the 2005 Franco-Spanish summit.[13] In the central Mediterranean, Libya has become a destination country for illegal immigrants, mostly from sub-Saharan Africa, and a transit point to Europe. The EU mission to Libya estimated that there were between 0.75 and 1.2m illegal immigrants in Libya.[14] Libya shares some 4,400km of border with six states, including three poor and unstable sub-Saharan states, namely Sudan, Chad and Niger. Its Mediterranean coast is 1,770 km long, which adds to the difficulty of precluding clandestine boats from embarking on their trips to Malta and Italy, particularly to the islands of Sicily, Pantelleria and Lampedusa.

Terrible twins: terrorism and the Middle East conflict

The end of the Cold War has not led to significant positive shifts in the region's main conflicts. The rise in terrorist activity, particularly since September 11, is a significant problem. Excluding casualties in Iraq, the total number of deaths from terrorism in the Near East was 726 in 2004, compared with 636 in Europe and Euro-Asia combined.[15] Terrorism is often linked with the Mediterranean region, because of associations – accurate or otherwise – with Islam, although Muslim leaders rightly insist that the association is false. The other destabilising problem is the Middle East conflict, which affects relations in the entire region and has led to increased terrorist activity. The EU rightly insists on the need for north–south co-operation in countering terrorism, although such co-operation is not easy. Major differences have emerged regarding acceptable definitions, with certain Arab states reluctant to designate organisations such as Hamas or Lebanese Hezbollah as terrorist groups, while the EU includes both in its list of terrorist organisations.[16] Hamas won the local elections in the Palestinian territories held in December 2005 and has overtaken Fatah as the main Palestinian political force, following the 2006 parliamentary elections. This result makes it considerably more difficult for the EU to argue that it would not have direct contact with Hamas, who now possess a democratic mandate to govern. The first signs – in terms of continued aid, while still insisting on a Hamas commitment to end all violence – suggest that the EU's preference would be to find some way to engage all actors in the wider conflict. In addition, it should be remembered that, despite the enormity of the definitional gap that exists between the EU and its Middle Eastern counterparts, such difficulties have not been permitted to fully obstruct practical anti-terrorist co-operation in many areas.

However, the lack of a common definitional basis is not the only concern in operationalising counter-terrorist co-operation within the wider region. As part of the 'War on Terror', certain governments have been perceived as being prone to restricting civil liberties, often disregarding international human rights conventions and the obligations they impose on them. This is despite the fact that such repressive action is often blamed for encouraging extremism and terrorism. Certain states, in effect, 'took advantage' of their anti-terror laws to strengthen their hold on power. For example, in Tunisia, a 2003 anti-terror law contains a broad definition of terrorism, which could be misused to prosecute persons for the peaceful exercise of their right to dissent, and outlines harsh penalties, including the referral of civilian suspects to military courts.[17] Human rights activists have also been harassed in Tunisia.[18] Human rights NGOs report similar developments in other Middle Eastern and North African states. In 2004, back sliding on human rights, resulting from counter-terrorist actions, also became evident in Morocco, which had previously been considered to be one of the more advanced promoters of such rights.[19] Given the EU's high-profile advocacy of human rights and the civil liberties agenda, such developments are potentially troubling for developing co-operation.

The Middle East problem injects political and economic uncertainty throughout the Mediterranean region. The diplomatic efforts of 'The Quartet' (the US, the EU, Russia and the UN) are focused on finding a lasting solution, while Palestinian reform and the Israeli withdrawal from Gaza and possibly parts of the West Bank offer a glimmer of hope. However, at the time of writing, the region was plunged into a further bout of political uncertainty, following the rapid establishment of Kadima, the tragic stroke that debilitated Israeli Prime Minister, Ariel Sharon, and the aforementioned Hamas victory. As a result, the 'road map' to peace is out of sync. That said, on 20 December 2005, UN Under-Secretary-General for Political Affairs, Ibrahim Gambari, informed the UNSC that the plan is still the agreed framework for reaching lasting peace in the Middle East.[20] Apart from its involvement in 'The Quartet', the EU has shown its readiness to become involved in a practical manner in helping solidify peace. On 14 November 2005, the Council established an EU Police Mission in the Palestinian Territories (EUPOL COPPS), which aims to provide enhanced support to the Palestinian Authority in establishing sustainable and effective policing arrangements.[21] A day later, Israel and the Palestinian Authority concluded an 'Agreement on Movement and Access', establishing agreed principles on the Rafah crossing point. This enabled the EU to undertake the third party role proposed in the Agreement and to launch the EU Border Assistance Mission at the Rafah crossing point.

Terrorism and the Middle East conflict are also the two most potent obstacles to much-needed reform in the region. The 2003 Arab Human Development Report observes that regressive governments in the Arab world 'have found a new justification (terrorism) for their ongoing warnings about the perils of freedom'.[22] It also noted that 'the occupation of Palestinian and other Arab lands exerts a direct and continuous burden on the economies of affected countries and diverts resources from development to military and security objectives'.[23] Furthermore, although the Middle East problem does not fall directly under the EMP's purview, it has, in effect, obstructed the development of a security dialogue, leading to the abandonment of the Charter for Peace and Stability, which was supposed to be the main achievement in the political basket. In addition, while the Middle East conflict continues to dominate the agenda, lesser long-standing conflicts and tensions cannot be ignored. These include tensions over Cyprus, traditional Greek–Turkish rivalry in the Aegean and intra-Arab tensions, such as those between Morocco and Algeria over the Spanish Sahara. This has poisoned efforts towards the realisation of an 'Arab Maghreb Union', which would have contributed significantly towards realising the EMFTA by 2010.

Weapons of mass destruction

In a 1996 RAND study, Lesser and Tellis painted a bleak picture of the scale and likely development of WMD proliferation in the Mediterranean region. They concluded that nowhere was the prospect of the spread of WMD likely to have a more pronounced effect on strategic perceptions than around the Mediterranean, given that many of the world's leading WMD proliferators are arrayed along Europe's southern periphery. They observed that key states south and east of the Mediterranean either possessed or were in the process of acquiring WMD, along with the means for delivering them across the Mediterranean. At the time, they singled out Egypt, Iran and Iraq as having the capability of developing long-range missile technology, claiming that Egypt also had active chemical-weapons and long-range missile development programmes. The report claimed that Libya and Syria possessed chemical weapons (Libya also had a biological capability), and that Algeria had been pushing ahead with development of a nuclear infrastructure. One important conclusion was that, within ten years, it was possible that every southern European capital would be within range of ballistic missiles based in North Africa or the Levant, with Turkish population centres already exposed to missiles based in Syria and Iran (and, at the time, Iraq).[24]

Since the publication of the RAND report, the situation has improved marginally in some cases and regressed in others. The military occupation of Iraq and Libya's decision to dismantle its WMD programmes effectively 'neutralised' two states known to be pursuing or which had the potential to pursue such programmes. Significantly, these developments did not result from the EU's Mediterranean policies, but from the Anglo-American intervention in Iraq. As Michele Dunne argues, Libya's change of heart on WMD was influenced by the US led 'War on Terror' and the looming war in Iraq, which raised fears in Tripoli that 'it was in the sights of influential neo-conservatives in Washington'.[25] That said, in fairness, mention must be made of France, Germany and the UK's efforts, supported by the rest of the EU, in pressurising Iran to dismantle its programme to produce nuclear weapons grade material, a matter of continuing controversy at the time of writing. Iran's military programmes are a threat not only to stability in the strategically important Gulf and Middle Eastern regions, but also, potentially, to the EU. According to Guy Bechor, Iran is developing the Shihab-4 missile, successor to the Shihab-3, while Syria, aided by North Korea and Iran, is reported to be sharpening the accuracy of its SCUD D missiles. With a range of 650 km, these can reach most of Turkey and Cyprus, the outer fringes of Greece, as well as neighbouring states.[26]

Part of the problem in this area is that the technology is not difficult to attain. States may acquire it independently or by procuring it from other states, as the 2004 Abdul Qadeer Khan affair showed. Many states can supply nuclear reactors and technology initially for peaceful uses, which is considered to be the first step in building a military programme, as has been seen in the debate over Iran's longer-term intentions. Argentina has built a nuclear reactor in Egypt, which could enable it to build one bomb a year.[27] Egypt has not yet acquired nuclear weapons, and has so far been largely compliant with IAEA requirements. However, it has failed on a number of occasions to report some nuclear activities (albeit involving only small quantities of nuclear material), in accordance with its obligations under the NPT Safeguards Agreement.[28] In 2002, it was reported to be considering developing a uranium enrichment plant with the help of China.[29] Egypt and Israel have not ratified the Nuclear

Test Ban Treaty: Egypt claims that it would ratify it only if Israel accepted the NPT. Most Muslim countries in the Middle Eastern region claim to support the creation of a WMD-free Middle East zone and are ready to halt their own WMD programmes, on condition that Israel removes its atomic weapons. As a rule, compliance with international conventions in the Mediterranean region is generally weak: Iraq and Libya are known to have violated the NPT; Egypt, Lebanon and Syria have not signed the Chemical Weapons Convention (CWC); Israel signed the CWC, but has not ratified it and has not signed the 1972 Biological Weapons Convention.

The struggle for resources

Very serious tensions, possibly leading to conflict, may arise as a result of the struggle for resources, involving water and fisheries, as well as offshore rights to prospect for oil and gas. Due to the narrowness of the Mediterranean Sea, only Cyprus has declared a 200 nautical mile exclusive economic zone (EEZ). Spain, France and Morocco apply such zones on their Atlantic coastlines, but not in the Mediterranean. Lack of agreement over the delineation of the continental shelf involves nearly all the Mediterranean countries, particularly Italy, France, Spain, Libya, Tunisia, Malta, Morocco, Greece and Turkey.[30] This presents serious obstacles to gas and oil explorations in contested regions. As world demand for energy resources rises and economic growth in the Mediterranean shore states increases, impacting further on their consumption of fossil fuels, these territorial issues become more crucial. Another contributory factor has been the development of deep-sea drilling, which brought potentially oil and gas rich, but hitherto inaccessible, areas within reach. Water resources present another problem. Roberto Aliboni observed that, in the early 1990s, several Mediterranean leaders referred to the scarcity of water as a potential trigger for war in the region.[31] Economic growth and the demographic explosion are making the problem even more acute. Aliboni summarises the situation around key rivers in the Mediterranean region thus: disputes over the Nile involve eight countries, notably Egypt and the Sudan; the Jordan river dispute involves Israel, Jordan and Syria; the Tigris–Euphrates river system involves Turkey, Syria and Iraq. Aliboni concludes that, while water may not be regarded as a direct cause of conflict, water disputes and the lack of solutions to the problem could worsen already tense relations.

In the case of fishing resources, it is noteworthy that, in 2005, both Tunisia and Libya extended their 'exclusive fishing conservation zone' beyond their territorial seas, bringing to five the number of states that claim such a zone.[32] The others are Algeria (1994), Malta (1978) and Spain (1997).[33] The Libyan zone starts above a straight line drawn from Misratah in the west to Benghazi in the east, effectively designating the Gulf of Sidra as internal Libyan waters. This pushes Libyan control over an area considered to be international waters.[34] The extended Tunisian fishing zone engulfs the small Italian isles of Pantelleria and Lampedusa, stopping about fifteen nautical miles from their coastlines.[35] The declaration of these fishing zones gives their respective states control only over fishery resources. However, tensions arise when fishermen of other nationalities are deprived of their traditional fishing grounds. Lesser Mediterranean tensions have also erupted suddenly around tiny rocks and atolls. These mostly uninhabited rocks are pivotal in the delineation of both EEZs and the continental shelf. Nearly all the states of the Mediterranean region, with the exception of Malta and Tunisia, have unresolved border issues with their neighbours. The best-known ones are those involving Spain and the UK over Gibraltar, which finds its replica in Spanish–Moroccan relations over Spain's North African enclaves of Cueta and Mellila. In July 2002, Spain sent troops to the disputed and deserted, half-a-mile-long island of Perejil (or Leila, as it is known in Morocco), after Moroccan soldiers had landed on it.[36] The island, situated around 200 meters from Morocco's shore, had not been formally claimed by Spain until then. This incident was reminiscent of the 1996 Imia (Turkish Kardak) affair that forced the US to broker a Greek and Turkish military withdrawal from a group of uninhabited islands in the Aegean that were claimed by both.[37]

Responding to the security challenges in the Mediterranean

The security challenges the EU faces in the Mediterranean region require a combination of responses, embracing economic, political and military options. Lacking the necessary military means, the EU has traditionally relied on its economic strength and market size, acting as a 'civilian power'. Before considering the development of EC/EU political involvement in the region, there are a number of general concerns to be noted. For example, the EU and the US concur on the promotion of democracy in the Mediterranean region, though both are occasionally ambivalent as to the levels of pressure to be applied, depending on their differing interests. The EU and the US garb their foreign policy objectives in idealistic terms, ostensibly to encourage more peaceful inter-state relations, but, in doing this, they also 'promote substantive interests'.[38] Citizens in the Arab world are also aware that Western governments support existing authoritarian regimes, while pressing for democratic reforms, a case of double standards. In addition, the EU's Mediterranean partners perceive democracy in terms of its impact on their regime's survival and can therefore be reluctant to promote far-reaching democratic reforms.

Additionally, EU policy has often suffered from a lack of agreement among its own member states. For example, French support for the Algerian government during the civil war, which started in 1992, obstructed the emergence of a coherent EU response.[39] US policies in the region often have a similar effect. For example, Washington's rapprochement with Libya appears not to include stringent conditions on the improvement of democracy and human rights. As this is a central EMP requirement, it may help explain why Libya has been slow to commit itself as a fully fledged partner as yet. Furthermore, the US is pursuing the 'Greater Middle East Initiative' in the Mediterranean region and beyond, concluding free trade agreements with a number of the littoral states.[40] The latter agreements do not pose real economic threats to the EU. In fact, they could be helpful if they catalyse economic growth in these states. However, they may also dilute the EU's leverage over its Mediterranean partners.

Before assessing the detail of the EMP, it is worth placing the developments in some form of historical context. The EC's engagement as a 'civilian power' in the Mediterranean region began when it concluded Association Agreements with Greece and Turkey (1961–63), a process it has continued with most of the other Mediterranean states. In 1972, the EC launched a more streamlined Global Mediterranean Policy (GMP) and proceeded to extend formal preferential trading arrangements with all the Mediterranean states. However, the GMP and other EC/EU initiatives have had to adjust to new challenges emanating from the region, often leading to the impression that it is more spectator than participant in the events of the wider region. While the GMP was useful in consolidating the traditional regional trade patterns, thus strengthening interdependence between the two shores of the Mediterranean region, in the political domain the EC fared less well. For example, the Euro-Arab Dialogue, which the EC had helped establish in 1975, despite Washington's objections, died prematurely following the 1979 Egypt–Israel Camp David Accord and the internal divisions this provoked in the Arab world. The EC's perceived leanings towards the Arab World and its 1980 Venice Declaration on the Middle East led to a deterioration of its relations with Israel.[41]

As a result, the member states tended to venture no further than to issue periodic declarations on their major concerns, often with great difficulty and after a lot of internal wrangling. To use Ambassador Ischinger's distinction, applied in the context of the EU's current policy dilemmas, it developed a 'declarative', as distinguished from an 'operational', foreign policy, earning it the frequently applied epithet of being 'an economic giant but a political pygmy'.[42] The EU has found it difficult to shake off this derogatory image. In fact, various non-EU initiatives, such as the 'Five plus Five' arrangement in the Western Mediterranean, the Mediterranean Forum and NATO's Mediterranean Dialogue, had already made a modest start before the EU even launched EMP in November 1995. Kagan has likened the EU's current foreign policy to the chorus in a classical Greek tragedy: 'It comments on the action. It reacts with horror and praise. It interacts in various ways with the protagonists. But the singers themselves play no part in the plot'.[43] The conclusion to be drawn is that a 'civilian power' approach on its own was often insufficient to handle the security challenges it faced. Lacking the unified military capabilities, the strength and diplomatic prestige of the US, and relying primarily on its soft power approach, the EU could not assume a leading diplomatic role in the region. These developments help expose the limits of the 'civilian power' approach.

The success and failures of the EMP

When the EMP was launched in 1995, the Middle East problem was purposely left out of its purview because of its disruptive potential, although it was thought that the

EMP would help strengthen the broader conditions for a lasting peace in the region. However, it made the security dialogue within the first basket of the Barcelona process more difficult. Symptomatic of this was the fact that the proposed Euro-Mediterranean Charter for Peace and Stability had to be abandoned after years of almost complete stalemate. Senior officials of the EMP had begun to draft the Charter after the 1995 Barcelona meeting. In 1997, the Ministers agreed that work on the Charter should continue 'in order to submit as soon as possible an agreed text for approval at a future Ministerial Meeting *when political circumstances allow*' (emphasis added).[44] Representatives of the Arab states had decided that they would not approve the Charter before the Middle East problem had finally been resolved.

Human rights, democracy and the rule of law are emblematic of the EU's overall approach. They are stressed in all EMP Ministerial declarations, are regularly cited by the European Parliament in its resolutions[45] and emphasised by the Commission, which noted the importance of 'main-streaming' human rights in the EU's external relations.[46] Such issues also play a pivotal role in the Commission's EMP work programme, submitted in April 2005.[47] Human rights clauses have been inserted in EC/EU agreements with non-member countries since 1989. Consistent with this policy, a 'political conditionality' or 'essential element clause' became a basic feature of all EMP Association Agreements. Such clauses were intended to help the EU pursue a positive engagement on reform with Mediterranean non-member states. This non-coercive approach, together with the EU's self-imposed limitation of issuing demarches, in preference to suspending the Association Agreements' provisions, has prompted criticism that the EU's human rights policy in the Mediterranean is ineffective.[48] Such criticism has wider implications, as the promotion of democracy and human rights is also important to the EU's 'civilian power' approach.

As Youngs argues, the EU's 'non-coercive' approach is a deliberate one, because the EU prefers 'positive engagement' and 'partnership'.[49] He describes European approaches, at both the regional and national level, as 'socio-economic, techno-governance [in] character, combining relatively innocuous grassroots initiatives with top–down cooperation purporting to "nudge" unthreateningly the outlooks of the entrenched elites'.[50] The European Council claims that the EU aims to be a *convincing* rather than an *imposing* power, with engagement and dialogue as the preferred means of interaction with third countries. The EU:

> has to seek a balance between persuasion and critical action. Promoting human rights involves building relations of trust, having a genuine exchange of views, setting conditions for fruitful cooperation and offering assistance to meet them, but being willing to indicate clearly when red lines have been crossed.[51]

Indeed, in contrast to the criticism of the EU as essentially passive (noted earlier in the chapter), Madeleine Bunting has praised this non-coercive approach, claiming that the costs in changing Iraq seem to be swaying opinion against the use of force as an instrument of change, towards the peaceful European approach.[52] Yet, how can EU policy effectiveness be increased? Youngs stresses that the EU's highly formalised and institutionalised partnerships tend to work to their own internal momentum, isolated from outside events. EU policies must, therefore, be more alert to grasp the opportunities that present themselves for promoting human rights.

Mainstreaming human rights in the EU's external relations has led to calls for the involvement of Euro-Mediterranean civil society and other initiatives, such as a dialogue of civilisations and the Euro-Mediterranean Parliamentary Assembly. A modest financial outlay to support NGOs and the promotion of democracy and human rights was established in 1999, when, on the insistence of the European Parliament, the European Initiative for Democracy and Human Rights (EIDHR) was created. Currently, it has an annual outlay of approximately €100m, to support human rights, democratisation and conflict prevention activities. The supported programmes are to be carried out in partnership with NGOs and international organisations. In contrast to the task it confronts, which may have worsened in the era of the 'War on Terror' (as noted earlier), such a figure is not extensive, though nevertheless helpful. The magnitude of the task of effectively promoting human rights and democracy in the Mediterranean region is such that it can only be accomplished if supported by stronger policy instruments, such as a democracy clause, accompanied by an EU readiness to invoke it appropriately.

The promotion of civil society projects and its wider involvement in the EMP raises a number of other issues. Civil society in the majority of the EU's Mediterranean partners mainly consists of NGOs that have emerged within the framework of semi-restrictive laws on freedom of association. Many of these NGOs are not only permitted but also encouraged by their respective governments, in order to confront social problems that the states are unable to cope with. As Brumberg observes, many of these NGOs in the Arab World are the result of a deliberate policy of 'partial inclusion', whereby regimes extend recognition to a large number of NGOs, allowing the opposition to 'blow off steam', while withholding the freedom to more broadly based, popular movements that could seriously challenge their authority.[53] Brumberg adds, 'for wily "reformists" such as Egypt's Mubarak, it is better to have 5,000 small civil society organisations than five big ones, since many competing NGOs impede social activists' cooperation'.[54] More poignantly, Ottaway observes:

> Political parties (in the Arab World) embracing democracy remain weak, their leaders isolated in downtown offices, while Islamist organisations set up headquarters in lower-class sections of town. Pro-democracy intellectuals in general shun political parties and prefer to set up NGOs . . . These organisations can generate quickly visible activities, such as conferences and receive attention abroad. But these groups are not generally able to speak to the general public in their own countries . . . Ideologically, the Arab street belongs much more to the Islamist preachers than to democracy activists.[55]

Thus, a more productive civil society dialogue could only be achieved if non-official Islamist NGOs are successfully targeted. However, these are difficult to locate or engage, both because little is known about them and because such contacts are certainly to be obstructed by the government in question.

It seems that the EU's best chance of success is to encourage a 'top–bottom' reform process. The kind of democratic reforms that the EU wishes to encourage in the Mediterranean region are outlined in a Regional Strategy Paper and Regional Indicative Programme.[56] Following this, a Country Strategy Paper and an associated National Indicative Programme (NIP) was negotiated with each partner state, detailing the reforms that each had to achieve. However, a 2004 report, evaluating the effect of the MEDA programme in Egypt found that the Union's strategy makes little explicit mention of other EU objectives, namely stability, based on democratisation and conflict prevention. The same report states that the results achieved have been mixed, with the overall impact of such programmes limited by the slow pace of reform within Egypt.[57] Such failures may help explain the European Parliament's request to be involved in the evaluation of the human rights assessments carried out by the Commission within the ambit of the ENP.[58] The Commission has already set up human rights sub-committees, with a view to ensuring more commitment to reform.

Other potential improvements include improving the Mediterranean partners' joint ownership of the Partnership, in which the EU is still the main agenda setter. In addition, conflicting goals have often obstructed EU policy making and these must be ironed out. For example, securing the co-operation of the Mediterranean partners in implementing free trade seems to have diminished the EU's leverage to coax them towards deeper political reforms. The effectiveness of the EU can also be strengthened if the partners' economic dependence on the EU is substantive enough to make non-compliance costly. Increased financial aid to the Mediterranean partners, to help them overcome the problems of restructuring, particularly in the agricultural sector, may increase the attractiveness of compliance – and the cost of non-compliance. Effectiveness also requires coherence on the part of the EU member states and a willingness to act decisively. However, the resurgence of a petrodollar surplus in the Mediterranean region blunts the EU's economic instruments for inducing reform.

Conclusion: EU security options in the Mediterranean region

This chapter has focused on the main security challenges that the EU faces in the Mediterranean region. Enlargement has provided it with more assets to confront the 'arc of instability' that surrounds it, from the borders of Russia in the north to its southern frontiers in the Mediterranean region. Although the accession of Cyprus and Malta does not add, in a substantive way, to the assets and resources needed to confront these challenges, both states contribute towards increasing the EU's sensitivities in the region. Since both Cyprus and Malta are small island states, they tend to focus more on their immediate regional environment than on wider global perspectives. For this reason, and particularly if Cyprus manages to free itself from focusing almost exclusively on its internal problems, the two EU Mediterranean states can stimulate a stronger focus on Mediterranean issues within the main EU institutions.

The ENP is a welcome development, which, if properly implemented, could improve the functioning of the EMP, while increasing the EU's effectiveness in the Mediterranean region in a number of areas. However, a 'civilian power' approach on its own may not be sufficient and the EU needs to develop ESDP further, in order to offer a suitable response across the range of possible instruments at its disposal. At the same time, it is worth emphasising that the main challenges that the EU faces in the Mediterranean region cannot be solved by military means alone – if at all. Under the ENP, the Commission has prepared a number of country reports and, on this basis, Action Plans were negotiated with Israel, Jordan, Morocco, Tunisia and the Palestinian Authority, aiming to promote political and economic reform, as well as modernisation and development.[59] On 21 February 2005, the European Council reached agreement on the positions to be adopted by the EU within the Association Councils and the EU–Palestinian Authority Joint Committee to implement these Plans. Action Plans are also to be negotiated with Algeria and Egypt, as well as Lebanon once the situation improves. These Plans are careful to take into account the individual needs of each partner. The ENP offers rewards to all of the Union's partners that carry out the agreed measures, in terms of increased access to the internal market and Community programmes. Hence the effectiveness of this policy hinges on the correct evaluation of the Plans' implementation and the ability of the EU to take timely decisions. The European Parliament wishes to be involved – together with the Commission – in evaluating these Action Plans, while the Commission has appealed for continued and comprehensive support from the member states.

The purview of the ENP and the EMP is being extended, to include other matters, such as energy security, migration and WMD proliferation. However, it is short sighted to rely solely on this policy instrument. There is much to be developed on the EU side, which, in turn, will help reduce the Union's risks. For example, increased energy efficiency and the development of alternative energy resources helps to lessen the EU's external dependence and reduce risks in this sector. It also provides innovations that can be useful to the southern riparian states, in order to satisfy their increasing energy needs as they move up the development ladder. The promotion and implementation of democracy programmes attacks not only some of the root causes of terrorism, but also of illegal immigration. The promotion of the dialogue of civilisations, through such institutions as the Alexandria-based Anna Lindh Foundation, is useful, but its limitations must be equally recognised. The dialogue primarily involves elites, but civil society in the region cannot be ignored, for such a dialogue can be fully effective only if it filters down to the grass roots in the societies it is meant to influence.

Immigration is a good example of how internal and external EU policies need to be co-ordinated. It requires policy instruments beyond the ENP and EMP, securing compliance from the southern littoral states to take action to curb this phenomenon. It requires co-operation and co-ordination, as well as coherence, at an EU level and the sharing of information among EU member states on the basis of solidarity. Additionally, it depends on the readiness of the member states to combine their military assets, in order to safeguard security in their territorial waters, through adequate patrolling and help and rescue missions, and to prevent organised crime networks from carrying out their activities with impunity. Last but not least, it calls for a properly designed and implemented EU emigration policy.

In the case of terrorism, tightening the network of collaboration and intelligence sharing amongst the EU member states and their Mediterranean partners is important. More useful will be the resolution of the older conflicts that fuel this phenomenon, primarily the Middle East problem and authoritarianism in key Mediterranean partners. Anti-terrorist measures in the EU's Mediterranean partners should not be allowed to strangle NGOs and individuals struggling for democracy. At the same time, terrorism must not be viewed as a threat to the EU, but as a common threat faced by all states. In combating terrorism, military means, under the aegis of the ESDP, can also become useful in failed states, in order to restore order and open the way to humanitarian efforts. As the EU itself recognises, regional conflicts need political solutions, but military assets and effective policing may be needed in the post conflict phase, such as the EU is doing in Gaza. Civilian crisis management helps restore civil government. The EU is particularly well equipped to respond to such multi-faceted situations.

Finally, in terms of WMD proliferation, the EU calls for the strengthening of multilateral non-proliferation regimes and verification methods, to ensure compliance,[60] as well as the mainstreaming of non-proliferation policies into the EU's wider relations with third countries. This could be done by introducing a non-proliferation clause into agreements with these states. This proposal follows the path of the 'democracy' clause in the Association Agreements. Deeper scrutiny as to how this new conditionality will be implemented is required, in the light of the pitfalls in the implementation of the human rights and democracy conditionality identified in this chapter.

Notes

1 For details on the Euro-Mediterranean Partnership, see http://europa.eu.int/comm/external_relations/euromed/bd.htm.
2 The ten partners are Jordan, Lebanon, Syria, Egypt, Tunisia, Algeria, Morocco and the Palestinian Authority, Turkey and Israel.
3 Euro-Mediterranean Partnership, *The Barcelona Declaration and Work Programme* (Brussels, 1995), pp. 137–8.
4 European Commission, *Wider Europe – Neighbourhood: A New Framework for Relations with our Eastern and Southern Neighbours* (Brussels, 2003).
5 See *Conclusions of the 2590 General Affairs Council* (Luxembourg, June 2004).
6 Council of the European Union, *Conclusions of the Thessalonica European Council* (Brussels, June 2003).
7 EU crude oil imports, as of 2004: Saudi Arabia 12.8 per cent; Libya 9.6 per cent; Algeria 3.7 per cent; Iraq 2.64 per cent; Syria 1.7 per cent; Kuwait 1.14 per cent; Egypt 0.5 per cent; Tunisia 0.34 per cent; Russia 25.9 per cent; Norway 20.02 per cent, www.europa.eu.int/comm/energy/oil/crude/index_en.htm.
8 European Commission, *Towards a European Strategy for Security of Energy Supply* (Brussels, November 2000).
9 For details on state profiles, see www.eia.doe.gov/emeu/cabs/algeria.html
10 *Organised Illegal Immigration into the European Union* (The Hague: Europol, 2005).
11 *European Union Organised Crime Situation Report 2004* (The Hague: Europol, 2005), pp. 13–14.
12 Philippe Fargues (ed.), *Mediterranean Migration Report 2005* (Florence: European University Institute, 2005). He claims that statistical information on irregular migrants originating from the Mediterranean non-member states is almost non-existent.
13 'Immigration: initiative conjointe franco-espagnole auprès de l'Union européenne', *Fenêtre*

sur l'Europe (18 October 2005), www.fenetreeurope.com/php/page.php?section= actu&id=4717.
14. European Commission, *Technical Mission to Libya on Illegal Immigration 27 November to 6 December 2004* (Brussels, January 2005).
15. There is no reliable data on terrorist casualties in the Mediterranean region. The source quoted here is Paul Wilkinson, 'International terrorism: the changing threat and the EU response', *Chaillot Paper*, 84 (October 2005).
16. *Council Common Position on the Application of Specific Measures to Combat Terrorism* (Brussels, November 2005).
17. For details on Tunisia, see *Human Rights Watch: World Report 2005*, http://hrw.org/english/docs/2005/01/13/tunisi9801.htm.
18. *Tunisia: Intimidation of the Tunisian League for Human Rights Must Stop* (London, Amnesty International, 2005).
19. *Morocco: Human Rights at a Crossroads* (London, Human Rights Watch, 2004), http://hrw.org/reports/2004/morocco1004/.
20. 'Despite missed deadline, Quartet peace plan still valid, UN envoy', *UN News Centre*, 20 December 2005, www.un.org/apps/news/story.asp?NewsID=16998&Cr=Middle& Cr1= East.
21. *Council Joint Action on Establishing a European Union Border Assistance Mission for the Rafah Crossing Point (EU BAM Rafah)* (Brussels, 2005), p. 28.
22. *Arab Human Development Report 2003* (New York, United Nations Development Programme, 2003), p. 22.
23. Ibid., p. 23.
24. See Ian O. Lesser and Ashley J. Tellis, *Strategic Exposure: Proliferation Around the Mediterranean* (Santa Monica: Rand Publications, 1996).
25. Michele Dunne, *Libya: Security is not Enough* (Washington, DC: Carnegie Endowment for International Peace, 2004), p. 2.
26. Cited in 'Why Israel should not attack Iran', *Defence Update: International Online Defence Magazine* (12 December 2005), www.defense-update.com/2005_12_01_defense-update_archive.html.
27. For details, see 'Egypt's budding nuclear programme', *The Risk Report*, 2:5 (1996), www.wisconsinproject.org/countries/egypt/nuke.html.
28. *2005 Report by the Director General to the Board of Governors of the IAEA on the Implementation of the NPT Safeguards Agreement in the Arab Republic of Egypt*, (Vienna: IAEA, 2005).
29. For details, see 'Egypt profile: nuclear chronology 2000–03', *Nuclear Threat Initiative* (October 2005), www.nti.org/e_research/profiles/Egypt/Nuclear/1697_1743.html.
30. For further background, see Claudiane Chevalier, *Governance of the Mediterranean Sea: Outlook for the Legal Regime* (Malaga: World Conservation Union Centre for Mediterranean Cooperation, 2005).
31. Roberto Aliboni, 'Water as a factor of conflict: challenges around the Mediterranean Basin', *L'acqua nei paesi arabi: il contesto giuridico, politico e storico-culturale Conference*, Naples (22–24 February 2001).
32. *Oceans and the Law of the Sea: Report of the Secretary General* (New York: United Nations, 2005), p. 9.
33. Chevalier, *Governance of the Mediterranean Sea*, p. 45.
34. The Reagan Administration considered the Gulf of Sidra to be international waters and carried out naval exercises to challenge Libyan sovereignty over the Gulf.
35. Chevalier, *Governance of the Mediterranean Sea*, p. 45.
36. 'Spanish offer on disputed Isle', *CNN.com/World*, 18 July 2002, http://edition.cnn.com/2002/WORLD/europe/07/18/spain.morocco/.
37. For the official Greek position, see www.mfa.gr/english/foreign_policy/europe

southeastern/turkey/turkeys_claims_imia.html. For the Turkish counterclaims, see www.mfa.gov.tr/MFA/ForeignPolicy/Regions/EuropeanCountries/EUCountries/Greece/GreeceLinks/the_Kardak_Dispute.htm.
38. Roberto Aliboni and Laura Guazzone, 'Democracy in the Arab countries and the West', *Mediterranean Politics*, 9:1 (Spring 2004), p. 87.
39. Ulla Holm, 'Algeria: France's untenable engagement', *Mediterranean Politics*, 3:2 (Autumn 1998), pp. 104–14.
40. The US concluded free trade agreements with Israel (1985), Jordan (2000) and Morocco (2004) and an Egypt–Israel–US Trade Partnership in 2004.
41. For details of the Declaration, see www.knesset.gov.il/process/docs/venice_eng.htm.
42. Ambassador Wolfgang Ischinger, speech, 'Reconciliation instead of rifts', August 25 2005, info.org/relaunch/politics/speeches/082905.html.
43. Robert Kagan cited Charlemagne, 'Europe's Cassandra complex', *The Economist* (27 October 2005), p. 51.
44. For details, see Euro-Mediterranean Partnership, *Conclusions of the Second Euro-Mediterranean Ministerial Conference* (Malta, 1997).
45. See, for example, *European Parliament Resolution on the Euro-Mediterranean Partnership* (Brussels, 2005).
46. For details, see *Reinvigorating European Union Actions on Human Rights and Democratisation with Mediterranean Partners: Strategic Guidelines* (Brussels, 2005).
47. European Commission, *Tenth Anniversary of the Euro-Mediterranean Partnership: A Work Programme for the Next Five Years* (Brussels, 2005).
48. *European Parliament Resolution on the Euro-Mediterranean Partnership*.
49. Richard Youngs, 'Europe's uncertain pursuit of Middle East Reform', *Carnegie Papers*, 45 (June 2004), p. 8.
50. Ibid., p. 13.
51. *EU Annual Report on Human Rights 2005* (Brussels, 2005) para. 3.7.
52. Madeleine Bunting, 'Regime change, European-style, is a measure of our civilisation', *The Guardian* (26 September 2005).
53. See Daniel Brumberg, 'Liberalization versus democracy: understanding Arab political reform', *Carnegie Working Papers*, 37 (May 2003), p. 6.
54. Ibid., p. 7.
55. See Marina Ottaway 'Democracy and constituencies in the Arab world', *Carnegie Papers*, 48 (July 2004), p. 4.
56. For details of both programmes, see http://europa.eu.int/comm/external_relations/euromed/rsp/rsp02_06.pdf
57. For full details, see *Evaluation of the European Commission's Country Strategy for Egypt* (La Hulpe, Belgium: MWH, 2004), http://europa.eu.int/comm/europeaid/evaluation/reports/med/951647_vol1.pdf.
58. *European Parliament Resolution on the Euro-Mediterranean Partnership*.
59. The Action Plans, as well as the Commission's ENP *Strategy Paper*, are published on the Commission web-page, http://europa.eu.int/comm/world/enp/document_en.htm.
60. See *EU Strategy against the proliferation of Weapons of Mass Destruction* (Brussels: December 2003).

13

A successful Stability Pact: European Union policy in South-east Europe

Anthony Welch

Introduction

Since the early 1990s, the UN, EU and major donor states have undertaken a growing number of 'peace and nation-building' operations. However, when facing each new challenge, this international community of states seems to struggle with the enormity of the task, while forgetting old lessons, as if approaching the problem for the first time.

Their efforts since Yugoslavia's violent break up have gone a long way in managing the ethnic hatred and political inequalities that contributed to the Balkan conflicts. However, the hatred remains, held in check by the continuing presence of NATO and EU forces and by the lingering, but diminishing, effect of massive economic aid and reconstruction, injected in the wake of the conflicts. This is clearly evident in Kosovo, which will be used to illustrate the problems in resolving these issues.

Under the two administrations of George W. Bush, and in the aftermath of September 11, US policy priorities have shifted from the Balkans towards the Middle East and the 'War on Terror'. Thus, the EU, already a large contributor to the region, has now assumed the primary position in funding and managing reconstruction and development in the Balkans. In addition, the Stability Pact for South Eastern Europe, a framework for building co-operation and peace in the region, has gained prominence as a vehicle for transforming the region from conflict to peace and prosperity.[1]

The Stability Pact

Although the Dayton Accords[2] of 14 December 1995 provided for a political settlement to the conflict in BiH and sought to promote long-term stability in the region, achieving this in practice was more difficult than the drafters hoped. The Dayton Accords envisioned a post-conflict democracy, with internationally recognised human rights and fundamental freedoms, which provided that 'all refugees and displaced persons have the right freely to return to their homes of origin'.[3] However, given the continuing difficulties experienced on the ground, the months immediately after the signing of the Dayton Accords did nothing to convince the troops and administrators that these aims were readily attainable.

In 1999, UNSC Resolution 1244, which initiated the Kosovo peace-building process, echoed Dayton in its desire to see the 'protection and promotion of human rights', together with 'the safe and unimpeded return of all refugees and displaced persons to their homes in Kosovo'.[4] As with Dayton, the reality on the ground has fallen short of expectations. Since June 1999, sporadic vicious attacks against Serbs remaining in or returning to Kosovo have continued. In March 2004, when nineteen civilians died and hundreds of Serb homes and churches were burnt in riots, there were fears that a form of reverse ethnic cleansing was underway. Apart from targeting ethnic Serbs, the post-conflict backlash was also aimed at the Roma, Ashkali and other minorities, whom some Albanians accused of having supported Serb rule. As a result, many minorities lived under virtual siege and few who fled Kosovo returned.[5] In 1999, more than 200,000 Serbs left Kosovo, fearing revenge attacks from the ethnic Albanian majority. By summer 2004, only about 10,000 had returned.[6]

In an effort to bring the whole process of peace and nation building together in the Balkan region, the Stability Pact was launched in June 1999. It sought to encompass the desires of Dayton and UNSC Resolution 1244, while providing a broader political agenda, in order to achieve 'lasting peace, prosperity and stability for South East Europe'. In essence, the Pact's aims are to foster democracy, the rule of law, respect for human rights and fundamental freedoms; to preserve multinational and multi-ethnic diversity; and to ensure the safe and free return of all refugees and displaced persons.[7] Some of these ideals were 'already actively promoted by many countries in the region, having taken root throughout, including in the Federal Republic of Yugoslavia'.[8] However, the Stability Pact's democratic and multicultural norms are being promoted in a region that has recently experienced the brutal consequences of ethnic nationalism and cultural divisions.

Reality of ethnic divides

What most people remember about Yugoslavia's break up and the ensuing wars was the predictability of the conflict, given the historically deep ethnic hatreds in the region. That image suggests, to most casual observers, that conflict in the Balkans is impossible to solve. The rationale for this reaction was illustrated by an encounter I had with a Croatian Government Minister and his well-educated and articulate wife at the British Embassy in Zagreb in the early 1990s. During a polite, but, on my part, somewhat naïve, conversation, I asked her why the Croatians and Serbs were fighting, when they had lived together in apparent harmony for so long. Her face clouded with anger and she said, 'You do not understand, we always hated them, we were just *made* to live alongside them. They want to steal our religion and our culture – we must destroy them before they destroy us. It is the same with the Muslims.' The cold reality of her words seemed to doom any compromise or solution to the conflict that engulfed the citizens of Croatia, regardless of ethnicity. Later, in Kosovo, I witnessed the results of similar sentiments when spending the Christmas of 2000 as the UN Regional Administrator in the divided city of Mitrovica. Over a two-day holiday period, eight murders took place in my area of responsibility. All eight victims were ethnic Serbs, and included an eighty-year old couple, who were dragged from their home before having their throats cut. Those killings were followed by reprisals by elements of the Kosovo Serbian population on Kosovar Albanians in the area. This, in turn, fuelled riots in February 2001, when Albanian demonstrations resulted in the injury of 130 civilians and twenty French NATO soldiers.

However, ethnic hatred is only one source of conflict in the Balkans. Social and economic hardship and the lack of a secure future bring desperation and uncertainty, which can turn to violence. Ethnic differences were used as a tool by various parties in the region to turn uncertain economic and social prospects into national conflict for personal gain. Political and criminal motivation may have been the spur, but the ethnic nationalist feelings, so engendered, took on a life of their own. Gagnon suggests that 'violent conflict along ethnic cleavages is provoked by elites to create a domestic political context where ethnicity is the only politically relevant identity. It thereby constructs the individual interest of the broader population in terms of the threat to the community defined in ethnic terms'.[9]

In the forty-plus years before the conflicts erupted in the Balkans, ethnic differences existed, but so did political and economic stability. Then, in the wake of Tito's death in 1980, strong political control waned and the reality of economic and social transition from Communism began. That transition was interrupted by conflict, delaying many difficult economic and political decisions. Today, the situation is actually worse, as the heavy international intervention, in the wake of conflict, has dissipated and the flow of international aid and reconstruction has diminished as donor funds shift to new crisis areas. This scaling down of effort has revealed a devastated political and economic system, where citizens of these newly independent states see few options for recovery or growth. Thus, the hatred continues to smoulder, and occasionally flare, as people look for explanations to their seemingly never-ending misfortune. Susan Woodward, however, rejects the notion that Yugoslavia was a disaster waiting to happen, upon which Europe accidentally stumbled. She suggests that 'the most recent wars in the Balkans tell less about the region as a vortex and more about the inability of the international community to act in concert when serious political problems appear in that neighbourhood'.[10] Woodward believes that the EU, along with the UN, the US and NATO, by failing to act decisively, exacerbated and prolonged the bloodshed.[11]

International aid and reconstruction: the Balkan experience

Among the first steps in nation-building, swiftly following the restoration of physical security, is reconstruction. For the last ten years, the EU, its member states, the US and the wider international community have been providing significant economic and material assistance to the Western Balkans.

In 2001 the Commission adopted a Country Strategy for BiH to cover the period 2002–06, which provides a framework for EU assistance in the area. Assistance of more than €300m has been committed under the Community Assistance for Reconstruction (CARDS) programme, supporting BiH's participation in the Stabilisation and Association Process (SAP). In 2005, a further €49.4m was agreed for the CARDS programme. This was used for strengthening state institutions, public administration reform, democratic stabilisation and economic and social development.[12]

Since 1991, the EU has been at the forefront of the reconstruction effort and is by far the single largest donor, providing assistance to Kosovo and the South-eastern European region as a whole. In 1999, the Commission provided €378m in emergency humanitarian assistance for the victims of the Kosovo crisis, and a further €127m for reconstruction programmes immediately after the conflict. In 2000–01, the EU continued to support Kosovo, with further tranches of €360m and €350m respectively.[13] In addition, some 36,000 soldiers from EU states have served as members of KFOR, 80 per cent of the total force. Eight hundred civilian police from EU member states have served in the province and over 100 NGOs have provided assistance there.[14]

In BiH, more than €2.5bn of EU funds has been committed since 1991. From 1991 to 2000, humanitarian assistance provided by the Commission's Humanitarian Aid Office (ECHO) totalled €1.032bn and, in the period 1996–2000, BiH received assistance under the OBNOVA and PHARE programmes amounting to €890.7m. Additionally, the EU member states contributed over €1.8bn in assistance between 1996 and the end of 2001. Since CARDS was set up, a total of €375.3m was invested in these states.[15]

While the US has also been a key actor in this region, in recent years, it has reduced its presence and financial commitment to the region, partially prompted by the long-held belief that the Balkans is actually a 'European' problem. USAID's budget for BiH has fallen from $79.9m in 2001 to $44m in 2004.[16] More and more, the US has focused on key security interests in the Middle East and Asia. In a statement to the House International Relations Subcommittee on Europe, on 27 March 2003, Thomas C. Adams, Acting Coordinator of US Assistance to Europe and Eurasia, said:

> In the wake of the tragic events of September 11, 2001, the countries of Central Asia assumed a much greater importance for the US. [South-eastern Europe] is now experiencing steady, if at times slow, progress in efforts to achieve democracy, market reform, overcome the destruction and dislocations of the Balkan wars, and meet the grave challenges of crime and poverty . . . For the long-term health of the region, we see the need to promote economic growth, led by the private sector.[17]

As a result of this switch of emphasis, all the leading international mediators in the Balkans are now European, with the EU central to the region's reconstruction and development efforts. This means that the age-old problem of winning the peace, having won the war, is a challenge that the EU now faces without significant US assistance. As Carr and Callan note, the task is never easy:

> The decentralised nature of authority in intra-state conflicts leaves international institutions with difficulties regarding accountability and responsibilities . . . missions can then drift as the intervening forces become the authority to regulate the behaviour of factions within the state.[18]

Importantly, the approach to the Balkans and its problems will dictate European strategy for spreading stability and influence beyond EU borders over the coming years.

Central to economic assistance is the process of reconstruction. Although infrastructure damage in Kosovo may have seemed more manageable than in BiH, the impact of more than ten years of neglect by the Yugoslav authorities was underestimated by the international community. A combination of neglect, bomb damage and a major migration of people from the countryside to the cities meant that electricity and water services collapsed in the early stages of reconstruction and, even today, continue to falter and fail for days on end. As late as October 2005, Pristina, the capital of Kosovo, was experiencing power cuts of between three and five hours a day, with the attendant loss of water through pump failure. Even in late 2006, some areas of the province continued to suffer from electricity and water restrictions, with parts of Pristina having the water supply cut off between midnight and 5am. This is despite the UK's Department for International Development (DFID) spending £18.5m (and the EU millions more) on engineering works in the first five months after the Kosovo conflict.[19] In addition, both organisations spent similar sums on schools, hospitals and clinics. Infrastructure repair has been dramatic, but basic utilities and services are still far below par for a territory that is part of the European continent. Significantly, such utilities have yet to return to the level seen under Belgrade's rule.

The problem is not limited to Kosovo. Ten years into the implementation of the Dayton Accords and the reconstruction process in BiH, signs of infrastructure weakness are still evident. Despite massive international reconstruction efforts, many cantons and municipalities still cannot deliver essential services. While the World Bank estimates that a large proportion of public expenditure goes towards health care, services remain far below the European average and, in some cases, are non-existent. World Bank reports place public sector expenditure in BiH at around 63 per cent of GDP – a full 20 per cent higher than the regional average. However, this expenditure is heavily weighted in favour of security expenditure and pensions benefits paid to war invalids and the bereaved families of soldiers.[20] Meanwhile, other public sector employees, such as police and teachers, suffer wage cuts or long periods of work without pay.[21] Between 1996 and 2000, the Bosnian public sector spent $9.2bn on wages and transfers, which is more than 48 per cent of the average annual GDP. Nevertheless, unemployment hovers around 41 per cent and social benefits for workers are non-existent, a harsh transition from the former socialist system.[22]

In the political arena, the international community recognised early on the need to reconfigure the existing system, starting with elections. This political foundation was to become the structure on which social and economic reform could be built. The ultimate goal was a level of stability where, once again, joining economic and political Europe – and even entering the EU – might be possible. It is a sad fact that the first flush of enthusiasm for the democratic process has waned. In all the countries of the former Yugoslavia there is a spreading disillusion about the advantages of western democracy. In many ways the actions of the international community can be blamed for this. The rush to elections, so favoured by the US, was readily embraced by their European partners. This quick implementation left little time for either the fledgling politicians or the electorate to consider or prepare for the process of democracy.

In considering how to design the system, the international organisations in charge, the UN, EU and OSCE, ignored the traditional and cultural ways of determining choice (such as family voting) and rushed forward with a system designed to instantly modernise and democratise. Good intentions abounded and, given the traditional pace of change, might even be commended, but the problem remained that the reasoning behind the new political system was never properly explained to the Balkan citizens. Instead, the processes in both BiH and Kosovo were presented as a *fait accompli*, resulting in immediate suspicion among the electorate, who largely believed they were designed to benefit a new class of elite power-brokers, in the form of the international community and their chosen local representatives.

Yet, the process moved forward with some degree of success in terms of technical implementation. People registered, people voted, the process was monitored by the international observers and deemed to be free and fair. They adhered to international standards for voting anonymity, lack of intimidation and clear rules and regulations governing the process.[23] Unfortunately, the electoral process did not produce the desired stable political foundation on which future progress could be built. Instead, in many cases, those seeking office fell back on the old way of doing business, using extortion, bribery and violence to pursue power.

Technical experts on elections often dismiss the reasons why the outcome was less than adequate as irrelevant. However, the reality is that the international community had invited and expected the people of the Balkans, during a period of difficult transition, to set aside nationalist feelings and place their trust in a process that took less than two years to develop. Furthermore, this was a process in which the people and leaders had little authority or responsibility. In other words, the UN, EU, OSCE and others expected a process that had taken European states centuries to develop to be fully operational and accepted, in the Balkans, in just a few years. Furthermore, it was expected that the local political leadership would adopt a system fully developed by outsiders. Without clear acceptance from all parties and ethnic groups from the beginning, it was too easy for all sides to simply blame others or to transfer responsibility to the UN and EU administrations.

This attitude is illustrated by the findings of a recent survey into the perceptions of security among the local communities. In Kosovo it found that the UN administration was seen as 'an arrogant bureaucracy . . . feeding on itself'. The UN Interim Mission (UNMIK) was 'getting in the way [of progress]'.[24] In addition, a report by Lesley Abdela, former Deputy-Director Democratisation and Head of NGO and Civil Society Development for the OSCE in Kosovo, stated that:

the local population has felt impeded rather than liberated by UNMIK despite UNMIK's remit . . . they felt completely excluded from the process of trying to find new solutions. They were neither employed – other than as drivers and interpreters – nor consulted. A frustrated or unhappy populace inevitably turns to alternative power brokers and fixers to achieve what the international organisations have failed to do. It was not hard for militant and criminal elements to increase support for the view that this is our country – now it's time you foreigners left.[25]

The election processes were viewed by many as confusing. As recently as the 2004 BiH Municipal Elections, the Office for Democratic Institutions and Human Rights (ODIHR) found that there was a continuing primacy of ethnicity in the election campaign, a tendency for the major political parties to criticise the integrity of the electoral system and an election system which few voters understand.[26]

In Kosovo, in particular, the rift between the main ethnic groups remains wide, with constructive dialogue yet to fully take place. In recent elections less than 1 per cent of Serbs eligible to vote did so.[27] Following the elections on 23 October 2004, Soren Jessen-Petersen, the UN Secretary-General's Special Representative for Kosovo was moved to say that 'more harmonious ethnic relations must be a key goal. We must now work with the legitimate representatives of all communities, and we must also reach out to those who decided not to vote or who felt intimidated not to cast their ballots'.[28]

Inevitably, after the elections, the problems were compounded. Once elected, many politicians seemed incapable of engaging in issues that were important to their electorate's daily lives. Often, they followed the time-honoured route of ensuring that their relatives and friends were looked after first and their clan or ethnic group second, leaving communities a long way behind. This failure to break with past tradition was evident on every level and left individual citizens with a clear example of why the new democratic system simply did not work. All Balkan politicians, even the best ones, were in danger of being tarred with the brush of 'incompetence' and 'corruption'. Abdela quotes a senior international police officer serving in Kosovo:

> The creation of the new joint administration initiatives between the UN and the various political factions has a number of people very concerned. [These politicians] are a certified, bona fide gang of thieves, with links to organised crime elements throughout Europe, Asia and North America. They are extremely dangerous people . . . they will be the ultimate winners in this charade . . . It would be laughable to turn an entire country over to such a gang of thugs if it wasn't so sad for the common people who have to live here.[29]

In some cases, problems were just too large for politicians to handle and tried and tested methods appeared the most expedient way to get through. In other cases, the international administrations failed the men and women they had helped put into office. This failing was not always based on the individual or individual actions, but more on the need to contain the local situation and to ensure that the particular region did not flare up. Kai Eide, the Permanent Representative of Norway to NATO and Balkans expert, in his 2004 report on the state of the UN mission in Kosovo, argued 'the efforts of the international community had become a static, inward-looking, fragmented and routine operation'.[30] The international community appeared to be in disarray, without direction and internal cohesion. Instead, UNMIK was simply used to keep a lid on tensions.[31] The International Crisis Group agreed:

> UNMIK's structure and mandate are now exposed as inappropriate to prepare Kosovo for the transition from war to peace, from socialism to the market economy, and from international political limbo to final status . . . Unable to agree on what that final status should be, it relied on the naïve assumption that delaying the decision would allow passions to cool . . . This lack of resolve left the majority Albanian and minority Serb communities locked in a confrontation that was suppressed, never resolved.[32]

Somewhere along the way, the interests and future of the Balkan people have been lost.

The impact of economic uncertainty and poverty

The good intentions and generosity of international donors have, sadly, also contributed to the growing economic and political problems across the Western Balkans. Nevertheless, the argument for continued engagement remains strong.

BiH is the second poorest state in Europe, just ahead of Albania. Kosovo remains a UN Protectorate and economic data is scare, but, given the desire of the international community to reduce their commitments, Kosovo is likely to join its neighbours at the bottom of the economic ladder. Croatia and Slovenia, meanwhile, bask in the relative success of their economic and political transitions. Nonetheless this success, particularly in Croatia, masks underlying ethnic tensions and the spectre of nationalism. The failure to arrest General Ante Gotovina, who led the operation to take the Krajina in 1995, stalled the start of EU membership negotiations until September 2005. In addition, the return of the Serbs remains problematic. Before the conflict 12 per cent of the Croatian population was Serbian; it is now just 4.5 per cent.[33] The government was slow to end discriminatory practices in property repossession, occupancy rights and reconstruction assistance. Things are, however, improving. Prime Minister Ivo Sanader has worked hard to improve the overall climate in the country and to encourage Serbs to return and integrate. Reconstruction assistance is now being granted to an increasing numbers of Serb applicants.[34] The greatest hindrance to his aspirations remains the sluggish economy and continuing job discrimination.[35]

Serbia remains the economic and political powder keg of the region. The relative success of ultra-nationalists in the 28 December 2003 parliamentary elections demonstrated that nationalist sentiments continue to run high and much is still to be done.[36] This perpetuates continuing concern among Serbia's neighbours over its history of expansionist policies. Nevertheless, a recovering Serbian economy could spell both political and economic relief for the region. Time and patience are required to achieve this.

It is not just poverty that threatens political stability in the Balkans; it is also the perceived lack of a future and declining social status. As stated by a director of a local

NGO in Pristina, 'Kosovo is secure but we are living in a bubble'.[37] Currently, irregular diaspora payments and small family businesses keep many households afloat. However, the massive influx of funds into BiH and Kosovo from the international community has distorted domestic spending patterns, resulting in an actual threat to the stability of the states themselves, and hence to the region and Europe more widely. Expectations have risen, and now the impact of those expectations is being felt by a weak political system with an even weaker leadership. To illustrate, in Kosovo, the UN has been paying stipends to 5,000 workers at the Trepca mines and smelting plant in north Mitrovica since late 1999, even though the works were closed for safety reasons in 2000. Any time UN international administrators move to stop the payments or suggest transitional arrangements to decommission the facilities, howls of protest from both the Albanian and Serbian communities ensue. As a result, the unsatisfactory situation continues. Eventually, the problem will be turned over to local leaders, who will be beholden to their own ethnic groups and therefore be completely unable to resolve the issue. Thus, stalemate will continue and stand as a symbol of mistrust and dissatisfaction for both parties – a ready source of blame for the daily troubles faced by individual citizens.

It is only through the hope of economic alternatives or visible progress that these problems can be overcome. It is therefore axiomatic that many of the people in the Balkans look to the EU for solutions. Currently, the steady drift of young people out of the region is a blight on society and a visible sign of the loss of hope in the future. Although many young people dream of living in the US, most find it easier to move to the EU. This emigration, legal or otherwise, is seen as the only escape from a jobless, dead-end future. Most people, however, prefer, or are forced by poverty, to stay at home. Their memories of a stable life and a time when their Yugoslav passport allowed them to travel easily throughout Europe, when international investors came seeking opportunities and their university education was respected throughout Europe are manifested in the dream that someday their homeland might join the EU.

However, there are ways of offering hope, both in terms of financial stability and personal achievement. Immediately following the conflict in Kosovo, a primary DFID objective was to seek ways of putting the maximum number of people back to work. The key to receiving DFID assistance was to demonstrate a substantial number of potential employees (beyond relatives) and a sense of fair business practice, which would benefit the community. As a result, more than 2,500 people were employed in the first few months after the war, which directly improved the lives of over 12,000 citizens across Kosovo.[38] Even today many of those businesses continue to trade successfully, providing vital employment, personal dignity and hope.

Why to act and how to act

The importance of these issues is their impact on both security and economic concerns in the EU and US. One conclusion to draw is that decreasing European and US aid and development funding is mirrored by a waning political commitment to the Balkans. Woods suggests that development assistance, which gives priority to human development targets, is at risk from the new imperative to use aid as a counter-terrorist weapon. She believes that this imperative, coupled with budget pressures in the major donor states, will almost certainly ensure that new aid will slow down whilst 'development agencies, with their more stable budgets, will be urged to give priority to the development needs of the countries at the front line of the "War on Terror"'.[39] As a result, as financial commitments decrease, the Western Balkans could become increasingly isolated from the rest of Europe. This isolation is exacerbated by Slovenia and Hungary recently joining the EU, Bulgaria and Romania joining in 2007 and Croatia starting accession negotiations in September 2005. Thus, the gulf between the richer and poorer Europeans is rapidly becoming the gulf between the EU and the Western Balkans.

Such a divide directly impacts on the EU's long-standing border control problems. Failure to maintain constructive and long-term engagement in the Balkans will result in continued economic immigration into the EU. The EU currently receives approximately 1.5m immigrants per year from states outside the accession process, while mobility within the EU shows that, in an average year, only about 1.5 per cent of employed people move between regions within their state or from another member state.[40] Furthermore, as economic decline continues in South-eastern Europe, political tensions will grow. The threat of conflict is then exacerbated and the likelihood of further military intervention rises. Given individual states' current worldwide commitments, particularly those of the UK and US, increasing Balkan commitments would strain an already overtaxed military. The added economic burden of having to provide further humanitarian aid to the region would not help an already stretched international development regime, which continually fears the onset of donor fatigue.

In addition, the issue of religiously inspired terrorism now weighs heavily in the minds of many Europeans. This concern, coupled with the close relationship between ethnic divides and religious differences in the Balkans, adds to security fears. However, the fear of religious extremism in the Balkans has been proven, in the majority of cases, to be misplaced. Although Muslim states such as Saudi Arabia have invested heavily in reconstruction throughout the Balkans, the secular culture of the region has remained. In a Pristina bar, I spoke to a young Kosovar Albanian about his religious beliefs. He readily professed himself to be a Muslim. I commented that he was drinking beer and chatting to western dressed women. 'Ah yes', he said with a smile, 'but we are all rock and roll Muslims!' However, a 2003 study by the Kosovar Institute for Policy Research concluded that neglect by UN administrators, with 'rigid stereotypes' about Islam and its practitioners, threatens the 'tolerant Islamic traditions' of Kosovo. With education improvements progressing slowly, conservative Islamic traditions, funded by groups from Saudi Arabia, may gain a foothold. An example of this is the Islamic Endowment Foundation's support for thirty Koran Schools in rural areas of Kosovo.[41]

This is not to say that concern over terrorism is naïve or unfounded. As Iraq, Afghanistan and the West Bank show, terrorism is born out of failed states, a sense of injustice and economic desperation, not simply religious fundamentalism. The potent ingredients that feed the growth of fundamentalism are present in BiH, Albania and Kosovo. In BiH, the effective use of Mujahideen fighters during the war, particularly in the Zenica area, left a legacy that concerns European states. These concerns and the fragile nature of the Western Balkans reinforce the importance of seeing the region through its period of transition. To do this, the EU needs to assume a leadership role. It must finish what the wider international community started, both politically and economically, and do its utmost to prop up the fragile democracies it helped create. The remaining international institutions (the OSCE across the region, the Office of the High Representative in Bosnia and the EU Pillar in Kosovo specifically) must demonstrate a collective vision for the Balkans based on the needs of the people. Pressure must be applied on local leadership to make difficult decisions and agree a common way forward that includes accountability for their actions. The EU must focus on promoting good governance and the rule of law.

This is one key element in the EU's effort to tackle the threat of organised crime, including trafficking in drugs and people, which is emerging from the region. In a November 2002 speech, Chris Patten, then EU External Relations Commissioner, said that he saw organised crime, trafficking and corruption in the Balkans as having an enormously negative impact on social, political and economic conditions. The problem was exacerbated by the perception that these issues were not taken seriously by the political establishment, which was often part of the problem.[42]

Although many of these concerns are effectively captured in the mission and approach of the Stability Pact, practical implementation remains difficult. For example, the Pact's Working Table One incorporates many of the issues of democracy, governance and human rights inherent to a successful approach, but is struggling to make headway. Working Table Two, which focuses on trade and infrastructure development, also has far to go. While the data is incomplete, it suggests that exports of goods and services constitute less than 10 per cent of imports, with a significant share involving domestic sales to foreigners (troops and international organisations), whose presence is bound to diminish over time. A small, landlocked economy such as Kosovo cannot be expected to grow in isolation, relying on its small domestic market. Effective integration in international trade broadly requires three elements: appropriate trade and foreign exchange policies, effective market and trade related institutions and market access.[43] Yet, in Kosovo, these avenues have yet to be established in any significant manner.

Economic reconstruction, recovery and development are the objectives assigned to the EU under Pillar IV of UNMIK's structure. Pillars I and II – police, justice (formerly humanitarian affairs) and civil administration – are run by the UN. Pillar III – democratisation and institution building – is run by the OSCE.[44] Through Pillar IV and its broader economic aid programme across the Balkans, the EU must continue the process of regenerating and modernising economic structures. They have created a Joint Interim Administrative Structure with local and international representatives, a Central Fiscal Authority, a Tax Collection Service, a Border Service, Banking and Payments Authority and a Department of Reconstruction.[45] Although the Pillar has suffered its fair share of criticism and false starts, it has done a remarkable job in providing technical and financial assistance to the province. However, it also suffers from the inevitable drift into the bureaucratic desire to self-perpetuate and become politically risk averse. International organisations attempt to bring order to chaos by throwing people and money at the problem, rather than seeking effective longer-term action and collaboration from local partners.

International organisations have been necessary players in bringing expertise, security and resources into the Balkans. Nonetheless, the most important measure to achieving stability and peace is to prioritise reducing unemployment across the region. Since 1999, unemployment in Pristina and other towns across Kosovo has been exacerbated by large-scale migration from the undeveloped countryside, pushing unemployment levels to approximately 57 per cent, with 70 per cent of sixteen to twenty-four year olds out of work.[46] However, building bureaucracies, either foreign or domestic, is not the best solution, as their priorities can often serve as obstacles to progress. This collision of priorities was highlighted in Kosovo. In my role as Mitrovica's UN Regional Administrator, a factory owner came to request the UN vehicle storage and servicing site for northern Kosovo be moved out of his privately owned factory. His intention was to restart production, in order to fulfil manufacturing orders from FYROM and Albania. He provided documentary proof of the orders and indicated he could re-employ some 200 semi-skilled workers. Despite my enthusiasm for what appeared to be an easy demonstration of faith in the decimated city, I found UN Headquarters in Pristina completely opposed to the idea, on the grounds that UN requirements were a priority. The logic was justified with the attitude of, 'after all *we* are running this place'. Exasperated, I delivered the news to the factory owner, but assured him that, as the UN was restructuring its operations in the coming months, the situation could change. Apparently I was wrong; the factory was still in UN hands two years later. In the wider political context, this attitude also seems to prevail. Ambassador Kai Eide also highlighted the importance of a sense of ownership: 'UNMIK should accelerate and expand the process of involving Kosovo residents in executive and support roles . . . greater local involvement in the reserved areas would also provide the Provisional Institutions for Self Government with relevant experience.'[47]

EU states currently second civil servants to Balkan states to work with counterparts in various Balkan ministries. However, the programme has met with criticism regarding its focus and overly bureaucratic procedures. One report suggested that the UN and EU missions throughout the Balkans should be rationalised as quickly as possible, and be supplanted by small multi-disciplined advisory teams, working alongside ministers and local civil servants.[48] The objective would be to instil a sense of ownership and responsibility among local leaders for institutional changes. The local community should be encouraged to use its expertise, to make and learn from their mistakes and to take responsibility for their actions. These advisory teams should report to Strasbourg and Brussels on the economic, political, human rights and cultural progress of their assigned country, whilst standing back, as far as practical, from day-to-day administration.[49] This streamlined intervention will help to replace the lame duck leadership identified by Kai Eide, and instil a sense of direction and respect.

International attitudes and approaches aside, it is clear that one of the major constraints on private sector development in the region is the legacy of socialist attitudes, outmoded equipment and approaches. The Balkans suffer from being neither a low-cost environment, nor having the modern technology to boost productivity and allow it to compete in Europe. In order to move forward, the states must capitalise on their high skills level to streamline costs across all key sectors, including textiles, mining, retail and commercial agriculture.[50] Again, these actions come saddled with difficult decisions and high political costs, but the EU member states are no strangers to similar choices and could be strong supporters, advisors and financers for the fledgling Balkan democracies.

Coupled with this is the problem of creating a proper regulatory and banking environment to support private investment. The principal obstacles to this are property rights and an ailing public service run by an imposed bureaucracy. In the wake of the 1999 Kosovo conflict, many wealthy members of the Kosovar Albanian diaspora attempted to return to and invest in Kosovo. As the current plethora of abandoned factories and building sites illustrate, after months, sometimes years, of trying to get through the UN/EU bureaucracy, many simply gave up and returned to their adopted countries and more fertile investment opportunities. The EU needs to redouble its efforts to work alongside the local population to overcome regulatory and bureaucratic obstacles, so that opportunities can be capitalised on. Encouraging diaspora investors and marketing to the broader investment community are vital to recovery.

The EU–Western Balkans summit at Thessaloniki in June 2003 re-emphasised the importance of Small and Medium-sized Enterprises (SMEs) and invited the Balkan states to sign-up to the principles enshrined in the European Charter for Small Enterprises, thus bringing them in line with EU and candidate states in sharing good practice in small enterprise policy. The sum of €200m has been allocated to the Balkans for economic reform and development measures and, in 2003, a programme dedicated to enhancing the competitiveness of SMEs in border regions was also launched.[51]

For the states in the Western Balkans, these approaches are also vital to eventual EU membership. Albania, BiH, FYROM and Serbia and Montenegro are all potential EU candidates. A key element in converting this potential into reality is the EU's SAP, encouraging country-specific reforms, as well as regional co-operation. The SAP consists of three main mechanisms: trade measures to encourage imports and exports, thus stimulating economic growth; contractual links, eventually resulting in the conclusion of an SAA; and substantial financial assistance to underpin the SAP's aims. This assistance, through the Country Strategy Papers and associated National Indicative Programmes, amounted to about €4.6 billion between 2000 and 2006.[52]

A proposed stepping stone to enhance trade may be to develop a 'Confederation of Balkan States', including Albania, BiH, Bulgaria, Croatia, FYROM, Romania and Serbia and Montenegro. Its aim would not be political union, but a vehicle for economic co-operation, in order to bring the states up to modern and competitive EU standards. The restoration of inter-regional trade that took place throughout the old Yugoslavia should be encouraged, particularly as most people in the Balkans agree that economic co-operation is the one area where leaders have always been able to work together, even in the darkest times.

Conclusion

The Balkans can be rebuilt. The justification is clear, and the path, although difficult, is not impossible. However, it is clear that the necessary stamina and political will among EU and US leaders is in doubt. Furthermore, new challenges will continue to demand increasingly expensive commitments, both financially and materially. Therefore, it is even harder to see how the Balkans will remain among international development priorities.

It is likely that the EU will have to go it alone in the Balkans. Achieving social and economic cohesion within Europe is one of the EU's great historical achievements. This project is on-going, with two more states to join in 2007. However, it is unclear how it can continue to enlarge without giving sufficient consideration to the one region that has been the source of so much conflict and has absorbed so many European soldiers, policemen, administrators and euros over the last ten years. To move forward without resolving these vexing issues in the Western Balkans seems almost futile.

To ensure success, the EU needs a cohesive approach to the region based on existing programmes and institutions. Closer ties to regional and European entities such as NATO should be encouraged through vehicles like PfP, but not simply as a reward for allowing coalition troops to be stationed or exercised on their territory. In addition, the EU should re-direct the efforts of the European Agency for Reconstruction away from localised or state-based reconstruction programmes towards a regional approach. The Stability Pact could widen its reach to become an employment and cohesion vehicle to encourage economic growth and help curb migration. Finally, the remaining Balkan states should be formally included in the post-2004 EU enlargement plans, along with Bulgaria, Croatia, Romania and Turkey. A realistic and achievable target date for the Western Balkan enlargement should be set, without appearing to be a far-off empty promise. Perhaps 2025 would be an appropriate date.

Through a cohesive, consistent and dedicated effort by its concerned neighbours, the tensions in the Western Balkans can be overcome, rather than simply managed. It may take two or more generations to achieve, but the investment in peace and stability will bear fruit and contribute to the growing prosperity found in the EU today; a prosperity only achieved after decades of hard work to put aside differences which plummeted to similar depths of despair.

In 2002, Chris Patten said that the EU intervention in the Balkans 'should have been the hour of Europe but we blew it. We could have acted decisively to ensure a peaceful dissolution of the old Yugoslavia but we didn't. We could have shown real leadership and vision but we were found wanting'.[53] Europe cannot afford to make this mistake again. In the more volatile world of the twenty-first century, the EU must have the courage and fortitude to act decisively when faced with the challenge of creating order out of chaos and stability out of strife. This is a challenge it must meet – to bring South-eastern Europe out of conflict and into the EU.

Notes

1 *Stability Pact for South Eastern Europe* (Brussels: Special Co-ordinator, 2004), www.stabilitypact.org/about/default.asp.
2 Formally know as *The General Framework Agreement for Peace in Bosnia and Herzegovina*.
3 *The General Framework for Peace in Bosnia Herzegovina* (Brussels: Office of the High Representative and EU Special Representative, 1995), pp. Annex 7, Art 1, www.ohr.int/dpa/default.asp.
4 *UNSCR 1244 (1999)* (New York: United Nations, 1999), p. 1.
5 *Kosovo (Serbia and Montenegro) The March Violence: UNMIK and KFOR Fail to Protect the Rights of Minority Communities* (London: Amnesty International, 2004).
6 See www.civpol.org/portal/html.
7 *Stability Pact for South Eastern Europe*.
8 Ibid.
9 V. P. Gagnon, 'Ethnic nationalism and international conflict: the case of Serbia', *International Security*, 19:3 (Winter 1994–1995), pp. 130–66.
10 S. Woodward, 'International aspects of the wars in former Yugoslavia', in J. Udovicki and J. Ridgeway (eds), *Burn this House: The Making and Unmaking of Yugoslavia* (London: Duke University Press, 1997), p. 248.
11 J. Mitric, 'Reviews', *The Slavic and East European Journal*, 43:4 (1999), p. 760.
12 'The EU's relations with Bosnia and Herzegovina: Fact Sheet', http://europa.eu.int/comm/external_relations/see/bosnie_herze/index.htm#3; 'Bosnia, European Commission sign assistance agreement worth €49.9m', www.onasa.com.ba/NewsFlow/web/guest.nsf.
13 'The EU's relations with the State of Serbia and Montenegro: fact sheet', http://europa.eu.int/comm/external_relations/see/fry/kosovo/index.htm.
14 Ibid.
15 Ibid.
16 'USAID: Europe and Eurasia', www.usaid.gov/locations/europe_eurasia/countries/.html.
17 T. Adams, *US Assistance Programs in Europe: An Assessment* (Washington, DC: US Department of State, 2003).
18 Fergus Carr and Teresa Callan, *Managing Conflict in the New Europe* (Basingstoke: Palgrave, 2002), p. 195.
19 *Emergency Aid: The Kosovo Crisis. Report by the Comptroller and Auditor General* (London: National Audit Office, 2000), p. 19.
20 *Country Assistance Strategy for Bosnia and Herzegovina 2000–2002* (Washington, DC: World Bank, June 2000).
21 'Bosnian Serb police: badly paid, rarely paid', *Agence France Presse* (7 February 2001).
22 Foreign Trade Chamber of Bosnia Herzegovina, *Country Profile: Unemployment Statistics*, www.komorabih.com/en/economybih/economy-bih.
23 *The ODIHR Election Observation Handbook* (Warsaw: OSCE/ODIHR, April 1999), Annex A.
24 A. Donini, L. Minear, I. Smillie, T. Van Baarda and A. Welch, *Mapping the Security Environment: Understanding the Perceptions of Local Communities, Peace Support Operations and assistance Agencies* (Medford MA: Feinstein International Famine Center; Tufts University, 2005), p. 31.
25 L. Abdela, *Kosovo – Missed Opportunities, Lessons for The Future: A Report prepared for the OSCE Mission in Kosovo* (Strasbourg: OSCE, 2000), pp. 3–4.

26 *International Observer Mission: Municipal Elections 2004; Bosnia and Herzegovina. Statement of Preliminary Findings and Conclusions* (Sarajevo: OSCE/ODIHR, October 2004), pp. 1–3.
27 R. Pinto, Elida Reci, Senada Keserovic, Nevenka Cuckovic, Zivko Dimor and Petar Ivanovic, *The SME Sector in the CARDS Countries: A Panorama and Country and Regional Level. Report to EU/EBRD/UNMIK* (London: UNMIK, May 2004).
28 Ibid.
29 Abdela, *Kosovo – Missed Opportunities, Lessons for The Future*, p. 4.
30 United Nations Administration in Kosovo: Press Release, www.unmikonline.org/news.htm#2501.
31 Ibid.
32 *Collapse in Kosovo Europe Report No 155* (Brussels: International Crisis Group, April 2004).
33 'Stormy memories: marking the tenth anniversary of Croatia's capture of Krajina', *The Economist*, 376: 8437 (30 July–5 August 2005), pp. 37–8.
34 *A Half-hearted Welcome: Refugee Returns to Croatia. Europe Report No. 138*, (Brussels: International Crisis Group, December 2002), p. 1.
35 'Stormy memories'.
36 *Collapse in Kosovo*, p. 1.
37 Donini et al., *Mapping the Security Environment*, p. 29.
38 *Kosovo Emergency Humanitarian Assistance Programme: Report on Activities*, 26 March 1999 – 31March 2000 (London: Department for International Development, April 2000).
39 Ngaire Woods, *The Shifting Politics of Foreign Aid* (Oxford: Global Economic Governance Programme, 2005), p. 14.
40 H. Krieger, *Migration*, (Brussels: European Foundation for the Improvement of Living and Working Conditions, 2004), pp. 3–8.
41 I. Blumi, *Political Islam among Albanians: Are the Taliban coming to the Balkans?* (Pristina: Kosovar Institute for Policy Research and Development, July 2003).
42 Chris Patten, Speech at UK Conference on Organised Crime, 2 November 2002.
43 C. Michalopoulos, *Kosovo's International Trade: Trade Policy, Institutions and Market Access Issues*, Report to the UK Department for International Development (London, Department for International Development, 2003), pp. 3–4.
44 *History of EU Pillar within UNMIK*, www.euinkosovo.org/pDefault.asp?id=78&Lang=2.
45 Ibid.
46 *United Nations Development Programme Fact Sheet 1: Unemployment*, www.kosovo.undp.org/Factsheets/factsheets/unemployment_may2003.pdf.
47 Kai Eide, *Report to the United Nations Secretary-General on the United Nations Interim Mission in Kosovo* (New York: United Nations, 2004), p. 8.
48 *Thessaloniki and After: The EU's Balkan Agenda* (Brussels: International Crisis Group, June 2003).
49 Ibid.
50 European Stability Initiative, *Preventing the Crisis of 2004: The Western Balkans and the boundaries of Europe. Wilton Park European Conference* (11 October 2002).
51 Pinto et al., *The SME Sector in the CARDS Countries*, pp. 7–8.
52 Ibid.
53 Chris Patten, *Organised Crime*.

Conclusion: the security implications of EU enlargement

David Brown[1]

When considering enlargement's wider impact on the EU's security agenda, this volume has highlighted two central issues: *internal cohesion* and *external projection*. Internal cohesion refers to the institutional and policy base on which the EU's security acquis rests, while external projection relates to how the enlarged EU behaves both within its immediate environs and at a global level. Before considering the impact that enlargement has had on each, it is worth sketching out their general contours.

Firstly, the issue of size affects both elements (as CFSP and ESDP, the main mechanisms for external projection, are potentially constrained by the existing level of internal cohesion). There is a lingering concern that an organisation of twenty-five states, each with their own interests and agendas, will have greater difficulty in attaining the necessary level of consensus. Valasek has argued that, even in a veto system, such increases do not really matter, as it only takes one state to block a proposal – 'it is said to have made the EU unmanageably large. Perhaps, but even if that were the case . . . it is irrelevant'.[2] However, that seems a little complacent. While it only takes two states to generate a disagreement, particularly on issues that touch on sensitive national security concerns, the chances of disagreement and delay increase exponentially as the number of participants increase. Although – as has been demonstrated in a number of chapters in this volume – the increase in numbers has not, as yet, overtly affected the process of integration (particularly in the internal security sphere, as denoted by the 2004 Hague Programme), it would be unwise to downplay this quantitative element too much. In this case, size does matter.

Secondly, internal cohesion refers to the impact that widening the membership has had – and will continue to have – on pre-existing policies across the security spectrum, both internal and external. Given the issues that dominate the security agenda, including terrorism and illegal trafficking, it may not be possible, in the longer term, to maintain such a clear distinction between the internal and external conceptions. At the national level, there has already been some convergence and the European level may have to follow suit, amending the Pillar structure accordingly.[3] This relates not only to how pre-existing policy proposals per se are affected, where the impact has not been even, but also how the EU's institutional structures adapt to manage the wider membership base and ensure that the necessary leadership is provided.

If internal cohesion relates to the impact that widening membership has had on pre-existing policy areas, external projection is more concerned with the challenges that confront the EU as its external frontiers expand. These are not necessarily new; at the end of the day, Russia has been an issue on the CFSP agenda since its inception. However, the EU's new geographical – and geopolitical – position has brought such relations into even sharper focus. The EU has already attempted to delineate its roles and responsibilities within what it has termed its 'neighbourhood' – a contested concept, in practical terms, but one that has been taken to embrace, in policy terms, the newly independent states of the post-Soviet space, the Southern Caucuses and the Southern Mediterranean.[4] This volume has focused primarily on three areas within such a 'neighbourhood' – relations with the FSU, particularly Russia, Turkey and the Greater Middle East and the Balkans. Implicitly, relations with the US are also important here, given its perceived global remit, which has expanded further as a consequence of operationalising the 'War on Terror'. By examining what impact, if any, enlargement has had on the EU's relations with its 'neighbourhood', we can also determine the room for manoeuvre that the EU has to achieve its desired aim of creating 'a ring of countries, sharing the EU's fundamental values and objectives'.[5]

These are separable, but not separate, concerns. As was noted above, the level of internal cohesion effectively provides the base from which the EU projects its interests and values into the wider international system, both within its immediate 'neighbourhood' and at a global level. In addition, the shifting coalition of forces within the EU is likely to affect the nature of relations with the aforementioned states, particularly given certain new member states' role as cheerleaders for continued enlargement, both east – towards Ukraine, in the case of Poland – and south, into the Balkans. Continuing the process of enlargement, even beyond the stated ambition to embrace Romania and Bulgaria by 2007 and, potentially Turkey and Croatia in the longer term, will, in itself, affect the cohesiveness of the institutional base. Furthermore, constantly looking to distant horizons cannot be at the expense of pre-existing commitments. In effect, a balance must be struck and adhered to, both here and across the security agenda as a whole.

Internal cohesion: a solid base?

When attempting to take a wider look at the impact on internal cohesion, the temptation to generalise must be avoided, as much as possible. At the end of the day, enlargement has not had a uniform impact on the EU's security agenda. In part, it is dependent on the nature of the issue at hand, the level of concern felt by individual states and the perceived sense of commonality. For example, Jorg Monar has noted the sense of 'common concern' in relation to border management, although, even here, there has been insufficient consensus to make a European Border Guard a reality in the short term. In contrast, David Brown has questioned the existence of a sense of substantive solidarity in relation to the development of a European counter-terrorist framework, given the uneven impact of the perceived threat. In relation to counter-terrorism, the lack of an actual common threat – in spite of the rhetoric – was evident before enlargement took place, although the inclusion of an additional ten states has stretched the sense of commonality still further. This highlights another factor that must be borne in mind when appraising the enlarged EU's security agenda, namely the state of progress prior to accession. The enlarged EU did not begin with a clean sheet; there is an inherited legacy from the EU fifteen that may affect longer-term progress.

It is also not the case, as was perhaps understandably thought before enlargement, that the inclusion of ten new member states would automatically weaken the EU's claim to be an effective security actor. Obligations cannot rest solely with the new member states. As was noted in the foreign policy sphere, where 'enlargement did not create new dividing lines (but) redistributed power within the existing groups', closing the acrimonious gap that was evident over the 2003 Iraq invasion 'will have to be a two way process'.[6] Reality has proved to be far more complex than the somewhat simplistic assumption that, in all cases, the new member states would be in a worse position than the EU fifteen. In fact, given the rigours of the accession process, it would have been surprising had that proved to be the case. A number of examples in this volume demonstrate clearly this greater complexity. For example, Alistair Shepherd notes that, in the military sphere, many of the new member states are closer to achieving the target of allocating 2 per cent of their GDP to defence spending, although this is, perhaps, of greater symbolic importance, given the actual figures involved. In the field of human rights, a central component of the EU's external image, Karim Khan and Anna Kotzeva point out that the new member states have a more advanced position in areas such as minority rights.

That said, given the centrality of the protection of human rights, continued attention must be given to ensure a satisfactory level of protection exists, both internally and externally. It is important that the EU considers both dimensions here. The EU Programme for the Prevention of Violent Conflicts, for example, has prioritised external considerations over the internal dimension, implicitly suggesting that everything within the EU is rosy. Karim Khan and Anna Kotzeva offer the reassurance that, even after the leverage inherent in the accession process has understandably diminished, human rights protection will not slip off the new member states' agenda. However, it may not be sufficient to assume that the rigours of the 'War on Terror' will, in effect, replace that leverage, even though it will ensure such matters remain within the public eye. As has been demonstrated in a number of cases, from the institution of Guantanamo Bay to the 2005 controversy over extraordinary rendition, the security implications of the terrorist threat may actually lead to a 'weakening' of the overall human rights protection, as each state adjusts the balance between security and civil liberties as it sees fit. Also, in order to be taken seriously in the wider international arena, the EU needs to ensure that it has put its own house in order on such matters.

There is a further issue worthy of consideration when exploring the advocacy of human rights and democratic practices, both within its immediate 'neighbourhood' and further afield. This is the balance to be struck between human rights and other considerations, such as the imperatives of economic and wider political co-operation, which has always been difficult to get right. The geopolitical shift inherent in the enlargement process, combined with the EU's assertion of its Neighbourhood Policy, give such challenges an even higher profile. The record here is mixed, at best. For those already involved, or hoping to become part of, the EU accession process, the protection of human rights will be a central consideration. This can be seen in Turkey's efforts to adhere to the relevant elements of the *acquis communautaire*, as demonstrated by the 2006 Justice Ministry decision not to proceed with a prosecution of noted author Orhan Parnuk.[7] The process of enlargement itself can suffice as an impetus here: 'The EU exercised soft power . . . to great effect, but without really trying. This is because the power derived from the fact of its existence, rather than from an active foreign policy'.[8] However, with states beyond the immediate or even long-term reach of the accession process, such as Russia, the foundation on which the EU can project its values is shakier. Given the change in Russian economic fortunes – Trenin estimates that the Russian economy will continue to grow by approximately 5–6 per cent per annum and notes that they have effectively repaid all of the Soviet era debt[9] – enforcing the EU's values is considerably more difficult. In fact, as Dmitry Polikanov has argued, the economic dimension to EU–Russia relations has even taken precedence over the development of a wider security agenda, let alone the issue of human rights. In addition, as Graeme Herd and Anne Aldis have pointed out in relation to the PMR, even where the territory has not been recognised as a legitimate state, let alone considering its human rights record, trade has continued to take place.

There is a further factor to take into consideration here, namely the continuing instinct of the EU for engagement, rather than isolation. This has been demonstrated throughout this volume. It can be seen in their approach to the enlargement process generally, in their relations with Russia (where the determination of the EU to ensure a continued dialogue has, at times, muted criticism of what it views as Russia's undemocratic practices and disproportionate security measures) and is inherent in the Barcelona Process of dialogue with key players within the Middle East. The decision to continue aid to the Palestinian Authority in January 2006, in the wake of Hamas' election victory,[10] is only one example of this wider trend. As such, it shows that enlargement has not shifted the EU significantly from its preferred position. Kagan has asserted that this is less of a choice, given the EU's noted lack of a 'stick' to balance off the potential 'carrots' at their disposal.[11] Yet, it remains to be seen whether a greater level of military involvement, dependent on progress within the ESDP sphere, will ultimately make any difference to the EU's long-standing preference for engagement.

A further theme that has clearly emerged from a number of chapters in this volume relates to the importance of implementation. While this is not a problem exclusive to the EU, closing the 'implementation gap' that exists between rhetoric and reality is essential, if the EU is to fully develop and maintain its credibility within the wider security sphere. This has been a problem that has dogged the EU for some time; in fact, the record of the EU fifteen in certain key areas, such as counter-terrorism, was unimpressive. However, increasing the membership, particularly to states that, generally, tend to have a less well-developed administrative and judicial framework, is not necessarily conducive to tackling this problem. A further complication relates to a lingering culture of corruption in certain states. As Paul Holtom has demonstrated in the case of the Baltic States, the first step is to recognise corruption as a serious problem; only when such a political realisation has been made can the problem begin to be tackled effectively, both through legislative efforts and, if required, judicial proceedings. When the continuing burden of adapting to the expansive *acquis communautaire* across the whole gamut of EU activity is factored into the equation, it becomes all the more important to keep the 'implementation gap' under supervision. It is not sufficient to simply have good intentions in this area; as Paul Holtom has noted, 'well meant legislation does not implement or enforce itself'. While the horizon may be crowded by moves to further widen the membership, pre-existing commitments cannot be ignored.

Leadership will be required, both on the part of the EU institutions and individual member states, to ensure that they are able to successfully balance some of the competing agendas already noted. At present, as demonstrated particularly in the internal security sphere, the widening of membership has not led to a notable slowing down of the integration process. However, if, in the longer term, consensus proves more difficult to attain, except at the level of the lowest common denominator, the need to consider alternative institutional arrangements will become even more pressing. One suggestion, made in this volume by Alistair Shepherd, concerns the possibility of creating some form of *directoire* in the external security arena. He raises a number of possible permutations for such a body, depending on whether it is located inside or outside the formal EU structures and in relation to its membership, be it fixed or variable. There are echoes here of an earlier debate between the UK and France, primarily, over the wider process of variable geometry, with the latter advocating, effectively, a fixed pioneer group of states and the former believing that the nature of the issue at hand should dictate the membership. While such considerations have proved to be exceptionally controversial in the external security sphere, some form of *directoire* has arguably already been established on more than one occasion within the internal security apparatus.

On both occasions, it began life outside the formal confines of the EU. For example, in order to circumvent opposition from, notably, the UK over the abolition of internal border controls, the Schengen process was initiated (and later formally adopted within the EU structures as part of the Treaty of Amsterdam arrangements). Additionally, possibly as a direct consequence of enlargement, a further example has been established in the counter-terrorist field, the G5. While such meetings have taken place outside the EU's formal structures, the implicit hope is that, by gaining agreement between five of the larger states, consensus will be easier to attain within the JHA Council. Time will tell whether the G5 can operate as such a conduit. That said, there may be lessons to be learned here, in terms of operationalising such an arrangement within the external sphere.

In terms of the membership of such a *directoire*, given the difficulties inherent in proposing one such arrangement, it may prove even more problematic to have a series of differentiated bodies. It also remains to be seen if such a variable arrangement could guarantee the consistency of leadership sought at the outset and ever-more important in an EU of twenty-five states. Freedman notes that, even if a core group was not determined from the outset, in reality, a *de facto* fixed membership will become apparent in the external sphere – 'to the extent that there is a European foreign policy, it will be set by the governments of the larger European states'.[12] Herein lies a further problem. Although a smaller group is, on average, more likely to attain a consensus than a twenty-five state forum, such consensus cannot be guaranteed, even amongst the larger European states. For every Iranian Troika initiative, there is a rancorous split over the possibility of military intervention in Iraq. While greater leadership is required, how it manifests itself remains to be seen. In addition, the potential for the process itself to cause further animosity cannot be ruled out.

External projection: in the neighbourhood?

Although the thorny issue of leadership will be difficult to resolve, it cannot be ignored, as the EU faces up to a series of challenges in its 'neighbourhood'. The EU is right to try and stabilise its immediate environs by attempting to engage its neighbours, so as to persuade them to adopt a similar outlook to its own. In fact, its long-term stability – as well as the credibility of the CFSP – will depend, to a large extent, on how it manages this task. Having already considered the impact that enlargement has had – and will continue to have – on the internal cohesiveness of the EU, it is worth turning our attention to the other theme of this volume, the process of external projection. It is worth taking each of the key relationships – Russia, Turkey and the Greater Middle East and the Balkans – in turn.

Russia

This is, in a sense, *the* key relationship, not only for the EU, in terms of realising its objective of securing a stable 'neighbourhood', but also for the new CEE member states, given their recent history. As such, this is reflected in the number of chapters contained within this volume that focus on different, yet connected, aspects of the wider EU–Russia relationship, from the Chechen issue to arms trafficking in the Baltic region. This relationship colours a wide array of EU activities, from energy security to counter-terrorism, from the advancement of CFSP to the future of the EU's enlargement process, in relation to both the Ukraine and Moldova. Wherever the EU turns, Russia seems to be there. As a result, how this relationship develops longer term will affect the effectiveness of the EU's entire security agenda.

That said, the prospects for productive partnership do not look good. Part of the problem here is that Russia does not want to be viewed as part of the EU's wider 'neighbourhood'. In contrast, it effectively wishes to view part of the EU's 'neighbourhood' as its own 'sphere of vitally important interests'.[13] The development of the ENP, an inevitable consequence of the EU's shift further eastwards, has, therefore, almost been viewed as a challenge by elements of the Russian political elite and an incentive for them to be more, not less, active in the region. As Vladimir Putin notes, 'the absence of an effective Russian policy in the CIS or even an unjustified pause will inevitably entail nothing more than the energetic occupation of this political space by other more active states'.[14]

Such an attitude has manifested itself in a number of different ways. It can be seen in Russia's sensitive reaction to the EU's exhortations to resolve the Chechen crisis by peaceful means, even if, as Tracey German has noted, such messages are subsequently weakened, both by the EU's desire to engage and to advance the overarching economic relationship that has developed to a more considerable level than any security relationship. It can also be seen in the diplomatic to-ing and fro-ing that took place in the Ukraine in 2004, where Russia and the EU found themselves on opposite sides of the election campaign. This issue is likely to remain a considerable source of angst for both sides. Following the 'Orange Revolution' of December 2004, Ukraine has moved up the enlargement agenda, helped along by encouraging words from the likes of Poland. While the EU should not – and has not – rushed to formally embrace the Ukraine within the already extensive accession process, a move that would not be well received by Russia, equally it cannot distance itself too much either. If the democratic process in the Ukraine is to be consolidated, some indication of longer-term EU membership may be necessary, because, as Rosaria Puglisi notes, the ENP process is not sufficient to meet the Ukraine's expectations. In fact, she believes that a signal from the EU regarding the Ukraine's longer-term membership chances is essential to help stabilise the Ukrainian political situation. Once again, a difficult balance will have to be struck between competing security objectives, with certain of the new CEE member states lobbying in favour of Ukrainian inclusion.

The situation is complicated further because of the scale of potential Russian leverage available. In the field of energy security, the December 2005–January 2006 dispute between Russia and the Ukraine raised fears – perhaps unfounded – in the EU regarding their level of Russian energy dependency. A similar concern has been raised in the US regarding their dependence on the wider Middle East.[15] This is not the first occasion that such disagreements have taken place, although it is significant that, on this occasion, it has caught wider public imagination, a possible consequence of the EU's greater involvement in that region. However, the possibility of energy as an effective bargaining chip in wider relations needs to be taken in context. While the Ukraine and other EU states, particularly CEE states, rely, to a large extent, on Russian supplies, Russia equally relies on the demand for natural gas to fuel its steady economic revival. As Maddox has noted, 'if the ability to turn gas taps on and off is one of its strongest cards, then it holds few cards'.[16] Unfortunately, for the EU, that is not the case. In Moldova, for example, accession negotiations cannot begin until the situation regarding Transdniestra has been fully resolved. However, such a resolution is impossible without the acquiescence of the Russian government, given their diplomatic, economic and military ties with the region. Graeme Herd and Anne Aldis have recognised this, noting that the frozen conflict – which has belatedly emerged onto the EU's radar, helped to prominence by the next stage of enlargement, involving Romania and Bulgaria – has given Russia a 'mischievous way to cause trouble'. Kaliningrad is another example where continued good relations with Russia are essential. In the wider sphere of the 'War on Terror', the skilful portrayal of the Chechen crisis as part of a wider Islamist movement, occasionally regardless of the facts on the ground,[17] has left Russia as a key ally, not only of the EU, but the wider international community, in combating terrorism. In fact, in an interesting geopolitical analysis of post-September 11 developments, Dannreuther has suggested that Russia forms part of what he terms a 'secular alliance', along with China, India and, after the terrorist attacks on Washington and New York, the US.[18] Given certain member states' noted difficulties in relation to the integration of Muslim communities, such as, for example, France and the Netherlands,[19] and the reaction against possible Turkish membership on religious and cultural grounds, it is interesting to speculate as to whether the EU could find itself as part of that alliance also. Longer term, as during the Cold War, the emergence of a common enemy allowed potentially competitive partners to overcome some of their other difficulties and maintain a coherent and united front.

The likelihood of that will also depend, in part, on the attitudes of the new member states. Given their history, they have more reason than most to be wary of Russian intentions and actions. Former Polish President Aleksander Kwasniewski has noted, 'Russia is not ready to propose a new chapter in its relations with all of us.'[20] Alistair Shepherd has also drawn attention to subtle differences in the security stance of several of the new member states, who are less prepared to view Russia even as a reluctant partner. However, there is a danger in placing too much emphasis on their words, at the expense of actions on the ground. As Paul Holtom has acknowledged, even when relations between the Baltic states and Russia were tense, over, for example, the treatment of the Russian diaspora and the delineation of borders, the arms trade continued. An even more significant example can be found in relation to Chechnya, suggesting that the desire for smoother relations and the imperatives of the 'War on Terror' have effectively outweighed the legitimate concerns of the new member states for the moment. In May 2005, a year after EU enlargement had taken place, the following statement was issued at the end of the annual EU–Russia summit: 'the leaders of the EU and Russia addressed in a constructive spirit, internal developments in the EU and Russia, including the situation in Chechnya'.[21] Rather than presage a toughening of the EU's stance towards Russia, as might have been expected in the newly enlarged EU, there was acceptance of the Russian view that Chechnya is an internal matter. While, once again, it is worth reminding ourselves that we are still in the initial phase of the enlarged EU and therefore such nascent trends could easily be reversed, it is significant that, as yet, enlargement has not led to a substantively more robust EU policy towards Russia. Having initially argued that Russia should not be treated differently, including it within the first plans for the ENP – 'Russia is of course much more than a neighbour, since it is a strategic partner, but it is also a neighbour'[22] – the EU has had to accept that Russia is a more significant player in its 'neighbourhood' and, thus, has to be treated accordingly.

Turkey and the Greater Middle East

It is, of course, not the only player – and, in fact, not the only 'neighbourhood'. Turkey stands at the gateway to an equally controversial extension of the EU's geographical reach: the Greater Middle East. Given the range of security issues associated both with Turkey's application, including Cyprus and Iraq, and with the wider Southern dimension – as explored in depth in Roderick Pace's chapter – there is no way that this region can be ignored. In addition, as with Russia, there is also a substantive economic dimension to consider, centring on energy resources. At the end of the day, 'the assumption that oil prices and supplies matter only to the Americans has always been absurd'.[23] While the geopolitical equilibrium of the EU seems to have tipped further eastwards, continued efforts, through both the EMP and Turkey's own application, will ensure that some form of regional balancing act is carried out.

The advantages and disadvantages of Turkish membership have already been well explored in this volume. As such, there is no need to go into them in depth here. The controversy engendered by Turkey's application – and the eventual form that takes, whether it be full membership or some form of 'privileged partnership'– is likely to colour both intra-EU relations and relations between the EU and the wider region for some time to come. In time, it is to be hoped that the debate will move beyond some of the more contentious and, possibly, inappropriate objections, such as the predominance of Islam within Turkey. Not only are there substantial Islamic communities within a number of EU member states already, but the EU, as part of its human rights agenda, advocates the principle of tolerance. In addition, given Turkey's secular status – with an Islamic governing party that has showed its determination to accede to the EU as soon as possible – such fears should be allayed. Article 2 of the Turkish Constitution elevates secularism to the level of constitutional obligation – 'Republican, Nationalist, Populist, Statist, Secularist and Revolutionary-Reformist' – while the Armed Forces have been tasked, not only with protecting territorial integrity, but also the state's secular character.[24] While there are genuine concerns about Turkey's long-term applicability, this need not be one of them. As the process deepens, it is to be hoped that all parties can progress beyond such cultural considerations.

Even though Turkey is formally on the membership track, doubts remain as to whether it will make it to the finishing line. However, having waited for a considerable period of time to even commence negotiations and bearing in mind that no formal applicant has ever been refused (even the UK managed to attain membership at the third time of asking!), Turkish expectations regarding their long-term European future have been raised. The EU will have to bear that in mind when it considers the larger question that was posed by Bill Park – will Turkey ultimately be a bridge or a barrier to the Greater Middle East? It would be naïve to assume Turkey's continued acceptance of its role as *de facto* barrier, effectively insulating the EU from some of the wider tensions associated with the Middle Eastern region, if some semblance of progress is not made in Turkey's membership application.

That said, the EU cannot avoid the question of the Greater Middle East, even if the Turkish 'bridge' is effectively withdrawn. The EU has made that mistake in the past. When it established the EMP, it assumed that it could, in some way, hermetically seal the process from the probable impact of the Middle East peace process, simply by not including it on the formal agenda (Tracey German has noted a similar trend with regard to Chechnya). As Roderick Pace has pointed out, it has managed to obstruct progress, particularly in the political basket of the EMP process, regardless of whether it was a formal agenda point or not. Regardless of Turkey's long-term future – although Turkish membership would give the EU a geographical footprint in the region – the EU must at least attempt to take on a more active role in the region, building on initiatives such as the Troika negotiations in Iran and its role within the Quartet.

However, as with the Russian 'neighbourhood', there are potential limitations on the extent to which the EU can actively involve itself. Having already *de facto* accepted a Turkish sphere of influence as part of the Ankara document, in order to ensure their acquiescence with the Berlin Plus arrangements, there is a further potential complication to be considered – the US. While the US has been happy, on occasion, to encourage a more activist role on the part of the EU, particularly in relation to defence spending, there are limits even to their support. A senior UK official related a discussion that took place between a number of EU member states' representatives and their US counterparts relating to the French-led operation in the DRC. The discussion centred on the meaning of the phrase 'where NATO, as a whole, is not engaged'. The French, already sensitive to the idea that they effectively had to seek the permission of the US – through NATO – to conduct such operations (a position accepted and effectively enshrined in the UK 2003 Defence White Paper),[25] felt that such an obligation had been met. From their perspective, it was clear that neither NATO, nor the US, were engaged. The US representatives took a different position – as they had global interests, and had not specifically ruled out an interest in the area, the European states should assume that they were engaged.[26]

That attitude – whether representative of the official US position or not – demonstrates the wider context in which the EU has to operate. Whether it would accept such a term or not (and given the way it is viewed by a number of Arab governments, the term could even be said to be ironic), the Middle East has long been regarded as a US 'sphere of influence'. This is particularly the case with regard to the Arab–Israeli peace process, where its genuine 'special relationship' with Israel has guaranteed the US the primary role in overseeing attempts at peace negotiations. This situation has remained, despite the widening of the process by the 'unilateralist' George W. Bush, to include the UN, Russia and the EU as part of the Quartet. While the EU will have to respond to the geographical imperative of enlargement to take on a more active role in the region, a question mark remains as to what shape this greater involvement will take.

The Balkans

There is no need, however, for relations between the EU and the US to follow the competitive route that seems to be developing with Russia, for example. Not only has the accession of the ten new member states strengthened the 'Atlanticist' wing of the EU – a matter that will be returned to momentarily – but the example of the Balkans also demonstrates that they can easily work together in a reasonably co-operative and constructive fashion. It is appropriate that this volume is bookended by separate chapters on the Balkans, given its central importance, both to the long-term stability of Europe and to the credibility of the ENP. While, to the east, the EU's attempts to secure a stable 'neighbourhood' are viewed with some degree of suspicion by Russia, and, in the Middle East, the potential obstacles are too numerous to mention, the Balkans offers a genuine opportunity to make a significant contribution. In reality, it may prove to be the EU's real 'neighbourhood', regardless of the substantive NATO involvement in the same region.

As Martin Smith demonstrates in his chapter, the competitive edge that may have existed between the two organisations in terms of their respective enlargement processes has been replaced by practical and co-operative arrangements on the ground in the Balkans. At the end of the day, both organisations' future credibility depends, to some extent, on their ability to stabilise the Balkan region, shepherding the Balkan states towards a peaceful and democratic inclusion within the wider 'European family'.[27] Philip Gordon noted that the Balkans 'arguably saved NATO from obsolescence in the 1990s',[28] and it is significant that, even with the move to take NATO fully 'out of area', the organisation, as of January 2006, had more troops in the Balkan region than in Afghanistan.[29] Similarly, the EU is committed, not only in terms of the number of troops and military operations undertaken in the region, but also in terms of the longer-term enlargement trend, with Croatia likely to be followed by a number of neighbouring Balkan states into the formal accession process. For example, as part of the 2006 Austrian EU Presidency, an invitation was tendered to BiH, Serbia, Albania and FYROM to attend informal Ministerial meetings for the first time.[30] Additionally, the long-term settlement of Kosovo's status is likely to depend, in part, on the 'impression that Kosovo was somehow moving forward and was not doomed to remain forever a forgotten, poverty stricken corner of Europe'.[31] As part of a four-stage process to Kosovan independence suggested by the International Commission on the Balkans in April 2005, EU membership would constitute part of the 'full and final sovereignty' of the region.[32]

Yet, the possibility for conflict to reignite, particularly as progress is made in determining Kosovo's final status, underlines the scale of the task still to be confronted in the region. Difficult decisions still have to be taken, particularly in the political and economic spheres, and the EU will have to walk a fine line between its commitment to external projection (as seen in the developing process of enlargement) and its own internal cohesion. As with the Ukraine and Turkey, it has to hold the carrot of membership near enough for it to act as an incentive for reform, but far enough away that expectations are not unduly raised. Not only that, but – in a lesson that echoes with Roderick Pace's conclusions on the EMP – it must balance its own institutional interests with those of the local players on the ground. Anthony Welch, drawing on his years of practical experience working in the region, has noted that 'somewhere along the way, the interests and future of people in the Balkans have got lost'. There is a need to empower, as much as possible, the local parties, so that they can invest in their own future. One of his suggestions is to establish a regional economic forum, so that intra-regional trade can flourish. Whether this will prove possible, given that the process of EU enlargement has already, *de facto*, separated those on the inside track from those still on the outside of any formal process, remains to be seen. However, in order to meet the economic expectations of the wider region, itself a precursor of greater political stability, it may be worth giving such suggestions greater consideration.

He also offers a salutary lesson regarding the effectiveness of the international community within the wider spheres of nation building. Much invective has been directed at the US in the aftermath of the 2003 invasion of Iraq, regarding its failure to properly plan or man the post-conflict phase of operations,[33] and, indirectly, at the UK, for failing to insist on such planning arrangements as a quid pro quo for their involvement.[34] Implicit in the suggestion that Iraq would have been better served in the hands of the wider international community is the assumption that such failings are, somehow, uniquely American in design. The Balkan example suggests not only that the problem is larger than simply one 'Made in the US', but also that the international community at large does not always swiftly learn the lessons of history. With distinct echoes of what has taken place in Iraq, Anthony Welch notes how the international community has underestimated the scale of the problem in the region, both political and economic. He also queries the sense of a strategy that effectively saw a 'race to democratise', when the institutions and the people of the region were not fully involved or prepared for such a transition. While the international community equally stand condemned for taking too much of a stake in the governance of the region – suggesting, as in Iraq, that they are damned if they do and damned if they don't – the end result of such a process has been the effective disenfranchisement of the remaining Serbs within Kosovo. As was noted earlier in the volume, less than 1 per cent of Serbs voted in the 2004 elections, a point reinforced by Judah, who traces an effective boycott of the electoral process by the Serbian minority from 1999 on. In some senses, while the international community has not learned the lessons of Balkan nation building, in terms of lowering expectations and ensuring stability on the ground, the Sunni Muslims in Iraq have learned from the Serbian example. While initially determined to boycott the newly established democratic procedures in Iraq, they have subsequently realised that participation is the only way to protect their interests in the longer term.[35] In that sense at least, the Iraq experience has moved quicker than in the Balkans. Such lessons place into context the assumption that the EU – and other international bodies – would be better placed than the US to undertake such nation building tasks in the future. While Klaus Naumann is right to insist that Europe would not be satisfied by a *de facto* division of labour with the US that left them with 'clearing up work',[36] the Balkan record demonstrates that they may not be a more effective substitute for the US either.

The US and the global agenda

The likelihood of the EU fulfilling what states such as France view as its destiny, as a counter-balance or alternative pole to that of the US, is ever more unlikely, following the 2004 enlargement process. Not only has the widening of membership, per se, the potential to undermine the longer-term effectiveness of the CFSP, but two noted trends in the political stances of the CEE states, in particular, may eventually spell the end of the dream of a more active global CFSP. Firstly, 'for the accession states to warm up to the CFSP, the EU will need to take a more active role in its eastern neighbourhood'.[37] Rather than look to pastures new, the CEE states are unsurprisingly concerned with matters much closer to home. As the examples above show, there is a substantive agenda for the EU to get its teeth into on its periphery, particularly in relation to the Balkans, but also in terms of managing effectively its longer-term accession process, without seeking foreign dragons to slay elsewhere.

Secondly, the CEE states tend to fall firmly into the Altanticist camp and, as such, are uninterested in transforming the EU into an effective 'rival' of the US. Valasek has attempted to relocate them to, effectively, the centre ground of transatlantic relations, noting that 'if some European are indeed from Venus and Americans from Mars, most accession states can best be described as Earthlings'.[38] However, their steadfast support for the US invasion of Iraq, in the face of considerable diplomatic (and occasionally undiplomatic!) pressure from elements of 'old Europe' suggest otherwise. In fact, if you compare the two letters of support that emerged from within the 'new Europe' camp prior to the invasion, it is notable that the 'Vilnius Ten' letter was, as Alistair Shepherd puts it, 'a more strongly worded statement' of support than the joint effort of existing and accession states combined. While he offers two possible explanations for this apparent strengthening of position, a third option may be that elements within the pre-existing EU fifteen were not as prepared to robustly defend the US as the accession states. It is unlikely that, even as the new member states become more deeply immersed in the mechanisms of the EU, they are about to change such long held views. Socialisation has its limits; one needs only to look to the example of the UK, a member of the EC/EU for over thirty years, to see that. As such, a more limited focus, prioritising areas around their own 'neighbourhood' may be the way forward for the EU.

The post enlargement security agenda: striking a realistic balance

That may, in time, prove to be no bad thing. Not only is there a substantive job still to be done, but the EU – as with the UK in the aftermath of the Second World War – has to recognise its limitations and develop a more realistic security agenda. This sense of realism pervades this volume. It is present in the calls from a number of authors for the EU to meet its pre-existing commitments before seeking out new challenges. It also relates to the suggestion that the EU takes the opportunity presented to it by an unprecedented enlargement to appraise its current position and tackle some of the long-standing problems that have bubbled away under the surface and which enlargement has crystallised. When considering the future scope of enlargement, the same sense applies, with a common theme being the need for the EU to create realistic timetables that protect the internal coherence of the EU, without either overly delaying or creating inflated expectations on the part of those wishing to join. As Dmitry Polikanov noted with respect to the development of an EU–Russia security relationship, small steps may be all that is possible at this stage. Rather than lament such developments, the EU should approach this potentially sensitive relationship – and others – in a patient and constructive manner.

Not only is there a need for a realistic appraisal of the wider EU security agenda; there is also a need for balance, in itself a difficult state to maintain. This sense of balance is reflected throughout this volume, whether it be the need to ensure regional balance, between east and south, or between the need to engage and the desire to uphold and project the EU's values in a confident and robust manner. It is inherent in the need to focus, not only on the continued efforts of the new member states to fulfil their obligations, but in the requirement for the older members of what was the EU fifteen to be held to account as well. Balance is required in ensuring pre-existing commitments, across the security sphere, are met, rather than side-stepped in favour of new initiatives and activities. And, ultimately, it is inherent in the tension between the desire for internal coherence and the on-going process of enlargement, as part of a wider external projection of EU values and influence. Getting the balance right across all of these areas will be a difficult task. However, failing to do so, will ultimately undermine, not only the EU's sense of security, but also its longer-term credibility as a security actor.

Notes

1 The views expressed here are personal and do not represent the opinions or views of the British Government, Ministry of Defence or the Royal Military Academy Sandhurst.
2 Tomas Valasek, 'New EU members in Europe's security policy', *Cambridge Review of International Affairs*, 18:2 (2005), p. 217.
3 For details of the national level, see Derek Lutterbeck, 'Blurring the dividing line: the convergence of internal and external security in Western Europe', *European Security*, 14:2 (2005).
4 For details on the European Neighbourhood Policy, see http://europa.eu.int/comm/world/enp/index_en.htm.
5 Ibid.
6 Valasek, 'New EU members in Europe's security policy', p. 218.
7 Steve Bryant, 'Turkey in clear over freedom of speech trial', *The Times* (23 January 2006), p. 34.
8 Lawrence Freedman, 'The transatlantic agenda: vision and counter-vision', *Survival*, 47:4 (Winter 2005–06), p. 29.
9 Dimitri Trenin, 'Pirouettes and priorities: distilling a Putin doctrine', *The National Interest* (Winter 2003–04), p. 78.
10 Stephen Farrell and Richard Beeston, 'EU hands Hamas lifeline, but White House acts to cut aid', *The Times* (31 January 2006), p. 34.

CONCLUSION

11 For details of his thesis, see Robert Kagan, *Paradise and Power: America and Europe in the New World Order* (London: Atlantic Books, 2003).
12 Freedman, 'The transatlantic agenda', p. 31.
13 Andrei Kozyrev cited Janusz Bugajiski, 'Russia's new Europe', *The National Interest* (Winter 2003–04, p. 85.
14 Vladimir Putin cited Derek Averre, 'Russia and the European Union: convergence or divergence?', *European Security*, 14:2 (June 2005), p. 192.
15 See George W. Bush, *State of the Union address* (Washington, DC: White House, 2006), www.whitehouse.gov/stateoftheunion/2006/index.html.
16 Bronwen Maddox, 'Obnoxious, but gas war is not Putin's worst crime', *The Times* (4 January 2006), p. 28.
17 For details, see Julie Wilhelmsen, 'Between a rock and a hard place: the Islamisation of the Chechen separatist movement', *Europe–Asia Studies*, 57:1 (January 2005).
18 Roland Dannreuther, 'The geopolitical impact of terrorism', *Transnational Terrorism: A Global Approach*, RUSI Conference, London (16–17 January 2006).
19 For more details, see Timothy M. Savage, 'Europe and Islam: crescent waxing, cultures clashing', *The Washington Quarterly*, 27:3 (Summer 2004).
20 Kwasniewski cited Valasek, 'New EU members in Europe's security policy', p. 220.
21 *EU–Russia Annual Summit Conclusions* (Moscow, May 2005), http://europa.eu.int/comm/external_relations/russia/summit_05_05/index.htm.
22 Gunther Verheugen cited Averre, 'Russia and the EU', p. 181.
23 Freedman, 'The transatlantic agenda', p. 30.
24 For details, see Sevgi Drorian, 'Turkey: security, state and society in troubled times', *European Security*, 14:2 (2005).
25 For details, see *Delivering Security in a Changing World: Defence White Paper* (London: Ministry of Defence, 2003).
26 Interview with author, RMAS (October 2004).
27 For a discussion of issues relating to NATO's longer term development, see Martin A. Smith (ed.), 'Where is NATO going?', *Contemporary Security Policy*, 25:3 (2004). It contains a number of articles written by contributors to this volume.
28 Philip H. Gordon, 'Reforging the Atlantic alliance', *The National Interest* (Fall 2002), p. 92.
29 The figures were 16,000 NATO peace-keepers in Afghanistan, compared to 40,000 in Kosovo. See Christina Lamb, 'The bandits wait for the British', *The Sunday Times* (29 January 2006), p. 25.
30 Rory Watson, 'Viennese set to repel Turks' new advance on the West', *The Times* (2 January 2006), p. 26.
31 Tim Judah, 'Kosovo's moment of truth', *Survival*, 47:4 (Winter 2005–06), p. 75.
32 For details, see International Commission on the Balkans, *The Balkans in Europe's Future*, www.balkan-commission.org.
33 For example, see Paul Bremer, *My Year in Iraq: The Struggle to Build a Future of Hope* (London: Simon & Schuster, 2006).
34 See Sir Christopher Meyer, *DC Confidential* (London: Weidenfeld & Nicolson, 2005).
35 For details of the 2005 election process, see Paul Rogers, *Iraq and the War on Terror: Twelve Months of Insurgency 2004–2005* (London: IB Tauris, 2005); in relation to the parliamentary elections, whose results became available in January 2006, see BBC News, 'Iraqi Shias win election victory', http://news.bbc.co.uk/1/hi/world/middle_east/4630518.stm.
36 General Klaus Naumann cited Anthony King, 'The future of the European Security and Defence Policy', *Contemporary Security Policy*, 26:1 (April 2005), p. 53.
37 Valasek, 'New EU members in Europe's security policy', p. 226.
38 Ibid., p. 225.

Select Bibliography

Official Documentation

European Union

COUNCIL OF THE EUROPEAN UNION
Declaration on Chechnya made by the Presidency on behalf of the European Union (Brussels, 1995).
The Barcelona Declaration and Work Programme (Brussels, 1995).
European Union Consolidated Version of Treaty on European Union (Brussels, 1997).
Common Strategy of the European Union of 4 June 1999 on Russia (Brussels, 1999).
European Union Energy Outlook to 2020 (Luxembourg, 1999).
EU Programme for Prevention of Violent Conflicts (Göteborg, 2001).
EU–NATO Declaration on ESDP (Copenhagen, 2002).
A Secure Europe in a Better World, European Security Strategy (Brussels, 2003).
Declaration by the Presidency on behalf of the European Union on the Presidential Elections in Chechnya (Brussels, 2003).
European Union Strategy against the Proliferation of Weapons of Mass Destruction (Brussels, 2003).
NATO/EU Consultation, Planning and Operations (Brussels, 2003).
Capability Improvement Chart II/2004 (Brussels, 2004).
Council and Commission Action Plan Implementing the Hague Programme on Strengthening Freedom, Security and Justice in the European Union (Brussels, 2005).
Council Regulation Concerning the Introduction of Some New Functions for the Schengen Information System, including in the Fight against Terrorism (Brussels, 2004).
Council Regulation Establishing a European Agency for the Management of Operational Co-operation at the External Borders of the Member States of the European Union (Brussels, 2004).
European Union Plan of Action on Combating Terrorism (Brussels, 2004).
The Hague Programme: Strengthening Freedom, Security and Justice in the European Union (Brussels, 2004).
EU Annual Report on Human Rights 2005 (Brussels, 2005).
Reinvigorating European Union Actions on Human Rights and Democratisation with Mediterranean Partners: Strategic Guidelines (Brussels, 2005).
The EU-Ukraine Action Plan (Brussels, 2005).

EUROPEAN COMMISSION
Towards a European Strategy for Security of Energy Supply (Brussels, 2000).
Communication from the Commission to the Council: The EU and Kaliningrad (Brussels, 2001).
Country Strategy Paper 2002–2006: National Indicative Programme 2002–2003 – Russian Federation (Brussels, 2001).
Communication from the Commission to the Council and the European Parliament: Towards Integrated Management of the External Borders of the Member States of the European Union (Brussels, 2002).
Wider Europe – Neighbourhood: A New Framework for Relations with our Eastern and Southern Neighbours (Brussels, 2003).
European Neighbourhood Policy: Strategy Paper (Brussels, 2004).
Communication from the Commission to the Council and the European Parliament on Relations with Russia (Brussels, 2004).

SELECT BIBLIOGRAPHY 223

Preparedness and Consequence Management in the Fight against Terrorism (Brussels, 2004).
Proposal for a Council Decision on the Exchange of Information and Cooperation Regarding Terrorist Offences (Brussels, 2004).
Report from the Commission on the Council Framework Decision on Combating Terrorism (Brussels, 2004).
Proposal for a Council Decision on the Transmission of Information Resulting from the Activities of Security and Intelligence Services with Respect to Terrorist Offences (Brussels, 2005).
Report from the Commission on the European Arrest Warrant and the Surrender Procedures between Member States (Brussels, 2005).
Tenth Anniversary of the Euro-Mediterranean Partnership: A Work Programme for the Next Five Years (Brussels, 2005).
The Hague Programme: Ten priorities for the Next Five Years (Brussels, 2005).

EUROPEAN PARLIAMENT
Committee on Foreign Affairs, Human Rights, Common Security and Defence Policy European Parliament Report on the Implementation of the Common Strategy of the European Union on Russia: Rapporteur: Arie M Oostlander (Brussels, 2000).
Committee on Foreign Affairs, Human Rights, Common Security and Defence Policy Report with a Proposal for a European Parliament Recommendation to the Council on EU-Russia Relations: Rapporteur: Bastiaan Belder (Brussels, 2004).
European Parliament Legislative Resolution on the Proposal for a Regulation of the European Parliament and of the Council Establishing a Community Code on the Rules Governing the Movement of Persons across Borders (Brussels, 2005).
European Parliament Resolution on EU–Russia Relations (Brussels, 2005).
European Parliament Resolution on the Euro-Mediterranean Partnership (Brussels, 2005).
European Parliament Resolution on the Results of the Ukraine Elections (Strasbourg, 2005).

EUROPOL
Terrorist Activity in the European Union: Situation and Trend Report – October 2001–Mid-October 2002 (The Hague: Europol, 2002).
Terrorist Activity in the European Union: Situation and Trends Report – October 2002–15 October 2003 (The Hague: Europol, 2003).
Terrorist Activity in the European Union: Situation and Trend Report – October 2003–17 October 2004 (The Hague: Europol, 2004).
European Union Organised Crime Situation Report 2004 (The Hague: Europol, 2005).
Europol Annual Report 2004 (The Hague: Europol, 2005).
Organised Illegal Immigration into the European Union (The Hague: Europol, 2005).

International organisations

European Convention on Human Rights (Strasbourg: Council of Europe, 1950).
Convention against Torture and other Cruel, Inhuman or Degrading Treatment or Punishment (New York: UN, 1985).
Study on NATO Enlargement (Brussels: NATO, 1995).
Arab Human Development Report 2003 (New York, United Nations Development Programme, 2003).
International Observer Mission: Municipal Elections 2004; Bosnia and Herzegovina. Statement of Preliminary Findings and Conclusions (Sarajevo: OSCE/ODIHR, 2004).
Council of Europe Convention on the Prevention of Terrorism (Strasbourg: Council of Europe, 2005).
Final Report on the 2004 Presidential Elections in Ukraine (Warsaw: OSCE, 2005).

Secondary Sources

Books

Aggestam, L. and Hyde-Price, A. (eds), *Security and Identity in Europe: Exploring the New Agenda* (Basingstoke: Macmillan, 2000).
Aldis, A. and Herd, G.P. (eds), *Soft Security Threats and European Security* (London: Routledge, 2005).
Andreani, G. Bertram, C., and Grant, C., *Europe's Military Revolution* (London: CER, 2001).
Blumi, I., *Political Islam among Albanians: Are the Taliban coming to the Balkans?* (Pristina: Kosovar Institute for Policy Research and Development, 2003).
Bretherton, C. and Volger, J., *The European Union as a Global Actor* (London: Routledge, 1999).
Brodin, A. (ed.), *Russian Transit Trade in the Baltic Sea Region* (Centre for European Research, Goteborg University, 2002).
Buzan, B., Waever, O. and de Wilde. J., *Security: A New Framework for Analysis* (London: Lynne Rienner, 1998).
Cosgrove, C. and Twitchett, K. (eds), *The New International Actors: The UN and the EEC* (London: Macmillan, 1970).
Cottey, A. and Averre, D. (eds), *New Security Challenges in Postcommunist Europe: Securing Europe's East* (Manchester: Manchester University Press, 2002).
Croft, S., Redmond, J., Rees, W. and Webber, M. (eds), *The Enlargement of Europe* (Manchester: Manchester University Press, 1999).
Davis, I., Hirst, C. and Mariani, B., *Organised Crime, Corruption and Illicit Arms Trafficking in an Enlarged EU: Challenges and Perspectives* (London: Saferworld, 2001).
de Lobkowicz, W., *L'Europe et la sécurité intérieure* (Paris: La documentation française, 2002).
Duke, S., *Beyond the Chapter: Enlargement Challenges for CFSP and ESDP* (Maastricht: EIPA, 2003).
Gartner, H. and Cuthbertson, I.M., *European Security and Transatlantic Relations after 9.11 and the Iraq War* (Basingstoke: Palgrave, 2005).
Gartner, H., Hyde-Price, A. and Reiter, E., *Europe's New Security Challenges* (London: Lynne Reiner, 2001).
German, T., *Russia's Chechen War* (London: Routledge, 2003).
Gordon, P.H. and Shapiro, J., *Allies at War: America, Europe and the Crisis over Iraq* (New York: McGraw-Hill, 2004).
Grabble, H. and Hughes, K., *Enlarging the European Union Eastwards* (London: Royal Institute for International Affairs, 1998).
Hagman, H., *European Crisis Management and Defence: The Search for Capabilities* (Oxford: Oxford University Press, 2002).
Henderson, K. (ed.), *Back to Europe: Central and Eastern Europe and the European Union* (London: University College London Press, 1999).
Holtom, P., *Arms Transit Trade in the Baltic Region* (London: Saferworld, 2003).
Ingham, H. and Ingham, M. (eds), *EU Expansion to the East: Problems and Prospects* (Northampton: Edward Elgar, 2002).
Joenniemi, P. (ed.), *Confidence-Building and Arms Control: Challenges around the Baltic Rim* (Aland: The Aland Islands Peace Institute, 1999).
Judah, T., *Kosovo: War and Revenge* (New Haven: Yale University Press, 2000).
Kagan, R., *Paradise and Power: America and Europe in the New World Order* (London: Atlantic Books, 2003).
Kuzio, T., *EU and Ukraine: A Turning Point in 2004?* (Paris: Institute for Security Studies, 2003).
Lansford, T. and Tashev, B. (eds), *Old Europe, New Europe and the US* (Aldershot: Ashgate, 2005).
Latawski, P. and Smith, M.A., *The Kosovo Crisis and the Evolution of Post Cold War European Security* (Manchester: Manchester University Press, 2003).
Lindberg, T. (ed.), *Beyond Paradise and Power: Europe, America and the Future of a Troubled Partnership* (London: Routledge, 2005).

Lindstrom, G., *EU–US Burdensharing: Who Does What?* (Paris: EU Institute for Security Studies, 2005).
Lindstrom, G., *The Headline Goal* (Paris: EU-ISS, April 2005).
Lumpe, L. (ed.), *Running Guns: The Global Black Market in Small Arms* (London: Zed Books, 2000).
Mahncke, D. (ed.), *Old Frontiers, New Frontiers: The Challenge of Kosovo and Its Implications for the European Union* (Bern: Peter Lang, 2001).
Missiroli, A., *Bigger EU, Wider CFSP, Stronger ESDP? The View from Central Europe* (Paris: EU Institute for Security Studies, April 2002).
Nugent, N. (ed.) *European Union Enlargement* (Basingstoke: Palgrave, 2004).
Peterson, J. and Pollack, M.A., *Europe, America, Bush: Transatlantic Relations in the Twenty-first Century* (London: Routledge, 2003).
Pierre, A.J. (ed.), *Cascade of Arms: Managing Conventional Weapons Proliferation* (Washington, DC: Brookings Institution Press, 1997).
Ross, C. (ed.), *Perspectives on the Enlargement of the European Union* (Leiden: Brill Publishing, 2002).
Salmon, T.C. and Shepherd, A.J.K., *Towards a European Army: A Military Power in the Making?* (London: Lynne Rienner, 2003).
Sharp, J.O. (ed.), *About Turn, Forward March with Europe: New Directions for Defence and Security Policy* (London: Rivers Oram Press, 1996).
Simon, J., *NATO Expeditionary Operations: Impacts upon New Members and Partners* (Washington, DC: NDU Press, March 2005).
Smith, D.J. (ed.), *The Baltic States and Their Region: New Europe or Old?* (Amsterdam/New York: Rodopi, 2005).
Smith, J. and Jenkins, C., *Through the Paper Curtain: Insiders and Outsiders in the New Europe* (London: Blackwell Publishing, 2003).
Smith, K., *EU Foreign Policy in a Changing World* (London: Polity, 2003).
Sperling, J. (ed.), *Two Tiers, Two Speeds: The European Security Order and the Enlargement of the EU and NATO* (Manchester University Press, 1999).
Wood, B. and Peleman, J., *The Arms Fixers: Controlling the Borders and Shipping Agents* (Oslo: International Peace Research Institute, 1999).
Zaborowski, M., *From America's Protégé to Constructive European: Polish Security Policy in the Twenty-First Century* (Paris: EU-ISS, December 2004).

Journal articles

Aliboni, R. and Guazzone, L., 'Democracy in the Arab countries and the West', *Mediterranean Politics*, 9:1 (Spring 2004).
Allen, D. and Smith, M., 'Western Europe's presence in the Contemporary international arena', *Review of International Studies*, 16:1 (1990).
Austin, K., 'Illicit arms brokers: aiding and abetting atrocities', *The Brown Journal of World Affairs*, 9:11 (2002).
Avci, G., 'Turkey's slow EU candidacy: insurmountable hurdles to membership, or simple Euroscepticism?', *Turkish Studies*, 4:1 (2003).
Averre, D., 'Russia and the European Union: convergence or divergence?', *European Security*, 14:2 (June 2005).
Baev, P., 'Putin's Western choice', *European Security*, 12:1 (Spring 2003).
Bauer, S., 'The EU Code of Conduct on Arms Exports – enhancing the accountability of arms export policies?', *European Security*, 12:3–4 (2003).
Bebler, A., 'Corruption among security personnel in Central and Eastern Europe', *Journal of Communist Studies and Transition Politics*, 17:1 (2001).
Berenskoetter, F.S., 'Mapping the mind gap: a comparison of US and European security strategies', *Security Dialogue*, 36:1 (March 2005).

Berryman, J., 'Russia and the illicit arms trade', *Crime, Law and Social Change*, 33 (2000).
Brown, D., 'Defending the fortress? Assessing the European Union's response to trafficking', *European Security*, 13:1–2 (2003).
Brumberg, D., 'Liberalization versus democracy: understanding Arab political reform', *Carnegie Working Papers*, 37 (May 2003).
Bugajiski, J., 'Russia's new Europe', *The National Interest* (Winter 2003–04).
Buzan, B. and Diez, T., 'The European Union and Turkey', *Survival*, 41:1 (Spring 1999).
Cimbalo, J., 'Saving NATO from Europe', *Foreign Affairs*, 83:6 (November/December 2004).
Clarke, M. and Cornish, P., 'The European defence project and the Prague summit', *International Affairs*, 78:4 (October 2002).
Cornish, P. and Edwards, G., 'The strategic culture of the European Union: a progress report', *International Affairs*, 81:4 (July 2005).
Cornish, P. and Edwards, G., 'Beyond the EU/NATO dichotomy: the beginnings of a European security culture', *International Affairs*, 77:3 (July 2001).
Cottey, A., Edmunds, T. and Forster, A., 'Military matters beyond Prague', *NATO Review* (Autumn 2002).
Crowe, B., 'A common European foreign policy after Iraq', *International Affairs*, 79:3 (2003).
Daalder, I.H., 'The end of Atlanticism', *Survival*, 45:2 (Summer 2003).
Drorian, S., 'Turkey: security, state and society in troubled times', *European Security*, 14:2 (2005).
Dunay, P., 'The half-hearted transformation of the Hungarian military', *European Security*, 14:1 (2005).
Dyczok, M., 'Was Kuchma's censorship effective? Mass media in Ukraine before 2004', *Europe–Asia Studies* (forthcoming, 2006).
Edmunds, T., 'NATO and its new members', *Survival*, 45:3 (Autumn 2003).
Freedman, L., 'The transatlantic agenda: vision and counter-vision', *Survival*, 47:4 (Winter 2005–06).
Galeotti, M., 'Russia's criminal army', *Jane's Intelligence Review*, 11:6 (1999).
Gordon, P.H., 'Reforging the Atlantic alliance', *The National Interest* (Fall 2002).
Greene, O., 'Examining international responses to illicit arms trafficking', *Crime, Law and Social Change*, 33 (2000).
Heisbourg, F., 'Europe's strategic ambitions: the limits of ambiguity', *Survival*, 42:2 (Summer 2000).
Herd, G.P. and Tracy, T., 'Democratic civil-military relations in Bosnia Herzegovina: a new paradigm for protectorates?', *Armed Forces & Society*, 32:1 (Winter 2005).
Hill, C., 'The capability–expectations gap, or conceptualising Europe's international role', *Journal of Common Market Studies*, 31:3 (1993).
Hills, A., 'Border security in the Balkans: Europe's gatekeepers', *Adelphi Papers*, 371 (2004).
Holm, U., 'Algeria: France's untenable engagement', *Mediterranean Politics*, 3:2 (Autumn 1998).
Howorth, J., 'France, Britain and the Euro-Atlantic crisis', *Survival*, 45:4 (Winter 2003–04).
Hyde-Price, A., 'The antinomies of European security: dual enlargement and the reshaping of European order', *Contemporary Security Policy*, 21:3 (December 2000).
Judah, T., 'Kosovo's moment of truth', *Survival*, 47:4 (Winter 2005–06).
Karp, A., 'Small arms: back to the future', *The Brown Journal of World Affairs*, 9:1 (2002).
Kirisci, K., 'Between Europe and the Middle East: the transformation of Turkish policy', *Middle East Review of International Affairs*, 8:1 (March 2004).
Kuniholm, B., 'Turkey's accession to the European Union: differences in European and US attitudes and challenges for Turkey', *Turkish Studies*, 2:1 (Spring 2001).
Leino, P., 'A European approach to human rights? Universality explored', *Nordic Journal of International Law*, 71 (2002).
Linden, R.H., 'Twin peaks: Romania and Bulgaria between the EU and the United States', *Problems of Post-Communism*, 51:5 (September/October 2004).
Lo, B., 'Beslan: a people's trauma', *The World Today*, 6:10 (October 2004).

SELECT BIBLIOGRAPHY

Lutterbeck, D., 'Blurring the dividing line: the convergence of internal and external security in Western Europe', *European Security*, 14:2 (2005).
Marsh, N., 'Two sides of the same coin? The legal and illegal trade in small arms', *The Brown Journal of World Affairs*, 9:1 (2002).
Medvedev, S., 'Rethinking the National Interest: Putin's turn in Russian Foreign Policy', *Marshall Center Papers*, 6 (August 2004).
Menon, A., From crisis to catharsis: ESDP after Iraq', *International Affairs*, 80:4 (2004).
Missiroli, A., 'EU–NATO cooperation in crisis management: no Turkish delight for ESDP', *Security Dialogue*, 3:1 (March 2002).
Oguzlu, H.T., 'The clash of security identities: the question of Turkey's membership in the European Union', *International Journal*, 57:4 (Autumn 2002).
Oldberg, I., 'The emergence of a regional identity in the Kaliningrad oblast', *Cooperation and Conflict*, 35:3 (2000).
Onis, Z., 'An awkward partnership: Turkey's relations with the European Union in comparative-historical perspective', *Journal of European Integration History*, 7:1 (2001).
Onis, Z., 'Domestic politics, international norms and challenges to the state: Turkey–EU relations in the post-Helsinki era', *Turkish Studies*, 4:1 (2003).
Onis, Z., 'Turkey, Europe and the paradoxes of identity', *Mediterranean Quarterly*, 10:3 (1999).
Onis, Z. and Yilmaz, S. 'The Turkey–EU–US triangle in perspective: transformation or continuity?', *Middle East Journal*, 59:2 (Spring 2005).
Ottaway, M., 'Democracy and constituencies in the Arab World', *Carnegie Papers*, 48 (July 2004).
Park, B., 'Turkey, Europe, and ESDI: inclusion or exclusion?', *Defense Analysis*, 16:3 (December 2000).
Park, B., 'Strategic location, political dislocation: Turkey, the United States, and Northern Iraq', *Middle East Review of International Affairs*, 7:2 (June 2003).
Park, B., Turkish policy towards northern Iraq: problems and perspectives, *Adelphi Papers*, 374 (May 2005).
Park, B., 'Iraq's Kurds and Turkey: challenges for US policy', *Parameters*, 34:3 (Autumn 2004).
Pesmazoglu, S., 'Turkey and Europe, reflections and refractions: towards a contrapuntal approach', *South European Society and Politics*, 2:1 (1997).
Phythian, M., 'The illicit arms trade: Cold War and post-Cold War', *Crime, Law and Social Change*, 33 (2000).
Pinelli, C., 'Conditionality and enlargement in light of EU Constitutional developments', *European Law Journal*, 10:3 (May 2004).
Polikanov, D., 'Russia's secret weapon: myth or reality', *BASIC Reports*, 85 (March 2004).
Puglisi, R., 'Clashing agendas? Economic interests, elite coalitions and prospects for co-operation between Russia and Ukraine', *Europe–Asia Studies*, 55:6 (2003).
Puglisi, R., 'The rise of the Ukrainian oligarchs', *Democratization*, 11:3 (Autumn 2003).
Raba, T., 'Enhancing export controls in transit states', *The Monitor: International perspectives in Nonproliferation*, 8:2 (2002).
Sadurski, W., 'Charter and enlargement', *European Law Journal*, 8:3 (September 2002).
Savage, T.M., 'Europe and Islam: crescent waxing, cultures clashing', *The Washington Quarterly*, 27:3 (Summer 2004).
Serry, R., 'NATO's Balkan odyssey', *NATO Review* (Winter 2003).
Serry, R. and Bennett, C., 'Staying the course', *NATO Review* (Winter 2004).
Smith, M.A. and Timmins, G., 'The European Union and NATO enlargement debates in comparative perspective: a case of incremental linkage?', *West European Politics*, 22:3 (July 1999).
Smith, M.A. (ed.), 'Where is NATO going?', *Contemporary Security Policy*, 25:3 (2004).
Steinberg, J.B., 'An elective partnership: salvaging transatlantic relations', *Survival*, 45:2 (Summer 2003).
Suvarierol, S., 'The Cyprus obstacle on Turkey's road to membership in the European Union', *Turkish Studies*, 4:1 (2003).

Thomson, J., 'US interests and the fate of the Alliance', *Survival*, 45:4 (Winter 2003–04).
Timmins, G., 'Strategic or pragmatic partnership? The European Union's policy towards Russia since the end of the Cold War', *European Security*, 11:4 (Winter 2002).
Trenin, D., 'Pirouettes and priorities: distilling a Putin doctrine', *The National Interest* (Winter 2003–04).
Udum, S., 'Turkey and the emerging European security framework', *Turkish Studies*, 3:2 (Autumn 2002).
Valasek, T., 'New EU members in Europe's security policy', *Cambridge Review of International Affairs*, 18:2 (2005).
Whitman, R., 'No and after: options for Europe', *International Affairs*, 81:4 (2005).
Wilhelmsen, J., 'Between a rock and a hard place: the Islamisation of the Chechen separatist movement', *Europe–Asia Studies*, 57:1 (January 2005).
Wilkinson, P., 'International terrorism: the changing threat and the EU response', *Chaillot Paper*, 84 (October 2005).
Wivel, A., 'The security challenge of small EU member states: interests, identity and the development of the EU as a security actor', *Journal of Common Market Studies*, 43:2 (2005).
Wojtowicz, K. 'Non-military security issues in Central Europe', *International Relations*, 18:1 (2004).
Woodward, R., 'Establishing Europol', *European Journal on Criminal Policy and Research*, 1:4 (1993).
Youngs, R., 'Europe's Uncertain Pursuit of Middle East Reform', *Carnegie Papers*, 45 (June 2004).

Index

Abdela, Lesley 196
Abkhazia 72, 73, 75
acquis communautaire 21, 41, 46, 50, 88, 91, 93, 210
Ad Hoc Committee for Border Guard Training (ACT) 61
Adamkus, Valdas 152
Afghanistan 15, 16, 20
  EU new member states and 30
Agadir Free Trade Area (AFTA) 175
Air Borders Centre (ABC) 61
Al Qaeda 43
Albania 9, 10
  economy 198
  human rights concerns 87, 90
  membership of EU 217
  support for Iraq intervention 22
Aldis, Anne 3, 210, 213
Algeria 177, 181, 182
Aliboni, Roberto 181
Amsterdam, Treaty of 40, 54, 56, 88, 211
'Ankara document' 161
Anti-Terrorism Crime and Security Act (2001) 91, 94
Antyufeyev, Vladimir 74
Arab Human Development Report 179
Area of Freedom, Security and Justice (AFSJ) 3, 43, 54
ARGO programme 61–2
Armenia, 160
  human rights concerns 90
arms trafficking 99–104, 119, 177
  in Baltic states 105–11
  in Transdniestria (PMR) 75
Asmus, Ronald 15
Austria 7, 31
Azerbaijan 160–1
  human rights concerns 90
  membership of GUAM 150
Aznar, José Maria 60

Baev, Pavel 139
Balkans, Western 5, 9–14, 16, 17, 20
  aid and reconstruction 193–8
  border controls 200
  economic conditions 198–9
  ethnic conflict 193
  EU policy in 191–205, 217–18
  organised crime 69–82
  terrorism 200–1
Baltic states 9, 211
  arms trafficking 100, 105–11
  see also Estonia; Latvia; Lithuania
Baltic Task Force on Organised Crime 45, 111
Barcelona Process 26
Barroso, Jose Manuel 144
Bechor, Guy 180
Belarus 25
  Single Economic Space proposal (SES) 149–50
Belder report 136, 137, 140
Belgium
  counter-terrorism issues 44
  European Border Police proposal 57
Berlin Plus arrangements 11, 12, 13, 24
Berlusconi, Silvio 136
Beslan terrorist attack 122, 137
Bigo, Didier 43
Bingham, Lord 94, 95
Biological Weapons Convention 181
Black Sea Economic Cooperation Organisation (BSEC) 150, 160
Black Sea Naval Cooperation Task Group (BlackSeaFor) 160
Blair, Tony 33, 60, 134, 144
Boag, Ian 78
border security 3, 54–67, 125, 200
Borisavijevic, Ivan 78
Bosnia-Herzegovina (BiH) 9–14, 17, 71–2

Bosnia-Herzegovina (*cont.*)
  democratisation 195–8
  economy 198–9
  EU aid 194–6
  EU operations in 158
  human rights concerns 87, 90
  membership of EU 217
Bot, Bernard 137
Brown, David 2, 104, 208
Bruggeman, Willy 44
Brumberg, Daniel 185
Bulgaria 9, 10
  border management systems 66
  counter-terrorism policy 45
  economy 200
  military capabilities 27, 28
  organised crime 72
  support for Iraq intervention 22
Bunting, Madeleine 184
Burns Nicholas 15
Busek, Erhard 71
Bush, George W. 163

Callan, Teresa 195
Capability Improvement Chart II 32
Carr, Fergus 195
Caspian Basin 25–6
Caucasus 25
Central and Eastern Europe (CEE) 3, 7, 165
  influence on EU security policy 174, 219
  relations with Russia 24–5
  support for ESDP 24
  support for Iraq intervention 20, 22–3
Centre for Land Borders (CLB) 61
Ceuta 177, 182
Chalyi, Oleksandr 149
Charter of Fundamental Rights of the European Union 88, 89, 90–1
Chechnya 4, 25, 72
  illegal arms trade 75
  in EU-Russia relations 120, 129–41, 213, 214

Checklist for the Root Causes of Conflict 86–7
Chemical Weapons Convention (CWC) 181
Chirac, Jacques 23
Chizhov, Vladimir 140
Cimbalo, Jeffrey 11
Clarke, Michael 14
Code of Conduct on Arms Exports see European Union Code of Conduct on Arms Exports
Common Foreign and Security Policy (CFSP) 2, 10, 20, 34, 116, 130, 131, 140, 158, 207, 208, 212, 219
Community Assistance for Reconstruction programme (CARDS) 194
'Confederation of Balkan States' proposal 203–4
Congo, Democratic Republic
  EU mission to 158, 216
Convention on the Prevention of Terrorism 94
Conventional Arms Exports Working Group (COARM) 104
Conventional Forces in Europe Treaty (CFE) 119
Cooper, Robert 77
Copenhagen criteria (1993) 87, 88, 91, 165
Cornish, Paul 14
Council of Europe 89–90, 92, 125
  counter-terrorism 38–50, 208–9
  'implementation gap' 39, 41–2, 45–7, 210
  prioritisation of 39–41
  Russia's accession 133
  see also terrorism
crime see arms trafficking; drugs trafficking; immigration, illegal; organised crime
Croatia / Croats 10
  arms trafficking 105
  economy 198

human rights concerns 87
membership of EU 217
relations with Serbs 192
support for Iraq intervention 22
Cyprus 3, 9, 26, 186
defence budget 31
exclusion from ESDP 27
exclusive economic zone 181
membership of EU 160, 174
threatened by WMD 180
Czech Republic 7, 9
counter-terrorism policy 45, 47
defence budget 31
military capabilities 27, 28
organised crime 69
support for Iraq intervention 22

Dannreuther, Roland 214
Dayton Accords (1995) 191
Denmark
counter-terrorism policy 43
support for Iraq intervention 22
directoire concept 33, 211
drugs trafficking 125, 201
Dubrovka theatre siege (2002) 135, 138
Dunne, Michele 180

Eastern Sea Borders Centre (ESBC) 61
Egypt 180–1
Eide, Kai 197, 202, 203
Ekeus, Rolf 76
Emerson, Michael 133
energy security 176–7, 181, 187
Espersen, Lene 69
Estonia
arms trafficking 100, 105, 106, 108, 109, 110
counter-terrorism policy 45
defence budget 31
military capabilities 27
relations with Russia 24, 119, 124
support for Iraq intervention 22
see also Baltic states

Euro-Mediterranean Free Trade Area (EMFTA) 174, 175, 179
Euro-Mediterranean Parliamentary Forum (later Assembly) 175, 185
Euro-Mediterranean Partnership (EMP) 4, 174, 175, 176, 182, 183–6, 215, 216
European Arrest Warrant (EAW) 40, 41
European Border Guard proposal 55, 57–60, 110, 208
June 2002 Action Plan 60–3
European Charter for Small Enterprises 203
European Commission 93, 187
counter-terrorism policy 41–2, 46, 48, 49
European Commission Humanitarian Aid Office (ECHO) 194
European Community Global Mediterranean Policy 183
European Convention for the Prevention of Torture and Inhuman or Degrading Treatment or Punishment 91, 96
European Convention on Human Rights (ECHR) 89, 90, 92, 93, 125, 133
European Council 9, 184, 187
European Court of Human Rights (ECtHR) 90, 91, 93
European Court of Justice (ECJ) 90
EU Crime Prevention Network (EUCPN) 82
European Defence Agency 126
European Initiative for Democracy and Human Rights (EIDHR) 185
European Neighbourhood Policy (ENP) 26, 78, 87, 147–8, 149, 152, 153, 159, 210, 214, 217
relationship with Euro-Mediterranean Partnership 175, 176, 186, 187
European Parliament 93
European Police Office (Europol) 39–40, 44, 45, 46, 48, 59, 123
illegal immigration 177

European Rapid Reaction Force (ERRF) 28, 158, 161–2
European Security and Defence Policy (ESDP) 1, 2, 14, 17, 20–35, 158, 187, 188, 207, 210
  Iraq War (2003) 22–3
  leadership within 32–4
  military capabilities of new members 27–32
  policy toward Russia 24–5, 117
  regional priorities 25–6
  Turkey's exclusion from 161, 162
European Security Strategy (ESS) 11, 12, 21, 116, 159
  nature of security 25
European Union Border Assistance Mission 179
European Union Code of Conduct on Arms Exports 99, 100–1, 108, 109, 110
European Union Common Strategy on Russia (CSR) 123, 130, 131, 132, 133
European Union Constitution 11, 34, 35, 47, 89, 96, 116
European Union Force (EUFOR) 97
European Union General Affairs Council 133, 153
European Union Police Mission (EUPM) 28, 29–30
European Union Police Mission in the Occupied Territories (EUPOL COPPS) 179
European Union Programme for the Prevention of Violent Conflicts 209
European Union Satellite Centre 126
European Union –Ukraine Action Plan 151, 153
European Union –Ukraine Parliamentary Co-operation Committee 152
External Borders Agency (FRONTEX) 55, 62, 63–4, 65

Faull, Jonathan 42
Ferrero-Waldner, Benita 144, 152
Finland 7
  counter-terrorism issues 44, 46
Fischer, Joschka 22
fishing rights 181–2
'Five plus Five' arrangement 183
Flint, Caroline 42
Fomin, Nikolay 79
Former Yugoslav Republic of Macedonia (FYROM) 10, 11, 12, 13, 17
  EU peacekeeping missions 28
  human rights concerns 87
  membership of EU 217
  support for Iraq intervention 22
Framework Convention for the Protection of Minorities 89
Framework Decision on Combating Terrorism 40, 42, 46
France
  counter-terrorism policy 43
  ESDP leadership role 33
  European Border Police proposal 57
  minority rights 89
  opposition to Iraq intervention 22, 23
  relations with Russia 117, 135–6
  relations with US 216
  support for Algeria 182
Frattini, Franco 43, 46, 66
Freedman, Lawrence 212
FRONTEX *see* External Borders Agency (FRONTEX)

G5 meetings 44, 45, 50, 211
Gagnon, V. P. 193
Gambari, Ibrahim 179
Geoana, Mircea 75
Georgia 25, 73, 78, 126, 160
  Chechen issue 129
  human rights concerns 90
  relations with Russia 137
German, Tracey 5, 213, 216
Germany 31
  ESDP leadership role 33

INDEX

European Border Police proposal 57
membership of GUAM 150
opposition to Iraq intervention 22, 23
support for Iraq intervention 22
views on Turkish membership of EU 157
Gibraltar 56, 182
Gillard, Emanuela-Chiara 100
Gordon, Philip 217
Gorebnko, Leonid 107
Gotovina, Ante 198
Greece
  arms trade 108
  counter-terrorism conventions 42
  EC Association Agreement 183
  relations with Turkey 161, 182
  threatened by WMD 180
Greene, Owen 101
Group of States against Corruption (GRECO) 100, 108
GUAM organisation 150
Gul, Abdullah 164

Hague Programme (2004) 38, 39, 46, 47, 48, 49, 50, 66, 207
Hain, Peter 50
Haukkala, Hiski 134
Headline Goal 2010 21, 158
Helsinki Headline Goal (HHG) 20, 28, 29
Herd, Graeme 3, 210, 213
Holtom, Paul 3, 211, 214
human rights 86–97, 178–9, 184, 209
  EU's internal standards 88–9
  legal framework 89–91
  terrorism 91–7
Hungary 7, 9
  defence budget 31
  economy 200
  military capabilities 27, 28
  support for Iraq intervention 22
Hyde-Price, Adrian 9

Imia / Kardak affair 182
immigration, illegal 2, 57, 60, 63, 201
  in EU-Russia relations 116, 124
  in Mediterranean region 177–8
Implementation Force (IFOR) 9
International Atomic Energy Agency 27
International Commission on the Balkans 217
International Criminal Court (ICC) 70
International Crisis Group 198
International Security Assistance Force (ISAF) 15
interoperability 32
Interparliamentary European Security and Defence Assembly *see* Western European Union (WEU)
Iran
  development of WMD 180
  EU policy towards 27
Iraq 181
Iraq War (2003) 20, 22–3, 33, 34, 160, 180, 209
Ireland 41
  Schengen opt-out 55, 56
Israel 170, 179, 181
Istanbul terrorist attacks (2003) 163
Italy 31
  counter-terrorism policy 41, 43
  defence budget 31
  European Border Police proposal 57
  support for Russia's human rights record 136
  support for Iraq intervention 22
Ivanov, Viktor 116, 123, 130

Jackson, Bruce 22
Jacobovits de Szeged, Adriaan 80
Judah, Tim 218
July 7th terrorist attacks (2005) 124, 125
Justice and Development Party (Turkish) (AKP) 157, 158, 163–4, 166

Justice and Home Affairs (JHA) 2, 42, 46, 47, 123, 124, 147, 211

Kadyrov, Akhmad 136
Kagan, Robert 168, 183
Kaliningrad 24, 26, 106–7, 111, 214
Kasinski, Colonel Marian 59
Kazakhstan
  Single Economic Space proposal (SES) 149–50
Keohane, Daniel 44
Khan, Karim 5, 209
Khasavyurt peace accords 131
Khodorkovsky, Mikhail 136
Khoroshkovsky, Valery 149
Kolerov, Modest 81
Kosovo 10, 16, 17, 191
  democratisation 195–8
  economy 198–9, 202
  EU aid 194–6
  EU new member states and 30
  membership of EU 217
  riots (March 2004) 192
Kosovo Force (KFOR) 10, 13, 194
Kotzeva, Anna 5, 209
Kuchma, Leonid 146, 147, 148, 150
Kurds 160, 161, 165, 167–8
Kwasniewski, Aleksander 152, 214
Kyulev, Emil 72

Laeken European Council 57
Laitinen, Colonel Ilkka 63
Latvia
  arms trafficking 100, 105, 106, 108, 109, 110
  defence budget 31
  military capabilities 27
  Russian minorities 119, 124
  support for Iraq intervention 22
  see also Baltic states
Lavrov, Sergey 116, 138
Lebanon 181
Lesser, Ian O. 179
Libya 177–8, 179, 181, 182

Lithuania
  arms trafficking 100, 105, 106, 108, 109, 110
  defence budget 31
  military capabilities 27
  support for Iraq intervention 22
  Ukranian membership of the EU 151–2
  see also Baltic states
Lo, Bobo 138
London bombings (2005) *see* July 7th terrorist attacks
Ludford, Sarah 46
Luxembourg
  counter-terrorism conventions 41, 42

Macedonia *see* Former Yugoslav Republic of Macedonia (FYROM)
Maddox, Bronwen 213
Malta 3, 9, 26, 174, 186
  counter-terrorism policy 45
  defence budget 31
  exclusion from ESDP 27
  fishing rights 181
Marakutsa, Grigori 73
Margelov, Mikhail 81
Maskhadov, Aslan 136
'Mediterranean Boat People' crisis 177
Mediterranean Forum 183
Mediterranean region 3–4
  illegal immigration 177–8
  in EU security policy 174–88
  natural resources 181
  terrorism 178–9, 188
  Weapons of Mass Destruction (WMD) 179–81
Medium-term Strategy for the Development of Relations between the Russian Federation and the European Union (MTS) 130, 131–2
Melilla 177, 182
Middle East 169, 174, 175, 178–9, 183–4, 215–16
  'Greater Middle East Initiative' 182

INDEX 235

'Road Map' 27
Weapons of Mass Destruction (WMD) 180–1
Minsk Group 160
Moldova 25, 126, 213
  human rights concerns 90
  membership of GUAM 150
  organised crime 3, 72, 74, 75
  sanctions against Transdniestria (PMR) 76–7
  Ukraine border 5, 76, 78–82
Monar, Jorg 3, 42, 208
Montenegro
  human rights concerns 87, 90
Montis, Cesare de 80
Moscow theatre siege *see* Dubrovka theatre siege (2002)
Multinational Peacekeeping Force for South-Eastern Europe Brigade (SEEBRIG) 160

Nagorno Karabakh 72, 126, 160–1
Nantoi, Oazu 75
NATO Response Force (NRF) 15, 16
Naumann, Klaus 218
Nemkov, Lt. Col. V. 75
Netherlands
  counter-terrorism conventions 42, 48
'Nettuno' border operations 60–1
Neukirch, Claus 75
Non-Proliferation Treaty (NPT) 126, 180–1
North Atlantic Council (NAC) 8
North Atlantic Treaty Organisation (NATO)
  agreement with EU (Copenhagen, 2002) 24
  agreement with EU (July 2003) 14
  agreement with EU (Dec, 2003)
  Article 5 24
  Balkan interventions 9–14, 217
  expansion 117
  'incremental linkage' with EU 7, 8–9
  Iraq War (2003) 160

  operations against Serbia 132
  relationship with EU 2, 10–11, 14–17, 29
  role beyond Europe 15–16, 215
  Turkish membership 158, 161
nuclear weapons *see* Weapons of Mass Destruction (WMD)

Ocalan, Abdullah 167
Odysseus Programme 56, 57
Office for Democratic Institutions and Human Rights (ODIHIR)
Oostlander report 133, 134
Operation Allied Force 43
Operation Althea 28, 29–30, 97
Operation Concordia 28, 30
Operation Proxima 28, 30
Organisation for Security and Co-operation in Europe (OSCE) 11, 12, 75, 76, 79, 81, 125, 196, 201
  see also Office for Democratic Institutions and Human Rights; Stability Pact
organised crime 2, 3, 69–82, 119, 125, 177, 201
Osica, Olaf 27
Ottaway, Marina 185
Ozal, Turgut 162

Pace, Roderick 3, 4, 215, 216, 218
Palestine 179, 210
Park, Bill 5, 215
Parnuk, Orhan 210
Partnership and Co-operation Agreements (PCA) *see* Russia; Ukraine
Partnership for Peace (PfP) 69, 80, 161
Patten, Chris 140, 201, 204
Paulauskas, Arturas 151
Peleman, Johan 108
Permanent Partnership Council *see* Russia
Phythian, Mark 99, 107
Pillar Three *see* United Nations Interim Mission (Kosovo) (UNMIK)

Plan of Action on Combating Terrorism 27
Poland 4, 7, 9, 20
  border issues 61, 62
  contribution to Operation Iraqi Freedom 30
  counter-terrorism policy 45, 47
  defence budget 31
  demands for greater influence 33
  EU Constitution 96
  military capabilities 27, 28
  relations with Russia 24
  support for Iraq intervention 22
  Ukraine border concerns 26
Polikanov, Dmitry 5, 210, 220
Pologne, Hongrie Assistance à la Reconstruction Economique (PHARE) 108, 194
Portugal 174
  counter-terrorism issues 44
  support for Iraq intervention 22
Powell, Colin 160
Prague summit (2002) 15, 23–4
Pridnestrovskaya Moldavskaya Respublika (PMR) *see* Transdniestria
Prodi, Romano 175
Prum, Treaty of 44
Puglisi, Rosaria 5, 213
Putin, Vladimir 115, 120, 121–2, 134, 135, 136, 137, 138, 213

Risk Analysis Centre (RAC) 61, 63
Romania 9, 10, 26
  border management systems 66
  counter-terrorism policy 45
  economy 200
  military capabilities 27, 28
  relations with Moldova 78–9
  support for Iraq intervention 22
Rop, Anton 70
Rumsfeld, Donald
  'new'/'old' Europe concept 22, 23, 46

Russia 4
  armed forces 123
  arms trafficking 105
  Chehen issue 129–41
  human rights issues 90, 133, 136, 139
  Military Doctrine (2000) 117, 118
  National Security Concept 117–18
  organised crime 111, 119, 124, 125
  Partnership and Co-operation Agreement (PCA) 116, 122, 124, 130, 131, 133
  Permanent Partnership Council 123
  relations with CEE states 24–5
  relations with European Union 115–27, 129–41, 207, 212–13, 214, 220
  relations with Moldova 78–9, 80, 81
  relations with Transdniestria (PMR) 74, 77
  Single Economic Space proposal (SES) 149–50
  terrorism 116, 120, 122, 124–5, 137–8
  White Book 117, 118
Rybachuk, Oleh 151

Sadurski, W. 96
St Malo Agreement 158
Sanader, Ivo 198
Schengen Agreement 3, 43, 44, 55, 69
  Schengen Borders Code 56, 64–5
  Schengen system 55–6, 62
Schröder, Gerhard 134, 135
Schuster, Rudolf 152
Scoreboard initiative 40, 42
Semper Vigilia border operations 61
September 11 terrorist attacks 38, 91
  impact on EU-Russia relations 135–6
Serbia / Serbs
  economy 198
  human rights concerns 87, 90
  membership of EU 217

INDEX

NATO operations against 132
  relations with Croats 192
Shepherd, Alistair 2, 214, 219
Single Economic Space proposal (SES) 149–50
Slovakia 9, 20
  defence budget 31
  military capabilities 27, 28
  support for Iraq intervention 22
Slovenia 9, 10
  attitude to NATO 23
  counter-terrorism policy 45
  defence budget 31
  economy 198, 200
  military capabilities 27, 28
  support for Iraq intervention 22
Smirnov, Igor 72, 73, 76, 77, 80
Smith, Martin 2, 7, 217
Socor, Vladimir 80
Solana, Javier 10, 40, 77, 97, 129, 138, 144, 152
South-East European Co-operation Initiative Regional Centre for Combating Trans-Border Crime 71, 160
South Ossetia 72, 73, 75
Spain
  counter-terrorism policy 43
  defence budget 31
  demands for greater influence 33
  European Border Police proposal 57
  fishing rights 181
  illegal immigration 177
  support for Iraq intervention 22
  territorial disputes 182
Special Immigration Appeals Commission (SIAC) 92, 93, 94, 95, 96
Stabilisation and Association Agreements (SAA) 87
Stabilisation and Association Process (SAP) 194
Stabilisation Force (SFOR) 14, 97

Stability Pact for South-Eastern Europe 71, 79, 160, 191, 192, 201
Stoicov, Iurie 75
Stratan, Andrei 79
Strategy Against the Proliferation of Weapons of Mass Destruction 27
Sweden 7
  counter-terrorism issues 46
Syria 175, 180, 181

Tampere European Council 56
Tarasyuk, Boris 79, 147, 151
Technical Aid to the Commonwealth of Independent States (TACIS) 123, 131, 144
Tellis, Ashley J. 179
terrorism 2, 15, 43–4
  anti-terrorism legislation 91–7
  in Balkans 200–1
  in EU-Russia relations 116, 120, 124–5, 135–6
  human rights issues 86, 91–7
  in Mediterranean region 178–9
  see also counter-terrorism
Timmins, Graham 7, 131
Titov, Vladimir 81
torture 94–7
Torture Convention see United Nations Convention Against Torture
Transdniestria (PMR) 72–82, 213
  organised crime 72, 74
  status of 72–5
  relations with other states 76–7, 79–81, 151
Treaty on European Union (TEU) 2, 42, 88, 90
Trenin, Dimitri 210
Tretyakov, Vitaly 140
'Triton' border operation 60
Turkey 4
  Cyprus question 26, 158, 160
  EC Association Agreement 183
  exclusion from ESDP 161

Turkey (*cont.*)
  human rights concerns 86, 87, 90, 93, 96–7
  Iraq War (2003) 160
  Kurdish issue 160, 161, 165, 167–8
  membership of NATO 158
  natural resources 181
  relations with the EU 157–70, 214, 215–16
  relations with Greece 161, 182
  relations with United States 162, 163–4
  security culture 165–6
  threatened by WMD 180
Tyhypko, Serhiy 149
Tymoshenko, Yulia 151, 153

Ukraine
  contribution to Operation Iraqi Freedom 30
  European Neighbourhood Policy (ENP) 147–8, 149
  human rights concerns 90
  membership of GUAM 150
  Moldovan border 5, 73, 75–6, 78–80
  Orange Revolution (2004) 137, 144–5, 146, 151, 152
  Partnership and Cooperation Agreement (PCA) 146–7
  Polish border 26
  relations with EU 144–54, 213
  relations with Russia 137
  Single Economic Space (SES) 149–50
'Ulysses' border operation 60
United Kingdom
  anti-terrorism laws 91–3
  counter-terrorism policy 41, 43, 48
  Department for International Development (DFID) 195, 199
  ESDP leadership role 33
  nature of security 25
  relations with Russia 135–6
  Schengen opt-out 55, 56
  support for Iraq intervention 22

United Nations 10, 125, 199
United Nations Conference on the Illicit Trade in Small Arms and Light Weapons 103
United Nations Convention Against Torture 94, 95, 96
United Nations Interim Mission (Kosovo) (UNMIK) 196–7, 198, 202
  Pillar I 201
  Pillar II 201
  Pillar III 25, 38, 40, 41, 201
  Pillar IV 201
United Nations Panel of Experts on Small Arms 101
United Nations Police Mission (Bosnia) 11
United Nations Protection Force (UNPROFOR) 9
United Nations Protocol against the Illicit Manufacturing of and Trafficking in Firearms 101, 108
United Nations Security Council (USNC) 27
  Resolution 1244 192
  Resolution 1441 21
  Resolution 1566 94
United States
  leadership in NATO 23–4, 216
  policy in Balkans 13–14, 194, 199–200
  relations with Europe 11–12, 168, 219
  relations with Turkey 162, 163–4
  rejection of International Criminal Court 70
  role of NATO 15–16
  support for Iraq intervention 22

Verbruggen, F. 43
Villepin, Dominique de 22
'Vilnius Ten' 22, 219
Voronin, Vladimir 74, 75, 76, 77, 80, 81

Vries, Gijs de 40
'War on Terror' 4, 11, 38, 44, 45, 118, 163, 168, 178, 180, 185, 200, 209, 214
Weapons of Mass Destruction (WMD) 4, 15, 118, 119
  in Mediterranean region 179–81
Welch, Anthony 5, 218
Western European Union (WEU) 11, 159
Wolfowitz, Paul 163

Wood, Brian 108
Woods, Ngaire 200
Woodward, Susan 193

Yanukovich, Viktor 147, 148, 149, 150
Yastrzhembsky, Sergey 123
Youngs, Richard 184
Yushchenko, Viktor 79, 81, 145–6, 148, 153

Zakaev, Akhmed 125, 136